Latin America

Johns Hopkins Studies in Globalization

Christopher Chase-Dunn, *Series Editor*

Consulting editors: Volker Bornschier, Christine Gailey, Walter L. Goldfrank, Su-Hoon Lee, William R. Thompson, Immanuel Wallerstein, and David Wilkinson

Latin America and Global Capitalism

A Critical Globalization Perspective

WILLIAM I. ROBINSON

The Johns Hopkins University Press
Baltimore

© 2008 The Johns Hopkins University Press
All rights reserved. Published 2008
Printed in the United States of America on acid-free paper
2 4 6 8 9 7 5 3 1

The Johns Hopkins University Press
2715 North Charles Street
Baltimore, Maryland 21218-4363
www.press.jhu.edu

Library of Congress Cataloging-in-Publication Data
Robinson, William I.
Latin America and global capitalism : a critical globalization perspective /
William I. Robinson.
p. cm.—(Johns Hopkins studies in globalization)
Includes bibliographical references and index.
ISBN-13: 978-0-8018-9039-0 (hardcover : alk. paper)
ISBN-10: 0-8018-9039-X (hardcover : alk. paper)
1. Latin America—Economic integration. 2. Globalization—Economic
aspects—Latin America. 3. Capitalism. I. Title.
HC125.R543 2008
337.8—dc22 2008014466

A catalog record for this book is available from the British Library.

Special discounts are available for bulk purchases of this book. For more information,
please contact Special Sales at 410-516-6936 or specialsales@press.jhu.edu.

The Johns Hopkins University Press uses environmentally friendly book
materials, including recycled text paper that is composed of at least 30 percent
post-consumer waste, whenever possible. All of our book papers are acid-free,
and our jackets and covers are printed on paper with recycled content.

CONTENTS

What in the world is happening? So goes the saying, a common refrain to capture the winds of change that have swept the planet in recent years challenging our established frames of reference. These dramatic changes along with the sense that the tempo of change itself has sped up and that the world is getting ever smaller are captured by the concept of *globalization*, which some social scientists view as the master concept of the new millennium. The present study is part of the emerging field of globalization studies, specifically, what Rich Appelbaum and I have termed *critical globalization studies* (Appelbaum and Robinson, 2005), and what I had previously referred to as new transnational studies (Robinson, 1998, 2003). I have been writing about globalization since the early 1990s. It is, in my view, a concept with tremendous explanatory power. The explosion of research that has taken place on the topic points to the ubiquity of its effects. All disciplines and specializations in the academy, it seems, have become implicated in globalization studies, from ethnic, area, and women's and cultural studies, to literature, the arts and social sciences, history, law, business administration, and even the natural sciences. The proliferating literature on globalization reflects the intellectual enormity of the task of researching and theorizing the breadth, depth, and pace of changes under way in human society in the early twenty-first century.

We find within globalization studies two broad categories: (1) those studying specific problems or issues as they relate to globalization and (2) those studying the concept of globalization itself, that is, theorizing the very nature of the process. In the present volume I attempt to span these two categories, to reiterate and further advance a theoretical understanding of the nature of the process, and to examine in-depth the sets of problems and issues that Latin America faces in the new century as they relate to globalization. As López-Alves and Johnson (2007) have observed, the literature on globalization offers few systematic references to Latin America. Beyond the community of scholars in and on Latin America, the region is largely absent from the mainstream comparative and theoretical literature on global transformation.

This book builds on my ongoing research into globalization. My particular theory of global capitalism, based on the three planks of *transnational production*, a *transnational capitalist class*, and a *transnational state*, has been laid out in two previous books: *Transnational Conflicts* (Robinson, 2003) and *A Theory of Global Capitalism* (Robinson, 2004a). A theory of globalization is a template for understanding numerous processes in the social world. In recent years I have applied my theory of global capitalism to a number of empirical cases, among them, Central American (2003), the Horn of Africa (2004), South Africa (2005), the U.S. invasion of Iraq (2005a, 2005b), Latino/a immigrants in the United States (2006), and U.S. interventionism and imperialism (2007). In the present book I employ this theory of global capitalism to explore and explain the momentous changes that have swept Latin America in recent decades.

Latin America entered into a tumultuous season of change and uncertainty early in the new century. The new transnational order has its origins in the world economic crisis of the 1970s, which gave capital the impetus and the means to initiate a major restructuring of the system through globalization over the next two decades. The region has been deeply implicated in this process. The mass movements, revolutionary struggles, nationalist and populist projects of the 1960s and 1970s were beaten back by local and international elites in the latter decades of the twentieth century in the face of the global economic downturn, the debt crisis, state repression, U.S. intervention, the collapse of a socialist alternative, and the rise of the neoliberal model (the diverse popular projects and movements had their own internal contradictions as well). Economically, Latin American countries experienced a thorough restructuring and integration into the global economy under the neoliberal model. But by the turn-of-century the model was in crisis in the region, unable to bring about any sustained development, or even to prevent continued backward movement. Politically, the fragile polyarchic ("democratic") systems installed through the so-called transitions to democracy of the 1980s were increasingly unable to contain the social conflicts and political tensions generated by the polarizing and pauperizing effects of the neoliberal model. The erosion of the "Washington consensus," economic stagnation, a string of revolts among popular classes, an electoral comeback of the Left, a new "radical populism," the revival of a socialist agenda, attempted coups, and renewed U.S. interventionism—all seemed to be the order of the day.

The larger backdrop to heightened turbulence in Latin America has been the integration of the region into the new global capitalism. This book, hence, examines the process of globalization that has swept Latin America from the late 1970s and on. It documents and analyzes, from the perspective of global capitalism theory, recent crisis and change in Latin America in historical perspective, and with an eye toward providing a theoretical framework and analytical and conceptual tools for understanding the current period of turbulence and possible futures. It focuses on the region's changing relationship to the global system, evolution of its political economy, novel social and political dynamics in the age of globalization, and prospects for the future. It also looks at resistance movements and alternative projects, including three brief case studies. My hope is that this is an accessible study, not definitive or exhaustive, but one that highlights the major changes that have occurred, and links the study of globalization with the study of Latin America and the notion of a global crisis. It is intended to provide an overview, a framework, and an interpretation that I hope will spark others to continue delving into the ideas and analysis presented here. In particular, left for ongoing research is a comparative focus on the convergences as well as specificities of Latin American America's integration into the new global system in relation to other regions. The rise of globalization studies has served to reassert not only the centrality of historical analysis and the ongoing reconfiguration of time and space but also the importance of a holistic approach to any understanding of human affairs. In my view, globalization is the underlying dynamic that drives social, political, economic, cultural, and ideological processes around world in the twenty-first century. New economic, political, and social structures have emerged—in Latin America and elsewhere—as each nation and region becomes integrated into emergent transnational structures and processes. There is a new configuration of global power that becomes manifest in each nation and the tentacles of which reach all the way down to the community level. Each individual, each nation, and each region is being drawn into transnational processes that have undermined the earlier autonomies and provincialisms. This makes it impossible to address local issues—if not indeed any issue of social, political, or intellectual importance—removed from the global context. I will argue in what follows, moreover, that crisis and transformation in Latin America are part of a deeper crisis of global capitalism.

I was involved from 1999 to 2003 in a global crisis working group, first convened by the Transnational Institute in Amsterdam, that brought together scholar-activists from five continents for a series of meetings and culminated in the publication of our proceedings (Freeman and Kagarlitsky, 2004). It was through this working group that I began to think about the nature of the crisis in the global system, a crisis that more generally I believe to be civilizational, in the sense that its scope is all of humanity and its non-resolution could well result in a collapse of our present global civilization, for better or worse. My role in the working group was to research Latin America. That work (Robinson, 2004b, 2004c) constituted the immediate origins of the present study. Clearly, the contradictions of global capitalism are explosive. It is at times of crisis rather than stability and equilibrium in a system that the power of collective agencies to influence history is enhanced. We stand at an historic crossroad, a moment of chaos, which presents grave dangers to humanity but also new opportunities.

The truth, as Hegel said, *is in the whole.* That said, if there is any one caveat to highlight here, it is that in a slim volume such as this simplification is unavoidable. I can only shine a spotlight on a select few of the trees that make up the forest and must inevitably omit entirely a look at other trees, no matter how much they may be integral to the forest. In the end, any intellectual endeavor is open-ended: a work in progress. My approach—to look at Latin America as a whole—inevitably understates complexity and divergence and overstates the extent to which general statements can be made. There is no single, homogenous Latin America. Nonetheless, the exercise remains valid—indeed, useful and vital—insofar as there *are* underlying structural shifts that have produced clear region-wide patterns of change. There is a general pattern across all of Latin America of transition to global capitalism, even if each country and region has experienced this transition on the basis of its own particular constellation of social forces, historical circumstances, and contingent variables. I am concerned in the present study with identifying this underlying unity among varied patterns of change, with extrapolating from divergent experiences to uncover these general patterns and categories of events—such as the spread of nontraditional exports, the rise of transnational capitalists from among the region's dominant groups, the debt crisis and the preponderance of global financial markets, and the upsurge of new resistance movements across the region. These general patterns point to underlying causal processes of capitalist globalization.

Returning to the dual themes of crisis and *critical* globalization studies, there can be little doubt that we are living in troubling times in the "global village." The system of global capitalism that now engulfs the entire planet is in crisis. There is consensus among scientists that we are on the precipice of ecological holocaust, including the mass extinction of species; the impending collapse of agriculture in major producing areas; the meltdown of polar ice caps; the phenomenon of global warming; and the contamination of the oceans, food stock, water supply, and air. Social inequalities have spiraled out of control, and the gap between the global rich and the global poor has never been as acute as it is in the early twenty-first century. While absolute levels of poverty and misery expand around the world under a new global social apartheid, the richest 20 percent of humanity received in 2000 more than 85 percent of the world's wealth while the remaining 80 percent of humanity had to make do with less than 15 percent of the wealth, according to the United Nation's oft-cited annual Human Development Report (UNDP 2000). Driven by the imperatives of over accumulation and transnational social control, global elites have increasingly turned to authoritarianism, militarization, and war to sustain the system. Many political economists concur that a global economic collapse is possible, even probable.

In times such as these intellectuals are called upon to engage in a *critical* analytical and theoretical understanding of global society: to contribute to an understanding of history and social change that may elucidate the inner workings of the prevailing order and the causal processes at work in that order that generate crisis. They are also called upon to expose the vested interests bound up with the global social order, the discourses through which those interests are articulated, and the distinct alternatives to the extant order that counter-hegemonic agents put forward. Intellectual production is always a collective process. Let us not lose sight of the social and historical character of intellectual labor. All those scholars who engage in such labor or make knowledge claims are *organic* intellectuals in the sense that studying the world is itself a social act, committed by agents with a definite relationship to the social order. Intellectual labor is social labor; its practitioners are social actors; and the products of its labor are not neutral or disinterested.

In recent years I have proposed a rationale and minimal guidelines for critical globalization studies and have called on intellectuals to "exercise a preferential option for the majority in global society" (Robinson, 2006c). Globalization is not a neutral process. It involves winners and losers and new relations of power and domination. We need organic intellectuals capable of theorizing the changes that have taken place in the system of capitalism, in this epoch of globalization, and of providing to popular majorities these theoretical insights as inputs for their real-world struggles to develop alternative social relationships and an alternative social logic—the logic of majorities—to that of the market and of transnational capital. In other words, critical globalization studies has to be capable of inspiring emancipatory action, of bringing together multiple publics in developing programs that integrate theory and practice.

Let me now summarize the layout of this book. In Chapter 1, I summarize my theory of globalization and introduce several new angles and propositions not previously presented elsewhere. Chapters 2, 3, and 4 then turn to Latin America, documenting and analyzing the transformation of Latin America's political economy as it has integrated into the new global production and financial system. The focus is on sets of nontraditional exports that are incorporated into new global circuits of accumulation and on some of the fundamental changes in the social structure and class relations bound up with that integration. I examine in particular the spread of nontraditional agricultural exports and agro-industry (Chapter 2), the reorientation of industry and rise of maquiladoras; transnational tourism; and the export of labor and import of remittances (Chapter 3). Chapter 4 reviews some of the most salient transnational processes in the region, in particular as they relate to class, state, nation, and transnational migration. Chapters 5 and 6 present an overview of the global crisis. Chapter 5 focuses on three dimensions in particular: the crises of social polarization–social reproduction; of over accumulation; and of legitimacy and hegemony. It then turns to how that crisis has manifested itself in Latin America. I argue that we have entered the twilight of neoliberalism; the battle is under way for what will replace this moribund model. Chapter 6 looks at the rise of resistance movements and counter-hegemonic projects in Latin America, challenges and dilemmas they face, and prospects for the future. I look in this final chapter at the situation in several countries and present three more detailed case studies: the continent-wide indigenous struggle; the immigrant rights movement in the United States, spearheaded by Latino/a immigrants; and the Bolivarian Revolution in Venezuela.

Finally, let me reiterate that all intellectual production is collective, and its results are social products. The present study is no exception. The list is vast indeed of people who contributed in a variety of ways, including those who have had a significant influence on my own intellectual and political development as well as those tied more immediately to the ideas and content put forward in this study. All I can do here is make mention of a few, especially my lifelong friend Kent Norsworthy, who read over the entire manuscript and provided chapter-by-chapter editorial suggestions, and my graduate research assistants at the University of California at Santa Barbara who contributed in a variety of ways, among them Veronica Montes, Cosme Caal, Amandeep Sandhu, Edwin Lopez, and Xuan Santos. I would like to express my gratitude to my friend and senior colleague Christopher Chase-Dunn at the University of California–Riverside, the series editor of the Johns Hopkins University Press's Themes in Global

Social Change. In addition to serving as an intellectual inspiration, Chris has provided me (and many of my peers) with important collegial support in crucial moments of my own professional and career development. Marielle Robinson-Mayorga gave me moral support and showed much patience during the several years that the manuscript was under preparation.

I am also grateful to (in alphabetical order): Vilma Almedra; Paul Almeida; Richard Appelbaum; Andres Beiler; Walden Bello; Judith Blau; Honor Bragazon; Peter Brogan; friends and colleagues at the Instituto de Altos Estudios Diplomáticos Pedro Gual of the Venezuelan Foreign Ministry, among them, Jonhy Balza and Eleonora Quijada; the team at Desde Abajo in Bogotá, Colombia; Daniel Dessain; Jonah Gindin; friends and colleagues at the San José, Costa Rica branch of the Latin American Social Science Faculty (FLACSO); and especially Abelardo Morales; John Foran; Sam Gindin; Fernando López-Alves; Margarita López-Maya, and Luis Lander at the Universidad Central de Venezuela in Caracas; Esteban Pino Cavello; Adam Morton; Leo Panitch; Marielle Robinson-Mayorga; Fred Rosen; Manuel Rozental; Xuan Santos; colleagues at the U.K. Society for Latin American Studies; my friends, colleagues, and students at the University of Costa Rica, especially in the Department of Political Science, in particular Carlos Sandoval at the Department of International Relations; friends and colleagues at the National University of Costa Rica, in Heredia, and in particular Jorge Cáceres; friends and colleagues at the Department of Political Science at the University of Chile; and Catherine Walsh. I gratefully acknowledge research grants from the Academic Senate and the Institute for Social, Behavioral, and Economic Research—both of the University of California at Santa Barbara—that helped fund portions of this study. The University of California's Education Abroad Program approved my summer 2004 Visiting Scholar exchange with the University of Chile that allowed me to conduct important research in South America. My apologies to any individuals and institutions I may have forgotten to mention here. I bear sole responsibility, as a matter of course, for all of the shortcomings of this study, of which no doubt there are many.

This book is dedicated to the immigrant rights movements in the United States and elsewhere, to the battles that these "new nomads" of global capitalism are forced to wage on a daily basis, in innumerable instances, against displacement, humiliation, exploitation, exclusion, and injustice. Their struggles for dignity and social justice, beyond inspirational, place them at the cutting edge of resistance to the dehumanizing effects of the system.

AD	Democratic Action Party (Venezuela)
AID	Agency for International Development (United States)
ALBA	Bolivarian Alternative for the Americas
APEC	Asia Pacific Economic Conference
ASOCOLFLORES	Colombian Association of Flower Exporters
CAFTA	Central American Free Trade Agreement
CARHCO	Central American Retail Holding Company
CARICOM	Caribbean Economic Community
CBI	Caribbean Basin Initiative
CEO	chief executive officer
CIM	Mercosur Industrial Council
CONAIE	Confederation of Indigenous Nationalities of Ecuador
CORPEI	Corporation for the Promotion of Exports and Investments (Ecuador)
CSN	South American Community of Nations
CTV	Confederation of Venezuelan Workers
EAP	economically active population
ECLAC	Economic Commission for Latin America and the Caribbean
ECPAT	End Pornography and Trafficking of Children for Sexual Purposes
ELD	export-led development
EPZ	export-processing zone
EU	European Union
FARC	Colombian Armed Revolutionary Forces
FDI	foreign direct investment

FEDEPRICAP	Federation of Private Sector Entities of Central America and Panama
FEDEXPORT	Ecuadoran Federation of Exporters
FSLN	Sandinista National Liberation Front (Nicaragua)
FTZ	Free Trade Zone
GATT	General Agreement on Tariffs and Trade
GCC	Global Commodity Chain
GDP	Gross Domestic Product
GEXPORT	Guatemalan Nontraditional Exporters Association
GM	genetically modified
HTA	Home Town Association
ICE	Immigration and Customs Enforcement (formerly INS)
IDB	Inter-American Development Bank
IFI	International Financial Institution
IGO	Intergovernmental Organization
IIRSA	Initiative for Regional South American Integration
ILO	International Labor Organization
IMF	International Monetary Fund
INS	Immigration and Naturalization Service
ISI	import-substitution industrialization
IT	information technology
MERCOSUR	South American Common Market
MNC	multinational corporation
MST	Landless Rural Workers Movement (Brazil)
MVR	Fifth Republic Movement (Venezuela)
NAFTA	North American Free Trade Agreement
NEM	New Economic Model
NGO	nongovernmental organization
NIDL	new international division of labor
NTAE	nontraditional agricultural export
OECD	Organization of Economic Cooperation and Development
OPEC	Organization of Petroleum Exporting Countries
PAN	National Advancement Party (Mexico)
PCMLA	Program for Mexican Communities Living Abroad
PDVSA	Petroleos de Venezuela, Venezuelan Petroleum Company
PPP	Plan Puebla Panama
PPT	Homeland for All Party (Venezuela)
PRD	Democratic Revolutionary Party (Mexico)

PRI	Institutional Revolutionary Party (Mexico)
PROEXPORT	Fund for the Promotion of Exports (Colombia)
PROEXTANT	Corporation for the Promotion of Nontraditional Agro-Exports (Ecuador)
PT	Workers Party (Brazil)
PUSV	United Venezuelan Socialist Party
PYMEs	pequeñas y medianas empresas (small and middle-sized firms)
RR	Roundup Ready
TCC	Transnational Capitalist Class
TNC	transnational corporation
TNS	transnational state
UN	United Nations
UNCTAD	United Nations Conference on Trade and Development
UNDP	United Nations Development Program
UNESCO	United Nations Education, Science, and Cultural Organization
UNICEF	United Nations International Children's Education Fund
UNT	National Workers Union (Venezuela)
WB	World Bank
WEF	World Economic Forum
WEPZA	World Economic Processing Zones Association
WSF	World Social Forum
WTO	World Trade Organization
WTTC	World Travel and Tourism Council

Latin America and Global Capitalism

CHAPTER ONE

An Epochal Shift in World Capitalism

Most scholars and laypeople alike would agree that if we are to understand the social world of the twenty-first century we must come to grips with the concept of globalization. The term first became popularized in the 1980s. During the 1990s there were raging debates about whether it was a useful concept for the social sciences and humanities. By the new century the concept had clearly earned its place, and debate turned more squarely to the theoretical significance of globalization. Most researchers would agree that there are two intertwined dimensions of this process: increasing interconnections among peoples and countries worldwide, or an objective dimension, and an increased awareness worldwide of these interconnections, or a subjective dimension. The rise of globalization studies has served to reassert the centrality of historical analysis and the ongoing reconfiguration of time and social space to any understanding of human affairs. But if globalization is modifying how we have traditionally gone about studying the social world and human culture, it is because as a real-world process it is reaching into the deepest, most remote and most local level in every corner of the planet, modifying social, cultural, and political life everywhere.

Critical Globalization Studies and Levels of Analysis

If academics and intellectuals are to play a meaningful part in addressing the urgent issues that humanity faces in the twenty-first century—war and peace, social justice, democracy, cultural diversity, and ecological sustainability—it is incumbent upon us to gain an analytical understanding of globalization as the underlying structural dynamic that drives social, political, economic, and cultural processes around the world. My colleague Richard Appelbaum and I put out the following call several years ago for *critical globalization studies:*

> We believe that the dual objective of understanding globalization and engaging in global social activism can best be expressed in the idea of a *critical globalization studies*. We believe that as scholars it is incumbent upon us to explore the relevance of academic research to the burning political issues and social struggles of our epoch,

to the many conflicts, hardships, and hopes bound up with globalization. More directly stated, we are not indifferent observers studying globalization as a sort of detached academic exercise. Rather, we are passionately concerned with the adverse impact of globalization on billions of people as well as our increasingly stressed planetary ecology. Moreover, we believe that it is our obligation as scholars to place an understanding of the multifaceted processes of globalization in the service of those individuals and organizations that are dedicated to fighting its harsh edges. We are not anti-globalists, but we are staunchly opposed to the highly predatory forms that globalization has assumed throughout history, and particularly during the past quarter century. (Appelbaum and Robinson, 2005:xiii)

This book centers on critical globalization studies. It is an attempt to explain the changes that have swept Latin America in recent decades through my particular approach to globalization, a *theory of global capitalism*, which sees globalization as a qualitatively new stage in the history of world capitalism (Robinson, 2004a). If earlier stages brought us colonial conquest, a world economy and an international division of labor, the partition of the world into North and South, and rising material prosperity amidst pauperization, this new era is bringing us into a singular global civilization—one in which humanity is bound together as never before, yet divided into the haves and the have-nots across national and regional borders in a way unprecedented in human history. This new transnational order dates back to the world economic crisis of the 1970s and took shape in the 1980s and 1990s. What we are experiencing is an epochal shift; it is a transnational phase that is coming to supersede the national phase of capitalism as a social system. An epochal shift captures the idea of changes in social structure that have systemic importance in that they transform the very way that the system functions.

Why consider the new phase an epochal shift? Neither global interconnections nor world capitalism are unique to the globalization epoch. A global capitalism approach sees globalization as a recent phenomenon involving novel processes and structures, and yet that approach also argues that the recent changes are embedded in long-term historical processes. This long-term perspective on social change, or the *longue durée,* is concerned with structures as patterns of relationships that people develop over decades, centuries, and even millennia. Structures are enduring, and change at this level is imperceptible at the day-to-day level of our social experience.

At what point and under what circumstances do structures become qualitatively modified or entirely new structures emerge? Moments of transition are spurred by crisis. The world capitalist system entered into crisis in the 1970s, precipitating a transition to a new epoch, or stage, in its evolution. Our attempt to discern a new stage is what some have called a "*stadial* perspective" (Laibman, 2005) that sees history as constituted by ongoing quantitative change and moments of qualitative change within a larger totality that is open-ended. To speak of stages in the ongoing evolution of world capitalism does not imply there is a predetermined script. Rather, we can identify particular periods in which processes of change produce new material circumstances upon which collective agencies operate and new structural arrangements that they confront. Change in structure is rarely, if ever, an evolutionary process of linear succession or development. It often involves ruptures produced during periods of rapid or revolutionary change that can be quite unpredictable.

History is open-ended precisely because collective human agency and contingency are central to it. Analysis of agency and contingency is *behavioral* or *conjunctural* analysis—what people say and do, policies, social movements, short term changes in social and economic indicators, and so forth. As Latin America experienced rapid change in recent decades, for instance, many observers tried to explain them through behavioral or conjunctural analysis. But to gain a deeper comprehension of changes we must combine insights of conjunctural analysis with *structural* analysis or a study of underlying structures. These structures are independent of intentionality. Structural analysis frames conjunctural analysis. The distinction between structural and behavioral accounts of social processes and historical phenomena is not one of "right" and "wrong" but of the level of explanation we wish to provide. The greater the level of abstraction in our analysis, the greater the historic explanation we will provide. Particular historical structures that emerge, such as those in Latin America during the late twentieth and early twenty-first centuries, are shaped by the dynamic, manifold, and ongoing interplay of agency with the underlying historical processes that constitute deep structure, such as the laws of capitalist development and globalization as the current stage in the development of the world capitalist system.

We want to theorize the deeper, underlying structures to noticeable political events and social processes, such as the string of electoral victories for members of the left wing that swept Latin America early in the new century, the rise of militant indigenous social movements, the spread of transnational tourism throughout the region, or the heightened influence of global financial markets. Much of this book is concerned with documenting and analyzing these noticeable changes. But I am also concerned with making sense of them by placing this conjunctural analysis in the context of long-term and large-scale processes the explanation of which requires structural analysis of the historical system of world capitalism. In the present study I engage in structural-conjunctural analysis in order to explore the globalization of Latin America. This chapter summarizes the global capitalism approach. It traces the crisis and restructuring of world capitalism from the 1970s into the twenty-first century, and the rise of novel transnational processes and structures, as the backdrop to an historically informed analysis of Latin America's relationship to the larger global system. I will discuss this relationship in the following chapters, showing that what has taken place in recent decades is the region's reinsertion into global capitalism under a new model of economy and society.

Periodizing World Capitalism

Periodization of capitalism is an analytical tool that allows us to grasp changes in the system over time. It rests on several core observations about the nature of capitalism, especially the dynamic of expansion built into the system. Capitalism is not a system that rests on simple reproduction, in which what we have at the end of a socioeconomic cycle (however measured or spaced) is the same as when the cycle began. The dynamic of a tributary system, for instance, is based on a cycle in which ruling groups appropriate for their own consumption surpluses produced by exploited groups such as peasants or slaves. A tributary system may well engage in imperial expansion, and indeed most (among them the Roman, the Chinese, and the Aztec) build up great empires. But this outward expansion was based on an ever-greater extension of the areas and peoples incorporated in the payment of tribute so that conceptually the dynamic remained one of simple reproduction. In distinction, the capitalist system is characterized by expanded reproduction, so that what we have at the end of a given socioeconomic cycle is greater than when the cycle began. Indeed, if it is not greater the system faces a crisis.

This expanded reproduction is what Marx, among others, calls *accumulation*. The surplus that is appropriated from exploited classes, whether workers, peasants, or slaves, is not simply used for the consumption of the ruling groups but goes (at least a portion of it) to investment in a new round of accumulation that involves an expansion of the capitalist production process or the web of capitalist relations. In the words of Wallerstein (following Marx), capitalism is about the "endless accumulation of capital" (2004). There is a history of debates in the social sciences on the nature of accumulation and reproduction under noncapitalist and capitalist systems that I cannot take up here (but see, inter alia, discussion in Wolf, 1997). Robert Cox (also following Marx) refers to "modes of reproduction" in making the distinction between simple and expanded reproduction and refers to expanded reproduction as "development." He notes that the mode of reproduction comprises

> the processes whereby societies are extended through time by giving birth to, raising and educating a new generation and placing its members in their economic and social roles. Throughout much of human history, reproduction often seemed to have been a circular process, constantly repeated, through which the same structure of society was reproduced. Agrarian-based societies reproduced themselves in the forms either of small subsistence communities or of peasant villages part of whose product was extracted by a dominant political-religious class that took no part in material production but saw to the reproduction of the social-political order. Reproduction tended to be a circular, no-growth, nonaccumulative process. Development implies a reproduction process with both accumulation and a consequential change of structure. . . . Development was initiated through the capitalist mode. In capitalism, the labor hired by the capitalist produces more than is required for its own reproduction. The surplus is taken by the capitalist who uses it, not for consumption and conspicuous display ... but for investment in expanding the capacity to produce in the next cycle. . . . The term capitalist is used here exclusively in this sense as a mode of development that breaks the cycle of continuous reproduction and introduces a purposive time dimension, an upward spiral of accumulation, investment, expanded reproduction. (Cox, 1987:406, n. 7)

But along with its tendency toward expansion, capitalism has another essential aspect. The essence of capitalism is production undertaken through a particular form of social interaction: the *capital-labor relation*—or capitalist production relations—in order to exchange what is produced, *commodities,* in a market for profit. For capitalist production to take place there needs to be a class of workers, or of people that have no means of production of their own, such as land with which to farm or tools and workshops with which to produce for themselves. And there needs to be a class of capitalists, or people who have come into possession of these means of production and in turn require a supply of labor in order to work these means of production so that commodities can be produced and sold for a profit. The capital-labor relation refers to the relationship between workers and capitalists as they come together in the process of producing goods that people want or need, so that these two groups of people, or class groups, form a unity. *Primitive accumulation* is the process by which people come to be separated from the means of production—such as through colonial conquest or the loss of land to creditors—thus creating the conditions for capitalist production to take place.

Production is a form of social power. It is our species' social power to collectively transform nature in order to meet our material needs and reproduce our existence. This power, what Marx called our "species being," became "power over" when some people came to control the labor of others and the social product that emerged from that labor. Different forms of class society over the millennia have exhibited different configurations of social power (different class structures, political institutions, ideological mechanisms, and so on). A major part of the story of globalization is that a new configuration of social power is emerging worldwide, that is, a shift in power relations globally among social classes and groups. The entire battlefield, so to speak, in which contenders engage in diverse social struggles, has shifted in recent decades.

The dynamic of expansion built into capitalism, and specifically the dual nature of this expansion, is crucial to understanding globalization as a new epoch. Capitalism is an expansionary system in a double sense: extensively and intensively. First, it has constantly extended outward around the world to new areas that were previously outside the system of commodity production and brought these areas into capitalist market relations, whether through mechanisms of political and military domination or through the economic compulsion of the market. This is capitalism's *extensive* enlargement. Second, capitalism expands by *commodifying* social relations, the process whereby capitalist or commodity production replaces pre- or noncapitalist forms of production. Commodification constantly deepens, so that human activities that previously remained outside of the logic of capitalist production are brought into this logic. When such commodity relations penetrate these spheres of social life formally outside of the logic of profit-making this represents capitalism's *intensive* enlargement. In the 500-year history of world capitalism the system has constantly deepened (its intensive expansion), and it has constantly extended outward around the world (its extensive expansion).

In my definition, the core of globalization, theoretically conceived, is the near-culmination of the 500-year process of the spread of the capitalist system around the world, its extensive and intensive enlargement. The final stage of capitalism's extensive enlargement began with the wave of colonizing of the late nineteenth and early twentieth centuries and concluded with the re-incorporation of the former Soviet-bloc and Third World revolutionary states in the early 1990s after their earlier attempts at withdrawal from the system. There are no longer any significant regions of the world that remain outside of the system. In the emerging global capitalist configuration, transnational or global space is coming to supplant national spaces. Capitalist relations, moreover, are deepening in the sense that they have penetrated and commodified at an accelerated pace ever more institutions of social and cultural life. In the closing decades of the twentieth century hundreds of millions of people—peasants, artisans, small and medium merchants, industrialists and other middle classes—were wrenched from the means of production, proletarianized, and thrown into a global labor market. This process has continued into the twenty-first century and is likely to accelerate. To be sure there are still many millions in the world who are not yet proletarianized, and for that matter, capitalist relations cannot ever fully do away with noncapitalist social relations lest society would be destroyed. The point here, however, is this: there is no longer anything external to the system, not in the sense that it is now a "closed" system but in that (1) there are no longer any countries or regions that remain outside of world capitalism or still to be incorporated through original accumulation and (2) there is no longer autonomous accumulation outside of the sphere of global capital. Harvard economist Richard Freeman observes:

> The most fundamental economic development in this era of globalization [is] the doubling of the global labor force. The doubling I am referring to is the increased number of persons in the global economy that results from China, India and the ex-Soviet Union embracing market capitalism. In the 1980s and 1990s, workers from China, India and the former Soviet bloc entered the global labor pool. Of course, these workers had existed before then. The difference, though, was that their economies suddenly joined the global system of production and consumption. . . . The entry of China, India and the former Soviet bloc to the global capitalist economy is a turning point in economic history. For the first time, the vast majority of humans will operate under market capitalism. (Freeman, 2005:1, 4)

In arriving at this "global moment" the capitalist system has gone through previous mercantile, competitive industrial, and corporate (or "monopoly") epochs in its evolution (see, inter alia, Robinson, 2004a; Weaver, 2000). Each of these epochs in the history of capitalism has involved an expansion of the system, a successive incorporation of new territories around the world through colonial conquest and imperialism. Each epoch has also involved an intensive expansion of capitalist relations into noncapitalist spheres that are opened up to commodity relations and has seen the establishment of sets of institutions that made this expansion possible and organized long-term cycles of capitalist development.

The first epoch, often referred to as the mercantile era, or what others have called the commercial era or the era of primitive accumulation, opened with the symbolic date of 1492, when the violent conquest of what would become the Americas linked the Old and New Worlds and made the world a single place. Humankind became one totality in the years that followed. Mercantilism was based on control of an expanding worldwide trade in commodities, often accompanied by diverse coercive mechanisms of organizing captive populations for the production of these goods and/or coercion in their appropriation. In the mercantile epoch European commerce gradually came to dominate much of the world while Latin America was forcibly and totally transformed and integrated into an "Atlantic economy" (Wallerstein, 1974; Stavrianos, 1981; Smith, 1991). This period runs to another symbolic year, 1789. The French Revolution ushered in the second epoch—that of competitive, or industrial capitalism—highlighted by the rise of the nation-state, the bourgeoisie, and the industrial revolution. The defining feature of competitive capitalism was a large number of small firms producing consumer (wage) goods and buying and selling in competitive markets. British historian Eric Hobsbawm in his seminal historical studies refers to this great sweep of modern history as the ages of revolution, capital, and empire (1962, 1977, 1987). The industrial revolution consolidated the supremacy of the capitalist system over diverse tributary, slave, kinship, and other noncapitalist (or pre-capitalist) systems around the world. The Atlantic world economy that had been constructed in the preceding epoch underwent a dramatic new round of expansion. The capitalist system had new needs, such as the search for new raw materials and inputs for factory production, and a superior ability over the mercantile era to expand through new military and economic powers.

The epoch of competitive industrial capitalism ran into the late 1800s and gave way on the eve of the twentieth century to the era of corporate capitalism, or what some termed monopoly capitalism. We do not have a symbolic date for the transition from the second to the third epoch. About 1870 the second industrial revolution got under way, characterized by new mass production techniques; the systematic application of science to industry; the rise of the chemical, steel, railroad, and other new capital-intensive lead industries; and the central role of bank (finance) capital. This was a time of great national concentrations of capital out of earlier local and regional capitalist enterprises, the rise of the joint-stock company (the corporate form), the consolidation of national markets, the crystallization of national capitalist classes that took control of these markets, and the appearance of the oligopolistic structure of modern capitalism that characterized this epoch.

The period from the 1870s to 1945 was also a time of intense worldwide class struggle, interstate conflict, imperialist conquest, and anticolonial resistance; indeed, it was a period of hyper-expansion not seen since the original conquest of the Americas. Hilferding (1910) and Lenin (1917) theorized imperialism at this time as a higher stage of capitalism involving the export of capital in which the two world wars of the first half of the twentieth century were the result of competition among the core capitalist countries over markets, resources, colonial possessions, and labor supplies around the world. From the late 1800s into the early 1900s vast regions of Africa, Asia, and the Middle East were colonized or semi-colonized and brought violently, and firmly, into the system—an expansion now legitimated by scientific racism and such vicious colonial ideologies as the "white man's burden" and reinforced by a near-universal color line. Between 1800 and 1878 European rule increased from 35 to 67 percent of the earth's land surface; another 18 percent was added in new waves of annexation between 1875 and 1914 (Hoogvelt, 1997:18). The "scramble for Africa" among European colonial powers and the carving up of Africa they undertook at the Berlin conference make 1884 stand out as a key date symbolizing the new round of worldwide imperialism and colonialism.

Lenin and Hilferding underscored an essential feature of this previous era in capitalism. Capitalist classes were organized in their respective nations and utilized their respective national states to advance their interests around the world in competition with other national capitalist classes. Hence one of the key features of the nation-state phase of world capitalism was the role of the nation-state in organizing classes. The nation-state was the cocoon of the bourgeoisie. Capitalist competition unfolded through the political structure of the inter-state system and accounted for a great deal of inter-state conflict. By mediating the boundaries of accumulation the nation-state shaped—and gave a definite territorial and geopolitical profile to—the worldwide patterns of uneven capitalist development that informed twentieth-century theories of world political and economic processes.

Corporate Capitalism as Keynesian Capitalism

In the aftermath of World War II corporate capitalism became reorganized around a new model. The ideas of the British nationals John Maynard Keynes and William Beveridge and the American Henry Ford combined to bring about a new social structure of accumulation within corporate capitalism (given Anglo-American domination in the twentieth century it is not surprising that the hegemonic model came from these two countries). A social structure of accumulation refers to a set of mutually reinforcing social, economic, and political institutions and cultural and ideological norms fusing with and facilitating a successful pattern of capital accumulation over specific historic periods (Kotz, McDonough, and Reich, 1994). The particular model or social structure of accumulation that would consolidate around the national corporate stage of capitalism was not clear from the 1890s into the 1940s, as fascist and social democratic versions on either extreme disputed for hegemony. The defeat of fascism paved the way in the post–World War II period for a Keynes-Ford-Beveridge model, what Munck simply calls the "KFB social order" (Munck, 2002:35), or what in popular parlance was known as New Deal capitalism, welfare capitalism, social capitalism, and so on.

John Keynes had broken with the assumption of classical economic theory that the natural state of the capitalist economy was an equilibrium brought about by market forces allowed to operate unimpeded. Keynes observed that the market on its own could not generate sufficient aggregate demand and argued that such demand had to be fomented in order to avoid more crises like the 1930s depression. His demand-side economic strategy emphasized state intervention through credit and employment creation, progressive taxation, government spending on public works and social programs, and so on, to generate demand and other mechanisms for regulating (and therefore stabilizing) accumulation. In this way governments could overcome crises, assure long-term growth and employment, and stabilize capitalist society. The Keynesian revolution swept through the industrialized capitalist world and formed the basis for economic policy for much of the twentieth century.

Another core aspect of corporate capitalism that took hold at this time was the Fordist regime of accumulation: a way of organizing the economy that was associated with a large number of easily organized workers in centralized production locations, mass production through fixed, standardized processes, and mass consumption (Lipietz, 1987; Harvey, 1990). It was known as "Fordist" because it became generalized following the lead of the automobile tycoon Henry Ford. He argued that capitalists and governments should stabilize the national industrial capitalist systems that had emerged in the previous century by incorporating workers into the new society through higher salaries, benefits, and secure employment coupled with tight control and regimentation of the workforce (Rupert, 1995). Ford himself was a bitterly anti-union industrial tyrant. Ford's initial shop-floor changes grew into Fordism as a "class compromise" between workers and capitalists mediated by the state, involving government measures to regulate capitalist competition and the class struggle.

The new model combined Keynesian macroeconomics and the Fordist regime of accumulation with a program of welfare epitomized by the famous *Beveridge Report,* presented to the British Parliament in 1942 by William Beveridge (*Beveridge Report,* 1942). The report was premised on the notion of a "social minimum" of consumption for all citizens: a social safety net, or more sociologically, the minimum required for *social reproduction.* The Beveridge program, a twentieth-century "social contract," included unemployment insurance, public health and education programs, social security (retirement pensions), disability payments, consumption subsidies or cash payments for the poor, and so on. This social welfare model is also associated with twentieth-century social democratic projects. Social democracy split from the anti-capitalist socialist movement. Its advocates believed that capitalism could be controlled through Keynesian, Fordist, and other state interventionist and redistributive mechanisms and eventually converted into socialism. Social democrats took power in many European and Third World countries in the post–World War II period and implemented sometimes far-reaching social welfare and redistributive programs without actually superseding capitalism itself. The particular type of welfare systems and the extent of social provisions varied from country to country. Nonetheless, the notion of a modicum of social solidarity and of the responsibility of states to assure the social reproduction of all members of society became embedded in the politics and culture of corporate capitalism; it became a social norm, or in Gramscian terms a "common sense" assumption about society.

The KFB social order arose not as the result of a particular design worked out by any one group, just as its breakdown and the onset of globalization was not the result of any design. Outcomes are the result of ever shifting historical constellations of social forces in struggle and cooperation that face the limits of material conditions and the possibilities opened up by ideology, imagination, and utopian visions. The KFB social order was the outcome of fierce class and social struggles from the late eighteenth century into the post–World War II period. Capital faced territorial, institutional, and other limits bound up with the nation-state system that imposed a series of constraints and forced it to reach an historic "class compromise" with working and popular classes. These classes could place demands on national states to constrain the power of capital and enforce a measure of social control over the capitalist production process because national states enjoyed a significant if varying degree of autonomy to intervene in the phase of distribution.[1] In this way it was possible to capture and redirect some of the surplus. In constructing a Fordist model of national capitalism, governments, universities, businesses, trade unions, and other bureaucracies followed Keynes' arguments that governments should intervene in the process of production and distribution by regulations and incentives, and by capturing and redistributing surpluses (wealth) through taxes, the credit system, and other mechanisms. Capitalists agreed to this arrangement because it was in their interests, and besides, they had little choice given the social upheavals against rampant market forces and the threat of further class conflict. The combination of Fordism and Keynesianism was essentially a model of accumulation based on a redistribution of wealth, on regulation, and on a (national) state supervised class compromise between capitalists and workers.

Diverse Keynesian models spread throughout the twentieth century from the cores of the world capitalist system to the former colonial domains in Latin America, Africa, and Asia. These countries tended to pursue a multiclass development model along radical Keynesian lines, often referred to as developmentalist, populist, or corporatist (Malloy, 1977). As we will see in the case of Latin America, developmentalist capitalism took on a form distinct from its First World New Deal and social democratic variants, often involving a much greater role for the state and the public sector; mass social mobilizations growing out of anti-colonial, anti-dictatorial, and national-liberation movements; and populist or corporatist political projects. Meanwhile, the so-called Second World developed a particular redistributive model of accumulation that some considered socialist and others "state capitalist," but always a part of the larger world capitalist system. The diverse First, Second, and Third World models were all predicated on a redistributive logic and on incorporation of labor and other popular classes into national historical blocs.

World capitalism developed in this period within the nation-state and through the inter-state system. Nation-states were linked to each other through the international division of labor and through commercial and financial exchanges in an integrated international market. The leading capitalist powers—that is, the victors in World War II—set up the Bretton Woods system in 1944 as a multilateral post-War system through which the trade and monetary relations of the capitalist world could be regulated in a stable manner. Bretton

[1.] I use the term nation-state to refer to a geographic/territorial-political (and perhaps in some ways culturally distinct) entity in the modern world, whereas I use the term *national state* to refer to the state ("government") of a nation-state, in distinction to other forms of state, such as the state of precapitalist empires.

Woods institutions included the International Monetary Fund (IMF) and the World Bank (WB), and the General Agreement on Tariffs and Trade (GATT) to regulate this international economic system. The system included a fixed exchange rate and capital controls by individual countries that gave little incentive to currency and international financial speculation (this "gold standard" meant that the U.S. government guaranteed the convertibility of dollars into gold at a fixed rate). In this way the system provided for more insulated forms of national control over economic and social policy and greater autonomy in internal capitalist development, even as the international market disciplined countries into supporting the international rules of exchange rates and exchange and reproduced the world capitalist power structure.

Crisis and the Restructuring of World Capitalism

The world economy experienced a sustained period of growth in the quarter century after World War II, the so called golden age of capitalism (Marglin and Schor, 1990). But the illusion of prosperity burst with the worldwide economic downturn that began in the 1970s and that threw national corporate capitalism into crisis (Cox, 1987; Webber and Rigby, 1996; Kolko, 1988). This crisis manifest itself economically in recessions, a decline in labor productivity, profit rates and profitable investment opportunities, stagflation (stagnation plus inflation, resulting from the refusal of workers to shoulder the crisis), unemployment, an energy crisis, widespread fiscal and balance of payments crises, rising international debt, and the decision by the Nixon administration in the United States to end gold convertibility of the dollar. This crisis manifest itself politically in a string of Third World revolutions (between 1974 and 1980 no fewer than fourteen Third World countries fell to national liberation movements [Halliday, in Hoogvelt, 1997:52]), an upsurge in class conflict, social movements, armed liberation struggles, and countercultures that reached a crescendo in the tumultuous events of 1968 and seemed to be developing by the 1970s into a system wide crisis of hegemony and political domination (Robinson, 1996a).

The social origin of this crisis was to be found in the relative strength that working and popular classes won worldwide in relation to capital after many decades of class and social struggles. Organized labor, increased taxes on profits and income, state regulation, revolutions in the Third World, and the explosion of social movements and counter-hegemonic cultural practices everywhere constricted private capital's real or perceived capacity for accumulation. The expansion of collective rights, the institutionalization of Keynesian-Fordist class compromise, and the prevailing norms of a "moral economy" that assumed capital and state reciprocities with labor and citizens and an ethnical obligation to minimal social reproduction—all of this burdened capital with social rigidities that had to be reversed for a new phase of capitalist growth. Capital and its political representatives and organic intellectuals organized a broad offensive—economic, political, ideological, military—that was symbolically spearheaded by the Reagan-Thatcher alliance. The Trilateral Commission, in its seminal 1975 report, *The Crisis of Democracy* (Crozier, Huntington, and Watanuki, 1975), diagnosed the problem as too much democracy and therefore not enough "governability" (read: social control and obedience). Emerging transnational elites from the centers of power in the world system launched a global counterrevolution that would be as much political and economic as social, cultural, and ideological, and that was still being fought out in manifold arenas in the twenty-first century.

In structural terms, this crisis was not merely cyclical. Mainstream business-cycle theories identify periodic swings from expansion to recession in the market economy. But world-system, critical political economy, international relations, and neo-Marxist theories have long pointed to the deeper cycles of expansion and contraction in world capitalism, sometimes called Kondratieff cycles (after the Russian economist who wrote about them in the early twentieth century), or observed fifty-year swings in the system, in which a period of expansion is followed by a period of contraction. Cyclical crises, in these accounts, eventually accumulate into more generalized crises involving social and political upheavals and ushering in periods of restructuring. Restructuring crises result in novel forms that replace historical patterns of capital accumulation and the institutional arrangements that facilitated them (see, inter alia, Aglietta, 1979; Kotz et al., 1994; Arrighi, 1994; Arrighi and Silver, 1999; Harvey, 1982; Frank, 1980; Lipietz, 1987; Amin, 1994). The world capitalist crisis that began in the 1970s is generally identified as the turning point for globalization and in my view signaled the transition to a new transnational stage in the system.

For much of the twentieth century all three "Worlds"—First World Keynesian capitalism, Second World state socialist-redistributive models, and Third World developmentalist capitalism—shared two common features: state intervention in the economy and a redistributive logic. The crisis that began in the 1970s could not be resolved within the framework of these post–World War II social structures of accumulation. Neither "socialism in one country" nor "Keynesianism in one country" was any longer a tenable project as we entered the globalization age. All three models began to face crises of legitimacy and political authority that evoked massive restructuring and integration into emergent global capitalism. In the First World there was a progressive breakdown of the Keynesian-Fordist welfare states. In the Second World the socialist–state redistributive projects experienced crisis and collapse in the 1980s and early 1990s. In the Third World developmentalist projects became exhausted as manifested above all in economic contraction and the debt crisis of the 1980s.

Globalization became a viable strategy as capitalists and state managers searched for new modes of accumulation. "Going global" allowed capital to shake off the constraints that nation-state capitalism had placed on accumulation and to break free of the class compromises and concessions that had been imposed by working and popular classes and by national governments in the preceding epoch. New technologies—particularly the communications and information revolution, but also revolutions in transportation, marketing, management, automation, robotization, and so on—were globalizing in the sense that they made it materially possible for capital to go global. It is important to recall, however, that globalization is not driven by a technological determinism. Capitalists (and governments) turned to inventing and applying new technologies in response to other processes going on in society that engender technological development, namely the drive, built into capitalism itself by competition and class struggle, to maximize profits by reducing labor and other factor costs. Deregulation, especially financial deregulation, made possible the use of this technology to develop new transnational circuits of accumulation. The decision by the U.S. government to abandon the fixed exchange rate system in 1973 effectively did away with the Bretton Woods system and, together with deregulation, opened the floodgate to a massive transnational capital movement and the meteoric spread of transnational corporations (TNCs). Capital achieved a newfound global mobility, or ability to operate across borders in new ways, which ushered in the era of global capitalism. The renewed power to discipline labor that this afforded transnational capital altered the worldwide correlation of class and social forces in favor of transnational capital. What had been international capital in the preceding epoch metamorphosed into transnational capital.

Emerging global elites and transnational capitalists set about to dismantle the distinct models associated with national corporate capitalism and to construct a new global "flexible" regime of accumulation. In broad strokes, Keynesianism was replaced by monetarist policies, deregulation, and a supply side approach that included regressive taxation and new incentives for capital. A new capital-labor relation based on deunionization, flexible workers, and deregulated work conditions replaced the Fordist class compromise. Social austerity and the law of the market in social reproduction replaced the welfare social contract. More specifically, the prospects for capital to accumulate and make profits were restored beginning in the 1980s by the following four key developments associated with capitalist globalization:

1. A new capital-labor relation based on the deregulation and "flexibilization" of labor.

2. A new round of *extensive* and *intensive* expansion. Extensively, the system expanded through the reincorporation of major areas of the former Third and Second worlds into the world capitalist economy, so that by the 1990s no region remained outside the system. Intensively, public and community spheres that formerly lay outside (or buffered from) the logic of market relations (profit making) were commodified and opened up to accumulation through privatization, state deregulation, and reregulation, including the extension of intellectual property rights, and so on.

3. The creation of a global legal and regulatory structure to facilitate what were emerging globalized circuits of accumulation, including the creation of the World Trade Organization.

4. The imposition of the neoliberal model on countries throughout the Third World, and also the First and former Second worlds, involving structural adjustment programs that created the conditions for the free operation of capital within and across borders and the harmonization of accumulation conditions worldwide. Through neoliberalism the world has increasingly become a single unified field for global capitalism.

Global Neoliberalism

The model for global restructuring rested on the assumptions of neoclassical economics that eclipsed Keynesianism and led to a particular set of social and economic policies known as neoliberalism. Neoclassical economics, with its doctrines of laissez-faire, comparative advantage, free trade and efficiency, became hegemonic in universities and governments across the First World. The theoretical rational for neoliberalism was first sketched by Friedrich Hayek and the Austrian school of economics and later refined by Milton Friedman and other neoclassical economists from the monetary school at the University of Chicago (the "Chicago boys") [see Hayek, 1978; Friedman, 1962, 1974]. It was implemented experimentally in Chile following the 1973 coup d'état that brought the dictatorship of Agusto Pinochet to power. But it was the governments of Ronald

Reagan in the United States (1981–1989) and Margaret Thatcher in the United Kingdom (1979–1990) that catapulted neoliberalism to the center stage of world capitalism, and international financial agencies (IFIs), such as the International Monetary Fund and the World Bank, that imposed the model on much of the Third World in the 1980s and 1990s through structural adjustment programs, in what came to be known as the Washington consensus (Williamson, 1990, 1993; Gore, 2000). Neoliberalism, in its heyday in the 1990s, had become dominant not just in the IFIs but in most international agencies and intergovernmental organizations, including such forums as the Organization of American States and the Organization for Economic Cooperation and Development, and the technical agencies of the United Nations, such as the World Health Organization, the Food and Agricultural Organization, and the United Nations International Children's Education Fund.

It was not so much the ideas or ideology of neoliberalism that converted it into the dominant model as it was the timing of its rise. The concrete program it prescribes was perfectly functional for transnational capital at the particular historic moment in which the major combines of capital worldwide were transnationalizing and seeking to develop new methods of accumulation and to impose new social relations of production—what Max Weber meant by a "fit between ideas and institutions." Neoliberalism is a concrete program and an ideology, a culture, a philosophical worldview that takes classical liberalism and individualism to an extreme. It glorifies the detached, isolated individual—a fictitious state of human existence—and her creative potential, which is allegedly unleashed when she becomes unencumbered by state regulation and other collective constraints on freedom. With the death of the collective, "there is no society, only the individual," as Margaret Thatcher was to famously declare. Neoliberalism as an ideology legitimates individual survival, everyone for herself, and the law of the jungle. The means of survival are to be allocated strictly on a market basis; in its ideological construct, neoliberalism sees these markets not as created and structured through state and societal relations of power and domination but as products of nature. Followed to its logical conclusion, neoliberalism as a prescription for society would mean the end of social reciprocity, of collective redistribution of the social product, an end to the family, and eventually to the species itself.

The globalization of exchange and production mandates a convergence in economic policies and institutions, of socioeconomic systems. Apart from its ideological and philosophical dimensions, programmatically global neoliberalism involved twin aspects, rigorously pursued by global elites with the backing of a powerful and well-organized lobby of transnational corporations. One was worldwide market liberalization and the construction of a new legal and regulatory superstructure for the global economy. The other was the internal restructuring and global integration of each national economy. The combination of the two is intended to create a "liberal world order," an open global economy, and a global policy regime that breaks down all national barriers to the free movement of transnational capital *between* borders and the free operation of capital *within* borders in the search for new productive outlets for excess accumulated capital.

The first of these aspects, worldwide market liberalization, accelerated dramatically with the Uruguay Round of General Agreement on Tariffs and Trade (GATT) negotiations in the 1980s, which established a sweeping new set of world trade rules to regulate the new global economy based on (1) freedom of investment and capital movements; (2) the liberalization of services, including banks; (3) intellectual property rights; and (4) a free movement of goods. Transnational elites also promoted regional integration processes, including the North American Free Trade Agreement (NAFTA), the European Union (EU), and the Asia Pacific Economic Conference (APEC), among others. The World Trade Organization (WTO), created in 1995 following the Uruguay Round, was perhaps the most potent symbol of the liberalized global economy. With its independent jurisdiction and unprecedented powers to enforce the GATT provisions, it was the first supranational institution with a coercive capacity not embedded in any particular nation-state but rather directly in transnational functionaries and a transnational corporate elite.

The second of these aspects, economic restructuring programs, was designed in the 1970s and 1980s by the IFIs and the think tanks of emerging transnational elites (see, e.g., Fishlow et al., 1978; Cox, 1983; Williamson, 1993) and accompanied by a new neoliberal development discourse (Robinson, 2002; 2003). These programs sought to achieve within each country the macroeconomic equilibrium and liberalization required by transnationally mobile capital and to integrate each nation and region into globalized circuits of accumulation. The model attempted to harmonize a wide range of fiscal, monetary, industrial, labor, and commercial policies among multiple nations, as a requirement for mobile transnational capital to function simultaneously, and often instantaneously, among numerous national borders. The program called for the elimination of state intervention in the economy and the regulation of individual nation-states over the activities of capital in their territories. Between 1978 and 1992 more than seventy countries undertook 566 stabilization and structural adjustment programs imposed by the IMF and the World Bank (George, 1992:xvi). These programs became the major mechanism of adjusting local economies to the global economy. What took place through these programs was a massive restructuring of the productive apparatus in these countries and the reintegration into global capitalism of vast zones of the former Third and Second worlds (Overbeek, 1993). Economic integration processes and neoliberal structural adjustment programs are driven by transnational capital's campaign to open up every country to its activities, to tear down all barriers to the movement of goods and capital, and to create a single unified field in which global capital can operate unhindered across all national borders (Chossudovsky, 1997; Green, 1995; Robinson, 2001a, 2001b).

Neoliberal restructuring, more specifically, involved two phases. The first was known as "stabilization," or a package of fiscal, monetary, exchange and related measures intended to achieve macroeconomic stability inside the adjusted country. This included abolishing subsidies for food, transportation, and utilities; cutting public employment; and social austerity measures, such as cuts in health and educational services. Stabilization was then followed by a second stage known as structural adjustment and comprising (1) liberalization of trade and finances, which opens the economy to the world market; (2) deregulation, which removes the state from economic decision making and from mediating capital-labor relations; and (3) privatization of formerly public spheres that could hamper capital accumulation if criteria of public interest over private profit are left operative. Grounded in the assumptions of neoclassic economics, these structural adjustment programs were justified by the need to generate a trade surplus to accommodate debt service payments and reduce trade deficits, the alleged inefficiency of the public sector, and the need to control inflation to close budget deficits and restore fiscal solvency and macroeconomic equilibrium. Trade liberalization and a reallocation of resources to the external sector are intended to increase exports and, by definition, result in a process of re-articulation and integration into the global economy. This opening to the world market is accompanied by the privatization of "inefficient" public sectors and internal liberalization, such as deregulation of financial systems and labor laws, in order to attract investment and allocate resources efficiently. Fiscal solvency is to be achieved through austerity programs involving expenditure reductions and revenue increases, which usually entails cuts in social programs, regressive taxes on consumption, the elimination of subsidies, public sector layoffs, and a rise in interest rates (for details, see Gelinas, 1998).

Notwithstanding the ideological claims of its promoters, the neoliberal model is driven more pragmatically by the breakdown of the earlier Keynesian-redistributive nation-state based accumulation strategies in the face of transnationalization and the need for a renovated policy regime capable of facilitating the new global model. Indeed, in the larger context, disequilibrium itself is a consequence of the breakdown of earlier national accumulation structures. The neoliberal program is rational vis-à-vis the *logic* of global capital accumulation, which is why the works of well-known economists who explain and defend neoliberalism from a neoclassical theoretical perspective are not merely "wrong" or ideological in the narrow sense (well-known studies are, inter alia, Balussa, 1981, 1989; Choski and Papageorgiou, 1986; Kruger, 1978; Sachs, 1989; Williamson 1990). The model generates the overall conditions for the profitable ("efficient") renewal of capital accumulation. Internal conditions of profitability are determined by compatibility of the local with the global environment. Adjustment creates the policy environment and the market signals for a shift in resources to external sectors. Economic reactivation in each adjusted country is achieved through the introduction or expansion of activities linked to the global economy and the integration of "national" accumulation circuits into globalized circuits. However, from the viewpoint of a broader *social logic* the model is irrational. With few exceptions, neoliberal adjustment programs have resulted in a fall in popular consumption, a deterioration of social conditions, a rise in poverty, immiseration and insecurity, heightened inequalities, social polarization, and resultant political conflict (see, e.g., Green, 1995; Cheru, 1989; Chossudovsky, 1997, 2005; Cornia, Jelly, and Stewart, 1987). The affirmation by neoclassical economists and their neoliberal policy counterparts that "free" markets produce efficient and socially beneficent results, it must be stressed, is entirely theoretical, not empirically based on the actual results of markets much less on the historical experience of capitalist development.

By synchronizing each national economic environment to an integrated global economic environment neoliberalism has served as the policy "grease" of global capitalism. To the extent that the model has been implemented it has kept the gears of the system in sync with one another. Greased by neoliberalism, global capitalism tears down all nonmarket structures that have in the past placed limits on, or acted as a protective layer against, the accumulation of capital. Deregulation made available new zones to resource exploitation, privatization opened up to profit-making public and community spheres, ranging from health care and education to police and prison systems. Nonmarket spheres of human activity—public spheres managed by states and private spheres linked to community and family—are broken up, commodified, and transferred to capital. As countries in the South integrate into global capitalism through neoliberal restructuring they become "emerging markets" that provide new market segments, pools of labor, and opportunities for transnational investors to unload excess capital, whether in productive or financial investment. By prying open and making accessible to transnational capital every layer of the social fabric, neoliberalism "dis-embeds" the global economy from global society, and the state cedes to the market as the sole organizing power in the economic and social sphere.

In Latin America the military dictatorships that came to power in Chile in 1973 and Argentina in 1976 launched the neoliberal process, which then became generalized in 1982 when Mexico announced its inability to service its debt and declared a moratorium on making payments, thus promulgating the international debt crisis. In 1985 Bolivia became the first country to implement a full-blown stabilization and structural adjustment program. In the ensuing years every single Latin America country, with the exception of Cuba, undertook neoliberal adjustment as globalization swept the continent, although the timing and the pace and extent to which each country embraced the neoliberal "economic reform" program varied. The next chapter explores the new transnational economic model in Latin America that neoliberal reforms helped bring about. Measured in terms of the sweeping transformation of the region's political economy, the juggernaut of neoliberalism was largely successful in the 1980s and 1990s.

But by the early twenty-first century neoliberalism had become largely discredited and was in crisis, as I will discuss in later chapters (see also Gore, 2000). In the face of the numerous problems and limitations associated with the model, policy makers from the international financial institutions (IFIs) and other agencies of what below I will refer to as the transnational state began to call for a new second generation of reforms. The new reforms were to involve legal and political changes that would create a more predictable institutional environment, including greater transparency in the activities of public and private economic agents (i.e., government ministries, stock markets, private firms, etc.), greater efficiency in tax collection (but not via a progressive system or taxation of profits), and "good government." They were also to include a new round of deregulation targeting labor markets, which were to be made flexible, and local capital markets and financial systems, which were to be opened up and integrated to a much greater extent to the global financial system. These new reforms were to include as well antipoverty programs that would not involve any systematic redistribution as in the earlier era but limited social programs targeting the most impoverished and funded by allocations from the IFIs or by regressive taxation on income and sales. The general idea was to sustain neoliberal capitalist globalization by correcting what transnational elites assessed to be weaknesses in the first generation of reforms. Those macroeconomic structural reforms were now seen as necessary but insufficient; institutional reforms were to be an indispensable complement of the workings of the market (Williamson, 2002; Naim, 1995), in accordance with the insights from institutional economics, which emphasizes the importance of institutions in assuring regularity and predictability in economic and other transactions (see Robinson, 2002).

A New Global Capital-Labor Relation

As capital became liberated from the nation-state and assumed new power relative to labor with the onset of globalization, states shifted from reproducing Keynesian social structures of accumulation to servicing the general needs of the new patterns of global accumulation. An emerging global social structure of accumulation came increasingly to be superimposed on, and to transform, existing national social structures, and at the core of the global structure was a new capital-labor relation. The restructuring of the labor process under globalization, what some have called the casualization or informalization of labor associated with post-Fordist flexible accumulation, involves new systems of labor control and diverse contingent categories of labor, the essence of which is cheapening and disciplining labor, making it "flexible" and readily available for transnational capital in worldwide labor pools. As the global economy integrates local economies into its chains of production, finance, and distribution, and as more and more work becomes subcontracted, outsourced, and flexibilized, workers around the world become appendages of these global networks, which relegate them to even more extensive forms of alienation than in previous capitalist labor relations. The new capital-labor relation that constitutes the essence of flexibility did not appear overnight; it has come about gradually through the ongoing rollback of earlier reciprocities and social wages involving great struggles and ongoing conflicts.

The new variants of capitalist labor relations have been broadly discussed in the globalization literature (see, inter alia, Berberoglu, 2002; Kolko, 1988; Harvey, 1990; Cox, 1987; Amin, 1994; Dicken, 1998; Barker and Christensen,

1998; Harrison, 1994; Lash and Urry, 1987; Yates, 2003; Lipietz, 1987; Ross and Trachte, 1990; Bowles, Gordon, and Weisskopf, 1990). They include subcontracting and contract labor, outsourcing, part-time and temp work, informal work, home-work, and telecommuting, the revival of patriarchal workshops and family labor units, sweatshops, and other oppressive production relations. While actual labor conditions still vary widely from country to country—and much more importantly, from sector to sector, and within distinct groups of workers within global production chains—there are general processes of "downward leveling" and deunionization, the lengthening of the working day and increases in absolute surplus value extraction, the increasing use worldwide of super-exploited immigrant communities, and new gendered and racialized hierarchies among labor. In general, we are witness to the Wal-Martization of labor. We have gone from the Ford factory worker under the old Fordist labor regime to the Wal-Mart service sector worker under the new flexible labor regime. The precarious Wal-Mart service workers who labor as a forced part-time employee, without benefits, heavily feminized, barred from unionizing, for wages that do not assure social reproduction, and so forth, give us the quintessential image of the new class relations of global capitalism.

There is also the rise of a new global "underclass" of supernumeraries or "redundants" who are alienated and not absorbed into the global capitalist economy and who are structurally under- and unemployed. Hundreds of millions of supernumeraries swell the ranks of a global army of reserve labor at the same time as they hold down the wages and leverage ability among those absorbed into the global economy. The supernumeraries are subject to new forms of repressive and authoritarian social control and to an oppressive cultural and ideological dehumanization. There is a systematic denigration in official discourse and Hollywood culture of the outcast and their depiction as "undeserving." This culture of global capitalism glorifies policing and militarization, constructs all those who resist, or even question the logic of the dominant order as incomprehensible, even crazed, *Others*. The intensified flow of peoples and symbols across borders and with it much greater physical, cultural, and symbolic mixing lays fertile ground for the racialization of class relations in new ways and in many different settings, for new or changing racist structures that involve both those integrated into globalized circuits of accumulation and those marginalized from such circuits.

Workers in the global economy under these flexible arrangements are increasingly treated as a subcontracted component rather than a fixture internal to employer organizations. In the Keynesian-Fordist order, labor supply and work force needed to be stable, which lent itself to a more regulated and protected capital-labor relation. In global capitalism, however, labor is reduced to an input just as any other, meaning that it needs to be totally flexible, available in large numbers that can be tapped, added to the mix, shifted, and dispensed with at will. A flexible labor regime allows capital to reduce labor costs and transfer more value to itself. The strategy is to reduce to a maximum all factor costs. Labor becomes an input just like any other and as a factor cost, reducing it to a maximum means its deregulation, flexibilization, and casualization. In these circumstances, labor is increasingly only a naked commodity, no longer embedded in relations of reciprocity rooted in social and political communities that were historically institutionalized in nation-states. The notion of responsibility, however minimal, that governments have for their citizens or that employers have toward their employees is dissolved in the face of this new class relation. In this age of "savage capitalism" unleashed from social constraints there is a veritable rollback of the historical or moral element in wage labor, driven by a culture of competitive individualism at whose fringe is a resurrected Social Darwinism in which norms and values of collective survival have all but disappeared.

These new systems of labor control rest in my view, in part, on the disjuncture between nation-state institutionality and capital's new transnational space. In the 1970s crisis, workers were unwilling to assume the burden of the crisis. But globalization brought about a change in power relations worldwide between capital and labor. Beginning in the 1970s capital began to abandon earlier reciprocities with labor forged in the epoch of national corporate capitalism precisely because the process of globalization allowed it to break free of nation-state constraints. Globalization facilitates these new labor patterns in a dual sense: first, capital has exercised its power over labor through new patterns of flexible accumulation made possible by enabling "third wave" technologies, the elimination of spatial barriers to accumulation, and the control over space these changes bring; second, globalization itself involves a vast acceleration of the primitive accumulation of capital worldwide, a process in which millions have been wrenched from the means of production, proletarianized, and thrown into a global labor market shaped by transnational capital. The entry of China, India, and the former Soviet bloc into the global economy resulted in a doubling of the global labor market, from 1.46 billion to near 3 billion workers by 2000, which resulted in a decline in the global capital/labor ratio to just 55 to 60 percent of what it had been (Freeman, 2005:2).

Novel Aspects of Global Capitalism

Globalization as a fourth epoch in world capitalism is marked by a number of fundamental shifts in the system, including (1) the rise of truly transnational capital and a new globally integrated production and financial system; (2) the transnationalization of classes and the rise of a transnational capitalist class as the hegemonic class worldwide; (3) the rise of a transnational state apparatus; and (4) novel relations of power and inequality in global society.

A Transnational Production and Financial System

Capital has come to achieve a newfound global mobility in a double sense, in that the material *and* the political obstacles to its unfettered movement around the world have dramatically come down. New patterns of accumulation opened up by globalizing technologies both require and make possible economies of scale that are truly global and require a more generalized commodification of the world economy. Enabling technologies have combined with liberalization of the world economy, neoliberal restructuring, and other changes in the state to lift the political barriers to global mobility. Since the 1970s, the emergence of globally mobile transnational capital increasingly divorced from specific countries has facilitated the globalization of production: that is, the fragmentation and decentralization of complex production processes, the worldwide dispersal of the different segments in these chains, and their functional integration into vast global chains of production and distribution.

World production is thus reorganized into new transnational, or global, circuits of accumulation through which values move instantaneously. National economies are reorganized and reinserted as component elements of this new global production and financial system (on the anatomy of this system, see Dicken, 1998; McMichael, 1996), which is a world economic structure that is qualitatively distinct from that of previous epochs, when each country had a distinct national economy linked externally to one another through trade and financial flows. This is a shift from international market integration to global productive integration. I have referred to this distinction elsewhere (Robinson, 2004a) as between a *world economy* (in which nation-states are linked to each other via trade and financial flows) to a *global economy* (in which the production process itself becomes globally integrated). At the same time an integrated global financial system has replaced the national bank-dominated financial systems of the earlier period. Global financial flows since the 1980s are qualitatively different from the international financial flows of the earlier period.

Globalization refers to a process characterized by relatively novel articulations of social power that were not available in earlier historic periods. The increasingly total mobility achieved by capital has allowed it to search out around the world the most favorable conditions for different phases of globalized production, including the cheapest labor, the most favorable institutional environment (e.g., low taxes) and regulatory conditions (e.g., lax environmental and labor laws), a stable social environment, and so on. This worldwide decentralization and fragmentation of the production process has taken place together with the centralization of command and control of the global economy in transnational capital. Transnational capital is the hegemonic fraction of capital on a world scale in the sense that it imposes its direction on the global economy and shapes the character of production and social life everywhere.

Although real power and control still remains rigidly hierarchal and has actually become more concentrated under globalization, the actual organizational form of economic activity is characterized by decentralized webs of horizontally interlocked networks in distinction to the old centralized hierarchies based on vertical integration. The rise of the global economy has been founded on the phenomenal spread since the late 1970s of diverse new economic arrangements associated with the transition from the Fordist regime of accumulation to new post-Fordist flexible regimes (see, inter alia, Harvey, 1990; Cox, 1987; Amin, 1994; Dicken, 1998; Lash and Urry, 1987; Hoogvelt, 1997; Lipietz, 1987; Fröbel et al., 1980). Subcontracting and outsourcing have become basic organizational features of economic activity worldwide. In the earlier epochs of capitalism, firms tended to organize entire sequences of economic production, distribution, and service from within. The *maquiladora,* or offshore, factories that are the epitome of the global assembly line are based on this type of subcontracting network. As the phenomenon of subcontracting and outsourcing spread in the 1970s–1990s, it was concentrated at first in low-skill, labor-intensive industries, such as textiles and apparel, toys, and electronics. But by the late 1990s the move to offshore production had spread to such advanced economic activities as the production of semiconductors, aerospace manufacturing, and network computing, and by the twenty-first century the outsourcing of services (both low end and high end) was well under way. It included the decentralized worldwide relocation of such jobs as telephone operators, graphic designers, accountants, computer programmers, engineers (Iritani, 2000:18), and even Hollywood movie production (Horn, 2005).

Subcontracting and outsourcing, along with a host of other new economic arrangements, such as formal and informal transnational business alliances, licensing agreements, local representation, and so on, make possible new subdivisions and specialization in production. These arrangements have resulted in the creation of vast transnational production chains and complex webs of vertical and horizontal integration patterns across the globe. The transnational corporations (TNCs) that drive the global economy are, according to Dicken, "also locked into *external* networks of relationships with a myriad of other firms: transnational and domestic, large and small, public and private" (1998:223). It is through such interconnections that small local firms and economic agents in one country may be directly linked to a global production network, even when such firms or agents serve only a very restricted geographic area. Such interrelationships between economic agents and firms of different sizes and types "increasingly span national boundaries to create a set of *geographically nested relationships from local to global scales*" (1998:223). The concepts of flexible accumulation and network structure capture the organizational form of globalized circuits (on this network structure, see, in particular, Castells, 2000).

Global production and service chains, or what sociologists have alternatively referred to as global commodity chains (Gereffi and Korzeniewicz, 1994) comprise a key concept in the study of globalization. These chains link sequences of economic activities in which each stage adds some value or plays some role in the production and distribution of goods and services worldwide. The structural properties of these chains or networks are *global* in character, in that accumulation is embedded in *global* markets and involves *global* enterprise organization and sets of *global* capital-labor relations, especially deregulated and casualized labor pools worldwide. Transnational capital, as organized into the giant TNCs, coordinates these vast chains, incorporating numerous agents and social groups into complex global networks.

While some academics continue to reject the notion of a qualitatively new global economy, those who are in a commanding position in that economy are clear on the novel configurations and processes that globalization entails. Among them, IBM's chair and CEO, Samuel Palmisano, affirmed in a 2006 article in *Foreign Affairs* that use of the very term "multinational corporation" suggests "how antiquated our thinking about it is." It is worth quoting Palmisano at some length:

The Multinational corporation (MNC), often seen as a primary agent of globalization, is taking on a new form. . . . This new kind of enterprise is best understood as 'global' rather than 'multinational'. . . . The MNC of the late twentieth century had little in common with the international firms of a hundred years earlier, and those companies were very different from the great trading enterprises of the 1700s. The type of business organization that is now emerging—the globally integrated enterprise—marks just as big a leap. . . . There were, of course, many recognizably global products throughout the twentieth century, from Coca-Cola to the Sony Walkman. . . . But by and large, corporations continued to organize production market by market, within the traditional boundaries of the nation-state . . . Starting in the early 1970s, the revolution in information technology (IT) . . . standardized technologies and business operations all over the world, interlinking and facilitating work both within and among companies. This combination . . . changed the sorts of globalization that companies found possible. . . . Simply put, the emerging globally integrated enterprise is a company that fashions its strategy, its management, and its operations in pursuit of a new goal: the integration of production and value delivery worldwide. State borders define less and less the boundaries of corporate thinking or practice. (127–129)

Competition in the new global economy dictates that firms must establish global as opposed to national or regional markets. Transnationally oriented capitalists promote a switch from "inward oriented development," or accumulation around national markets such as the Import-Substitution Industrialization (ISI) models that predominated in many Third World regions in the middle part of the twentieth century, to "outward-oriented development" involving export-promotion strategies and a deeper integration of national economies into the global economy. This switch involves the emergence of new economic activities and structures of production in each country and region integrating into the global economy (Robinson, 2001b; 2003; 1998/99). These new activities generally imply local participation in globalized circuits of accumulation, or in global production and service chains, such as maquiladora assembly operations, transnational banking services, or tourism and leisure, and so forth. Latin America has become swept up in these transnational processes. The new dominant sectors of accumulation in Latin America are inextricably integrated into global accumulation circuits. It is through these circuits that pockets of society that were pre-capitalist or that at least enjoyed some local autonomy vis-à-vis national and world capitalism just a few decades ago have since been largely subsumed by global capitalist relations. Capitalist relations are practically universal now in the region.

A Transnational Capitalist Class

Both dominant and subordinate classes are transnationalizing. Capital and labor increasingly confront each other as global classes. New urban and rural working classes linked to transnational production processes appear, as do newly "superfluous" masses, in most if not all countries of the world. A global working class has emerged that runs the factories, offices, and farms of the global economy—a stratified and heterogeneous class, to be sure, with numerous hierarchies and cleavages internal to it: gender, ethnicity, nationality, and so on. "Globalization in its modern form is a process based less on the proliferation of computers than on the proliferation of proletarians," observes Munck. "Massive proletarianization is at least as much a feature of globalization as the increased mobility of capital. It is an apparent paradox of the era of globalization that while the labor movement has never been weaker, workers have never been more important to capitalism" (2002:111, 185). Here I want to focus on a new transnational capitalist class, or TCC, comprised of the owners and managers of the TNCs and the private transnational financial institutions that drive the global economy (Sklair, 2002; Robinson and Harris, 2000; Robinson, 2004a). The TCC is a class group grounded in global markets and circuits of accumulation. Globalization acts in a dual manner in terms of the subjective dimensions of class formation worldwide. It acts as a centripetal force for capitalists, who must integrate their holdings and operations into global production chains if they want to remain competitive. This process is conducive to broadening subjective horizons and social-political sensibility. In contrast, globalization often acts as a centrifugal force for working and popular classes, who face new cleavages as they are drawn into self-defeating webs of competition with their homologues around the world. If earlier waves of capitalist development brought together increasing numbers of workers, the fragmentary nature of economic and social processes associated with global capitalism militates against intersubjective solidarities.

The globally integrated production and financial system underscores the increasing interpenetration on multiple levels of capital in all parts of the world, organized around transnational capital and the giant TNCs. It is increasingly difficult to separate local circuits of production and distribution from the globalized circuits that dictate the terms and patterns of accumulation worldwide, even when surface appearance gives the (misleading) impression that local capitals retain their autonomy. There are, of course, still local and national capitalists, and there will be for a long time to come. But they must de-localize and link to transnational capital if they are to survive. Territorially restricted capital cannot compete with its transnationally mobile counterpart. To paraphrase the academic slogan publish or perish, in the case of global capitalism, capitalists in any part of the world beyond the smallest of scale find that they must globalize or perish. As the global circuit of capital subsumes through numerous mechanisms and arrangements, these local circuits, that is, the local capitalists who manage these circuits, become swept up into the process of transnational class formation.

I have been writing about the process of transnational class formation and the rise of a TCC since the late 1990s (inter alia, Robinson, 1996a, 1996b, 2003, 2004a). The topic has become part of a collective research agenda, and the empirical evidence demonstrating the transnationalization of leading capitalist groups is now considerable (for a sampling, see, Sklair, 2002; Kentor, 2005; Kentor and Jang, 2004; UNCTAD, various years; Carroll and Carson, 2003; Carroll and Fennema, 2002). The following are some of the empirical indicators of the increasing interpenetration of national capitals: the sharp rise in foreign direct investment; the spread of TNC affiliates; the phenomenal increase in cross-border mergers and acquisitions; the increasing transnational interlocking of boards of directorates; the increasingly transnational ownership of capital shares; the spread of cross-border strategic alliances of all sorts; and the increasing salience of transnational peak business associations. There are important new mechanisms that facilitate the transnationalization of capital. The spread of stock markets, for instance, from the principal centers of the world economy to many if not most capital cities around the world, combined with 24-hour trading, facilitates an ever greater global trading and, hence, transnational ownership of shares. The global integration of national financial systems and new forms of money capital, including secondary derivative markets, has also made it easier for capital ownership to transnationalize.

With the rise of transnational production chains and circuits of accumulation, transnationally oriented capitalists in each country shift their horizons from national markets to global markets. Different phases of production, as they become broken down into component phases that are detachable and dispersed around the world, can be doled out to distinct economic agents through chains of subcontracting, outsourcing, and other forms of association. These agents become integrated organically into new globalized circuits, so that they are denationalized, in the material if not the cultural sense, and become transnational agents. The vast multilayered networks of outsourcing, subcontracting, collaboration, and so on increasingly link local and national agents to global networks and structures. It is worth citing again the chair of IBM:

> Everywhere, economic activity is turning outward by embracing shared business and technology standards that let businesses plug into truly global systems of production. . . . Because new technology and business models are allowing companies to treat their different functions and operations as component pieces, firms can pull those pieces apart and put them back together again in new combinations. These decisions are not simply a matter of offloading noncore activities, nor are they mere labor arbitrage. They are about actively managing different operations, expertise, and capabilities so as to open the enterprise up in multiple ways, allowing it to connect more intimately with partners, suppliers, and customers. New forms of collaboration are everywhere. . . . Small and medium-sized businesses everywhere, particularly, are benefiting: as new services—from back-office administration to sales support—create infrastructures once only affordable to large organizations, these businesses can now participate in the global economy. (Palmisano, 2006:130–133)

Increasingly, the TCC is a class group with subjective consciousness of itself and its interests. Its members increasingly socialize together in their private institutions and have developed a transnational class consciousness. In this sense it is a class-for-itself, whereas the global working class is a class-in-itself but not yet for-itself. David Rothkopf (1997:44–45), the director of Kissinger Associates, has observed:

> Business leaders in Buenos Aires, Frankfurt, Hong Kong, Johannesburg, Istanbul, Los Angeles, Mexico City, Moscow, New Delhi, New York, Paris, Rome, Santiago, Seoul, Singapore, Tel Aviv, and Tokyo all read the same newspapers, wear the same suits, drive the same cars, eat the same food, fly the same airlines, stay in the same hotels, and listen to the same music. [This integrated elite also includes] international bureaucrats . . . [who] coordinate policy . . . on global issues such as trade, the environment, health, development, and crisis management.

The TCC has increasingly exhibited a global political action capacity and placed itself on the world scene as a coherent actor. In the same way as business groups organize to orient national policy planning groups and lobby national governments, transnational business groups have become a powerful lobby able to impose their will on intergovernmental and supranational institutions. On the eve of the December 2005 Ministerial Conference of the World Trade Organization, for instance, the CEOs and chairs of several dozens of the largest

TNCs, at the initiative of the International Chamber of Commerce, wrote a highly publicized letter to the secretariat of the WTO laying out their collective demand that the organization's secretariat push for a deeper liberalization of the global economy. Among the signatories were representatives from France, Sweden, Morocco, the Netherlands, Hong Kong, India, Spain, Pakistan, Thailand, the United States, Japan, and the Philippines (the letter and full list of signatories was accessed on March 7, 2007, from http://news.ft.com/cms/s/328b4362-4ffd-11da-8b72-0000779e2340.html).

Dominant class relations have shifted worldwide. The struggle between ascendant transnational and descendant national fractions of dominant groups has often been the backdrop in recent decades to national political and ideological dynamics. Transnational fractions of local capitalist classes and bureaucratic elites vied for state power and in most countries won government control in the 1980s and 1990s, or at least came to capture powerful positions influencing state policy making via key ministries, such as foreign, finance, and central banks. Here there is a contradictory logic between national and global accumulation. On the one side are national fractions of dominant groups whose interests lie in national accumulation and traditional national regulatory and protectionist mechanisms. On the other are transnational groups tied to new globalized circuits of accumulation. Their interests lie in an expanding global economy. There is a tension between nation-centric class interests and those groups who develop new relationships linked to transnationalized accumulation. As conflicts arise between descending forms of national production and rising forms of globalized capital, local and national struggles should be seen as simultaneously global and internal. Transnational fractions, as they have captured governments around the world, or come to positions in which they can influence and redirect state policies, have utilized national state apparatuses to advance globalization, pursue economic restructuring, and dismantle the old nation-state social welfare and developmentalist projects. While pursuing the neoliberal model at home they have also pursued worldwide market liberalization and projects of regional and global economic integration. They have promoted a supranational infrastructure of the global economy. In Latin America transnational fractions utilized local states that they were able to capture, or at least influence, in the 1980s and 1990s to undertake internal restructuring and to latch their countries to the train of capitalist globalization.

The economic and the political merge through complex transnational processes in a broader project of hegemony. Restructuring gives an immanent class bias to agents of the external sector. These agents tend to fuse with political managers of the neoliberal state and in the latter decades of the twentieth century began to co-alesce gradually, in a process checkered with contradictions and conflict, into a transnationalized fraction of the elite, at whose help is a politicized leadership and a technocratic cadre steeped in neoliberal ideology and economics and sharing a familiarity with the world of academic think tanks, world-class universities, and international financial institutions. These transnationally oriented elites promote and often manage new globalized circuits of accumulation. They are expected to become hegemonic and to construct new national historic blocs that tie local social order to transnational order. The mechanics of this process can be quite complex and require "concrete analysis of concrete situations." To the extent that power in the global system has shifted from nationally oriented dominant groups to these emerging transnationally-oriented groups, any potential for counter-power or counter-hegemony must face this new reality of transnational power.

Transnationalization of the State

Globalization brings about not the end of the nation-state but its transformation into neoliberal national states. "How does the universe of capital relate to the form of Nation-State in our era of global capitalism?" asks Žižek. "Perhaps, this relationship is best designated as 'auto-colonization': with the direct multina-tional functioning of Capital, we are no longer dealing with the standard oppo-sition between metropolis and colonized countries: a global company as it were cuts its umbilical cord with its mother-nation and treats its country of origins as simply another territory to be colonized" (Žižek, 1997:43). Inversely, the role of the neoliberal state is to serve global (over local) capital accumulation, includ-ing a shift in the subsidies that states provide, away from social reproduction and from internal economic agents and toward transnational capital. These neoliberal states perform three essential services: (1) adopt fiscal and monetary policies that ensure macroeconomic stability; (2) provide the basic infrastruc-ture necessary for global economic activity (airports and seaports, communica-tions networks, educational systems, etc.); and (3) provide social order, that is, stability, which requires sustaining instruments of social control, coercive and ideological apparatuses. When the transnational elite speaks of "governance" it is referring to these functions and the capacity to fulfill them. This was made explicit in *The State in a Changing World*, the World Bank's World Develop-ment Report for 1997b, which points out that the aegis of the national state is central to globalization. In the World Bank's words, "globalization begins at home."

However, there are other conditions that transnational capitalists require for the functioning and reproduction of global capitalism. National states are ill equipped to organize a supranational unification of macroeconomic policies; to create a unified field for transnational capital to operate; to impose transnational trade regimes, supranational transparency, and so forth.

In recent years the construction of a supranational legal and regulator system for the global economy has been the task of sets of transnational institutions, the policy prescriptions and actions of which have been synchronized with those of neoliberal national states that have been captured by local transnationally oriented forces. There is a new transnational institutionality, a new transnational configuration of power, but this is a very incomplete, contradictory, and open-ended process. "One promising trend toward greater global stability is the growth of horizontal, intergovernmental networks among the world's regulators and legislators," observes Palmisano, the chair of IBM, in allusion to the network among national states and trans- and supranational institutions that I refer to as a TNS. "Built on shared professional standards and relationships among cross-national communities of experts, these networks are interesting analogues to new forms of organizing work in business, such as globally integrated supply chains, commercial 'ecosystems,' and open-source communities" (2006:135).

Transnational institutions attempt to coordinate global capitalism and impose capitalist domination beyond national borders. The IMF, for instance, by imposing a structural adjustment program that opens up a given country to the penetration of transnational capital, the subordination of local labor, and the extraction of wealth by transnational capitalists, is operating as a transnational state institution to facilitate the exploitation of local labor by global capital. We can conceptualize a TNS apparatus as a loose network comprised of inter- and supranational political and economic institutions *together with* national state apparatuses that have been penetrated and transformed by transnational forces; the network, moreover, has not yet (and may never) acquire any centralized form. My thesis on a TNS (Robinson, 2001a; 2004a) involves a threefold argument:

1. Economic globalization has its counterpart in transnational class formation and in the emergence of a TNS brought into existence to function as collective authority for a global ruling class.
2. The nation-state is neither retaining primacy nor disappearing but becoming transformed and absorbed into this larger structure of a TNS.

3. This emergent TNS institutionalizes new class relations between global capital and global labor or the new class relations and social practices of global capitalism.

Although it is true that nation-state power and autonomy have declined in relation to transnational power structures, this image is somewhat misleading since these transnational power structures are localized within each nation by concrete social forces that are materially and politically part of the emergent transnational power bloc. Transnational capital and its agents acquire their newfound power vis-à-vis (*as expressed within*) national states, which may act as transmission belts and filtering devices but are also transformed into proactive instruments for advancing the agenda of global capitalism. Moving beyond the dualist constructs of states and markets and the national and the global, governments undertake restructuring and serve the needs of transnational capital not simply because they are "powerless" in the face of globalization but because a particular historical constellation of social forces came into existence in the late twentieth century that presents an organic social base for this global restructuring of capitalism.

As in the past, when states forced the bourgeoisie to modernize whether they wished to or not, the TNS and local neoliberal states, despite the withdrawal of the latter from many areas, have organized and led dominant groups into capitalist modernization under globalization. The "free" market in global society means freedom of accumulation vis-à-vis institutional constraints and the social forces that have imposed these constraints. In this sense, the neoliberal state intervenes in order to support capital over diverse social forces that may constrain its freedom of accumulation. In Latin America, as elsewhere the nation-state system, remains highly functional to the process of capitalist globalization. The state played a leading role in the enormous transformations in Latin America. As in all major transformations of capitalism, state intervention in Latin America has been necessary, even *central,* to the development of a new model of accumulation. This transformation was not, as is often depicted in the literature, a crude imposition of international organizations representing the core powers. It was a process facilitated by the TNS that included the participation of national state apparatuses in Latin America and the active involvement of local dominant groups.

Transnational elites set about to penetrate and restructure national states, directly, through diverse political-diplomatic and other ties between national states and TNS apparatuses and functionaries, and indirectly, through the impositions of transnational capital via its institutional agents (IMF, World Bank, etc.) and the structural power that global capital exercises over nation-states. Local transnational nuclei, or pools, liaise with the transnational elite as "in-country" counterparts through a shared outlook and interest in new economic activities and through diverse external political, cultural, and ideological ties. These nuclei seek to advance the transnational agenda by capturing key state apparatuses and ministries, by the hegemony they are expected to achieve in civil society, and by the power they wield through their preponderance in the local economy and the material and ideological resources accrued through external linkages. Hence it is not that nation-states become irrelevant or powerless vis-à-vis transnational capital and its global institutions. Rather, power as the ability to issue commands and have them obeyed, or more precisely, the ability to shape social structures, shifts from social groups and classes with interests in national accumulation to those whose interests lie in new global circuits of accumulation.

The TNS played a key role in imposing the neoliberal model on the old Third World and therefore in reinforcing a new capital-labor relation. The IMF, by conditioning its lending on a deregulation and flexibilization of local labor markets, as it has often done, is imposing the new capital-labor relation on the particular country and, in the process, fundamentally transforming local labor markets and class and power relations. When the U.S. state invaded Iraq and imposed a property regime that gave free reign to transnational capital in the occupied country and promoted integration into global capitalism, it was internalizing in the occupied country global capitalist relations. In these ways the TNS imposes the new class relations and social practices of global capitalism, and the state as a class relation becomes transnationalized. In doing so, TNS apparatuses are able to apply what Gill and Law (1993), among others, have referred to as the structural power of transnational power over the direct power of states (1993): that is, the coercive discipline of the global market whose levers can be pulled by the IFIs or the core national states of the G-8 countries to open up space within each nation and region for global accumulation. It is through a TNS apparatus that global elites attempt to convert the structural power of the global economy into supranational political authority. States are subject to the structural power of transnational capital and the coercive discipline of the global economy even when transnationally oriented groups are unable to directly instrumentalize states.

The continued division of the world into nation-states constitutes a fundamental condition for the power of transnational capital because nation-states can only exercise jurisdiction/sovereignty within national borders. Transnational capital, however, operates beyond national borders and is thus not regulated by or responsible to any single political authority. This point is crucial: the continued existence of the nation-state system is a central condition for the power of transnational capital. For instance, transnational corporations during the early 1990s were able to utilize the institutions of different nation-states in order to continuously dismantle regulatory structures and other state restrictions on the operation of transnational capital in a process of "mutual deregulation." In this process, core or "hard" national states, as components of a larger TNS apparatus, play key roles in global restructuring. Transnational fractions among dominant groups are able to use these core states to mold transnational structures. This helps us understand the preponderant role of the U.S. national state in the integration of many Latin American countries into the global economy and society.

Although they do not disappear, national states experience dramatic fracturing and restructuring. As globalization proceeds, internal social cohesion declines along with national economic integration. The neoliberal state retains essential powers to facilitate globalization, but it loses the ability to harmonize conflicting social interests within a country, to realize the historic function of sustaining the internal unity of nationally conceived social formation, and to achieve legitimacy. Unable to resolve the contradictory problems of legitimacy and capital accumulation, local states opt simply for abandoning whole sectors of national populations. In many instances, they no longer bother to try to attain legitimacy among the marginalized and supernumeraries, who are isolated and contained in new ways or subject to repressive social control measures (such as, for example, the mass incarceration of African Americans in the United States).[2] A fundamental contradiction in the global capitalist system is a globalizing economy within a nation-state–based political system. A TNS apparatus is incipient and unable to regulate global capitalism or to ameliorate many of its crisis tendencies.

---

[2] The movement toward the decentralization of the national state, such as "devolution" of administrative powers from the central government to local governments in the United States, or the transfer to municipal governments of formerly central state activities in Latin America, should be seen in light of changes in the state under globalization. No longer able to sustain the activities that provide for popular legitimacy, central states attempt to abdicate social welfare responsibilities and the costs of continued social polarization through the decentralization of such functions to local authorities. This is the double movement of the state under globalization: "downward" to decentralized local levels and "upward" to emergent transnational space. Centralized states also attempt to privatize social reproduction by unloading it on NGOs.

Imperialism and Transnational Hegemony

National states remain major—perhaps *the* major—battlegrounds for contending social forces, and the larger TNS is *contested terrain*. Popular forces, even when they capture local states, must contend with the structural power of transnational capital and the authority structures of the TNS. This raises the matter of hegemony in twenty-first-century global society. The struggle for hegemony in the global system should not be seen in terms of a dispute *among* nation-states but in terms of the transnational social groups and their struggles to develop hegemonic and counter-hegemonic projects (Robinson, 2005). For most analysts hegemony is inextricably tied up with state power, and state power is conceived in terms of the nation-state. What is hegemonic in this construct is not a social group or bloc but a nation-state. In my view we need to move away from a statist conception of hegemony—from *statism*—and revert to a more "pure" Gramscian view of hegemony as a form of social domination exercised by social groups and classes operating through states and other institutions. This means replacing the whole notion of hegemony in international relations with a distinct conception of hegemony in global society. In contrast to the typical construct in the literature on international relations and world order, in which the (national) state is the point of backward linkage to society and forward linkage to the international order, I want to focus on the horizontal integration of classes and social forces that then operate through webs of national and transnational institutions. In this imagery, transnational capitalists and allied dominant strata integrate horizontally and in the process move "up" cross-nationally, penetrating and utilizing numerous national and transnational state apparatuses to forge their rule. A counter-hegemonic project led by popular classes would need to do the same.

Nation-state–centric analyses of international and transnational relations fail to appreciate the integrative character of global capitalism. They view hegemony in nation-state and state terms, and they fail to see how capitalist accumulation has shifted from a national form of organization and competition to a transnational form involving dynamics of conflict and contradiction between descendant national capitals and class interests and ascendant transnational capital and its class interests. In simplified terms, both national and transnational forms of accumulation exist in differing degrees in all nations. Class and social sectors whose interests are linked to the old state system still attempt to advance their interests and to shape the world more fully to those interests. But the material benefits connected to the remnants of the nation-centric system are subject to challenge from the class and social forces rooted in the new forms of globalized accumulation. These contradictions appear in a variety of forms and unfold differently depending on the particular histories and sets of relations unique to each country and region.

The transnational capitalist class (TCC) has been attempting to position itself as a new ruling class group worldwide since the 1980s and to bring some coherence and stability to its rule through an emergent TNS apparatus. The world politics of this would-be global ruling class is not driven, as they were for national ruling classes, by the flux of shifting rivalries and alliances played out through the interstate system but by the new global social structure of accumulation. What would a potentially hegemonic bloc—a globalist bloc—look like? At the center of such a globalist bloc would be the TCC, comprised of the owners and managers of the transnational corporations and private financial institutions and other capitalists around the world who manage transnational capital. The bloc would also include the cadre, bureaucratic managers and technicians who administer the agencies of the TNS, such as the IMF, the World Bank, and the WTO, other transnational forums, and the states of the North and the South. Also brought into the bloc would be an array of politicians and charismatic public figures, along with select organic intellectuals who would provide ideological legitimacy and technical solutions. Below this transnational elite would be a small layer, shrinking in some locales (such as the United States) and expanding in others (such as India and China), of old and new middle classes, high-paid workers, and cosmopolitan professionals who exercise very little real power but who—pacified with mass consumption—form a fragile buffer between the transnational elite and the world's poor majority. It is in this way that we can speak of a historic bloc in the Gramscian sense as a social ensemble involving dominant strata and a social base beyond the ruling group, and in which one group exercises leadership (the TCC) and imposes its project through the consent of those drawn into the bloc. Those from the poor majority not drawn into the hegemonic project, either through material mechanisms or ideologically, are contained or repressed.

All social orders in class society, and all historic blocs, involve in their genesis and reproduction an ongoing combination of consent and coercion. The problematic nature of its rule is revealed to the extent that an historic bloc—or dominant groups attempting to construct such a bloc—must rely more on direct domination or coercion as opposed to consent in securing its rule. "[It is necessary] to change the political direction of certain forces which have to be absorbed if a new, homogenous politico-economic historic bloc, without internal contradictions, is to be successfully formed," writes Gramsci. "And since two similar forces can only be welded into a new organism either through a series of compromises or by force of arms, either by binding them to each other as allies or by forcibly subordinating one to the other, the question is whether one has the necessary force, and whether it is 'productive' to use it" (1971:168). At best, such a globalist bloc achieved in the 1980s and 1990s a certain "restricted" as opposed to "expansive" hegemony in global society, less through the internalization by popular classes worldwide of the neoliberal worldview than through the disorganization of these classes in the wake of the juggernaut of capitalist globalization. Nonetheless, since the late 1990s, as I discuss in later chapters, it has been unable to reproduce even this "restricted" hegemony and has had to resort to increasing use worldwide of direct coercion in order to maintain its supremacy.

Globalization itself emerged as a restructuring of the system in response to a capitalist crisis. The opening of new spaces worldwide for accumulation through liberalization and restructuring helped offset the 1970s crisis of declining profits and investment opportunities. But this period of restructuring remained fluid and indeterminate, and by the late twentieth century the system was once again moving into crisis. In Chapter 4, I discuss the four interrelated dimensions of this crisis that I wish to highlight: (1) a crisis of social polarization and social reproduction; (2) a crisis of over-accumulation; (3) a crisis of legitimacy and authority, that is, of hegemonic reproduction and social control; and (4) a crisis of sustainability. This multidimensional crisis of global capitalism generated intense discrepancies and disarray within the globalist ruling bloc, which began to tear apart at the seams under the pressure of conflicts internal to it and from forces opposed to its logic. The more politically astute among global elites have clamored to promote a "post–Washington consensus" project of reform: a so-called globalization with a human face in the interests of saving the system itself (see, e.g., Stiglitz, 2002). But others from within and outside of the bloc called for more radical responses. In particular, the Bush White House militarized social and economic contradictions, and following the events of September 11, 2001, it launched a permanent war mobilization to try to stabilize the system through direct coercion.

Many interpreted militarization and renewed U.S. interventionism through theories of a "new imperialism," according to which the United States set about to renew a U.S. empire and offset the decline in its hegemony amidst heightened inter-imperialist rivalry (see, inter alia, Wood, 2003; Harvey, 2005; Foster, 2006; various entries in Appelbaum and Robinson, 2005). These interpretations confused capitalist competition with state competition and conflated disarray, factionalism, and parochial and sectoral interests among transnational capitalist groups and global elites with nation-state rivalries. The hallmark of "new imperialism" theories is the assumption that world capitalism in the twenty-first century is made up of domestic capitals and distinct national economies that interact with one another, and a concomitant realist analysis of world politics as driven by the pursuit by governments of their national interest. Yet the meaning of "national interest" is never made clear. Once we belie the realist notion of a world of national economies and national capitals then the logical sequence in "new imperialism" argumentation collapses like a house of cards, since the whole edifice is constructed on this notion (see my extended critique of these theories in Robinson, 2007b). By coming to grips with the reality of transnational capital we can grasp U.S. foreign policy in this new epoch in an organic, if not merely functional, relation to the actual structure and composition of the dominant social forces in the global capitalist system.

Interpreting the U.S. state as playing a leadership role on behalf of transnational capitalist interests is a more satisfactory explanation than that of advancing "U.S." interests, as we will see when applying the concepts of hegemony and world order to the study of Latin America. The U.S. state has taken the lead in imposing a reorganization of world capitalism. But this does not mean that U.S. interventionism seeks to defend "U.S." interests. As the most powerful component of the TNS, the U.S. state apparatus defends the interests of transnational investors and the overall system. The only military apparatus in the world capable of exercising global coercive authority is the U.S. military. The beneficiaries of U.S. military action around the world are not "U.S." but transnational capitalist groups. This is the underlying class relation between the TCC and the U.S. national state. It is in this way that the United States played a key role in the globalization of Latin America, more properly understood as U.S. tutelage of the region's restructuring and integration into global capitalism on behalf of a transnational project than as a project of "U.S." hegemony in rivalry with other core powers for influence in the hemisphere.

If the world is not divided into rival national economies and national capitals, do we still need a theory of imperialism? In the post–World War II period, and drawing on the tradition established by Rosa Luxembourg, Marxists and other critical political economists shifted the main focus in the study of imperialism from the classical focus advanced by Lenin and Hilferding on rivalry among core powers to the mechanisms of core capitalist penetration of

Third World countries and the appropriation of their surpluses. Imperialism in this sense referred to this exploitation and to the use of state apparatuses by capitals emanating from the centers of the world system to facilitate this economic relation through military, political, and cultural mechanisms. The relentless pressure for outward expansion of capitalism and the distinct political, military, and cultural mechanisms that facilitate that expansion and the appropriation of surpluses it generates is a structural imperative built into capitalism. We need tools to conceptualize, analyze, and theorize how this expansionary pressure built into the capitalist system manifests itself in the age of globalization. The class relations of global capitalism are now so deeply internalized *within* every nation-state that the classical image of imperialism as a relation of external domination is outdated. Failure to comprehend this leads to such superficial and misleading conclusions as, for instance, that the failure of popular projects to materialize under the rule of the Workers Party in Brazil or the African National Congress in South Africa is a result of a "sell out" by the leaders of those parties or simply because "imperialism" undercut their programs.

Today, imperialism is not about nations but about groups exercising the social power—through institutions—to control value production, to appropriate surpluses, and to reproduce these arrangements. The challenge for such a theoretical enterprise is to ask: how, and by whom in the world capitalist system, are values produced (organized through what institutions), how are they appropriated (through what institutions), and how are these processes changing through capitalist globalization? During the five hundred years since the genesis of the world capitalist system, colonialism and imperialism coercively incorporated zones and peoples into its fold. This historical process of "primitive accumulation" is coming to a close. The end of the extensive enlargement of capitalism is the end of the imperialist era of world capitalism. The system still conquers space, nature, and human beings. It is dehumanizing, genocidal, suicidal, and maniacal. But with the exception of a few remaining spaces—Iraq until recently, North Korea, etc.—the world has been brought into the system over the past half millennium. The implacable logic of accumulation is now largely internal to worldwide social relations and to the complex of fractious political institutions through which ruling groups attempt to manage those relations. We need a theory of capitalist expansion: that is, not only of the political processes and the institutions through which such expansion takes place, but also of the class relations and spatial dynamics it involves.

New Patterns of Global Inequality: From Geographical to Social Cartographies

As capitalism globalizes, the twenty-first century is witness to new forms of poverty and wealth, and new configurations of power and domination. Globalization has in many respects aggravated class, racial, and gender inequalities, and new social cleavages are emerging. One major new axis of inequality is between citizen and noncitizen, given not only a massive upsurge in transnational migration but also the increasing use worldwide of ethnic immigrant labor pools. The dominant discourse on global inequality is territorial, that is, inequality among nations in a world system. But global polarization is less territorial than social. Global society is increasingly stratified less along national and territorial lines than across transnational social and class lines (Castells, 2000; Cox, 1987; Hoogvelt, 1997; Robinson, 1998, 2002, 2003).

Certain forms of conceptualizing the North-South divide obscure our view of social hierarchies and inequalities across nations and regions. Hurricane Katrina ravaged New Orleans in 2005, for instance, lifting the veil of race, class, poverty, and inequality in the United States. The storm disproportionately devastated poor black communities who lacked the resources to take protection and whose Third World social conditions became apparent. A U.N. report released in the immediate aftermath of the hurricane observed that the infant mortality rate in the United States had been rising for the previous five years and was the same as for Malaysia, that black children were twice as likely as whites to die before their first birthday, and that blacks in Washington D.C. had a higher infant death rate than people in the Indian state of Kerala (UNDP, 2005).

Clearly we need to rethink the categories of North and South and the very concept of development. A sociology of national development is no longer tenable. In earlier epochs core and periphery referred to specific territories and the populations that resided therein. The center-periphery division of labor created by modern colonialism reflected a particular spatial configuration in the law of uneven development, which is becoming transformed by globalization. The transnational geographic dispersal of the full range of world production processes suggests that core and peripheral production activities are less geographically bounded than previously, while new financial circuits allow wealth to be moved around the world instantaneously through cyberspace just as easily as it is generated, so that exactly *where* wealth is produced becomes less important for the issue of development.

While the global South is increasingly dispersed across the planet so too is the global North. Rapid economic growth in India and China have created hundreds of millions of new middle-class consumers integrated into the global cornucopia even as it has thrown other hundreds of millions into destitution. Globalization fragments locally and integrates select strands of the population globally. The cohesive structures of nations and their civil societies disintegrates as populations become divided into "core" and "peripheral" labor pools and as local economic expansion results in the advancement of some (delocalized) groups and deepening poverty for others. We find an affluent "developed" population, including a privileged sector among segmented labor markets linked to knowledge-intensive, professional, and managerial activities; high consumption exists alongside a super-exploited secondary segment of flexibilized labor and a mass of supernumeraries constituting an "underdeveloped" population within the same national borders. This social bifurcation seems to be a worldwide phenomenon, explained in part by the inability of national states to capture and redirect surpluses through interventionist mechanisms that were viable in the nation-state phase of capitalism.

Unequal exchanges—material, political, cultural—implied in a social division of labor on a world scale are not captured so much in the concept of an *international* division of labor as in a *global* division of labor, which implies differential participation in global production according to social standing and not necessarily geographic location; such differential participation accounts for sweatshops in East Los Angeles and Northern Honduras, as well as gated communities in Hollywood and São Paulo. The great geographic core-periphery divide, a product of the colonial and imperialist era in world capitalism, is gradually eroding—not because the periphery is "catching up," but because of the shift from an international to a global division of labor and the tendency for a downward leveling of wages and the general conditions of labor. The international division of labor has gone through successive transformations in the history of world capitalism. For many, the most recent permutation involves the shift in manufacturing from North to South, so that in the "new international division of labor" (Fröbel et al., 1980) the North specializes in high-skilled and better-paid labor supplying advanced services and technology to the world market, while the South provides low-skilled and poorer-paid labor for global manufacturing and primary commodity supply. But this analysis, as Freeman observes, has become increasingly obsolete

> due to the massive investments that the large populous developing countries are making in human capital. China and India are producing millions of college graduates

capable of doing the same work as the college graduates of the United States, Japan or Europe—at much lower pay. . . . The huge number of highly educated workers in India and China threatens to undo the traditional pattern of trade between advanced and less developed countries. Historically, advanced countries have innovated high-tech products that require high-wage educated workers and extensive R&D, while developing countries specialize in old manufacturing products. The reason for this was that the advanced countries had a near monopoly on scientists and engineers and other highly educated workers. As China, India and other developing countries have increased their number of university graduates, this monopoly on high-tech innovative capacity has diminished. Today, most major multinationals have R&D centers in China or India, so that the locus of technological advance may shift. (2005:3)

There remain very real regional distinctions in the form of productive participation in the global economy, as we shall see for Latin America. But processes of uneven accumulation increasingly unfold in accordance with a social and not a national logic. Different levels of social development adhere from the very sites of social productive activity, that is, from *social,* not geographic, space. Moreover, privileged groups have an increasing ability to manipulate space so as to create enclaves and insulate themselves through novel mechanisms of social control and new technologies for the built environment. The persistence and, in fact, *growth* of the North-South divide remain important for its theoretical and practical political implications. What is up for debate is whether the divide is something innate to world capitalism or a particular spatial configuration of uneven capitalist development during a particular historic phase of world capitalism, and whether tendencies toward the self-reproduction of this configuration are increasingly offset by countertendencies emanating from the nature and dynamic of global capital accumulation.

To explain the movement of values between different "nodes" in globalized production, clearly we need to move beyond nation-state—centric approaches and apply a theory of value to transformations in world spatial and institutional structures (the nation-state being the central spatial and institutional structure in the hitherto history of world capitalism). The notion of net social gain or loss used by development economists has little meaning if measured, as it traditionally is, in national terms, or even in geographic terms. The distribution of social costs and gains must be conceived in transnational social terms, not in terms of the nation-state vis-à-vis the world economy, but transnationally as social groups vis-à-vis other social groups in a global society. Development should be reconceived not as a national phenomenon, in which what develops is not a nation, but in terms of developed, underdeveloped, and intermediate population groups occupying contradictory or unstable locations in a transnational environment.

Conceptualizing Global-Regional-Local Change as Regional Rearticulation to World Capitalism

Epochal changes in the system of world capitalism have had transformative effects on the world as a whole and on each region integrated in or re-articulated to the system. The birth of capitalism in Europe and its initial mercantile expansion reoriented nearly every society in the world toward newly formed webs of interconnection, including new world trading patterns, the demand for novel products, changes in the labor and productive activities of most peoples and civilizations, and an international division of labor. Mercantilism also involved the unprecedented deployment of coercion on a world scale to destroy whole civilizations, impose colonial authority, reorient production, and organize labor supplies. The transition from mercantilism to classical competitive capitalism brought with it a new wave of core expansion and colonization that similarly transformed the international division of labor, productive structures, classes, and polities around the world, and generalized the nation-state as the modern political and institutional form. As competitive capitalism gave way to corporate (or, monopoly) capitalism, each country and region again experienced dramatic economic, social, political, and related changes. In this way, world society has been continuously constituted and reconstituted by the spread of a social system at the world level, and gradations in this spread offer clues to patterns of change over time and place.

Each of these three earlier epochs of world capitalism has had major implications for Latin America (Weaver, 2000). Latin America has gone through successive waves of ever-deeper integration into world capitalism. With each new integration or reintegration there has been a corresponding fundamental change in the social and class structures of Latin America, and in the leading economic activities around which social classes and groups have exercised collective agency. The mercantile era saw the original creation of Latin America through conquest and colonial incorporation into the emerging world capitalist system. It was in the next epoch of competitive, industrial capitalism that Latin America won its independence, as the former colonies became nation-states with their own national elites and administrative apparatuses. In this epoch

Latin America broke loose from Spanish mercantile control and experienced a re-articulation to world capitalism based on export expansion under the new political and economic elites who led liberal revolutions and oversaw nation building. The epoch of corporate capitalism saw yet a deeper integration of Latin America into world capitalism through a major export boom and the rise of new industrial, commercial, and financial elites and new middle and working classes. The groups came together in multi-class populist and corporatist projects that sought development through import-substitution industrialization and modernization. Each phase of historical change in Latin America—and more generally in the world capitalist system—builds on preceding ones and retains important elements from them. Global capitalism is now having a similar transformative effect on every country and region of the world. Latin America is experiencing a transition to a new model of economy and society as the region becomes reinserted into the emerging global stage of world capitalism.

As transnational capital integrates the world into new globalized circuits of accumulation, it has broken down national and regional autonomies, including the earlier pre-globalization models of capitalist development and the social forces that sustained these models. Through internal adjustment and re-articulation to the emerging global economy and society, local productive apparatuses and social structures in each region are transformed, and different regions acquire new profiles in the emerging global division of labor. Integration into the emergent global system is the causal structural dynamic that underlies the events we have witnessed in nations and regions all around the world over the past few decades. The breakup of national economic, political, and social structures is reciprocal to the gradual breakup, starting in the 1970s, of a pre-globalization world order based on the nation-state. New economic, political, and social structures emerge as each nation and region becomes integrated into emergent transnational structures and processes. We want to pay particularly close attention to changes in the economic structure because they provide the material basis for related processes of change in practices and institutions, politics, class structure, and so forth.

The remolding of each national economy creates an array of contradictions between the old and new forms of accumulation. As each country experiences the transformation of its social relations and institutions, it enters a process conditioned by its own history and culture. Thus uneven development determines the pace and nature of local insertion into the global economy. Saskia Sassen has suggested that the international mobility of capital creates new specific forms of articulation among different geographic areas and transformations in the role played by these areas in the world economy: for example, zones of export processing, offshore banking, global cities as nodes of worldwide management and control. The particular *form* of re-articulation that emerges through transnational processes has varied from region to region. As national and regional productive apparatuses are fragmented, restructured, and integrated into the emergent global productive apparatus, each country and region acquires a new profile as components of a globally integrated economy. The webs and structures of globalized production exhibit numerous segments and mixes of geographically scattered activities with varied value-added contributions and levels of benefit for local communities.

This "economic regionalism," in which different regions acquire profiles in a changing global division of labor, is best seen as a fluid rather than a fixed structure and as a transition between decaying national productive systems and the further fragmentation and spatial reorganization of emerging global production systems. I consider Latin America here as a region within the global economy in the sense that Harvey refers to regions as relatively stable historical geographic configurations "that achieve a certain degree of structured coherence to production, distribution, exchange, and consumption, *at least for a time*" (2003:102, my emphasis). What sets a region off from other parts of the global economy, in Harvey's view, is uneven geographic development. I suggest, however, that more determinant (of causal priority) in conceptualizing regions within the larger unity of the emerging global economy and society than uneven accumulation, while still important, is the distinct configurations of social forces and of institutions that arise from these configurations. If we are to properly understand the role of local and regional economies and social and class structures, they must be studied from the perspective of their point of insertion into global accumulation rather than their relationship to a particular national market or state structure.

This does not mean ignoring local conditions, history, or culture. But the key becomes their relationship to a transnational system and the dialectic between the global and the local. It is crucial to stress in this regard that having distinct national and regional histories and configurations of social forces as they have historically evolved means that each country and region experiences a distinct experience under globalization. Moreover, these social forces operate through national and regional institutions. Hence there is variation in the process of globalization and concomitant processes of institutionalization of the new social relations and political structures of global capitalism. What we want to avoid in conceptualizing the dynamics and dialectics of global-regional-local change, nonetheless, is a reversion to the nation-state/inter-state system as the framework of analysis, to the notion of national and regional competition as causal to processes of uneven accumulation, and so on. Instead, we want to see how transnational social forces from above are able to reproduce and utilize regional distinctions to serve global accumulation and how transnational social forces from below continue to operate politically through local and national institutions in struggles against global capitalism.

Transnational processes and globalizing dynamics are filtered through particular nation-states and regions and unfold within a process of uneven globalization. Globalization is characterized by related, contingent, and unequal transformations. To invoke globalization as an explanation for historic changes and contemporary dynamics does not mean that the particular events or changes identified with the process are happening all over the world, much less in the same way. It does mean that the events or changes are understood as a consequence of globalized power relations and social structures. My study on contemporary development and social change in Latin America departs from the analysis of the larger global system. The complexity of the ongoing period of change in Latin America is grounded in the region's particular history, including individual national histories, and in the unique behavioral response of different agents to globalization and its repercussions.

We do not want to lose sight, however, that global capitalism is a concrete totality, but the world economy is not a general abstraction. On the one hand, it is the laws of capitalist development that drive the overall system and that also constitute the unifying basis and the common linkage of all the different constituent elements of the system, such as national and regional economies and social formations. On the other hand, the world economy becomes manifest in specific regions and their inter-relations. The study of one region, such as Latin America, is the study of a piece of a larger system. The larger system cannot be understood without looking at its pieces and how they fit together. Neither can any piece be understood outside of how it fits into the larger, and encompassing, system. National and regional studies (such as Latin America) constitute concrete and specific mappings (spatial-political) of the ways in which general tendencies of capitalism manifest themselves and are not discrete studies that are radically different as objects of investigation from other parts of the system.

A critical focus of globalization studies should be exploration into the dynamics of change at the local, national, and regional levels in tandem with movement at the level of the global whole. The concern should be on how movement and change in the global whole are manifest in particular countries or regions, but with the focus on the dialectic reciprocity of the two levels, that is, on the dialectic between historically determined structures and new transnational structures. The transition from the nation-state to the transnational phase of capitalism involves changes that take place in each individual country and region reciprocal to, and in dialectic interplay with, change of systemic importance at the level of the global system.

CHAPTER TWO

Nontraditional Agricultural Exports and Agro-Industry

Over the past five centuries Latin America has become ever more integrated into the world market. But this integration has taken place in periodic spurts and even occasional withdrawals—such as following the nineteenth-century wars of independence or during the Great Depression of the 1930s—rather than in step to a steady drumbeat. Spurts of deepening integration usually follow the onset of a new epoch in world capitalism and its corresponding waves of expansion. These spurts involve the introduction of new products exported from the region that tend to become leading axes of accumulation. Each cycle of integration into world capitalism is also associated with an extension of capitalist institutions and production relations in the region. The late twentieth century began a major new cycle of integration, corresponding to the globalization epoch, on the basis of a new set of exports that constitutes what I refer to as the transnational model.

Crisis of Developmental Capitalism and the Rise of the Transnational Model

The transnational model has replaced the previous popular/corporatist import-substitution industrialization (ISI)—or developmentalist—model, which in turn had replaced the oligarchic agro-export societies that came into place in the post-independence period. Earlier in the twentieth century social and political mobilization by popular sectors convulsed the region, culminating during the Great Depression of the 1930s in a general crisis of the prevailing oligarchic orders.

The popular/corporatist ISI model—which I will refer to simply as ISI—and attendant forms of political domination corresponded to maturation of national corporate capitalism at the world level. It was a regional-specific variant of Fordist-Keynesian national capitalism, with its regulatory and redistributive mechanisms and focus on nationally oriented accumulation. It was based on domestic market expansion, populism, and a strategy of import-substitution industrialization made possible by—and quite compatible with—the dramatic expansion of the world economy in this "golden age" of capitalism and with the increasing internationalization of capital in the form of multinational corporate investment. ISI ushered in a period of unprecedented industrial growth in Latin America during the decades after World War II. It involved a major role for the state in organizing national development plans and a set of Keynesian and other fiscal and monetary measures and incentives for private domestic capital to invest in industry and for international capital to invest locally. Other measures aimed to bring popular classes, particularly expanding urban working and middle classes tied to industrialization and the expansion of the state, into populist and corporatist coalitions under the hegemony of capital and traditional oligarchies. These measures included import tariffs, foreign exchange controls, multiple exchange rates, subsidies on credit and investments, expanding public sector and direct state investment in strategic sectors (e.g., infrastructure, utilities, steel, and energy), subsidies on mass consumption labor codes to legalize trade unions and regulate labor, social insurance programs, and public health and education (on ISI, see, inter alia, Bulmer-Thomas, 1996; Bruton, 1998; Baer, 1972).

The expansion of world capitalism also opened up new opportunities in the world market for Latin American exports, especially new export products such as beef and cotton in Central America, which expanded significantly at this time. Moreover, Mexico, Argentina, Brazil, Uruguay, Chile, and Colombia, among others, experienced significant industrialization. The rates of Latin American industrial growth during this period were unprecedented, averaging 6.9 percent per year between 1950 and the mid-1970s, higher than in the United States, the European Economic Community, and other developed countries (Weaver, 2000:129). For the region as a whole, manufacturing as a percentage of GDP increased from 19 to 24 percent, although this masks much higher rates of increase in some countries, such as from 18 to 26 percent in Brazil, from 23 to 32 percent in Argentina, from 19 to 24 percent in Mexico, and from 11 to 19 percent in Peru (Weaver, 2000:129).

ISI strategies elsewhere formed part of broad-ranging populist movements protagonized by autonomous national classes in a more precarious alliance with international capital. Such a model was possible as a result of the greater national autonomy in the pre-globalization age and was protagonized as much by export-oriented elites as by new industrial, financial, commercial, and bureaucratic elites whose interest lay in the buildup of national (and regional) markets and circuits of accumulation. The appearance of the new elites and middle and working classes altered the dominant power blocs throughout Latin America. New multi-class alliances formed around national political projects, often populism or corporatism under authoritarian arrangements (on populism, see Mouzelis, 1985; on corporatism and authoritarianism in Latin America, see, inter alia, Malloy, 1977). Surpluses were not only appropriated by national elites and transnational corporations but also redistributed through diverse populist programs, ranging from packets of social wages (social service spending, subsidized consumption, etc.), expanding employment opportunities, and rising real wages. Under corporatism the state attempted to organize distinct social sectors—so as to preempt their independent organization—to incorporate these sectors consensually into national historical blocs and to mediate class conflict under the overall hegemony of capital.

The worldwide crisis of Fordist-Keynesian capitalism discussed in Chapter 1 had its Latin American counterpart in an exhaustion and breakdown of the ISI model. The immediate causes of this crisis include such factors as the world economic shocks of the early 1970s, recession in core countries, and mounting debt burden and rising interest rates as the wave of international borrowing of the 1970s came to an end. But the underlying structural cause was the exhaustion of the patterns of accumulation based on expanded exports and ISI development. For those regions that focused more on an expansion of agro-exports, such as Central America, the world market was becoming saturated for these exports due to changing market demand, the failure of Third World producers to organize effectively to control global surpluses, the substitution of tropical food products by First World alternatives, and secular declines in the terms of trade (Robinson, 2003).

For those countries that experienced industrialization, ISI production depended on substantial imported inputs in the form of capital equipment, licensed technologies, intermediate products, and raw materials. Growth came to be dependent on a rising import bill and generated a squeeze on traditional exports, mounting foreign exchange shortages, balance of payments deficits, and macroeconomic disequilibrium. Growth was eventually arrested by fiscal and foreign exchange crises, which led to cycles of foreign borrowing in order to sustain production and a rising debt burden. Moreover the expansion of markets for ISI consumer goods was limited by inequality in income distribution and could not be compensated for by regional integration schemes, such as the Central American Common Market or the Latin American Free Trade Area.

The inherent urban bias in ISI spurred armed struggles in the rural areas, massive migration from the countryside to the cities, the proliferation of shantytowns, and expanding social struggles of workers, the poor, and the unemployed. Political stalemate spread throughout the region as the dominant power blocs unraveled. The inability of civilian regimes to contain these convulsions led to military takeovers in most of the region—Brazil in 1964, Argentina in 1966 and again in 1976, Peru in 1968, Chile in 1973, Uruguay in 1973—and authoritarian control of one form or another almost everywhere.

This breakdown of ISI culminated in a major downturn at the end of the 1970s that carried through into the 1980s, which became know as Latin America's "lost decade," characterized by negative growth rates in many countries, a decline in GDP per capita, plummeting standards of living, spreading poverty, and debilitating external debt (see Chapter 4). In South America military regimes launched the era of neoliberalism, implementing free-market policies and demobilizing the popular classes through mass repression. In Central America only after the revolutionary challenge was beaten back in the late 1980s and early 1990s did neoliberalism take hold. In Mexico, the government of President Carlos Salinas de Gortari ushered in globalization starting in 1988, although his predecessor, Miguel de la Madrid, had already taken steps in that direction. During the latter decades of the twentieth century, Latin American governments, under constant pressure from diverse constituencies, resisted particular aspects of structural adjustment packages, and at times the entire package, implementing instead heterodox (mixed) policies or even trying to resurrect ISI populist programs. But eventually every country (with the exception of Cuba) succumbed to pressure for structural adjustment and began to restructure and integrate into global capitalism. To take the example of trade liberalization, the average level of tariffs in Latin America dropped from 42 percent in 1985 to 14 percent in 1995, and nontariff restrictions that affected 38 percent of imports in the pre-neoliberal period were only affecting 6 percent of imports by the 1990s (IDB, 1997:42).

In the emergent transnational model of economy and society, ISI has been replaced by a neoliberal opening to the global economy and by what has been termed in international development discourse Export-Led Development, or ELD (Bulmer-Thomas, 1996; Green, 1995; Robinson, 1999), which favors new circuits of production and circulation linked to the global economy and is often organized along the lines of flexible accumulation.

As each country becomes integrated into the global economy new structures of production, new lead economic activities, and new sets of social relations emerge.

The supply of new commodities responds to new demands on the world market, shifts in world consumption patterns, a need for greater amounts of raw materials as part of the expansion and far-reaching restructuring of the world production base, a changing global division of labor, and the need for a host of financial and other services to facilitate global accumulation. Table 2.1 provides one indicator of this process of increasing outward orientation of Latin American countries as globalization took hold in the final decade of the twentieth century.

In the 1960s there were still major pockets of society that were pre-capitalist or that at least enjoyed some local autonomy vis-à-vis national and world capitalism. Of course these pre-capitalist areas often served as labor reserves and sources of low cost wage goods, so that we do not want to suggest a dualist or dichotomous structure. Nonetheless, in the twenty-first century global capitalism has penetrated nearly every nook and cranny so that capitalist relations are practically universal in the region. There is little space left for primitive accumulation in Latin America. As we will see, capitalist relations are penetrating in hothouse fashion through globalization into the last remaining pre- or noncapitalist preserves in Latin America, whether by means of free trade agreements, such as NAFTA, that are doing away with communal lands in Mexico; "ecotourist" projects that bring nature reserves into the global market; the conversion of small producer lands in South America to soy, flower, fruit, and vegetable plantations controlled by transnational agribusiness; and so on.

TABLE 2.1
*Trade in Goods as a Percentage of GDP, Latin
America and Select Countries*

	1989	1999
Latin America and Caribbean	10.2	18.2
Argentina	5.1	10.9
Brazil	6.3	8.4
Chile	24.0	23.7
Colombia	6.7	9.3
Costa Rica	19.9	40.6
Dominican Republic	21.4	29.0
Ecuador	15.5	20.1
Guatemala	11.5	16.6
Honduras	18.4	26.9
Mexico	14.1	35.6
Peru	7.5	12.2
Venezuela	22.6	26.6

Source: World Bank, 2001, table 6.1, p. 322.

The New Economic Model and Nontraditional Exports

Nontraditional exports became a centerpiece of ELD strategies throughout Latin America during the 1980s and 1990s. Bulmer-Thomas and his colleagues have referred to these strategies as the New Economic Model [NEM] in Latin America (Bulmer-Thomas, 1996). The NEM, which I refer to (with broader connotations) as the transnational model, entailed essentially the package of neoliberal structural adjustment measures—among them, trade liberalization, fiscal austerity, privatization, and labor market deregulation and flexibility—as the mechanism for a shift from inward-looking development to export-led growth. The debt crisis of the 1970s and subsequent neoliberal project institutionalized the new definition of development as participation in the world market and the transition from managed national economic growth to managed global economic growth. The "solution" to the debt crisis and stagnation was not only increased exports but also export diversification. Such new export profiles, in Latin America as elsewhere, became the path of integration into the globalized economy then emerging. These new export activities tend to form part of global commodity chains, or globally dispersed and decentralized production processes. Specialization in the world economy, rather than specialization of economic activities within a national framework, began to emerge beginning in 1970s as the criterion of development (McMichael, 1996:109). "Instead of countries specializing in an export sector (manufacturing or agriculture), production sites in countries specialize in a constituent part of a production process spread across several countries," notes McMichael. "The global decentralization and fragmentation of the production process indicates a shift from the production of national products to the transnational production of world products" (1996:92).

There has been a shift in Latin America from state-led development to state-promoted linkage to global production chains driven by transnational capital. Economic growth and social reproduction are coming to rest on a transformed set of productive structures and relations. The most dynamic economic sectors in Latin America are those linked directly to globalized circuits of production and distribution. Among these sectors are the following:

1. Nontraditional agricultural exports, including cut flowers in Ecuador, Colombia, and Costa Rica; fruits and wine in Chile; peanuts in Nicaragua; winter vegetables in Mexico, Guatemala, Peru, and elsewhere; soy in Argentina, Brazil, and Bolivia; cut chicken pieces from the Dominican Republic; shrimp farming in Honduras, and so on. There has been a major

influx of transnational agribusiness along with the transnationalization of domestic agribusiness. No national agricultural system has remained untouched by globalization.

2. New forms of participation in global manufacturing, including maquiladoras, which have spread throughout Mexico, Central America, and the Caribbean, and to a number of South American countries; local subcontracting and outsourcing networks managed by local investors and entrepreneurs to supply component processes and component capital and intermediate goods; joint ventures, alliances, and other forms of association between local and transnational corporate groups.

3. Transnational services, including an unprecedented boom throughout the continent of transnational tourist circuits; the rise of transnational banking, bond, and other financial markets; new transnational commercial establishments; and outsourced call centers.

4. The export of labor to other centers of the global economy and reverse flow of remittances. Latin American labor export is both internal—that is, from one country or region of Latin America to another—and external to the global labor market beyond Latin America.

Nontraditional exports and services are the face of global capitalism in the region. They utilize the region's comparative advantage in cheap labor as a basis for a "competitive" reinsertion into global markets. The social and production relations of global capitalism—including the new capital-labor relation based on informality, flexible and casualized labor, as discussed in Chapter 1, and the gendered nature of these relations—are evident in these new activities—in the maquiladoras, agro-export platforms, new offices, commercial establishments, and tourist facilities that have spread throughout Latin America. Yet these social and production relations also spread to older economic sectors and to areas of social life not *directly* connected to the global economy, so that the social relations and the culture of global capitalism are diffused throughout society. Existing social relations are disarticulated and replaced by new sets of relations shaped by the commercial, productive, and cultural processes of global society.

It appears that Latin America began a new cycle of capitalist development in the 1990s, following the lost decade of the 1980s, as a new model of globalized accumulation took hold. I will argue, however, that this new cycle exhibits deep structural and social contradictions and is politically unstable. A key underlying theme of this book is that the problematic nature of the global capitalism in Latin America reflects the larger crisis of the global capitalist system. First, in particular, the model is highly dependent on attracting mobile and often volatile transnational finance and investment capital, with a large component of financial speculation characteristic of the global casino. Second, the new export boom, based on a set of nontraditional activities that constitute regional participation in global production and distribution chains, is fragile as a consequence of global market competition, overproduction, and the impermanent nature of production sequences in the global economy. Third, the development model based on neoliberal integration into the global economy does not require domestic market expansion or an inclusionary social base and is therefore unable to couple the new accumulation potential with social reproduction. Fourth, the social contradictions generated by the model have led to heightened social conflict, popular class mobilization, the political instability of fragile polyarchic regimes, a new resistance politics, and the breakdown of neoliberal hegemony. The key argument is that the model was thrown into an economic crisis between 1999 and2002, and then this crisis unleashed counter-hegemonic social and political forces that discredited neoliberalism and brought about a new period of popular struggle and change.

This sweeping scenario is unpacked in this and the following two chapters. Let us start by looking more closely at what has been in fact an export boom in Latin America from the 1980s and on, comparable to the export booms of earlier epochs, such as the late 1800s and then again after World War II.

Nontraditional Agricultural Exports

Agricultural systems, land tenure, rural life, and class structure have been profoundly transformed in Latin America through globalization. This transformation has taken a distinct path in each country and sub-region based on particular histories, but there are clear patterns common to Latin America. Among these are (1) increasing domination of agriculture by transnational agribusiness (which includes local investors and agribusiness capitalists); (2) the accelerated replacement of noncapitalist by capitalist forms of agricultural development; (3) the concomitant displacement of the peasantry and its conversion into a rural proletariat along with an increase in rural to urban and transnational migration; (4) the flexible and casualized nature of work in the new agro-export platforms; (5) the predominance of female workers in these platforms; and (6) the articulation of local agricultural systems to the global supermarket, that is, to global agricultural and industrial food production and distribution chains.

While traditional agro-exports continue to predominate, they are diminishing in overall importance relative to nontraditional agricultural exports (NTAEs). The term nontraditional may refer to a product that has not been produced in a particular country before, such as snow peas in Mexico or cut flowers in Ecuador. Or it may refer to a product previously produced for domestic consumption and now exported, such as mangos and other tropical fruits in Central America. Or it may refer to the development of a new market for a traditional product, such as the export of Central American bananas to Eastern Europe (for these distinct meanings, see Barham et al., 1992:43). As used here NTAEs refers to the first and/or the second meaning. Some of these products, and other NTAEs exported from Latin America—fruits such as kiwis, passionfruit, and carambola (star fruit), and vegetables such as cassava, arugula, chicory, and baby vegetables—were once relatively unknown or exotic items in the North and were certainly too pricey for mass consumption. Other products such as winter vegetables were at one time produced only in temperate zones and were seasonally marketed. The new ability to outsource this production through global food commodity chains makes them available year round and presents seasonal market opportunities in temperate zones for tropical countries. The reduction in costs that has been achieved by the globalized "flexible" production of these items has made them more available and commonplace among consuming strata, particularly in the North, but increasingly also in the South. The consumption of broccoli, for example, increased 300 percent in the United States in the 1980s (see, e.g., AVANCSO, 1994:9–10). But the phenomenon also reflects the process of post-Fordist income polarization and new class consumption patterns beginning in the 1970s. This has involved a shift in production from standardized to more specialized products catering to segmented markets, entailing the rise of niche markets among a high-income and high-consumption sector of professional and middle strata worldwide increasingly fed by the "global supermarket" and consuming gourmet coffees, exotic fruits, and other specialty food products.

The rise of global supermarkets and the global reorganization of food production and distribution have involved the transformation of national and regional agricultural systems and their incorporation into global agricultural commodity chains (see, inter alia, McMichael, 1994, 1995, 1996; Bonnano et al., 1994; Thrupp, 1995; Goodman and Watts, 1997). Agribusiness firms, just as their manufacturing counterparts in the maquiladoras, use global sourcing strategies. The food trade, as McMichael (1996:100) notes, is one of the fastest-growing industries in the world, especially in processed foods and in fresh and processed fruits and vegetables. Companies stretch across the globe organizing producers on plantations and farms to deliver products for sale in higher-value markets around the world. The extension of transnational agribusiness and growth in worldwide trade of exotic fruits and vegetables are made technically possible by new mechanisms for transportation and refrigeration and by other innovations. "Cool chains," for instance, maintain chilled temperatures for moving fresh fruits and vegetables and allow perishables to be produced anywhere in the world and then marketed elsewhere with little regard for distances between production and consumption and the travel time between these two. The growth of NTAEs is associated as well with the relocation of labor-intensive branches of agribusiness to regions with a comparative advantage in terms of agricultural seasons, soils, and wage rates. By creating and operating in markets across the globe, agribusiness is able to make use of time-space compression in ways that result in the incorporation, transformation, and subordination of local agricultural systems. The operation of food markets across time and space means that global prices have a direct and often immediate bearing on local prices, thereby undermining the possibility of national-contained agricultural systems.

Compared with the production of domestic and traditional export crops, NTAE production takes place more fully under capitalist relations, and it entails much deeper market integration. There are several reasons for this. First, NTAEs require more systematic and much higher levels of financing than traditional crops. This draws producers more fully into the financial system, which itself is in the process of transformation and globalization. Second, NTAE production is highly dependent on an assortment of industrial inputs, from imported seeds and pesticides, to chemical fertilizers and farm equipment. Third, NTAE production involves more sophisticated techniques and technical know-how in planting, maintenance, harvesting, and handling than traditional crops. Technological knowledge is increasingly considered a fourth factor of production, after land, labor, and capital, and its centrality to NTAEs creates dependencies on market-based technical assistance. It is difficult to get around the need for such assistance, since the global market imposes new quality and esthetic demands that imply a more rigorous production process. Finally, NTAEs require insertion into a complex global marketing structure. Ultimately, global market control becomes the key to profitability in the NTAE industry. Global market relations thus penetrate the Latin American countryside through the spread of NTAEs. Peasants are drawn into webs of market relations and subsumed under a capitalist production regime that helps to further undermine what remains of pre-capitalist agriculture (see, e.g., Barham et al., 1992; Thrupp, 1995).[1]

Industrial, financial, and service activity comes to account for a steadily rising proportion of value added as the agricultural product increasingly becomes, conceptually, an input to industrialized production, financial sector, and service sector activity (see, inter alia, Goodman, Sorj, and Wilkinson, 1987). Value flows from the point of agricultural production to the points of control over marketing and financing. A number of researchers have observed that the global food regime has blurred the traditional boundaries between the primary, secondary and tertiary sectors of economic analysis (see, e.g., Gwynne, 1999). The system joins the primary agricultural sectors to industrial processing and to manufacturing industries, and both of these in turn flow into global distribution and marketing networks. Some analysts have labeled this integrated global food regime "Fordist agriculture" (Kim and Curry, 1993), but I think it is more accurate to see the emerging global food regime as a Taylorist flexible accumulation complex that links agro-industry and commercial circuits through new global network structures. Different parts in the system—production, packing, processing, technology supply, retailing, and consumption—are geographically dispersed around globe, networked, and transnational rather than international, as will become clear below.

The spread of NTAEs has been promoted by local states and transnationally oriented elites with financing and guidance (and often imposition through aid conditionality) from the Agency for International Development (AID) and the international financial institutions (IFIs), especially the World Bank.

---

[1] The "commodification of everything" has reached extreme proportions, epitomized in a new wave of *biopiracy* that swept Latin America in the early twenty-first century. The Central American Free Trade Agreement (CAFTA), for instance, opened the door for foreign ownership of the right to exploit Central America's abundant and diverse tropical flora. Under the treaty's intellectual property provisions the Central American governments were required to create legal provisions for what it euphemistically termed bioprospecting: the patenting of biological resources to the benefit of pharmaceutical and agro-industrial TNCs. Bioprospecting allows TNCs to seek plants with properties previously unknown to the TNC and then to legally claim a patent on the processes in which they are used. And such claims are notwithstanding the prior use of these plants by local and indigenous communities. As early as 1991, Costa Rica opened the doors to such biopiracy when the pharmaceutical TNC Merck bought from the government's National Biodiversity Institute the rights to some 500,000 species and microorganisms in the country's national parks. Under the terms of the contract Merck has automatic patent rights to any medicine or product developed from any substance discovered (Noticen, 2006a). Other TNCs, among them Monsanto, Syngenta, and Cristiani Burkard, were seeking in 2006 to launch bioprospecting operations in Guatemala and Panama (ibid.).

But portraying the emerging NTAE complexes in Latin America and else-where in the old terms of Third World agriculture plundering by First World transnational corporations (TNCs) is misleading. Dominant groups in the Third World are thoroughly integrated into these global networks, not just at the point of primary production, and are themselves stakeholders in the TNCs. The mod-ern capitalist structure that emerges is in contrast to the old oligarchic rural structure. NTAE activity has drawn in not a landed oligarchy but dynamic new entrepreneurial sectors, often urban-based, that are linked to the global econ-omy through finances and webs of relationships with TNCs (see, e.g., Conroy et al. 1996; Raynolds, 1994; Kay, 2002). It is clear that asymmetries in power and appropriation as values flow through global production and distribution chains are less inter-national than global, in which those losing and gaining values up and down the chain do not neatly correspond to First and Third World elites. As we shall see below, by way of example, Colombian flower growers also appropriate "high end" value in the global flower industry.

NTAEs tend not to displace traditional agro-exports but to displace basic grain production for the domestic market, under the rationale that grains do not earn foreign exchange and that the region has a comparative advantage in NTAEs. Liberalization results in a flooding of local markets with cheap grains that under-cut peasant production and accelerate the commodification of agriculture. The rise in food imports combined with the need to import much of the inputs, such as fertilizers, pesticides, and seeds, makes it very questionable to what extent NTAEs actually increase available foreign exchange earnings rather than result in a deepening cycle of debt. In addition, neoliberal programs eliminate diverse state supports for the peasant sector and privatize former state services for agriculture. Rising land values in NTAE production areas have been accompanied by declin-ing profitability of traditional activities, which combine to displace peasant pro-ducers. Over time the introduction of NTAE agro-industry leads to the heightened concentration of land, greater rural class differentiation, inequality, polarization, and a further proletarianization of peasants. They then become casualized farm and agro-industrial labor, as the Latin American countryside becomes more deeply implicated in the global economy (Robinson, 2003).

There are two principal patterns of NTAE production in Latin America. One is satellite production, in which TNCs or local firms contract out produc-tion to small producers (Glover and Kusterer, 1990; Conroy et al. 1996). In these instances, packers-exporters purchase crops from many individual farmers and market them through TNC-controlled commodity chains. These packers/exporters are often themselves TNCs or their local representatives, or are contractors or national groups who in turn operate within TNC marketing and other structures. Such satellite production is the principal direction in which transnational agribusiness has moved since the 1980s, as flexible accumulation structures made it possible for TNCs more generally to minimize risk in fixed investment. The contract farming arrangements implied in the satellite production system are inserted into the larger phenomenon of subcontracting and outsourcing associated with new decentralized modes of flexible accumulation. The second pattern, estate-plantation farming, has been called the new plantation system in Latin America. In this arrangement, local or transnational agribusiness firms directly organize production on large estates, generally hiring a small corps of permanent workers (among them, technicians, agronomists, administrators, and foremen) and large numbers of casualized part-time and seasonal workers. This is the system generally employed, for instance, by Standard Fruit (Dole) for pineapple production in Honduras, by national and transnational producers of melons in Guatemala, by flower producers in Ecuador and Colombia, and by TNCs producing fruits in Chile. Regardless of the particular arrangements, diverse agents involved in the NTAE industry are swept up into the transnational production chain and subordinated in various ways and degrees to the overall control of transnational capital, in particular the giant agribusiness firms that dominate the world food regime.

Historically, the introduction of new export crops in Latin America has driven peasants off their land and resulted in waves of rural strife and the social reorganization of the countryside. Recent de-peasantization, the capitalist transformation of agriculture, and the integration of local agriculture into the global agricultural regime have entailed little direct coercion. In earlier rounds of commercial agricultural expansion peasants and the indigenous were forcibly, and often violently, expelled from the land by oligarchs backed by state power. In contrast, peasant and indigenous alienation and proletarianization are being effectuated in the current epoch in most cases (Colombia is one glaring exception) strictly through the economic coercion of the market. The introduction of NTAEs often drives up land prices as outside investors, either nationals or transnational companies, rent or buy land in the local market. As a result, rents become out of reach of small producers and sharecroppers, or production costs and attendant difficulties rise for peasants who have few resources. Similarly, technical information is a key input in NTAEs. Under the neoliberal program it is no longer a state service provided for peasants but increasingly a commodity bought and sold in a capitalist agriculture market. Here, large local producers and TNCs—although the distinction is rarely clear, as local producers are often associated with TNCs through numerous arrangements—are at a distinct advantage, while peasants enter into relations of technical dependency. Moreover, the giant fruit companies themselves often supply technical assistance and professional consultants to producers under contract. Small producers also face an array of difficulties in competing with larger producers and agribusiness. They simply cannot exercise enough control over the gamut of factors and phases involved in production to remain competitive.

Just as there are local losers in NTAE industries, there are also winners. Local benefits include new employment and income opportunities, access to new consumer goods, social and productive infrastructure, and so on. But these benefits are very unevenly distributed. The NTAE industry has benefited a class of medium-level producers and local investor groups, often –urban-based. Many people in these groups have bought out their poorer neighbors thereby changing the class structure. It is interesting to observe the local social groups often involved in the NTAE industry. In the case of Central America or of Chile, for instance, local influence over the industry is exercised largely through finances. Under the neoliberal program state banks providing low-cost credit to peasant producers have been closed or restructured along market lines. Most credit for NTAEs comes from private banks, from TNCs that provide commercial credits for their contractors (or simply use their own capital for direct investment), and increasingly, from investment houses in urban areas, known as *financieras*. These *financieras* function like investment funds, where urban professionals and middle strata, along with capitalists, invest their money in shares. Urban import-export groups, such as those that own foreign automobile or computer dealerships, have entered NTAE production by organizing these *financieras,* which replace state credits that were established in the pre-globalization period of ISI and state-led development (for these details, see Robinson, 2003).

The following sections look at the cut-flower industry in Ecuador and Colombia, fruits and wine in Chile, soy in Argentina, and an array of new agricultural export products in Central America, as examples of the spread of NTAEs in Latin America.

Cut Flowers in Ecuador and Colombia

Flower cultivation and marketing became a global enterprise in the 1980s, and it is now one of the fastest-growing industries worldwide (Sawer, 2005; Korovkin,

2004; Seldeman, 2004). Previously, high transportation costs forced flower producers to locate close to retail markets. The spread of cheap air freight, refrigeration, superhighways, standardized container transportation systems, and so on, associated with the transportation revolution of recent decades, meant that the industry could shift to a strategy of minimizing production costs—in particular, labor costs—rather than transportation costs (Méndez, 1991). The result has been a relocation across the globe of flower production in accordance with ecological, labor, and other considerations, and a shift worldwide from high-markup, low-volume retailing, largely by small independent florists to cheap and high-sales volume flowers produced through globally outsourced chains and marketed increasingly by large and often transnational retailers, such as Krogers, Wal-Mart, Costco, and K-Mart. In 1977, for instance, only 13 percent of U.S. supermarkets sold flowers, but by the mid 1990s, 85–90 percent of large retailers sold flowers at least seasonally and came to account for 40 percent of U.S. flower sales (Sawer, 2005:59). By the 1990s more than sixty countries exported significant quantities of fresh cut flowers. South American flowers are marketed worldwide. While the United States and Europe are the two principal destinations, flowers are also sold as far away as Russia, the Middle East, and Asia, as well as to other Latin American countries (Argentina in particular). Miami has become the key port of entry for flowers from Latin America destined for the North American market, while Amsterdam is the chief port for European marketing.

Floriculture as an agro-industry first made its appearance in Colombia in 1969, and then in Mexico and Chile in the late 1970s. In the decade of the 1980s it was introduced into Bolivia, Costa Rica, Peru, and Ecuador. As systems for developing flower fields in new countries came into place in the 1980s the floriculture industry in these Latin American countries came to bring together such agents as Dutch flower breeders, Israeli manufacturers of computer driven drip irrigation systems, U.S.-based pesticide companies with transnational and local investors and flower producers (Sawer, 2005:60). Colombia is by far the largest Latin American producer—and the second-biggest exporter of flowers worldwide, after the Netherlands—and Ecuador the second-largest in Latin America and the fourth-largest worldwide. The spread of the flower industry in these two countries, as elsewhere in the region, came about also as a result of governments' concerted effort to promote nontraditional exports and achieve reinsertion into global markets. In Ecuador, the government created the Corporation for the Promotion of Exports and Investments (Corpei) in 1997 for the purpose of promoting such exports and attracting foreign investment. Corpei's board of directors is made up largely of government officials and representatives from the private sector, in particular, transnationally oriented financial and investment groups (see Corpei website at www.corpei.org). Similarly, the Colombian government agency for promoting nontraditional exports—Fund for the Promotion of Exports (Proexport)—was instrumental in fomenting the flower industry. Almost every Latin American state has created such government institutions dedicated to promoting nontraditional exports and to attracting foreign investment, which is indicative of the role not only of the neoliberal state as part of the larger TNS apparatus facilitating globalization, but also of the political influence of new transnationally oriented elites over these states. The new export-oriented entrepreneurial sectors have become highly organized in trade associations that work closely with these government branches, and with TNS agencies, such as the AID and the World Bank, to promote NTAEs and other globalized economic activities.

In Ecuador, the oil boom of the 1980s paved the way for the subsequent flower boom. The oil boom and its infamous Dutch disease[2] contributed to the stagnation of traditional agro-exports. The spread of commercialized agriculture and its oil-induced stagnation pushed thousands of peasants off their land and concentrated holdings, thus creating a huge labor supply that could be harnessed to corporate floriculture. The industry took off thanks to massive investment by the government—prodded on by the IFIs and local export-promotion business associations—in such infrastructure as roads, airports, power generation plants, and irrigation projects to encourage floriculture and other NTAEs (Whitaker and Colyer, 1990; Korovkin, 2004; Verdezoto, 2005). Table 2.2 shows the meteoric rise of the industry in Ecuador. By 2003, cut flowers had become the country's third-largest export, after petroleum and bananas, representing nearly 6 percent of total exports, and nearly 10 percent of nonpetroleum export earnings (Sawer, 2005:43–44). The flower industry consists of some 250 companies employing 60,000 workers and indirectly supporting another 110,000. Nontraditional exports, among them, cut flowers, fruit juice and preserves, shrimp, and garments produced in maquiladoras, grew from 11 to 40 percent of all exports between 1989 and 2001 (Sawer, 2005:56–57, table 4), indicating the shift to new core accumulation activities linking Ecuador to the global economy.

---

[2] "Dutch disease," a concept first developed by Corden (1982) in reference to the depression of other exports when the Dutch began exporting oil, refers to the frequently recessionary impacts of a booming resource-based export sector based on inflationary pressures and the appreciation of the real exchange rate generated by the booming sector, which in turn makes other exports less competitive or attractive. The phenomenon is most clearly seen in oil booms. In Mexico and Nigeria, for example, oil booms severely depressed the more traditional export sectors.

TABLE 2.2
Growth of Cut Flower Exports from Ecuador, 1985–2004

Year	Export Volume (in metric tons)	Value (in $million)	Flowers as Share of Total Exports
1985	531	.53	1.02
1990	7,682	13.6	0.50
1992	13,543	29.9	0.97
1994	22,479	59.2	1.5
1996	42,422	104.8	2.1
1998	57,770	162	3.9
2000	78,825	194.7	4.0
2002	80,650	289.3	5.8
2004	91,325	320.5	N/A

Source: Central Bank of Ecuador, as reported by Korovkin, 2004, table 1, p. 89; Sawer, 2005, table 1, p. 42.

In neighboring Colombia cut flowers were aggressively promoted in the 1980s by Colombian and foreign companies with support from the World Bank and other TNSs. In addition to its ideal climate for year-round flower cultivation, noted one World Bank report, two other factors made Colombia an ideal location: "the country is abundantly endowed with naturally fertile land" and "an abundance of low-skilled, largely female labor" (Méndez, 1991:7). The report fails to mention that the country has been experiencing a civil war since the 1960s, fought largely over land. Flowers have become the leading NTAE and the fourth- largest foreign exchange earner, after coffee, petroleum and coal, and garments. In 2005, exports of fresh cut flowers reached nearly $900 million, up from $700 million just one year earlier (Table 2.3). In that year, nontraditional exports—principally fresh cut flowers, garment assembly, metals and plastics, and jewelry and precious stones—surpassed traditional exports (oil and derivatives, coal, and coffee), accounting for a full 51 percent of the country's exports (Proexport, 2006:11). Three out of every four flowers marketed in the United States now come from Colombia. According to industry figures, floriculture employs directly nearly 100,000 workers and indirectly supports another 80,000 (Asocolfores website, www.colombianflowers.com).

Given its capital-intensive and industrial nature, floriculture is organized along corporate lines, controlled directly by domestic and transnational companies employing wage labor rather than being contracted out to small or medium producers. In distinction to fresh fruits and vegetables, flower production is a semi-industrial activity and has as much or more in common with the maquiladoras as with other NTAE activities. Flowers are grown in greenhouses equipped

TABLE 2.3
*Growth of Cut Flower Exports
in Colombia, 1965–2005*

Year	Value (in $million)
1966	0.02
1970	1.0
1975	19.5
1980	101.4
1985	140.8
1990	211.9
1995	475.8
2000	580.0
2002	672.0
2004	702.0
2005	899.9

Source: Proexport, 2006, p. 11.

with sophisticated irrigation, microclimatic control, and fertilization systems. The production process is labor-intensive, including incubation, nursing, fertilizing, cutting, sorting, cleaning, cold storage, and packing, and has a seasonal cycle distinct from other nontraditional agricultural products. Major production runs are organized around international holidays, such as Valentine's Day, Mothers Day, and Christmas. As a result, the industry is characterized by a core of permanent workers and a periphery of seasonal workers—and a high rate of labor turnover.

The spread of floriculture has wrought major social and class transformations in the Ecuadorian and Colombian countryside, as evidenced in the Andean highland zones (the "sierra") of Ecuador, where the industry is concentrated. The introduction of the flower industry to Ecuador constitutes a leading edge for the penetration of global capitalist relations into the countryside and has heightened the process of breakup and proletarianization of peasant and indigenous communities (see Chapter 1 for a theoretical discussion of these phenomena). Proletarianization began in the years after World War II with the expansion of traditional agro-exports and accelerated with the oil boom of the 1970s. What took place during this period was a semi-proletarianization of the peasantry, since most rural families sent out agricultural workers on an itinerant migrant basis and continued to farm on small plots as a supplementary source of family income and subsistence (Martínez Valle, 2000). However, the arrival of the flower industry helped change this pattern. The rescinding of the agrarian reform law in 1994 as part of the neoliberal program allowed for a rapid concentration of holdings as the production of domestic food crop declined and as large holders switched from raising cattle to producing flowers or to leasing or selling their lands to urban and transnational floriculture investors (Whitaker and Colyer, 1990:143, 145; Korovkin, 1997, 2004). Between 1990 and 2000 the amount of land brought into floriculture increased tenfold (Korovkin, 2004:89). Greenhouses, flower fields, and cutting and packing plants stretched in all directions as far as the eye could see when I toured the central sierra between Quito and Otavalo in February 2006.

Floriculture researcher Tanya Korovkin documents a sharp decline during the 1980s in cattle raising among large landholders and a decrease in the production of traditional food products for domestic consumption, such as potatoes, corn, barley, wheat, and beans (Korovkin, 1997:95, table 1; 2004:89) coinciding with the introduction and spread of the flower industry. The spread of the cut-flower industry fueled the crisis of peasant agriculture—fragmentation, declining yields, shrinking agricultural incomes, and a growing dependence on off-farm jobs. The arrival of the flower industry sharply inflated land prices. Only a little more than 50 percent of all flower workers own land, and of these, 83 percent of male workers and 94 percent of female workers own less than one hectare (Korovkin, 2004:98, table 3). As Korovkin documents, the flower industry employs young women and men, whose average age is 27 compared with age 45 for a previous generation of migrant and itinerant rural workers (2004:98). Proletarianization has been especially sharp among the younger work force, whose members no longer work the land. Contractors also draw on child labor, which is widespread in the Andean flower industry (U.S. Department of Labor, 2006:1). New economic activities such as the flower industry can potentially offer new opportunities for social mobility, and Korovkin is right to point out that proletarianization is not by definition a negative phenomenon in terms of living standards. The broader story here is the increasing class differentiation in the countryside as globalization generates both winners and losers. Yet despite new opportunities opened up by employment in the flower industry, as Korovkin also points out, in the case of Ecuador the combined minimum wages for a husband and wife that the industry paid is not enough to cover the basic food basket, and most flower workers have continued to live at or near the poverty line (Korovkin, 2004:99). Floriculture workers in Colombia face similar conditions as in Ecuador. In 2005, the minimum monthly wage of $130 was 200 percent below the poverty line for a family of four.

Flower companies have located installations in rural communities. The spread of floriculture has strengthened capital's presence in rural civil society and the influence of new technocratic and transnationally oriented elites. Flower producers in Ecuador have organized into a business association, EXPOFLORES, which has promoted neoliberal reforms and played an active role in securing government subsidies and IFI-funding infrastructure for the industry. On the other hand, as Korovkin has shown in her ethnographic research (2004), the changes associated with global capitalist penetration and the spread of the flower industry in the countryside has contributed to the "nuclearization" of extended family units, a breakdown of extended family and community networks, heightened insecurity, and a decline in the influence of popular sectors in rural civil society. While cautioning that they have managed to retain non-capitalist traits as part of their resistance to complete incorporation into the capitalist labor market, Korovkin observes that sierra agricultural peasant communities

> have been trapped and exploited by the growing capitalist economy. In the absence of meaningful agrarian reform, they had to confront the problems of land fragmentation and soil depletion. The result was erosion of their agricultural base, which forced them to sell their labor power in the construction and flower industries or to travel as petty traders to other parts of Ecuador and across the border to Colombia [and we may add, to the United States, Spain, and elsewhere; see Chapter 3]. In effect, what had been largely agricultural peasant communities in the middle of the twentieth century looked forty or fifty years later more like communities of wage earners and traders who owned small family plots of land. (1997:105)

The flower industry in both countries is organized through subcontracting and outsourcing chains—labor recruitment, transportation, warehousing, and so on—so that diverse local groups come to participate in the industry (Tamayo, 2006a:2). As part of their reform of their labor laws, the Colombian and Ecuadorian governments introduced legislation allowing for what has been loosely called *tercerización* or third-party arrangements, highly characteristic of new global capital-labor relations. This includes local temporary-worker agencies and labor recruitment firms, arrangements that, as in the United States and elsewhere, shift the employment responsibility from the industry to smaller groups whose labor violations are harder to denounce. An increasing number of workers in both countries are employed by labor subcontractors who hire workers for six-month, three-month, or one-month contracts—or even for just 10 to 15 days at a time. Short-term contract workers have no rights to social benefits, such as pensions, health and injury insurance, or maternity leave (VIDEA, 2002). These local agents of labor recruitment and control, along with land speculators and owners who rent to the flower industry, local supply firms, and so forth, form part of a bloc whose interests lie in the expansion of transnational circuits that draw the country deeper into the global economy.

Notwithstanding increased worldwide consumption, the global flower industry was already showing signs in the 1990s of saturation, similar to the pattern of earlier Latin America exports such as coffee, sugar, and cotton, as a number of Asian and African countries, among them Kenya, India, Malaysia, Malawi, South Africa, Zambia, and China, entered the world market as producers (Korovkin, 2003:22; 2004:90). This tendency for market saturation holds more generally as a cautionary note for NTAEs as a development strategy (Barham et al., 1992). As a result there has been a tendency in the Latin American floriculture industry to increase labor flexibility and to extract greater absolute surplus value by increasing the working day and amount of piecework required of each worker. As one worker in Ecuador described to Korovkin, typical of ethnographic reports on labor conditions in the industry:

> From mid-January until February eight we worked nearly round-the-clock. Sometimes we would leave at three in the morning and we would have to be back at work by 6:30 a.m. We'd come home only to say hello. . . . Many people also came down with tonsillitis because it would get so cold [in the post-harvest rooms]. Our output declined [from 25] to 15–16 'bunches.' The foreman threatened that he would not pay us overtime if we did not reach at least 20 'bunches' per hour. At any rate they never paid us our overtime. Out of the 300–350 [hours] that I would put in each season they would barely pay me for 200–250 [hours]. (Korovkin, 2004:93)

Workers in the flower industry also face significant health hazards as a consequence of the high levels of toxins emitted through the use of pesticides, fungicides, artificial fertilizers, and other dangerous substances. Up to 60 percent of the workforce in the Ecuadorian industry suffers from one or another work-related health problem, ranging from cancer to neurological damage, acute poisoning, blurred vision, conjunctivitis, chronic back and muscle pain, varicose veins and ulcers, persistent cough, headaches, memory loss, miscarriages, bronchitis, and tonsillitis (Tamayo, 2006a:3; Mena and Proaño, 2005; VIDEA, 2002). According to medical surveys in Colombia, nearly 66 percent of flower workers suffer from maladies associated with pesticide exposure (Watkins, 2001). A study of more than 8,000 workers on flower plantations near Bogotá found that the workers were exposed to 127 different pesticides, many of them highly toxic, and about 20 percent of them banned in the United States and Canada (VIDEA, 2002:9). The food chain and water supply in the Ecuadorian sierra and in Colombia's Sábana de Bogotá have been found contaminated as a result of leakage of toxins from flower fields and plants (Tamayo, 2006:3; Mena and Proaño, 2005; Watkins, 2001). In Ecuador, one report found that toxic runoffs are causing the extinction of some species of flora and fauna (VIDEA, 2002:10).

NTAE production transforms and transnationalizes subordinate groups, affecting relations among them and between them and the dominant groups. In the case of gender relations, a major portion, often an outright majority, of workers in the new transnationally integrated circuits in Latin America are women. Women predominate in the maquiladoras, the new agribusiness establishments, menial service work in the tourist industry, and so on. Carmen Diana Deere has termed the increasing prevalence of women in NTAE complexes in Latin America as the "feminization of agriculture" (Deere, 2005). The growth of women's employment in agriculture has been concentrated in NTAEs as the most dynamic sectors Latin American agriculture and agro-industry integrated into the global economy, especially the production and packing of fresh fruits, vegetables, and flowers. However, as Deere notes, there is also evidence of a feminization of smallholder production, as growing numbers of rural women become the principal farmers, associated with an increase in the proportion of rural female households, male absence from the farm (outmigration, off-farm pursuits, etc.), and the decreased viability of peasant farming under neoliberalism (Deere, 2005). In the larger picture we are seeing the highly gendered nature of the demise of the peasantry and the gendered nature of global labor markets.

Women and men are differentially incorporated into expanding nontraditional sectors. Sociologist Laura Raynolds has studied the increase of women's participation in NTAE production in Latin America and found that women often play a predominant role in the industry but remain gender segregated within it and generally receive less pay than men. In her case study on the Dominican Republic, she found that supervisory and professional jobs were reserved almost exclusively for men, who also ran machinery and packed containers, whereas women were concentrated in sorting fruits and vegetables, washing and labeling, and other assorted activities requiring (according to managers) a supposed natural female dexterity. In the fields, men tended to prepare land, plant, and apply chemical inputs, while women predominated in cultivating and harvesting. Raynolds found that women's overall earnings were typically below men's because of their limited access to better-paid supervisory and technical jobs and their concentration in seasonal activity (Raynolds, 1998).

The images of superexploitation and patriarchal domination of female employees who predominate among floriculture workforces in Latin America has been memorialized in the award-winning 2004 film production *Maria Full of Grace* (Marston, 2004) and the documentary *Love, Women, and Flowers* (Rodríguez, 1988). Sixty percent of the 60,000 flower workers in Ecuador are female (Sawer, 2005:47) as are some 70 percent of the approximately 100,000 flower workers in Colombia. The case of Ecuador is emblematic. Gender segmented labor markets in the new agro-export complexes result, on the one hand, from structural adjustment, unfavorable policies for domestic (especially smallholder) agriculture, the withdrawal of state public services, and the loss of land among peasant families in the countryside, which has led to a diversification of household income and new survival strategies. The crisis of peasant agriculture has led to male unemployment and outmigration toward cities (and abroad) and forced rural women to search for paid employment as a survival strategy (Korovkin, 2004:96; Deere, 2005). On the other hand, employers often prefer female workers because preexisting patriarchal structures provide capital with extra leverage over women workers.

Patriarchal relations are not eliminated by but grafted onto expanding capitalist relations, intensifying unequal power relations between men and women. Women seeking paid employment face fewer options than men, principally domestic service for middle and upper classes, the restaurant, itinerant trading in the informal sector, or maquiladora work. Once on the job, female flower workers are subject to systematic sexual harassment and assault. A mission sent to Ecuador by the International Labor Rights Fund found that more than 55 percent of flower workers have suffered some kind of sexual harassment, 19 percent have been forced to have sex with a coworker or superior, and 10 percent have been sexually assaulted (Mena and Proaño, 2005). And as has been widely discussed in the literature on women in the global economy, women face an intensified "double burden" of production and reproduction: as they enter the paid workforce they are still largely responsible for reproduction in the household (see, inter alia, Benería and Feldman, 1992).

The flower industry has resisted unionization, firing and blacklisting workers who have tried to organize and promoting pliant company unions. In 2005 there were only two unionized plants of a total of more than 400 in Ecuador (Tamayo, 2006a:1). Several hundred workers from the Rosas de Ecuador firm sustained a strike from 2003 into 2006, with the support of the Confederation of Indigenous Nationalities of Ecuador (CONAIE, see Chapter 5) [Tamayo, 2006a:1). In Colombia, workers at the Tuchany plant succeeded in forming a union, but subsequently management fired the organizers and disbanded the union. In 2001 workers at the Benilda plant formed the National Union of Flower Workers (Untraflores), but firing and blacklisting had reduced the union to just 45 members in 2006 (Global Exchange, 2006). The local and international press is full of accounts of workers struggles, labor conflict, and state and employee repression in the Colombian and Ecuadorian flower industry.

The flower industry in Colombia offers a case study of the TCC in Latin America. Flower cultivation was first introduced in the fertile mountain plateaus of Sábana de Bogotá in 1969 by a group of U.S. investors who formed the Floramerica Corporation (Méndez, 1991:12). But with World Bank support Colombian investors quickly moved into the industry, which by the 1980s was controlled by some 500 firms that are mostly owned by Colombians or by transnational investor groups with Colombian participation. These Colombian investors, organized into the powerful agribusiness guild, the Colombian Association of Flower Exporters (Asocolflores), turned aggressively to global marketing and to establishing overseas operations, including common handling companies in importing countries around the world (Méndez, 1991:10). Colombian growers and exporters, for instance, established in Miami the Colombian Flower Council in 1987 to promote flower consumption in the United States (see the Asocolflores website at www.colombianflowers.com). They also joined forces in 1996 with U.S. growers and importers to form the U.S.–Colombia Business Partnership to promote their collective interests.

What happened next is instructive. As Colombian exporters captured an increasingly larger share of the U.S. flower market, U.S. growers lobbied for import restrictions, leading to a trade war of sorts in the mid-1990s. But the process of transnationalization overcame national antagonisms among business groups from both countries. By 2000 growers and exporters in Colombia had reached agreement with growers and importers in the United States—many of whom have investments as well in the industry in South America—and resolved their differences. In that year they set up a transnational business association, the Flower Promotion Organization, to cooperate in expanding consumer demand in the United States and internationally (see the organization's website at www.flowerpossibilities.com). There was thus a merging of interests and organic alliances among Colombian and U.S. growers as they transnationalized. This is in contrast to the classical pattern of Latin American agro-exports, in which producers were subordinated to core purchasing and marketing firms and simply exported their products without operating transnationally. For example, in 1998 Dole Food purchased the biggest flower operation in Colombia,

Floramerica, and three other flower companies from Colombian investors, giving the company control of 25 percent of Colombian flower production. Dole is the world's largest supplier of fruits and vegetables; it and other leading agribusiness TNCs have a major stake in NTAEs and expanding agribusiness throughout the Americas. However, the Colombian case suggests that the relationship between the extra-regional TNCs and Latin American capitalists is not one of comprador, or managerial underlings, but of partnerships that promote the process of TCC formation. Colombian capitalists have thus found ways to tap into other phases in the global commodity chain as they transnationalize, capturing values further down the chain that they may lose through "leakages" closer to production.

We find a similar pattern in Ecuador, where flower producers have teamed up in a number of ways with transnational capital from abroad, including Dutch, U.S., and Colombian-based capital (Korovkin, 2004:89). The flower industry in Latin America is transnational not merely in the sense that it is integrated into new global circuits of production and distribution and involves TNC participation, but also in the sense that investors in the industry come from numerous countries and invest elsewhere in flower production as well (Sawer, 2005:61). Noteworthy here is the cross-investment by Ecuadorian and Colombian groups. Many Colombian growers, for instance, invested in Ecuadorian flower fields in the 1990s as the Andean Pact allowed freer movement of capital among member countries.

Fruits and Wines in Chile

Chile is the darling of the transnational elite, held up as a success story of neoliberalism and global capitalism. This story line, shown in the more critical literature to be seriously defective (see, inter alia, Winn, 2004; Collins and Lear, 1995; Green, 1995; Petras et al., 2004; Robinson, 1996c), hinges on the country's remarkable export expansion. Total exports jumped from $1.3 billion in 1973 to $39 billion in 2005, according to Chilean Central Bank data (see www.bcentral.cl/esp/), as the country became thoroughly reintegrated on a new basis into world capitalism, starting with the era of the Pinochet dictatorship (1973–1989) and accelerating under civilian regimes (1990–2008). Dynamic new export sectors that constitute the core of the country's new accumulation model include fresh and processed fruits, vegetables, wine, forestry products, and farmed salmon and other mariculture products. Of these new exports, the fruit sector is the most important, accounting for over 60 percent of Chile's agricultural and agro-industrial exports in the late 1990s, and nearly 80 percent if wine (as processed grapes) is included (Gwynne, 1999:213). Before the rise of fruiticulture Chile's primary agricultural exports were traditional crops—e.g., beans, lentils, and wool—that are now insignificant in the country's export profile. By 2004 fresh and processed fruits accounted for nearly 10 percent of all the country's exports, involving some 500 export companies and 8,000 producers. Table 2.4 shows the take-off of the fruit agro-industrial export industry.

Chile is held up, along with Costa Rica, as the most successful case of NTAE growth in Latin America. Chile has become the world's leading exporter of fresh table grapes and plums, the second-most important exporter of avocados, and the third-most important exporter of apples, kiwis, and pears. The country also exports significant quantities of peaches, raspberries, blueberries, nectarines, mandarins, apricots, and other fruits (Chilean Fresh Fruit Association, at www.cffa.org). As well, a portion of fruit production is processed and exported as canned goods, dried goods, frozen goods, and juice concentrates. Thus the fruit industry is agro-industrial; fresh fruit exports involve packing operations, and processed fruit production involves a major industrial phase (the same is true for mariculture, involving industrially organized fish processing and packing and for forestry, involving sawmills and paper, pulp, furniture, and related industries). In my June 2004 drive south from the Chilean capital of Santiago to the Central Valley, the heartland of the country's fruit and wine industry, I saw Santiago's skyscrapers give way to fields of fruits and vineyards as far as the eye could see, and ubiquitous packing and processing plants along the highway with the familiar logos of Dole, Unifrutti, and other fruit companies.

TABLE 2.4
Chile: Fresh and Processed Fruit Exports
(value, in US$ million)

Year	Fresh Fruit	Processed Fruits	Total
1975	N/A	N/A	40
1980	168	N/A	168+
1985	356	47	403
1990	716	232	948
1995	1,162	552	1,714
2000	1,386	474	1,860
2003	1,650	558	2,208
2004	1,911	718	2,639
2005	N/A	N/A	2,869

Source: Central Bank of Chile, www.bcentral.cl/esp/.

TABLE 2.5
Chile: Number of Export Products, Importing Countries, and Exporting Firms

Year	Products	Importing Countries	Exporting Firms
1975	200	50	200
1987	1,400	120	3,666
1990	2,300	122	4,100
1995	3,647	157	5,817
2000	3,749	175	5,666
2001	3,749	173	6,009
2002	5,160	158	6,118
2003	5,232	165	6,435
2004	5,238	171	6,636

Source: ProChile, Estadísticas de Comercia Exterior, available at www.prochile.cl/servicios/estadísticas/index.php.

Chile is the first country to have started neoliberal restructuring and globalization, and it is probably the "purest" neoliberal republic in the hemisphere in terms of its level of integration into global markets, deregulation, privatization, domination by private capital, the atomization of the working class, and the hegemony of neoliberal ideology and global capitalist culture. Chile's neoliberal transformation began earlier and is more "complete" than anywhere else in the hemisphere, perhaps the world. The entire Chilean productive structure has been reoriented from an accumulation strategy based on industrialization and the expansion of internal markets to diverse exports for the global market. Table 2.5 gives some indication of the country's re-conversion into a massive export platform for the global market.

Chile, thus, is the quintessential example of the new outward oriented development model based on nontraditional exports and a deeper insertion into the global economy.[3] In 2004, exports represented a full 75 percent of the GDP, according to Central Bank data. This extreme extraversion-globalization of the economy has as well profound class and social implications. The literature on Chile's export fruit industry was the first to identify the emergence of a new entrepreneurial class linked to Chile's NTAE sectors (Barham et al., 1992). This new exporting elite stands in contrast to the old landed oligarchy and national commercial and industrial elites of an earlier epoch. Chile has a powerful capitalist class organized into an array of general and specialized business

[3] However, two qualifiers in this analysis should be noted. First, Chile remains dependent on the export of its traditional export, copper (and mining)—the backbone of the twentieth-century Chilean economy—which in 2004 still accounted for just under half of export earnings, while nontraditional exports accounted for just over half. Second, unlike the Asian Tigers' skyrocketing exports in the late twentieth century, Chile still exports almost exclusively primary sector products and their derivatives.

associations. In the fruit industry alone, there are at least twenty national associations organized into the umbrella Chilean Fresh Fruit Exporters Association (Fedefruta), and the agro-industrial groupings, Association of Chilean Food Enterprises (Chilealimentos) and Federation of Chilean Food Processors and Agro-industrialists (Fepach). As in Ecuador and elsewhere, these new private sector associations are fused with the Chilean state in a number of ways. In fact, in 1997 the government began directly funding these business associations (USDA, 2005a).

As with floriculture in Ecuador and Colombia, and more broadly with NTAEs in Latin America, this "new entrepreneurial class" is made up in part of traditional landed oligarchies and agrarian bourgeoisies who have modernized and transformed into capitalist farmers, but even more so, of emergent transnationally oriented elites from outside agriculture, such as urban industrialists and financiers, international marketing and commercial groups, and professionals (such as agronomists and MBAs) with capital to invest (Barham et al., 1992:63; Gwynne, 1999:221). These new urban-based business groups thus link backward into agriculture and horizontally with banking, industrial, and commercial capital. In turn, these diverse Chilean capitalist groups have associated in manifold ways with transnational capital from abroad and at the same time are themselves investing in other countries in Latin America and beyond, fusing with capitalists from elsewhere and becoming a part of the TCC. Because fruit production is now a highly sophisticated technical process requiring substantial capital investment and know-how it tends to exclude smallholders. As a result there has been a steady concentration of land in fruit and other nontraditional sectors and the rise of a new class of dynamic agricultural entrepreneurs integrated into the global economy and fused in numerous ways with other transnationally oriented groups alongside a new casualized workforce and intensified social differentiation.

The Chilean fresh and processed fruit industry begins with some 8,000 farm businesses, the vast majority medium- and large-sized capitalist producers, including investment and holding companies that draw in Chilean and foreign investors. Next, the phase of industrial processing, packaging, cool storage, export, and so on, is controlled by five large TNCs, four large domestic fruit corporations, some 200 to 250 small- to medium-sized processing and export companies, and a handful of farmer consortia (Gwynne, 1999:216–218). In 1997 the TNCs included the following: Dole (formerly Standard Trading Company); Chiquita, operating through its Chilean subsidy, Frupac; United Trading Company; Unifrutti Traders; and Zeus (investors come from the United States, the United Kingdom, Switzerland, New Zealand, France, Argentina, South Africa, Japan, China, and elsewhere). These five TNCs were responsible for about 35 percent of fruit exports in the mid-1990s (Gwynne, 1999:218). The four largest Chilean fruit companies controlled some 20 percent of processing and exports in the 1990s and had developed international marketing networks. Companies representing consortia of large capitalist farmers began to invest in the 1990s in cool transport, storage, packing, and other forward-integration activities in the production chain. Finally, the small- to medium-sized export firms tended to specialize in specific fruit sectors and world market niches. The latter two categories controlled some 45 percent of fruit exports (Gwynne, 1999:218). Hence we see an increasing transnationalization of Chilean economic agents.

Underpinning the rapid growth of NTAEs is the exploitation of cheap peasant labor that has been proletarianized and semi-proletarianized, especially seasonal female wage workers (see, inter alia, Kay, 2002; Gwynne, 1999; Korovkin, 1992; Murray, 1997; Schurman, 2001; Bee and Vogel, 1997). In the table grape sector, male labor has predominated in harvesting and female labor in packing (Bee, 2000; Bee and Vogel, 1997). The ratio of permanent to temporary labor runs from 1:4 to 1:10 (Gwynne, 1999:222), although permanent labor also is flexible and casualized, and often permanent workers are forced to move from farms to packing houses and processing plants with little work stability. "When small-scale farmers were forced to sell out to the fruit TNCs, they received a small cash payment for the transfer of agricultural property and kept their house and garden (huerta). Then, if they did not migrate out of the region, they would be reincorporated into the table grape economy as providers of seasonal or permanent labor for the larger farms. . . . [T]hese peasant farmers effectively became part of the rural proletariat" (Gwynne, 2002:318). Just as we saw in the case of flowers in Ecuador, in rural settlements in Chile that service areas dominated by large-scale farms, notes Gwynne, "the sense of community has been lost as highly mobile patterns of life style have emerged." The population of one community he studied, Chanaral Alto, "varies between 2,000 and 14,000 during the year, depending on the labor requirements of large-scale farming. At the local scale, the nature of production is increasingly characterized by inequalities while rural communities are becoming more segmented, divided and transient." (1999:223)

As elsewhere, a majority of the new workers are women. In a phenomenon we see in Ecuador and elsewhere, the new casualized, feminized labor force for NTAEs draws on semi-urban workers who travel seasonally to farms and agro-industrial complexes. About one-third of Chile's agricultural workforce during the harvest season is urban or semi-urban (Barham et al., 1992:65). Only 7 percent of workers employed in the nontraditional export sectors in Chile are affiliated with a trade union (Kay, 2002:492). As with *tercerización* in Ecuador, seasonal and temporary workers in Chile are increasingly not even employed directly by capitalist farmers and agro-industrialists but by *contratistas* who are subcontractors (Korovkin, 1992; Kay, 2002). While in the early 1970s two-thirds of agricultural labor was permanent and a third temporary, by the late 1980s these proportions had reversed. Sixty percent of these temporary wage workers were employed in export fruiticulture, and up to 70 percent of these were women (Kay, 2002:481, citing various sources). These *temporeras*, as the temporary female workers are known, constitute a new form of agricultural labor in Chile and have played a key role in the dramatic expansion of fruit and wine exports (Barrientos, 1997). "The concept of *temporera* also carried political and ideological baggage as it represents the most unprotected sector of workers and illustrates the extreme effects of the neo-liberal model on the labor market," observe Bee and Vogel. "The temporary nature of the jobs excludes workers from the legal right to organize, it affects their pension and social security payments, contracts and job security guarantees, whilst giving employers total freedom to set wage levels and retain or dismiss workers freely according to their production schedules" (1997:85). Moreover, the horrendous work conditions, gender segmentation and sexual abuse, widespread occupational health hazards, low pay, and repression that we saw in floriculture has been broadly documented in Chile's NTAE industries as well (see, inter alia, Schurman, 2001; Winn, 2004; Collins and Lear, 1995). In most fruit-packing and seafood-processing plants, workers have to stand on their feet all day in cold, wet atmospheres performing repetitive motions at tremendous speed.

The rural population in Chile has gone from peons to small producers to rural proletariat in the latter half of the twentieth century, as the Chilean countryside has experienced three distinct phases in its transformation. Prior to the reformist and revolutionary periods (1964–1973) the countryside was characterized by the classical Latin American *minifundia/latifundia* or hacienda structure. A landed oligarchy controlled vast tracks of land, and a mass of peons on small parcels faced off with landlords in semi-feudal arrangements. The reformist period did away with this structure and to a certain extent democratized rural property, leading to a predominance of small and medium-sized cooperative and individual producers (Kay, 2002). The Pinochet and post–Pinochet era has resulted in a re-concentration of lands through new economic power relations, this time in the hands of large modern capitalist producers and agribusiness companies while the mass of rural dwellers has been drawn in as salaried employees and workers—a largely temporary and seasonal workforce that has been flexibilized and casualized (see, inter alia, Kay, 2002; Gwynne, 1999, 2002; Schurman, 2001; Murray, 1997; Korovkin, 1992; Winn, 2004; Bee and Vogel, 1997).

Mounting debt, government policy, land and credit markets, commercial networks, the mechanisms of contract farming for corporate agro-industrialists, exporters, and TNCs, and lack of access to technology, information, training, and inputs all conspired against smallholders and family farms (*parceleros*). These strictly market mechanisms—the normal progress of capitalist development freed from political interference—have resulted in a steady loss of land to capitalist farmers and agro-industries. Between 1986–88 and 1993–94 alone, the percentage of the country's fruit-producing lands in the hands of peasant farmers dropped from 22 to 15 (Kay, 2002:481). And as elsewhere, NTAEs have replaced food and domestic crop production. Between 1986 and 1998 the agricultural lands under traditional crop cultivation dropped by 33 percent while the area dedicated to fruits and vineyards increased by 33 percent and horticulture and flowers increased by 26 percent (Kay, 2002:479, table 3, and 480).

As Kay (2002) shows, the social and technical relations of production in the Chilean countryside by the 1990s had nothing in common with the former *latifundia*, having been transformed into capitalist agriculture thoroughly integrated into global capitalism. Through conversion to NTAEs, global capitalism has penetrated and transformed the Chilean countryside. Indeed, the Chilean government has even proclaimed "conversion"—a switch in agricultural land use from traditional production for the domestic market to NTAEs—as its policy and has actively fomented the spread of NTAEs through incentives and subsidies through its export promotion agency, ProChile, and other bureaus. Murray examined how this process played out from the 1970s and on in his detailed study of one typical region, El Palqui, in the north-central valley:

(1) From 1977 to 1984, the sector remained almost exclusively dedicated to the production of tomatoes and green beans destined for regional and national markets.

(2) Between 1984 and 1990, virtually every small farmer converted to the production of grapes for export. This was facilitated by the entrance of multinational and national export companies offering credit under...contractual conditions. . . .

There was a significant local "boom" in local income due to the favorable conditions existent at this time.

(3) From 1990 to the present day the sector has been characterized by an increasing "squeeze" on small growers. The main characteristics of this "squeeze" have been rising levels of debt, the sale of land and a consequent re-concentration in the ownership of reformed land-holdings. (Murray, 1997:50)

There is a highly revealing aside here. Murray (1977) and Korovkin (1992, 2004) note that as Chile and other new Southern Hemisphere fruit and vegetable exporters (Australia, New Zealand, South Africa, etc.) began to flood the global market, prices dropped precipitously in the 1990s. This global market stagnation, in turn, forced producers to upgrade technologically and organizationally, but such upgrading was entirely impossible for all but the largest producers with capital and economies of scale, thus accelerating a re-concentration of land and proletarianization of peasant producers. Of course this process is germane to capitalist development itself; it is the general mechanism whereby overproduction/ overaccumulation lead to recession that is "resolved" through a greater concentration and centralization of capital. In this case, such concentration and centralization is not national but transnational; global market stagnation reverberates into the Chilean countryside resulting in the development of transnationally oriented Chilean capitalists who deepen their integration into the global economy.

In the 1970s and 1980s much fruit production took place through contract farming, which is a consignment system whereby the exporter/distributor takes a percentage of the actual price the fruit fetches in global markets. But by the 1990s as land became concentrated and as the fruit companies moved down vertically into production, this system seemed to be giving way to more direct organization of production by the fruit TNCs or by large producers who deal directly with processors, exporters, and distributors. The Chilean link in the global production chain, according to Gwynne, is increasingly dominated *directly* by four TNCs—Dole, Chiquita, United Trading Company, and Unifrutti— alongside some significant Chilean distribution companies, while producers become differentiated by the bargaining arrangements with transnational distributors (Gwynne, 2002).

Chile has also become a world-class exporter of wine, moving into fifth place in 2003 and ahead of such countries as Germany, the United States, and Portugal, capturing some 5 percent of world market exports, as wine production more than tripled between 1992 and 2003 (Visser, 2004:7, 17). This is remarkable, since Chile exported insignificant amounts of the beverage in the mid-1980s. In part, there was a shift in wine marketing from domestic to foreign markets; the degree of internationalization of the Chilean wine industry is the highest in the world, amounting to over 45 percent in the late 1990s (Visser, 2004:21). But it is more a consequence of the dramatic expansion itself of wine production. Wine exports went from $18 million in 1980 to $845 million in 2004 (USDA, 2005b:25). The wine industry is highly concentrated. The top four wine firms in Chile, led by Concha y Toro, controlled 45 percent of exports in 2001 (Visser, 2004:24). In the 1980s and 1990s the global wine industry witnessed a sharp process of concentration, largely through mergers and takeovers, and of vertical integration of primary and secondary production, marketing and distribution (Visser, 2004:25). In Chile, wine producers set up two business associations to expand the industry: the Association of Fine Export Wine Producers (Chilevid) and Wines of Chile.

As with fruiticulture, foreign wine companies have invested in the Chilean industry, generally as joint ventures with Chilean wine producers. B. Philippe de Rothschild-Mouton from France has paired up with the Chilean wine giant Concha y Toro to form Almaviva. Robert Mondavi of California joined with Viña Errazuriz to set up Caliterra, and Mildara Blass of Australia with Santa Carolina to establish Dallas Conte. Such big names as Fetzer and Kendall-Jackson also entered joint ventures with Chilean wineries (Visser, 2004:26, table 10). Independent of its partnership with the Rothschilds of France, Concha y Toro produces and markets the Walnut Crest brand in the United States, making it truly a TNC. In the 1990s Chilean and TNC fruit companies also began to acquire direct ownership of vineyards (Gwynne, 1999:221).

In broader perspective, the globalization of the Latin American countryside reminds us, as sociologist Beatriz Cid Aguayo (2006) observes, that rural places "are not outside of the cycles of production and circulation of capital, culture, and ideology, but rather are fully integrated therein." Cid Aguayo refers to such rural localities as Chile's Central Valley, the Ecuadorian indigenous town of Otavalo (see below), and La Realidad, a rural nucleus of Zapatista activity in Chiapas, Mexico, as global villages in "a literal rather than metaphorical sense, as a way of referring to all small settlements that participate in the globalization of processes related to economy, ecology, culture, migration, technology and other aspects of life. . . . Classical definitions of rurality that describe it as a pre-industrial and pre-capitalist residue are no longer meaningful. There are no *truly* local places, since all are integrated in the global economy and the global circulation of culture, being in some way cosmopolitan" (3). In relation to fruit and wine, she suggests, the Central Valley of Chile "has become a neo-liberal global village . . . a node in the global foodscape" (9).

Argentina and the New Soy Republics of the Southern Co ne

The story of soy production in Argentina and the Southern cone is a textbook study in the overnight transnational corporate colonization of Latin American agriculture and a damning example of its social and environmental consequences. Soy production has experienced explosive growth in Argentina, Brazil, Bolivia, Paraguay, and Uruguay, expanding at a rate of 10 percent annually from 1995 to 2005 (AIDEnvironment, 2005:1). In the 1990s soy became the single-most important agricultural export of all four countries (Dros, 2004:9). The agents that control the global soy market have taken advantage of the extensive lands available in the Southern Cone, practically the only place in the world that could be targeted for a major expansion of output to meet booming world market demand. Here I will examine Argentina, which in a few short years went from an insignificant producer to the third-largest producer in the world, after the United States and Brazil, and the number one world exporter. In Argentina, as elsewhere in the Southern Cone, the spread of soy has taken place through a new transnational agribusiness model based on the application of biotechnology and genetic engineering as one of the core technologies that has spawned new forms of global accumulation and allowed capital to heighten its control over such accumulation.

Soy is one of the most important commodities in the global agribusiness trade, supplying worldwide one fourth of edible oils and over half of the oils and meals in animal feed (Dros, 2004:1). The United States, Brazil, and Argentina are the principal exporters of soy to the world market, accounting for 90 percent of world market supplies (Dros, 2004:7). As the demand for soy has increased rapidly worldwide, the area planted in soy in the major producing regions—the U.S. Midwest, the South American Southern Cone, and China—has expanded at the expense of other crops and natural ecosystems. Yet China and the United States have little arable land reserves so that expansion now takes place primarily in the Southern Cone.

Soy in Argentina and neighboring countries has experienced an explosive expansion—*invasion* would be more accurate—with frightening social and environmental consequences. As Table 2.6 shows, output in Argentina increased over elevenfold between 1980 and 2004, showing the most rapid growth after the government launched a self-declared "campaign" to promote production through a new transgenic (genetically modified, or GM) crop scheme. Already by the new century soybean production accounted for over 50 percent of Argentina's total agricultural output (in tonnage) and over 20 percent of its export earnings (Bisang, 2003:2; Pengue, 2005:315). The Argentine government has enjoyed a

Soybean crop areas in the Western Hemisphere, which accounts for 80 percent of world production and 90 percent of world exports.

windfall from a 20 percent tax on soy exports, so much so that the economic recovery in the wake of the 2002 financial crisis (see Chapters 4 and 5) can be attributed in large part to soy (Grau et al., 2005).

Around 70 percent of the Argentine soybean harvest is converted in oil-processing plants and mostly exported, providing 81 percent of the world's exported soybean oil and 36 percent of soybean meal. Global market demand for both products has boomed. Soy meal has become a leading animal feed and as world meat production increases, especially in China, so has the demand for soy meal. Major importers are the EU and China; although Japan, Mexico, Taiwan, Thailand, Indonesia, South Korea, Iran, Bangladesh, Russia, Morocco, and Egypt are also major importers.

Key and Runsten (1999) make a distinction between labor-intensive and land-intensive crops. In distinction to most NTAEs in Latin America, which are labor intensive, soybean production as organized in the Southern Cone is land intensive. Mechanized soy production generates only one job per 100 to 500 hectares (AIDEnvironment, 2005:3). The clearing of natural vegetation for soy, on the one hand, requires the short, intensive use of manual labor. Labor conditions in this phase are extremely poor, and cases of slavery have been reported (AIDEnvironment, 2005:3; Dros, 2004:30). On the other hand, between 1995 and 2005 the number of rural workers in Argentina halved, from 1 million to 500,000 (Valente, 2006). As I discussed in Chapter 1 and above, the transformation of the class structure under globalization involves an accelerated

TABLE 2.6
Soy Production in Argentina and Brazil
(bushels, million metric tons)

Year	Argentina	Brazil
1980	129	559
1985	268	581
1990	423	579
1996	411	1,003
1997	716	1,194
1998	735	1,150
1999	779	1,257
2000	1,021	1,433
2001	1,102	1,598
2002	1,304	1,910
2003	1,212	1,933
2004	1,433	1,947

Source: USDA, *World Statistics*, as reported by United
Soybean Board, available at www.unitedsoybean.org/
soystas2000/page_35.htm.

proletarianization, in which those dispossessed and alienated may move into the ranks of the super exploited in the new transnational accumulation circuits, such as the case of flower and fruit workers in Ecuador, Colombia and Chile, or into the ranks of the marginalized or superfluous population, as is the case of farmers and rural workers in Argentina.

The shift into soy farming has contributed to the disappearance of small and medium-sized businesses, a mass displacement of farmers, and a drop in the production of needed foodstuffs in a country once known for its food production, and an increase in urban and rural unemployment, which rose from 7.1 percent in 1989 to 15.4 percent in 2000 (Pengue, 2001:3). In just four years between the 1997/8 and 2001/2 agricultural seasons the following changes took place: sunflower production dropped by 31 percent; corn by 24 percent; sorghum by 24 percent; and wheat by 64 percent (calculated on the basis of SAGYPA data in Bisang, 2003, table 1). In the Pampas, soy has displaced dairy, fruit trees, horticulture, cattle, and other grains. In the face of declining per capita consumption of proteins and rising malnutrition, companies and the government have promoted a "let them eat soy" campaign to change diets to include more soybeans. In 2004 some 20 percent of Argentine children showed signs of malnourishment (Pengue, 2005:321). By 2004 soy occupied more land in Argentina than all other crops put together; in just seven years from 1997 to 2004 soy crops rose from 24 percent to over 50 percent of the country's total acreage under cultivation (Dros, 2004:14, 18). Remarkably, in 2004 the Food and Agricultural Organization listed Argentina, a country known historically as the granary of the world, as one of the thirty-five countries around the world facing a food crisis (FOEI, 2005:2). It remains more profitable for landowners to sell or rent their land for soy production than to grow crops for local consumption, and local supplies of milk, meat, and vegetables have been disappearing.

Soybean production began in the rich agricultural lands to the north, west, and south of Buenos Aires known as the Pampas, equivalent to the fertile plains of the U.S. Midwest. The crop spread from there almost overnight to more environmentally sensitive areas rich in biodiversity, such as the Tungas, Great Chaco, and the Mesopotamian Forest, in the provinces of the Northwest and the East, including Santiago del Estero, Salta, Chaco, Tucumán, Entre Ríos, and Misiones. As soy rapidly turns the countryside into a monoculture it has left a path of social and environmental devastation. The crop has resulted in widespread deforestation, nutrient depletion, soil degradation, the beginnings of desertification, and a loss of species as varied landscapes and diverse ecosystems become oceans of monoculture (Forest Working Group, 2005; AIDEnvironment, 2005; Pengue, 2005). The transgenic model under which it is produced is capital and input intensive, requires large extensions of land and economies of scale to be profitable and involves very little labor. Its introduction has led to the ruin of local farmers, a rapid concentration of land in agribusiness, un- and underemployment, an increase in inequality, poverty, malnutrition, and out-migration to the cities (Pengue, 2005, 2001, 2000; Bisang, 2003; AIDEnvironment, 2005; Forest Working Group, 2005).

As soy spread in the 1990s, the number of people living below the poverty line escalated and in 2000 the number of beggars and homeless people in the capital city jumped from 325,000 to 921,000. This escalation of poverty and marginality was not solely a consequence of rural transformation brought about by soy: the soy invasion was but one aspect of a vast neo-liberal restructuring and globalization of the country. Starting in 1991, President Carlos Menem (1989–1999) undertook sweeping neoliberal adjustment measures that paved the way for the soy boom, including lifting tariffs and quantitative restrictions on imported inputs, the deregulation and privatization of the country's marketing, storage, and transportation infrastructure, the convertibility of the peso with the dollar, and the exemption from taxes of capital goods for agricultural production.

The new agricultural model is based on the adoption of transgenic crops cultivated through the no-tillage system and is worth exploring in some detail, as it illustrates new patterns in the transformation along global capitalist lines of agriculture in Latin America and elsewhere. Argentine authorities released GM modified seed in soybean to the market for the first time in the agricultural cycle between 1996 and 1997 as it launched a "campaign" to convert the country into a world-class producer of the bean (Bisang, 2003:3–4; Pengue, 2000). The genetically engineered (GE) soy acreage increased from 20 percent of the national total in that season to 95 percent of total acreage in the 2003–2004 cycle (Pengue, 2005:317). The new GM seed contained a gene resistant to glyphosate, a herbicide effective on a wide range of flora. The new seed, produced by Monsanto, one of the largest agro-industrial TNCs in the world and a leader in biotechnology and genetic engineering, is known as Roundup Ready, or RR soybean, referring to a bean that is impervious to the herbicide glyphosate, known by its brand name, Roundup. Monsanto made it freely available in a strategy that many believe was intentionally aimed at having the country first become dependent on the seed before enforcing intellectual property rights and demanding patent and copyright payments and filing court cases for patent infringement (see, e.g., Balch, 2006; Editorial, Ram's Horn, 2005). The widespread and often indiscriminate use of glyphosate is blamed for the destruction of soil microbial life, leading to sterile soils where crop residues are no longer decomposed. Weeds that have developed glyphosate resistance require cocktails of highly toxic herbicides that have intoxicated rural workers and communities throughout through the soy producing provinces (Dros, 2004:17). Intensive aerial fumigation has contributed to serious health problems in soy producing communities. Monocultural practices make the food chain very susceptible to being wiped out from pathogens.

Zero tillage, meanwhile, refers to a major technological innovation know as direct seeding, supposedly a tool for reducing soil erosion on farms. Seeds are planted directly into the soil without the need for plowing. The planting requires new fumigation equipment and a special machinery known as zero tillage seed drills (for these details, see Bisang, 2003). Direct seeding is promoted as an environmentally friendly farming technique but, to begin with, it involves the mass spraying of herbicides prior to seeding in order to remove weeds, bacteria and funguses. Although it reduces the rate of erosion *initially* it generates other problems related to the intensification of agriculture it requires, including the emergence of new diseases and pests, a marked reduction of the levels of nitrogen and phosphates in the soil, and the rise of herbicide-resistant weeds. Moreover, the destruction of forests for increased soy acreage has led to water run-off, ironically accelerating the very soil erosion and desertification that direct tillage claims to reduce.

The introduction of RR soy did result in an improvement in yields at first but by the new century there were signs that the increase could not be sustained. First, by 2000 the first glyphosate-tolerant weeds appeared in the Pampas and raised the specter of soy rust, a fungus that can cut yields significantly. As Walter Pengue, an agricultural engineer at the University of Buenos Aires and one of the leading researchers on the soy industry in Argentina, has shown in his research, RR soybean requires more, not less, herbicide than conventional soybean. Evidence shows that RR soybean ends up producing 5 percent to 10 percent less yield per acre compared with other identical varieties grown under similar soil conditions (Pengue, 2001:3). But the slight loss of exportable yields is more than made up for by the fantastic profits generated by GM seed sales, patents, and copyrights; herbicides; innovative machinery (zero tillage seed drills, etc.); and other new inputs and technologies. Table 2.7 shows the rapid conversion from conventional agriculture to the new agricultural model.

TABLE 2.7
Soybean: Zero Tillage, Biocides, and Transgenetic Seeds, Argentina, 1980–2002

Year	Total Sown (million hectares)	Zero Tillage (million hectares)	Glyphosate Consumption (million Htl)	Transgenetic Seeds (million hectares)	Total Production (million tons)
1980/1	1.9	0	0	0	3.9
1985/6	3.3	0	0	0	7.1
1990/1	5.0	0.3	0	0	10.9
1995/6	6.0	2.2	0.8	0	12.4
1996/7	6.7	2.9	1.3	0.04	11.0
1997/8	7.2	3.6	2.9	1.8	18.7
1998/9	8.4	3.8	4.5	4.8	20.0
1999/0	8.8	5.0	6.1	6.6	20.2
2000/1	10.7	6.7	82.3	9.3	26.9
2001/2	11.3	8.7	81.5	10.3	31.0

Source: Bisang, 2003, table 2, p. 3.

The meteoric rise of soy production is intimately tied to the introduction and expansion of the transgenic technological model in Argentina and the Southern cone. While the introduction of transgenic technology allowed—at first—for an increase in yields, this expansion has taken place principally through the conversion of lands previously cultivated in other crops to soy and through clearing of new lands for soy planting. Because it requires vast tracks of land but very little labor, there is rapid concentration of lands in the hands of local and foreign agribusiness (some 16 million hectares of Argentine land have been sold to foreign companies that then often subcontract them out to local farmers or investors) [Pengue, 2005:318; Bisang, 2003]. Small producers become indebted for investments in machinery, chemicals, fertilizers, and other inputs required by NTAEs. The technological packet needed for transgenic soy production requires initial capital outlays that smaller producers can only acquire by going into debt. Pengue has shown in his study of the Pampas that 14 million hectares there were in debt to banks and big companies, and between 1992 and 1999 the number of farms in the Pampas decline from 170,000 to 116, 000 (a 30 percent reduction), while the average farm size increased from 243 to 538 hectares (Pengue, 2005:318). His study of the five main soy-producing regions found that the total number of farms dropped by 25 percent from 421,221 in 1988 to 317,816 in 2002.

The adoption of GM seeds meant that Argentine soy would be inextricably tied to the global agro-industrial complex dominated by a handful of powerful TNCs and their monopoly over transgenic seeds. The global trade and processing of soybeans is concentrated in a small number of TNCs, among them Archer Daniels Midland (ADM), Cargill, Bunge, and Louis Dreyfuss. Four TNCs (Monsanto, Atanor, Nidera, and Dow) control more than 80 percent of the glyphosate market in Argentina (Pengue, 2005:317). One of the characteristics of the "second green revolution" spearheaded by new biotechnologies is the privatization of agricultural knowledge inputs, codified through inputs or direct assistance and enforced by the TNS intellectual property rights regime, in distinction to the first green revolution, which involved the public diffusion of knowledge as a public good. In a globalization era where knowledge is a key factor of production its privatization becomes imperative if the logic of capital is to prevail. What this constitutes are new mechanisms for transnational corporate control over the productive use of agricultural resources and for the appropriation in new ways by transnational capital circuits of agriculture values. This new technology package shifts economic control to transnational capital. The conversion to high technology-intensive soy forces a paradigm shift in which knowledge monopolized by transnational capital becomes a new mechanism for the appropriation of agricultural values, a social relation codified in intellectual property rights (patent and copyrights) and reinforced by the TNS.

Traditional seed firms have merged with, or been taken over by TNCs dedicated to herbicide production and fine chemistry, which in turn have become more closely integrated with pharmaceutical companies that have pioneered genetic engineering techniques (Bisang, 2003:6). Hence Argentine agriculture as a case study of this new model has been restructured based on the dominant presence of TNCs that control the production of the most dynamic crops and a transfer to the local context of technology that locks the country into new global production chains bringing together agribusiness, chemical, pharmaceutical, and biotechnology sectors. Moreover, primary producers (farmers and subcontractors) become reequipped with new, patented technologies. In this process, the relations of production are transformed. The new agricultural model shifts agricultural values so that they flow through new production technology and commercial circuits, which dictate how such values will be generated (what to grow and how) in the first instance, and in the second, allow these values to be transferred and appropriated in new ways. The model is organized along flexible accumulation, through chains of subcontracting and outsourcing. Businesses dedicated to sowing, for instance, are now typically subcontracted to plant soy through zero tillage techniques. The supplier network comes to control the process. All this adds up to a transnational service center that generates a host of externalities (that is, inputs, services, and processes, external to the actual production of soy itself) that is able to capture agricultural values.

The soy agro-industrial cluster in Argentina and the Southern Cone brings together a powerful coalition of corporations, banks, private sector associations, governments, TNS institutions, large agribusiness farmers, and scientific and academic organizations. These diverse agents make up the transnational bloc behind "King soy." It is crucial to note, however—as I will continue to underscore—that when I refer to transnational capital this includes local contingents in Argentina and elsewhere of transnational capitalist groups who are integrating in new ways into the global capitalist bloc. Nation-state centric analysis is ill equipped to conceptualize these emerging transnational class relations and social structures. This is not a classical situation of core-periphery relations of dependency, because Argentine capital has as well fused with the transnational corporate complex that controls the soy global production chain. Bayer, Cargill, Monsanto, Nidera, Cyanamid, Pfizer, Dow Chemical, Novartis, and other well-known agro-industrial, chemical, and pharmaceutical TNCs all have a major stake in the Southern Cone soy industry, but so do powerful Argentine-based companies that operate beyond Argentine borders, among them PASA, Profertil, AgrEvo, Don Mario, La Tihereta, Relmo, and others.

Several Argentina companies taking advantage of technology transfer, cloning, and association with TNCs, have become major stakeholders in the national GM seed market and have expanded abroad, among them, Don Mario, La Tijereta, and Relmo (Pengue, 2001:2; Bisang, 2003:12, table 4). During the 1990s a dozen large Argentine firms participated in the supply of herbicides, biocides, machinery, and other inputs to the agricultural sector, especially fertilizers, which are applied to some 85 percent of sown surfaces (Bisang, 2003:7). These firms in turn entered into joint ventures and other cooperative agreements with foreign-based TNCs. The stocks of the largest producer of gas-based urea, for instance, Profertil, were held by the following: Repsol-TPF (33 percent), itself a TNC with Argentine and foreign owners; PASA (33 percent), an Argentine company that is part of the Argentine conglomerate, Perez Companc Group; and the rest owned by the foreign-based Agrium. PASA, AgreEvo, and other Argentine-based groups, many of whom operate outside of Argentine borders as well, have also entered into ventures with Cargill, Monsanto, ASP, and other foreign-based TNCs (Bisang, 2003:7). The bloc organized around the new globalized agricultural model also includes local agribusiness farmers and land leasers, machinery and equipment suppliers, supply and service subcontractors;

the crushing and oil industries, trading houses and transport companies that supply equipment/machinery and freight.

If the juggernaut of "King soy" is not brought under control, the Southern Cone could become a bleak dustbowl in the coming years.[4] Others Southern Cone countries such as Brazil, Paraguay, Bolivia, and Uruguay have faced a similar expansion of transgenic soy production and its consequences. The Argentine government announced in 2005 the goal of nearly tripling soy production in the coming years, from the 35 million tons registered in that year to 100 million tons (Pengue, 2005:316). If the Southern Cone countries expand the acreage of soy according to plan, global overproduction could read 150 million tons by 2020 (AIDEnvironment, 2005:1). The crop has already led to the total destruction of the Atlantic Forest in South Brazil and the disappearance of rainforests of Eastern Paraguay and of the Parana River basin that straddles Paraguay, the southern tip of Brazil, and the Missiones corridor in Argentina. River transportation has been tapped to extract the crop in new hinterlands. The "Hidrovia Paraguay-Parana"—the Parana River waterway—has been converted into one such aquatic transportation route that threatens the destruction of extensive floodplain wetlands and the numerous micro-ecosystems of the region (Pengue, 2005) and is expected to facilitate agro-export expansion further downstream. In Brazil, soy has already carved out vast fields of the Brazilian Amazon ecosystem.

In Brazil, soy quickly expanded in the 1980s and 1990s out of the three southern states of Rio Grande do Sul, Parana, and Santa Catarina and into the Center-West and North Amazonian regions (especially Mato Grosso, Rondonia and Tocantins). In the Brazilian Amazon the annual deforestation rate of primary and secondary forest for soy production is estimated to be about 700,000 hectares (AIDEnvironment, 2005:2). The Forest Working Group of Friends of the Earth found in a regression analysis of soy cropping and deforestation in Brazil that "deforestation rates are positively correlated (50%) to the increase in soy cropping and this correlation is extremely significant from the statistical

---

[4] Plans launched by the United States and Brazilian governments in early 2007 to vastly increase the world supply of biofuels would exacerbate many times over the destructive processes observed here. As Pinto, Melo, and Mendonca (2007) note, such an increase in ethanol and biodiesel production would require a vast expansion of the area under soy, sugar cane, corn, and palm production, turning South America into a giant plantation for the global biofuels market. Should these plans move ahead they could well obliterate small and medium producers and consolidate a new empire of corporate agribusiness, biotechnology, chemical and pharmaceutical TNCs in South America. The ecological devastation would undermine any gains in terms of a reduction in carbon-based fuels, and we would face a situation—absolutely absurd from any social logic yet consistent with the logic of capital—in which cars would replace human beings as the main consumers of world cereal output.

point of view (>99% probability)" [2005:8, see table 4]. Throughout the Southern Cone land clearing is often carried out by total removal of the original vegetation by a 100 meter drag-chain that is pulled by two bulldozers, or else through slash-and-burn techniques practiced in both forest areas and savannahs (AIDEnvironment, 2005:2), destroying biodiversity and setting the stage for heightened erosion and sedimentation on downstream wetlands and reservoirs along river systems.

Soybean cultivation in Bolivia took off in the late 1980s following a World Bank project to promote the crop's expansion. Soy rapidly became Bolivia's single most important agricultural export, accounting in 2004 for 27 percent of the country's total export revenues (Dros, 2004:18, 19). The Bolivian soy boom has made Santa Cruz the economic capital of Bolivia. The crop is controlled by new economic groups from the Eastern province of Santa Cruz and by immigrant Brazilian entrepreneurs in alliance with agribusiness TNCs, at the expense of the lowland indigenous communities that predominate in the region. This transnationally oriented Santa Cruz elite provides the major social base for the neo-liberal program and has consistently organized politically against the radical indigenous/popular movement and the leftist indigenous president, Evo Morales (see Chapter 6).

In Paraguay the amount of land planted in soy increased more than fivefold between 1997 and 2005 as the bean expanded from the east into the Chacos and the wetlands of the Western half of the country (Monahan, 2005). As in Bolivia, Brazilian immigrants play a major role in its production, underscoring the expanding transnational class relations in the region. By 2005 soy had come to represent an astonishing 10 percent of Paraguay's GNP and more than 50 percent of the country's exports (Monahan, 2005). Violent land struggles in soy-producing zones in Paraguay have broken out in recent years (Dros, 2004:35). In June 2005, for instance, police forcibly evicted 270 people from the Tekojoja community in the department of Caaguazu after local residents were unable to produce legal proof of ownership over land they had been farming for generations (FOEI, 2005:4).

Winter Fruits and Vegetables in Central America

While traditional agro-exports continue to predominate in Central America's agricultural production for export, they have diminished considerably in overall importance relative to NTAE, such as fruits, flowers, ornamental plants, winter vegetables, and spices (see, inter alia, Robinson, 2003; Brockett, 1998; Clark,

1995; Paus, 1988). If the rise of a global food regime is one part of the story of NTAEs in Central America the other is the role of the transnational elite in promoting them as part of the broader strategy of structural adjustment and re-articulation to the world economy. The Caribbean Basin Initiative (CBI), launched by the U.S. government in the 1980s as a strategy for countering revolution in the Isthmus, aimed to rearticulate the Caribbean Basin region to the global system through the establishment of new export industries, including duty free entry of certain exports to the U.S. market, tax breaks, guarantees, and other benefits for transnational capital investing in these industries. The AID set up a special office, the Support Project for Non-Traditional Agricultural Exports (PROEXAG) to promote NTAEs in the region (Friedmann, 1991:49; AID, 1991). AID monies throughout the 1980s and 1990s, although provided as official government-to-government aid, were allocated specifically to fund NTAE production and consistently channeled through a "parallel state"—a network of private business associations established throughout the region (Conroy et al., 1996, esp. chapter 3; Robinson, 2003, esp. chapter 2).

Costa Rica and Guatemala were among the first countries in the Caribbean Basin, along with the Dominican Republic, to adopt NTAE strategies. By the middle of the 1980s NTAEs had taken off, especially in these two countries, as Table 2.8 shows.

In 1991, an estimated 60 percent of NTAE producers in Central America were small farmers—a very different picture than the flower, fruit, and soy industries in South America. Medium farmers and larger individual farmers, national commercial/corporate operations, and foreign companies, made up the remainder (Conroy et al., 1996:96). However, the relative contribution of these groups in total value exported was highly skewed: for example, foreign companies accounted for 25 percent; medium- and large-sized national companies for

TABLE 2.8
Central American NTAEs to the World (in US$ million)

	1980	1985	1989	1994
Costa Rica	43	48	138	400
El Salvador	13	16	11	90
Guatemala	73	75	106	350
Honduras	42	60	53	70
Nicaragua	7	12	6	50
Central America	178	211	314	960

Source: For 1980–1989 data, Conroy et al., 1996, table 1.6, p. 21; for 1994 data, Brockett, 1998, figure 3.5, p. 56.
NTAE: nontraditional agricultural export.

about 40 percent; and small-sized farms for only 35 percent. Even when production is in peasant hands, local transnational groups gain control through financing and related servicing of NTAE activity, such as supply of inputs, which as well are largely controlled by TNCs and of local agents who are often distributors or local contractors for the TNCs.

The modern capitalist structure emerging in the Central American countryside through the spread of NTAEs is in contrast to the old oligarchic rural structure. NTAE activity has drawn in not a landed oligarchy but dynamic new entrepreneurial sectors, often urban-based, linked to the global economy through finances and webs of relationships with transnational corporations. The economic groups that dominate NTAEs in Central America include financial concerns, landlords, and transnational suppliers of land, credits, and inputs, purchasing, shipping and marketing agents. The bulk of value-added and the lion's share of profits in the NTAE industry lie in the pre- and post-farmgate phases. In the pre-farmgate phase financial concerns, landlords, and transnational suppliers, provide land, credits, and inputs for production, while in the post-farmgate phase brokers are heavily involved as cross-border agents arranging purchase, shipping, and marketing. The transnational strategy of promoting NTAEs is mutually reinforcing with the political objective of shoring up transnational groups in the region as internal agents of the neoliberal program and capitalist globalization.

Central America offers a prime example of how transnational capital exercises overall control of the entire production chain, and how the chain exercises a transformative effect on Central America in the context of the more general processes associated with globalization, including effects on the class structure. Let us look first at the structure of production within the chain, and particularly, at the point of production (inside-farmgate) and the distinct agents involved, and then at the larger transnational structures into which it is inserted. Central America is relatively less urbanized and industrialized than South America or Mexico and the peasantry constituted a major portion of the population—over 50 percent (Robinson, 2003)—as the region became swept up in globalization processes in the 1980s and on. As a result the satellite system (contract farming to small producers) prevailed at first for NTAE production, which allowed transnational firms to take maximum advantage of peasant production conditions, in particular, the exploitation of unpaid family labor (Fuentes, 1991).

Many NTAEs are short cycle labor-intensive crops that require ongoing care throughout the period of cultivation (especially vegetables), lending themselves to production regimes based on extended family labor. In this way the cost of labor is born by the small producer. Local producers are left with risks of hurricanes, floods, disease, political crisis, and market fluctuations, and when family labor is not the norm they must themselves organize labor supply, including controlling labor conflicts. United Brands/Chiquita has made extensive use of the satellite contract system in Honduras's melon producing region of Choluteca, among others, while the satellite-contractor form is also most prevalent in the Guatemalan highlands, where indigenous farmers plant broccoli, snow peas, and other winter vegetables. In El Salvador, larger growers of melon who are also packers have developed the satellite system with small growers in the Ahuachapan region (Friedmann, 1991; Conroy et al., 1996).

Estate-plantation farming is also prevalent in Central America. This is the system generally employed, for instance, by Standard Fruit (Dole) for pineapple production in Honduras, by national and transnational producers of melons in Guatemala, and by pineapple producers in Costa Rica. In the mid-1990s, some exporters began to shift more directly to controlled estate farming, as many small producers were proletarianized after being driven out of the NTAE sector and became employees of large-scale operations (Conroy et al., 1996:102). As Conroy and his colleagues have documented for El Salvador, melon is grown through a two-tiered system. Small growers sell their output to large growers who are also packers/exporters and who are usually tied to transnational fruit companies and suppliers. Large growers are able to pay themselves higher prices for their own output and lower prices for melons they purchase from small producers. They are able to prioritize the purchase and export of their own output and regulate the amount of fruit they buy from small producers, assuring a buffer against fluctuating demand and prices, as set by brokers and retailers in U.S. markets. Friedmann, in his study on melon production in Western El Salvador, found for 1990–1991 that small producers earned $3.98 per box of fruit, whereas large firms reported $9.46 per box. "The explanation for this difference is in the structure of production/marketing that prevails in the country, in which the large producers are also the exporters," he notes. "Their price reflects production and export yields" (1991:59).

Small producers, after having entered into debt to invest in their melon crops often find that they are unable to sell their output to the packers/exporters and have to sell on the local market or even discard their perishable produce due to the lack of buyers. "In essence, the small farmer who grows melons for export to the United States is a farm worker paid to work on his own fields, who additionally must personally assume 100 percent of the risks of crop failure, lessened quality, or market vagaries," note Conroy and his colleagues. "The clear winners from the globalization of the melon commodity chain are international shippers and brokers, or the giant fruit companies in the case of integrated enterprises" (1996:106). National agribusiness firms are the principal exporters of melons from El Salvador, among them, Frutas S.A. de C.V., Exfrusa, Melopac, Fruvex, Exsalva, El Salvador Fresh, and CAPECA. Here we see the transnational fraction of the Salvadoran bourgeoisie concentrated in this activity. "In studying the promotion of NTAEs in El Salvador, one observes that a principal objective has been the selection, preparation, and consolidation of a relatively small but very dynamic group of Salvadoran entrepreneurs well connected abroad," notes Friedmann. These groups "are the principal national protagonists of the NTAE industry and form the link between internal promotion and production and external demand" (Friedmann, 1991:59). In their study on the distribution of value-added in the melon commodity chain, Conroy et al. found for 1991 in El Salvador, the following: U.S. shipping and retailing captured 76.6 percent of revenues; international shippers, 9.1 percent; imported inputs, 5.1 percent; U.S. brokers, 2.6 percent; packer and exporter profit, 2.5 percent; miscellaneous in-country services, 3.5 percent; and finally, farmers profits accounted for only 0.6 percent of revenues from the commodity chain. In that year, a pound of Salvadoran melon retailed in the United States for 65 cents but about half a penny actually went to the farmer as income (Conroy et al., 1996:105–107).

NTAE production requires a large amount of inputs in the form of fertilizers and pesticides, equipment and seeds, which in turn means that producers must obtain large amounts of credit. As Fuentes notes for Guatemalan highland production with the introduction of NTAEs, "the use of agricultural credit for production became a common practice in a region in which it was formerly non-existent" (1991:35). A successful NTAE harvest can register high profit margins. But they are also a capital-intensive crop, involving high costs of production and high risk. A producer of snow peas, for example, risks about $4 thousand a hectare in costs versus only $250 to $375 for corn or $750 per hectare for mechanized coffee production (Barry, 1999:108). And the market for NTAEs is extremely volatile. NTAE product prices fluctuate dramatically from season to season in accordance with unstable demand and shifting supply. Peasants who shift from food and other traditional crops to NTAEs are quickly driven into debt. One bad crop or a precipitous drop in prices due to erratic world market conditions can wipe out small producers. Peasants, squeezed between suppliers of inputs and buyers of their produce, are often unable to sustain production, even after a season or two of success, and having become caught up in a web of market relations, face the threat of bankruptcy and the loss of their land. The stage is set for de-peasantization.

The NTAE industry in Central America has benefited a class of medium-level producers, many of whom have bought out their poorer neighbors thereby changing the class structure. This process is notable, for instance, in the Central Highlands of Guatemala and has contributed to a more general process of class formation among the indigenous population (AVANSCO, 1994). Fruit and vegetable brokers in U.S. and European ports also play a prominent role in the NTAE industry, generally as well-remunerated agents of the transnational fruit and retail companies. Shippers, often themselves subsidiaries of TNCs or contractors for them, are big winners, as are suppliers of inputs and in-country buyers, who may be local packers and exporters (themselves often large producers), local holding or financial companies, or, as is often the case, local agents of TNCs. Local packers/exporters have set up companies throughout Central America and in the practice tend to become junior partners of the transnational fruit companies. They purchase produce from local producers and sell to the TNCs, acting as intermediaries that link local groups to transnational capital (Fuentes, 1991).

As the NTAE industry progresses, TNCs have come to exercise ever-greater control, working their way backward from marketing to production. Three giant fruit companies dominate the industry in Central America. Chiquita, formerly United Brands (and before then, United Fruit Company), runs numerous subsidiaries in the region, from its Chiquita Tropical Products Company in Costa Rica, to PATSA in Honduras, and BASICO and BANACORP in Guatemala. Castle and Cook (which absorbed Standard Fruit in 1968) runs its own set of subsidiaries, as does Del Monte, which merged with and became an affiliate of R.J. Reynolds in 1979. Del Monte has established, among others, its COAGRO subsidiary in Guatemala and its PINDECO in Costa Rica. Other TNCs with a significant share of the Central American NTAE industry include Chestnut Hill Farms, Hanover Brands, Coca Cola, PolyPack, and Seaboard Corporation (AVANSCO, 1994:56–57; Brockett, 1998:57).

In Costa Rica, Del Monte exported 95 percent of that country's pineapple production in the early 1990s, while Dole accounted for 96 percent of pineapple exports from Honduras. In the least concentrated commodity in Costa Rica, cassava, the three largest firms out of 33 controlled one-third of exports. In papaya, Del Monte exported 94 percent of Costa Rican production, as well as a substantial quantity of mangoes and strawberries. TNCs control approximately 80 percent of Costa Rican fern exports, 50 percent of cut flower production, and

40 percent of macadamia nut exports. In Costa Rica's Guanacaste province, heavily targeted in the 1980s and early 1990s for NTAE production and held up as a showcase of NTAE success, local and transnational investors quickly acquired control over the industry. Corporations such as Laechner and Saenz—a holding company that owns Costa Rican dealerships of Xerox, IBM, Apple, Chevrolet, and Isuzu—and the fruit transnational, United Brands/Chiquita, began developing extensive plantations of melons, mangoes, miniature papayas, guanabana, irrigated cacao, and other nontraditional products (Conroy et al., 1996:38).

NTAEs tend not to displace traditional agroexports but to displace basic grain production for the domestic market, under the rationale that grains don't earn foreign exchange and that the region has a "comparative advantage" in NTAEs. Brockett has shown how NTAE expansion in the 1980s and 1990s resulted in a decrease in the ratio of food to export crop production. But this situation has been aggravated by the trade opening under neo-liberal adjustment that has resulted in a flood of basic grain imports, which almost doubled from 1980 to 1990 in Central America parallel to the introduction of NTAEs (Conroy et al., 1996:15). Revealingly, basic grain production dropped most in the 1980s precisely in those regions where NTAEs were introduced (Brockett, 1998:30). In Costa Rica, which has the most developed NTAE sector, food imports from the United States increased from 1,000 tons in the 1974/5 growing season to 235,000 tons in 1987/8 under U.S. Public Law 480 Program, which provides recipient countries with food aid earmarked specifically for the importation of U.S. agricultural commodity exports. By flooding local markets with cheap grains this program undercut peasant production and accelerated the commodification of agriculture in recipient countries (Garst and Barry, 1990). The rise in food imports combined with the need to import much of the inputs, such as fertilizers, pesticides, and seeds, makes it very questionable to what extent NTAEs actually increase available foreign exchange earnings rather than result in a deepening cycle of debt.

Scattered evidence from Central America suggests a similar gendering of agricultural labor that we have seen elsewhere. One study by the AID of NTAEs in Guatemala, Honduras, and Costa Rica revealed that women make up more than half of the labor force in those countries in harvesting, processing, and packaging (Raynolds, 1998:150). Guatemalan researcher Claudia Fuentes (1991) found, in another study detailing NTAE production in the Guatemalan highlands, where the population is principally indigenous, that women have predominated as hired laborers, although they are consistently paid less than their male counterparts (a number of other studies have found this as well; see, e.g., Fuentes, 1991; AVANSCO, 1994). She also found that, as family labor has become reorganized to produce NTAEs among small landholders, women and daughters have assumed a major portion of the labor involved, even as they continue to be responsible for traditional household chores within the gendered division of labor in the family. However, men predominate in selling output to local intermediaries (known as "coyotes"). In this way preexisting patriarchal structures, in which men take charge of the family's external relations, tend to reinforce male economic control over income earned through NTAEs (Fuentes, 1991).

CHAPTER THREE

Global Economy and Latin America, II

Industrial Subcontracting, Transnational Services, Tourism, and the Export of Labor

The turn toward globalization involves new types of export-oriented industrialization. Industrial development in the previous era was geared largely toward supplying national and regional markets. It was a strategy of import-substitution industrialization (ISI) that brought together national and multinational corporate investors and local states that invested directly in a country to produce consumer goods for the domestic market of that nation: for example a U.S. auto manufacturer made cars in Chile to sell to Chileans, often with direct state participation. From the point of view of multinational corporations and local industrialists, this activity was not primarily seeking cheap labor or resource-based export possibilities but was seeking out markets for modern consumer and capital goods by establishing production facilities in those markets. This meant that the ISI working class labored under Fordist arrangements: that is, a relatively privileged sector, almost exclusively male, unionization, regulated employment relations and progressive labor codes.

This form of transnational corporate activity continues under globalization—although generally the state has privatized its holdings and withdrawn from participation—but three new forms of transnational industrial activity overshadow it. One is the international reorientation of national industries established under ISI, or, new forms of local industrial production in which output is geared toward export to global markets. The second is subcontracted supply for global production chains. The third is the installation of the maquiladora industry, in which local investment takes place in order to produce industrial goods (whether intermediate or finished) for re-export to the global market. The new industrial activity takes place under flexible accumulation patterns and in particular with flexible labor. The role of these flexible industrial workers as laborers or creators of surplus value no longer has any relevance to their capacity to consume in domestic markets, whereas previously they were expected to participate in the consumption of consumer goods produced by ISI. The political corollary to this shift in labor from local to global markets and from the logic of Fordism to that of flexible accumulation is the expulsion of labor from national power blocs.

Table 3.1 gives a rough idea of the increasing export-orientation of Latin American industry.

At the same time, offshore assembling and subcontracting involve new forms of participation by Latin American capitalist groups and by small and middle-sized firms—often known by their Spanish acronym, PYMEs. These forms of participation have opened up space for local investors and small-scale entrepreneurs to integrate into transnational production chains. The industrial activity of transnational corporations (TNCs) generates demand for a host of suppliers as industrial production is increasingly fragmented and organized through networks of outsourcing and subcontracting. Hence TNC investment may give rise to industrial and service clusters that bring in these PYMEs,

TABLE 3.1

Manufacturing Exports f.o.b. as a Percentage of Manufacturing, Select Countries (aggregate value, at constant 2000 prices)

	1995	2000	2005
Argentina	15.8	18.2	22.6
Bolivia	19.8	36.7	15.8
Brazil	21.3	26.6	45.5
Chile	17.4	26.6	33.3
Colombia	28.9	36.6	49.8
Costa Rica*	26.7	97.8	98.0
Ecuador	24.3	61.6	92.0
El Salvador	15.9	21.4	28.1
Guatemala	23.8	34.1	49.0
Honduras	33.7	28.6	53.1
Mexico*	81.6	129.6	155.0
Nicaragua	22.6	8.0	11.5
Paraguay	15.8	15.0	26.6
Peru	10.4	15.1	27.0
Uruguay	24.3	28.1	28.7
Venezuela	12.1	13.0	20.4

Source: Calculated on the basis of ECLAC, *Statistical Yearbook for Latin America and the Caribbean*, 2006, tables 2.2.2.4 and 2.1.1.15.
   *The figures for Mexico total more than 100 percent because a portion of manufacturing exports in the in-bond industry is calculated by statistical agencies as manufacturing exports but not as part of the national manufacturing sector. The Costa Rican case appears skewed because the very high percentage of manufacturing value-added as exports results from the installation of a major INTEL computer chip plant in the country in 1997 and the export of high-value computer chips.

although these enterprises may be large as well. Some of these PYMEs may be newly created to supply TNC-organized production chains, and others may be previously existing and orient their output from national markets to transnational subcontracting or export markets (see, e.g., Schmitz, 1995; Schmitz and Knorringa, 2000; Altenburg and Meyer-Stamer, 1999; and for a Central America case study, Pérez Saínz and Andrade-Eekhoff, 2003). These two variants of globalized industrial activity are not mutually exclusive, as PYMEs also subcontract to maquiladora plants (Pérez Saínz and Andrade-Eekhoff refer to these local firms as submaquilas). In this section I will examine maquiladoras in Mexico and Central America as one case example of industrial activity in the new globalized economic model.

Maquiladoras and Industrial Subcontracting

The maquiladora phenomenon is often seen as the quintessence of the global economy and has become one of the most widely studied aspects of globalization. export processing zones (EPZs) are a type of free trade zone (FTZ). An FTZ is a site that is free from cross-border duties and taxes and generally from national regulations. EPZs, sometimes called *zonas francas,* are established as enclaves outside the customs territory of a particular country the chief attraction of which for transnational capital is the supply of abundant, cheap labor from the host country. Products are stored, processed, and manufactured free from the payment of import duties on equipment, machinery, and raw materials and with the intention of exporting most or all of the output to the world market. Firms in these EPZs, known as maquiladoras, or assembly plants, are provided with a generous package of incentives, generally including tax holidays, freedom from foreign exchange regulations, and most notoriously, even guarantees against unionization of the labor force (see, inter alia, Fröbel et al., 1980; Dicken, 1998). EPZs have spread rapidly as production has become transnationalized, from just a handful in the 1970s to several hundred in the early twenty-first century employing over 5 million workers in some fifty countries (excluding China, which has some 40 million to 50 million workers in its special economic zones, which do not share all the typical features of FTZs and EPZ). About 90 percent of the EPZs were located in Latin America and Asia, with the strongest concentration in the Greater Caribbean Basin (Dicken, 2003:180–81).

In their landmark 1977 study, *The New International Division of Labor,* Fröbel and his colleagues argued that the spread of maquiladoras was leading to a new international division of labor as core capital relocated low-wage phases of manufacturing to cheap labor zones in the Third World. In fact, in the same year as *The New International Division of Labor* was published in English (i.e., 1980), the export of manufactured goods from the Third World for the first time surpassed that of raw materials (McMichael, 1996:57). The study first drew attention to the now-notorious sweatshop conditions of super-exploitation, labor repression, the degradation of women, child labor, Taylorist control and dehumanization at the maquiladora factories, as the counterpart to "runaway factories" and rising structural unemployment in the traditional core. Although NIDL theory has been superseded by more recent theorizing on the global economy, and the 1977 study is now outdated, it remains a classic statement on the maquiladora phenomenon:

> Free production zones are industrial areas which are separated off from the rest of the country, located at places where labour is cheap and designated as sites for world market oriented industry. . . . Production in world market factories is highly vertically integrated into the transnational operations of the individual companies and involves non-complex production operations; the manufacturing of parts, assembling of parts, or final assembly . . . textiles and garments are one example. The employment structure in free production zones and world market factories is extremely unbalanced. Given a virtually unlimited supply of unemployed labour, world market factories at the free production zones, or other sites, select one specific type of worker, chiefly women from the younger age groups. The criteria used for the selection of workers are quite unambiguous: the labour which is employed is that which demands the least remuneration, provides the maximum amount of energy (i.e. fresh labour which can be expected to work at a high intensity) and which is predominantly unskilled or semiskilled. (22–23)

This description is still valid for much maquiladora production in the Greater Caribbean Basin, especially garment production. Although EPZ manufacturing around the world ranges from toys to sporting goods, optical instruments, and footwear, the vast majority of world maquiladora production is in textiles-garments and electronics, while a single industry tends to dominate EPZ activity in most countries where it becomes established. In Central America, maquiladora production is almost exclusively of garments, outside of Costa Rica, where electronics, consumer goods, telecommunications and pharmaceutical-medical equipment also represent a significant share (Jenkins et al., 1998:32–36; Dypski, 2002:121). Mexico presents a more complex case, although there too garments still predominated in the early twenty-first century.

Following the general tendency in the restructuring of capitalist production, the garment industry has undergone an increasing decentralization, segmentation, and sub-division of tasks in the production process. This includes the automation of some of these tasks and the transfer to low-wage zones around the globe of those tasks that are difficult to mechanize and that remain labor-intensive (sewing operations in particular are very-labor intensive). The garment industry has three major phases: fibers production, in which the general tendency is toward the production of technologically advanced synthetics; textile production, which remains highly labor-intensive; and a final retail phase. This complex global commodity chain (GCC), to evoke the concept developed by Gereffi and Korzeniewicz, is buyer driven—that is, dominated by huge transnational retail outlets, such as Sears Roebuck, J.C. Penney, the Gap, and so on (Gereffi and Korzeniewicz, 1994; Taplin, 1994; Dicken, 1998, chapter 9; Figueroa, 1996). In contrast, producer driven GCCs are those in which TNCs play the central role in coordinating production chains, including forward and backward linkages, "and is most characteristic of capital and technology-intensive commodities, such as automobiles, aircraft, semi-conductors, and electrical machinery." In turn, buyer driven GCCs are those in which "large retailers, brand-name merchandisers, and trading companies play the central role in shaping decentralized production networks ... typical in relatively labor-intensive consumer goods such as garments, footwear, toys, and housewares" (Gereffi, Korzeniewicz, and Korzeniewicz, 1994:7).

Mexico—From ISI to the Maquiladoras

The worldwide maquiladora phenomenon first became popularized when the "in-bond assembly," or maquiladora, industry became established along the U.S. Mexico border in the 1970s. The prototype of the maquiladoras, however, was actually established in Puerto Rico by U.S. corporations in the 1950s and 1960s under special concessionary arrangements provided by U.S. colonial authorities (see, inter alia, Fatemi, 1990; Sklair, 1993). The U.S.–Mexico border is a transnational region that Dicken refers to as one of the major "transborder clusters and corridors" of the global economy (2003:75–76), where one finds an intense geographic concentration and conglomeration of global economic activities. In 1965 the Mexican government set up its Border Industrialization Program to try to offset the recessionary effects, especially in the Northern border region, after the United States terminated the *Bracero* guest worker program and repatriated some half a million Mexican workers. The number of maquiladoras in Mexico grew from 50 plants in 1965 to close to 3,000 in 2004. As Table 3.2

indicates, the Mexican maquiladora sector experienced two sharp rises, first in the late 1980s, as outsourcing intensified under globalization and as Mexico adjusted and deepened integration into the global economy, and then after the North American Free Trade Agreement (NAFTA) went into effect in 1994, all but eliminating restrictions on the free movement of capital across North American borders and state regulation of transnational capital in Mexico. Although Mexico became a relatively industrialized country through its post-WWII ISI strategy, the maquiladora sector surpassed domestic industry as the most dynamic industrial process.[1]

In the 1990s maquiladora exports overtook oil as the country's top foreign exchange earner and came to represent nearly 90 percent of manufactured exports. According to some estimates, the maquiladora sector's share of the GDP reached 20 percent in 2000 (Brandt, 2003:12). The maquiladora sector still accounted in 2004 for over half of exports (*Business Week*, 2004).

In distinction to the typical pattern of EPZs, many of the maquiladora establishments along the U.S.-Mexico border have a "twin plant" on the U.S. side supplying parts to be further processed and/or receiving goods made on the Mexican side. This arrangement, in which the Mexican side may offer lower wages, lax regulations, and other benefits, grew out of the particular way in which the border region became a major nodal point of the global economy on the historical basis of the North American political economy. The twin plant on the U.S. side may be owned or contracted by a TNC that is not headquartered in the United States, such as Sony, and the operations on the Mexican side are often owned or run by Mexican and third country nationals operating under outsourcing and subcontracting arrangements, so that the whole border economy

---

[1] Moreover, Delgado-Wise and Cypher (2005) argue that what is conventionally characterized as domestic Mexican industry has actually come to constitute a "disguised maquila sector" since this industry may have its roots in the earlier ISI model and involve larger, more capital-intensive and technologically sophisticated levels of production but it has increasingly been reoriented toward the logic of the maquiladora sector: it relies on cheap and increasingly flexibilized labor; it absorbs maquila-made parts as inputs; and it carries on production with the same tax subsidies, fiscal exemptions, and export-market objectives as the maquila firms. "A significant and rapidly growing volume of production is generated by the maquila firms and then sent to the large TNCs throughout the interior of Mexico which incorporate maquila-made parts and components into finished manufacturing products" that are then exported, they observe. "At the same time a variety of programs are offered by the Mexican state to non-maquila firms that are engaged in export activity. These effects are so pervasive that roughly 38 percent of Mexican exports (45 percent of all manufacturing exports) comes from the disguised maquila sector" (2005:17). Moreover, this movement of inputs is often intrafirm transactions. Delgado-Wise and Cypher point out that the "indirect maquilazation activities" employ at least half a million workers, or 37 percent of all non-maquila manufacturing workers "who are normally assumed to be working in the national manufacturing sector." In this way all of Mexican industry is swept one way or another into the global economy. It would be worthwhile to undertake such research for industry in other Latin American countries.

TABLE 3.2
Maquiladora Plants and Jobs in Mexico, 1965–2004

	1965	1970	1975	1980	1985	1990	1993	1995	1998	2004
Number of Plants	65	120	454	620	760	1,938	2,172	N/A	3,051	2,810
Employment*	n/a	20.3	67.2	119.5	212.0	460.3	541.0	968.2	1,369	1,115

Source: Galhardi, ILO, 1998, tables 1.1 and 2.1; for 1998, 2004, INEGI, *Estadísticas Economicas*, available at www.inegi.gob.mx.
    *In thousands.

is a zone of transnational capital. NAFTA, in fact, encouraged TNCs from around the world to attain a toehold in Mexico in order to enjoy privileged access to the North American market. Far from a case of the United States seeking to construct a Western Hemisphere bloc in competition with Europe and Asia, the integration of Mexico into the North American political economy has had the effect of accelerating not regionalization but transnationalization. While the majority of maquiladoras are owned or outsourced by TNCs based in the United States, transnational capital in the Mexican maquiladora industry originates from several dozen countries, among them Mexico itself, Japan, Korea, China, Taiwan, Germany, France, Brazil, Holland, Sweden, and Dubai.

In the 1970s and 1980s, Mexican maquiladoras were concentrated along the border with the United States, especially in the border cities of Tijuana, Ciudad Juárez, and Mexicali, connected with "twin plants" across the border. But by the 1990s they were spreading south into central and even southern Mexico—what Sklair (1993) refers to as the march to the interior—where wages are lower and labor militancy and turnover is less. Puebla, Morelos, Guanajuato, the greater Mexico City area, the Yucatán peninsula, and the west coast state of Jalisco, figured prominently as new production sites. Investors took advantage of a huge new pool of peasant labor made available by the opening of the Mexican market to U.S. agricultural surpluses and the breakup of communal ejido lands under NAFTA and other neoliberal measures, such as the end of price supports and state credit for small producers, all of which has resulted in the displacement of hundreds of thousands of Mexican peasants. A part of these have migrated to the United States and elsewhere outside of the country and another part has migrated to Mexican cities (Jones, 2001). By the turn of the century, about one in every three maquiladora workers did not work in a border municipality.

By the 1990s a "new generation" of maquiladora plants became involved in more capital and skill-intensive production of electronics, computers, and components for cars, transforming components rather than just assembling them (Galhardi, 1998:4). If at first transnational corporate strategy was based on nothing more than seeking out cheap labor, by the late twentieth century a more decentralized yet integrated global economy based on flexible accumulation patterns meant that geographic location was increasingly driven by complex market conditions requiring product diversity, quality, and reliability, proximity to markets, and a host of other factor cost considerations beyond simple wage levels. By the late 1990s the Mexican maquiladora sector comprised a mix of flexible production plants (often linked to outsourcing networks in Mexico), mass production plants, and labor-intensive assembly plants (Galhardi, 1998:21). These plants undertook export-processing assembly, component supply subcontracting, and original equipment manufacturing. In the early twenty-first century approximately 40 percent of maquiladora operations were in electronics and electrical equipment, as measured by the number of workers, another 22 percent in automotive, close to 22 percent in textiles, and the remainder in chemicals, foodstuffs, footwear, and other activities.

Worker productivity in the Mexican maquiladoras rose sharply starting in the 1980s and even more sharply in the 1990s. According to one estimate productivity rose almost 48 percent from 1993 to 2001 (Brandt, 2003:13). Yet despite this increased productivity wages in the maquiladora sector actually experienced a secular decline since the late 1970s, when they peaked, into the late 1990s—precisely during the rapid rise in productivity (Galhardi, 1998:9, figure 2.1). Importantly, real wages for low-skilled workers in non-maquiladora manufacturing industries in Mexico, while they also experienced a decline in the 1980s, have remained consistently and significantly above—almost double—maquiladora wages, and actually started to grow again in the early 1990s even as maquiladora wages continued their decline (Galhardi, 1998:9; Delgado-Wise and Cypher, 2005:18). Breaking this down further, one researcher found that wages for *obreros* (low-skilled workers) and *técnicos* (skilled workers) both declined in the maquiladoras, while those for *empleados* (administrative and managerial positions) remained relatively stagnant (M. Gambril, as cited in Galhardi, 1998:10). What is all the more remarkable about this decline in maquiladora wages is that it also took place at a time in which the labor market in the border zone went from a situation of abundance to shortage—that is, as the border economy began to experience labor shortages.

There are two observations here relevant to the theoretical arguments of this book. First, the secular decline in maquiladora wages during a time of rising worker productivity and increased participation in capital and skills-intensive processes belies the argument made by apologists of capitalist globalization that wages and living standards will go up as productivity rises and as workers acquire "human capital" by upgrading their skills and their participation in higher capital and skills-intensive processes. Second, despite the ongoing shift to flexible accumulation, workers in Mexican domestic manufacturing still labored during the 1980s and 1990s under the old Fordist-developmentalist capital-labor relation that characterized the pre-globalization ISI model, including regulated labor, packets of benefits, and capital-labor relations mediated by political relations and the state. These workers became incorporated into accumulation processes in Mexico both as labor and as domestic market consumers, in distinction to the logic of the new capital-labor relation in which workers provide labor but are not strategic as consumers to accumulation. The earlier generation of industrial workers became incorporated into capitalist accumulation through a logic of production and reproduction in national accumulation circuits whereas the maquiladora generation—irrespective of their productivity, the capital-labor ratio, or their skills level—are incorporated through a logic of production alone as cheap labor within globalized accumulation circuits. At the same time, there is scattered evidence that Mexican domestic manufacturing is transforming in other ways; becoming "lean" establishments employing flexible labor and entering into wider and often transnational production chains and sub-contracting arrangements (see, inter alia, Videla, 2005, 2006).

This may be a general phenomenon. In his research on the EPZs in the Dominican Republic, for instance, Kaplinsky found that the boom in labor intensive export manufacturing led to "immiserizing employment growth, that is employment growth which is contingent upon wages falling in international purchasing power" (1993:1861). The Dominican government introduced EPZs in the early 1980s. By the end of that decade the country had become the world's fourth-largest EPZ economy measured in terms of employment (Kaplinsky, 1993:1855–1856) and by the end of the next decade it soaked up more than one-fourth of total foreign investment in the Caribbean region, outside of Mexico (Dypski, 2002:121). The Dominican maquila sector employed nearly 200,000 workers and generated close to $2 billion in value added (exports minus imports) [Sánchez-Anocochea, 2004:9]. As in Mexico, industrial output outside of the EPZs declined significantly as it rose within the EPZs. Between 1981 and 1989, manufacturing inside the EPZs increased from 23 to 56 percent of the country's total industrial employment as real wages in the maquiladora sector dropped by more than half during this period (ibid.:1860). And also as in Central America and Mexico, Dominican capitalists have significant participation in the maquiladora sector. Dominican-owned enterprises such as D'Clase Corporation, Bratex Dominicana, Interamericana Products, and Grupo M, are among the largest apparel producers in the Caribbean Basin and have invested abroad, including in Haiti and the United States (Sánchez-Anocochea, 2004:21–22).

As we have seen for NTAEs, women predominate among the maquiladora workforce. However, there has been increasing employment of men relative to women in Mexican maquiladoras, as the industry has become more capital and skills-intensive. Overall, the share of men employed in maquiladoras increased from less than 20 percent to about 35 percent from 1980 into the 1990s, and up to 50 percent in some sectors, such as transportation equipment (Galhardi, 1998:16, table 2.1). As Tiano (1994) and others show, these maquiladora jobs involving higher skills, status, and pay have tended to go to men, thus reproducing male domination and sex segmentation in the labor market in new ways. There is a large and growing body of literature on women, gender and the maquiladoras (see, inter alia, Fernández-Kelly, 1983; Tiano, 1994; Salzinger, 2003; Iglesias Prieto, 1997; Kopkinak, 1998; Cravey, 1998). Perhaps the most potent symbol of degradation of women under global capitalism is the chilling femicide that has taken place in the border city of Juárez, across from El Paso, Texas, where hundreds of women—many of them young maquiladora workers—have been brutally murdered since the 1990s and abandoned in the desert, mutilated and disfigured (see, inter alia, Gaspar de Alba, 2005; Alcala Iberri, 2004; Nathan, 1999; Portillo, 2001). Although explanations for the unsolved murders vary, most concur that the femicide is associated with the potent mix of globalization in the border region and patriarchal violence. In an environment of rapid change and mounting insecurity, women who work in the maquiladoras are reduced to commodities that can be discarded; their devaluation has made women in general ready targets for heightened violence in the public and private realms.

The future of the in-bond industry in Mexico is unclear. After the post-NAFTA boom the maquiladora sector experienced a downturn in the early twenty-first century, in part as a result of recession in the United States but also as a result of the relocation of plants—especially textiles and apparel—to China, Central America, and other lower-wage regions. Between 2000 and 2005 China had lured over 600 maquiladora plants to relocate to its industrial complexes (at U.S. $0.30 per hour), leaving 250,000 Mexican workers unemployed. In 2004 China overtook Mexico as the largest exporter of apparel to the U.S. market. Wages in the Caribbean Basin EPZs were significantly higher than their Southeast Asian counterparts when the maquiladora boom arrived in the Caribbean in the 1980s, as Table 3.3 indicates. The Caribbean maquiladora industry will surely retain an importance since the region enjoys proximity to the North American market; such market proximity may often be as or more important than prevailing wage rates. However, the relative decline in wages is likely to continue as globalization pits working classes from different countries in competition with each other.

TABLE 3.3
*Hourly Wages for Semi-Skilled Production Workers
in Export Manufacturing Industries, 1987*

	$/hr	US=100
Germany	15.93	116.6
United States	13.66	100
Thailand	0.35	2.6
Sri Lanka	0.29	2.1
Philippines	0.26	2.1
China	0.15	1.1
Costa Rica	0.95	7.0
Guatemala	0.88	6.4
Haiti	0.58	4.2
Honduras	0.53	4.2
Jamaica	0.63	4.6
Panama	1.77	13.0
Mexico	0.84	6.1
Dominican Republic	0.79	5.8

Source: World Bank, as cited in Kaplinsky, 1993, table 4, p. 1859.

Central America—From the Farm to the Sweatshop

Beyond Mexico, as the global economy emerged in the 1960s and 1970s, U.S. textile-apparel producers shifted the labor-intensive middle phase to the East Asian low-wage zone, and developed subcontracting (outsourcing) networks, whereby East Asian, particularly Taiwanese and South Korean, capital organized local production in consort with transnational capital.[2] By the 1980s and 1990s, this process had resulted in the integration into transnational accumulation circuits of East Asian capitalists themselves, who began to shift production to new low-wage zones, particularly mainland China, Southeast Asia, and Central America and the Caribbean, in the face of rising wage levels and other factor cost considerations in their home countries. The social dislocations generated by capitalist development in Central America as globalization proceeded from the 1960s and on, together with the disruptions caused by the political-military conflagration in that region, had generated a huge pool of available—and potentially revolutionary—labor in Central America by the 1980s and 1990s. Moreover, the region was ideally situated geographically for access to the U.S. market. This is the economic backdrop to the appearance of the garment industry in Central America. The political backdrop was the U.S. Caribbean Basin Initiative (CBI) program, which allowed factories operating in the region duty-free access to the

---

[2] This section draws heavily on Robinson, 2003, chapter 3.

U.S. market and provided further incentives for the massive influx of foreign capital from East Asia to Central America. The more conjunctural strategic objective of the CBI on the part of U.S. policy makers was the expectation that CBI-induced development would help subdue revolutionary movements in the region (for detailed discussion, see Robinson, 2003; Dypski, 2002).

There was a complex convergence of U.S. geopolitical interests with the evolving class interests of East Asian capitalists in the process of integration into transnationalized circuits and with the changing composition of social forces in Central America. From a structural perspective, the CBI was part and parcel of economic globalization, and illustrated how the U.S. state functions to facilitate the conditions for the globalization of production and to promote the interests of the transnational elite. The AID, for instance, funded and guided Central American states and local business foundations and think tanks in the establishment of free trade zones and the development of policies and programs conducive to maquiladora production. In this way, local elites operating in the state and in civil society became integrated into these emergent transnationalized circuits in Central America, which spurred on the development of transnational fractions among the elite. A nation-state-centric analysis of this situation, which would have "East Asian" capital competing with "U.S." and other national capitals, conceals the transnational essence of this phenomenon: in the complex global commodity chain, "U.S.," "East Asian," and local "Central American" actors are all component agents of *transnational* circuits of capital accumulation. They are experiencing a process of transnational class formation on the basis of an objective identity of interests and organic integration as they converge around sites for globalized production and services.

Tables 3.4 and 3.5 show the dramatic appearance of garment-assembly enclaves in Central America from the mid-1980s to the early twenty-first century. Between 1984 and 1991 every Central American country enacted laws creating EPZs and offering incentives ranging from tax holidays, import duty exemptions, guarantees for profit repatriations, and exemptions from labor laws (Tello and Tyler, 1997:43; Jenkins et al. 1998:19–25). Interestingly, legislation in all five countries contains provisions allowing maquiladora plants to locate anywhere in national territory (outside of the confines of the EPZs), so that in effect the entire Isthmus has been constituted as single mega-export processing zone.

Maquiladora production is generally not included in national trade statistics in Central America since the sector's transactions are considered external to national accounting. It is notoriously difficult for this reason to acquire precise data on plants, workers, exports, and value added, but researchers generally

TABLE 3.4
Garment Assembly Industry in Central America (as measured in imports to the United States in $million)

	1983	1986	1990	1993	1996
Costa Rica	64	142	384	653	706
Guatemala	4	20	192	552	809
El Salvador	6	11	54	251	721
Honduras	20	32	113	510	1,241
Nicaragua				3(1992)	232 (1998)

Source: U.S. Department of Commerce, as compiled by Gereffi, 1997, p. 2.

TABLE 3.5
Maquiladora Production in Central America (in $million, average five-year periods)

	1980–84	1990–94	2000–2003
Costa Rica*	10.4	507.5	3,172.2
El Salvador*	N/A	360.2	1,724.6
Guatemala**	N/A	88.5	483.6
Honduras**	N/A	107.6	613.4
Nicaragua**	N/A	6.5	117.9

Source: ECLAC, in Segovia, 2004, table 1, p. 14.
  *Exports, f.o.b.
  **Value-added.

placed the maquiladora labor force in Central America by the late 1990s as 300,000 to 350,000 for the five republics, including 50,000 in Costa Rica, 50,000 in El Salvador, 80,000 in Guatemala, 120,000 in Honduras, and 30,000 in Nicaragua, while other estimates ranged upwards to half a million when subcontractors to the maquiladoras are included (Willmore, 1997:61; Robinson, 2003; Brandt, 2003:6). Maquiladora export earnings for the region as a whole amounted to about $1 billion in 1996 out of total regional receipts of some $7.7 billion, or about 13 percent of the total (Jenkins et al., 1998:27–30). Seen from another angle, maquiladora products replaced traditional agro-exports as the chief product imported from Central America by the United States, which was still the region's principal trading partner. In the late 1990s, 51 percent of U.S. imports from Central America consisted of maquiladora products, largely clothing, while agricultural products represented only 37 percent (ILO, 1998:15). Moreover, there is evidence that the importance of maquiladoras to Central America has expanded significantly since the late 1990s (see, e.g., Tables 3.4, 3.5, 3.6, and 3.7; and WTO *Trade Policy Review* reports for various years). In sum, the maquiladoras account for a significant and rapidly growing share of the region's industrial output, employment, and foreign exchange earnings.

TABLE 3.6
Maquiladora Employment as a Percentage of Manufacturing Employment

	% of Manufacturing Employment		% of Manufactured Exports
	1990	1996	1996
Costa Rica	16	24	40
Honduras	11	36*	N/A
Nicaragua	45	33	60
El Salvador	N/A	28	45
Guatemala	N/A	38	30

Source: Jenkins et al., pp. 27–30.
*Figures for 1995.

TABLE 3.7
*Export Earnings (value added) from Maquiladora Production
(in $million) as a Percentage of Total Export Earnings*

	Net Earnings		As % of Earnings, 1996	Net Earnings, Other Years
	1990	1996		
Costa Rica	107	265	10	3,580** (2001)
Honduras	30	291*	25*	346 (2001), 560 (2002)
Nicaragua	0	53	8	74 (1997)
El Salvador	22	214	20	N/A
Guatemala	39	184	9	358 (1999)

Source: Jenkins et al., pp. 27–30, for 1996; WTO, *Trade Policy Review*, various years, for
other years.
 *Figures for 1995.
 **Value of total maquiladora exports before subtracting value of imports.

A very noteworthy aspect of the maquiladora industry in Central America, as
indicated in Table 3.8, is the high percentage of local entrepreneurial participation, as measured by the national origin of capital invested out of 791 maquiladora plants operating in the region in the mid-1990s. In Costa Rica, 21 percent
of maquila plants in the EPZs were owned by local investors; in El Salvador, 65
percent; in Guatemala, 43 percent; in Honduras, 32 percent; and in Nicaragua,
16 percent. Local capitalist developers were also heavily involved in constructing and administering EPZs and industrial parks in all five republics, and especially in Honduras and Nicaragua.

The high proportion of local participation in the maquiladora sector points
to the emergence of a new Central American entrepreneurial class more thoroughly
integrated into transnational production circuits than the old oligarchy, whose
external linkage was strictly market-based. It suggests less of a "comprador"

TABLE 3.8

National Origin of Capital in the Central American Maquiladora Industry as a Percentage of 791 Plants in EPZs, Mid-1990s

	Origin of Capital				
	Local	U.S.	Korean	Other	Other Asian*
Costa Rica	21	60	2	2	16
El Salvador	65	11	8	6	10
Guatemala	43	9	44	2	2
Honduras	32	36	21	10	1
Nicaragua	16	32	16	32**	5

Source: International Labor Organization, 1998, pp. 5–6.
    *Largely Central American and European.
    **Largely Taiwanese.

relation, in which local bourgeoisie are mere managers and administrators of transnational firms, than a relation between capitalists able to operate at the local or regional levels and those able to operate at the global level, and merits a brief theoretical digression here. Capitalists at the local and regional levels, such as maquiladora entrepreneurs in Central America, it would seem, come to participate in the global economy as subordinate partners dependent on global capitalists operating through the oligopolist TNC structures. But this does not justify nation-state centric conclusions because, among other reasons, in the "core" there are capitalists that operate only locally and in the "periphery" there are capitalist that operate regionally and globally. More fruitful approaches, although they cannot be pursued here, might be to explore the relationship between transnational capitalists in more competitive and in more monopolistic sectors of the global economy, just as political economists earlier identified the relations between capitalists in functionally integrated competitive and monopoly sectors within national accumulation processes (e.g., Baran and Sweezy, 1966). Capitalists in the competitive sectors, whether in the "First" or the "Third" world, increase the rate of exploitation or the transfer of value from labor to capital in the phases of accumulation they control in order to compensate for the transfer of value from their sector to capitalists in more monopolistic sectors in other phases. Clearly, what is required is to move beyond nation-state centrism and to apply a theory of value to transformations in world spatial and institutional structures, and to draw out the concomitant implications for transnational class relations.

The maquiladora sector in Central America exhibits the new forms of transnational collaboration between capitalists discussed in Chapter 1, especially subcontracting and outsourcing, as well as joint ventures, technical cooperation, licensing agreements, and local supply of TNC operations. Unlike TNC subsidiary production, which predominated in the pre-globalization period, these new forms bring local investors directly into TNC-organized global production chains and foment a more organic integration of Central American capitalists into the TCC (on forms of local-transnational collaboration, see Weersma-Haworth, 1996; ILO, 1998; Jenkins et al., 1998, Robinson, 2003). These novel relations that develop among transnational capitalists (even those operating only locally are transnational because they are incorporated into globalized circuits) are not "core-periphery" relations as seen through the lens of nation-state centrism. Hopkins and Wallerstein note that "core" and "peripheral" nodes within global commodity chains are competitive and monopolistic, respectively, and then go on to correlate core nodes in GCCs to core (nation) states in the world system and "peripheral" nodes to peripheral (nation) states (Hopkins and Wallerstein, 1994). But what we see as the apparel industry globalizes is the existence of competitive and monopoly phases of fragmented and decentralized production *within* nation-states. Apparel production in the United States, for instance, involves a more monopolistic sector constituted by the large chain retail outlets that set overall production and pricing. What apparently occurs is a disproportionate appropriation of value from productive capital by commercial and finance capital. And the competitive sector is constituted by the garment-production phase, involving competitive clusters of sweatshops in New York, Los Angeles, the southeastern states, and elsewhere, alongside monopolistic sector retailers who control production through market control, financial, pricing, subcontracting and other mechanisms (Taplin, 1994). We also see similar wage and labor conditions in some of these U.S. sweatshops as in the Central American sweatshops (see, e.g., discussion below).

"Contractors, who are near the beginning of the fashion-oriented chain, retain a periphery-like status even though they may be located in the United States," observes Taplin. "Like their overseas counterparts, domestic contractors capitalize upon large pools of low-wage labor, extracting value via wage-deepening tactics . . . production is fragmented *between* firms domestically, *between* firms globally, and *within* firms domestically" (1994:210, 220). On the other hand, profit margins in the garment maquiladoras in Central America are remarkably high: 40 percent return on investment in some cases (Petersen, 1992:39–40). Clearly, greater value added, or values transferred among nodes in GCCs, does not necessarily denote "core" and "peripheral" nation-state relations. "Peripheral" nodes operate in the United States and "core" nodes in Central America and nation-state-centric conclusions are not justified. To be internationally competitive, according to GCC theory, means precisely to decentralize distinct nodes across the globe in accordance with the whole matrix of factor cost considerations. As Taplin appropriately observer, "Because different production links in the commodity chain occur *within* the United States, a core country, it suggests that countries are not the most appropriate unit of analysis in talking about globalized production in apparel. Furthermore, industry sectoral differences demonstrate the saliency of local rather than national production systems as parallel commodity chains are integrated into global production networks" (Taplin, 1994:208).

A focus on the maquiladora industry in one country of the region, Guatemala, as a case study that reveals some general patterns in Central America and beyond as well as certain country-specific features of the sector, also shines empirical light on these larger issues of transnational class and state formation. The establishment of the maquiladora sector in Guatemala was the result of a concerted and coordinated effort by the AID, the World Bank, the Guatemalan state, transnational capitalists and their "home states," together with transnationally oriented Guatemalan business elites. These later had become organized into private sector associations, such as the Chamber of Business and the Guatemalan Non-Traditional Exporters Association (GEXPORT), dedicated to promoting nontraditional exports and neoliberal modernization. Shortly after its founding in 1982, GEXPORT set up a special commission, the Apparel Manufacturers Export Commission (VESTEX) to promote maquiladora operations in Guatemala. In 1984, the Guatemalan government, working closely with the AID and Guatemalan private sector associations, approved legislation to attract export-assembly investment. At the time the law was passed, there were only six factories assembling apparel for export employing barely 2,000 workers. By 1992 maquiladora production had become the fastest-growing sector of the Guatemalan economy, with more than 250 plants employing over 50,000 workers and exporting nearly $350 million in garments to the world market (Petersen, 1992:1).

In the structure of maquiladora production in Guatemala as part of a GCC, U.S.-based TNCs contracted nearly all of the garment production, led by such brand names as Liz Claiborne, Sears, Bugle Boy, Levis, and Phillips–Van Heusen. These suppliers in turn contracted out to South Korean, Guatemalan, U.S., German, and Israeli firms, and to a spattering of firms from other countries of origin. While this general pattern is typical for the region, Guatemalan production was dominated in the early 1990s by investment capital originating in South Korea, which accounted for nearly half of all output, while Guatemalan investors accounted for over 40 percent, and joint ventures between transnational and local investors, typical of maquiladora operations elsewhere in the region, was less significant (Petersen, 1992:46–49). South Korean investors included middle-sized Korean firms but also several TNCs, among them, Samsung, Sam Phoong, and Lucky Goldstar. It appears that South Korean investors picked Guatemala largely under the guidance of the South Korean government, which had developed close diplomatic relations with Guatemalan military regimes in the 1970s and targeted the country to be the nucleus for Caribbean-wide operations.

As part of the Korean government's drive to transnationalize the Korean economy, the Korean state, in much the same way as it organized and directed Korean capital inside the country in the 1960s and the 1970s, organized Korean capital's transnationalization in the 1980s and early 1990s. This included a search for new apparel export platforms. Once Guatemala was chosen as the major Western Hemisphere site in the wake of the CBI and the opportunities it presented, the Korean state provided a packet of services, including information bureaus, loans, subsidies, and tax breaks at the departure end in South Korea. It also provided a host of services at the arrival end in Guatemala, such as acting as liaison with the Guatemalan state, investor insurance, market studies, the establishment of Korean-Guatemalan air flights for the massive transfer of apparel plants to Guatemala and Guatemala-to-U.S. garment shipping arrangements. As researcher Kurt Petersen reports, the opening of a Korean factory in Guatemala marked the closing of one in Korea, in which "entire factories transfer their contents to Guatemalan warehouses and begin anew" (Petersen, 1992:139). As the life source of Korean factories, "the Korean embassy staff [in Guatemala] are advocates, spokespersons, mediators, and consultants for individual Korean factories" (ibid.:145). The embassy micromanaged the external and sometimes internal affairs of Korean investors, including acting as liaison with the Guatemalan government, settling labor disputes, and handling legal matters. Korean ambassador to Guatemala Key-Sung Cho played the archetypical role of a "chief executive officer" for Korean transnationals in Guatemala.

In this way, the Korean state was replicating at the transnational level, now in the service of global capitalism, the same role it played at the national level in the development of Korean capitalism. This was not a particularly "Asian" capitalist strategy and conforms to the expected relationship between capital and the capitalist state. The AID played a nearly identical role throughout the Greater Caribbean Basin in generating the conditions for capital investment, but the AID promoted less "U.S." capital than transnational capital in general. More specifically, in Guatemala AID officials solicited and served as guides to representatives from U.S.-based TNCs interested in contracting work or investing directly in the maquiladora industry, and the AID even contracted a former embassy official to work full time with GEXPORT to encourage collaboration between entrepreneurs in Guatemala and the United States (Petersen, 1992:28). While pursuing the logics of their own institutional strategies, U.S. and Korean officials in Guatemalan were thus on-the-ground activists of the transnational project in Central America. And both the U.S. and the Korean national states conducted this activity in coordination with the Guatemalan national state. In either case, national state apparatuses acted objectively to facilitate the transnationalization of capital. When the Korean state acts to transnationalize Korean capital, and when these activities are complementary to and coordinated with those of the U.S. and the Guatemalan state, it is engaging objectively in transnational state practices aimed at fomenting a globalized accumulation of capital.

In analytical abstraction, the international financial institutions (IFIs), the AID, and the Korean and the Guatemalan states should be seen as components of an emergent TNS apparatus that played the role, taken as a whole, that we would expect of the capitalist state: organizing the conditions for capital accumulation (promoting neoliberal reform, providing investment incentives, and so on), and overseeing the larger social, political, and cultural conditions under which this accumulation takes place (promoting peace processes and polyarchy, and so on). Ambassador Cho, AID officials, and Guatemalan state officials were in effect transnational state managers. Those agents involved in capital formation around this activity—South Korean, Guatemalan, and U.S. investors—are constituent members of an emergent transnational capitalist class. Indeed, members of this class begin to see subordinate classes, which are themselves transnationalizing, in the same light regardless of geographic location. "The Guatemalan *campesino* is very much like the Korean peasant," explained one Korean maquiladora factory manager. "They are docile. They work hard. And, they even have short names like our peasants" (cited in Petersen, 1992:150).

Guatemala led the way in the region's maquiladora sector, and became a staging point for the spread of operations into the "Northern triangle" (Guatemala, El Salvador, and Honduras). Perhaps the most phenomenal growth of the maquiladoras took place in Honduras, which had just one EPZ in Puerto Cortes in 1990, but within a few years had constructed five government-sponsored zones and five privately run industrial parks. Such well-known U.S.-based TNCs as Sara Lee, Osh Kosh B'Gosh, and Warners set up shop, along with Korean investors who arrived en masse from Sunny Industries, the Dong Bank Corporation, and the Hanil Group, among others, and Hong Kong, Taiwanese, and Singaporan investors (Norsworthy, 1993:78–79). Employment rose from 9,000 in 1990 to 20,000 in 1991, then to 48,000 in 1995, and to more than 100,000 by the twenty-first century, as the country went from a "banana republic" to a sweatshop republic. El Salvador also experienced an amazing growth of the industry. Maquila exports to the United States increased by 3,800 percent between 1985 and 1994, from $10 million to $398 million, while the number of workers shot up from 3,500 to 50,000 (Green, 1995:28). Costa Rica's maquiladora sector took off in 1986, after the government began an "industrial reconversion program" it negotiated with the IFIs, aimed at reorienting the country's industry from the domestic market to exports (Hansen-Kuhn, 1993:16). In the 1980s the sector almost exclusively produced apparel, but by the 1990s investors were assembling electronics, medical equipment, and other products requiring greater capital investment.

Workers in the Guatemalan maquiladoras, which resemble the typical working conditions in the sector throughout the Isthmus, labored typically in shifts that lasted 12 to 15 hours during the 1990s on primitive shop floors in sweatshop conditions, earning between two and four dollars per day. Most of the factories were set up makeshift in old warehouses that are poorly ventilated, poorly lit, and having dangerous fire hazards. Workers were generally locked in during working hours and labored in prison-like conditions, suffering numerous health traumas as a result of exposure to harmful chemical fumes and dust, overwork, and the near-total lack of safety conditions. Fainting and collapsing due to exhaustion and dehydration were commonplace. In 1992, less than half the factories had worker cafeterias, and few had any health facilities. Bathrooms were unsanitary and in disrepair, and workers required permission for bathroom breaks, provoking exasperation and indignation. Workers also suffered rampant abuses from supervisors, including routine sexual and physical assault, verbal abuse, and threats. The piece-rate system in place in most maquiladoras assured breakneck work for minimum and sub-minimum wages. Child labor was rampant, and the illegal dismissal of pregnant women was a regular practice. The lack of job security was compounded by an extreme anti-union atmosphere backed by the Guatemalan state, which promoted a union-free industry and worker docility as one of the key attractions for transnational investors (on the details, see Petersen, 1992).

These working conditions were replicated throughout the region (Robinson, 2003). In a visit to the maquiladoras in Nicaragua's Las Mercedes *Zona Franca,*

I observed rows of buildings that looked like vast warehouses. At 7:00 a.m. what appears to be an army of workers, the vast majority women, stream into the red chain-link gates that cordon off the *Zona Franca,* just a few minutes from the international airport, in the northeast corner of Managua. The atmosphere inside the plants is frighteningly regimented, as well as overcrowded, hot, stuffy, and poorly ventilated. There are separate areas for each of the assembly stages. Rows and rows of sewing machines dominate floor space, where hundreds of workers, almost all women, sit for 10–15-hour shifts, with one 15-minute break in the morning and a half-hour lunch break in the afternoon as their only rest time. On one side of the shop floor, workers use electric blades to cut thick stacks of fabric, while in another area industrial washing machines spew steam and noxious fumes into the air, while sweating workers, both men and women, load and unload bundles of clothing. Maquiladora workers are beset by a litany of occupational hazards and commonly suffer from such illnesses as tuberculosis, depression, asthma, allergic reactions, and intoxication from chemicals and noxious fumes. In addition, one survey reported that 40 percent of workers in the Honduran maquiladoras have been subject to physical punishment such as being pushed, hit, or beaten by a supervisor (Brandt, 2003:7).

In recent years, international labor and anti-sweatshop campaigns have brought attention to these sweatshop conditions in the Central American maquiladoras and to ongoing workers struggles. Although wages within the sector were above the national minimum in some countries, although not all, this did not mean that they amounted to a *living wage,* as called for by the international anti-sweatshop campaign. The average wage in the Nicaraguan maquiladoras, for example, was about $60 a month in 1999, whereas the calculated monthly salary to meet minimum basic needs of a family was $125. Moreover, charges levied by the anti-sweatshop movement of *absolute* exploitation of Central American maquiladora workers appear to be authentic. According to figures compiled by the National Labor Committee, a U.S.-based international workers rights organization, following a May 2000 visit to the Las Mercedes *Zona Franca* in Nicaragua, workers at the Chentex plant received just 18 cents for every pair of Kohl's "Sonoma" shorts that retailed for $24 in the United States (less than 1 percent of the retail price). They received just $0.28 for each $34 pair of Gloria Vanderbilt jeans they sewed (8/10th its retail price), $0.22 for each pair of $19.99 Arizona jeans for J.C. Penny, and so forth. Average wages at Chentex, including bonuses and overtime rates, were some $0.48 an hour. In its promotional material to attract investors, the Foundation for Investment and Development (FIDE), the chief business association representing new capitalist groups in Honduras (see Chapter 4), advertises the "fully loaded labor cost per hour" (that is, including all benefits and extras) at $0.63 (for these details, see Robinson, 2003, chapter 3).

Maquiladora work is quintessentially organized along the lines of flexible accumulation, under the new capital-labor relation discussed in Chapter 1. Work in the EPZ is extremely unstable and turnover is high. Workers are generally not hired permanently but on the basis of temporary renewable contracts, which in any event do not stipulate guarantees against dismissals, and are not officially covered inside the *zona francas* as by national labor laws. Moreover, this type of work is seasonal, dependent on fluctuating demand that regularly draws in and then expels just-in-time labor. Many firms fire workers at the end of peak seasons, as demand slacks off. In El Salvador's San Bartolo EPZ, one common practice is to fire workers at the end of the year and hire them again a few weeks later in order to avoid a "thirteenth-month" bonus payment (*aguinaldo* in Spanish) and other year-end benefits, which have a long traditional in Latin America.

The maquiladora sector is largely nonunion. Starting in the late 1990s there was an upsurge in workers' struggles throughout the region's maquiladora sector, leading to a number of agreements signed in the region between Labor Ministries conceding workers the right to form unions and "codes of ethics" and other statements by TNCs promising to respect international labor standards. However, these were for the most part more public relations maneuvers than real change in government or company policies. The mass firing of workers attempting organizing drives, the selective firing of identified leaders, and other forms of repression, were routine occurrences throughout the region in the 1990s as government and employers mounted a concerted effort to wipe out the labor movement and clear the way for the expected expansion of the sector. In 1998 workers at a Phillips-Van Heusen maquiladora in Guatemala, with the support of international labor rights organizations, forced the company to sign a labor contract after a six year unionization battle. The victory, however, was short lived. In December of that year, the company closed its doors, pleading "surplus capacity," and relocated the plant to Honduras, underscoring the difficulties that workers face in organizing in the age of transnational capital mobility. By 2004 there were still no functioning unions in El Salvador and Guatemala, while a handful of officially recognized unions in Nicaragua and Honduras were under attack.

The vast majority of workers in EPZ plants around the world are young women 16 to 25 years old. This is especially so with regard to unskilled and labor-intensive work in garments and electronics. The disproportionate, often almost exclusive, employment of women in the EPZs, who face super-exploitation and often blatant abuse, is a constant theme in the literature on the subject. Some 80 percent of maquiladora workers in the Central American EPZs are women (Willmore, 1997:61). In 1990 a business group in El Salvador, epitomizing the convergence of female degradation, labor exploitation, and dehumanization that have made the maquiladoras infamous, placed an advertisement in *Bobbin,* the trade magazine of the U.S. spinning industry, vaunting "Rosa Martinez." "You can hire her for 57 cents an hour," stated the caption below a picture of a young Salvadoran woman at work behind a sewing machine. "Rosa is more than just colorful. She and her coworkers are know for their industriousness, reliability, and quick learning" (as cited in Barnet and Cavanagh, 1994:325): A study on maquiladora workers in Guatemala City found that at least four-fifths were women between the ages of 14 and 24 who suffered extreme gender discrimination on top of the conditions faced by their male counterparts. They were routinely harassed sexually and dismissed for pregnancy. "My ideal worker is young, unmarried, healthy, thin and delicate, lives close, and does not have previous experience," explained one personnel manager. "If they have experience they come with many vices. They do not like to follow orders. We like to teach them ourselves. Old people are also not good because they are sick often and do not look good anymore." Another manager complained, "Nothing disturbs our production more than women getting pregnant. These women are irresponsible. They do not seem to be able to control themselves" (as cited in Petersen, 1992:42–43, 93).

The new transnational model of accumulation profoundly alters as it transnationalizes the local social structure. The maquiladora sector has acted as a magnet drawing in labor far beyond the immediate peripheries of the EPZs, heightening the flow of rural-to-urban migration and bringing changes to local communities. "Once young people leave the peasant world, they usually do not want to return, and even become magnets that attract other relatives and friends," note one team of Honduran researchers. "The migration of males is provoking a scarcity of field hands that is in turn causing an increase in the pay rate for day laborers" in the agricultural sector, while the flow of young women into the maquiladoras has placed upward pressure on the salaries of domestic workers in the cities. "For men as well as women, working in a factory is both more lucrative and more prestigious than working in the fields or in the kitchen" (Del Cit et al., 1999:29–30). Moreover, young men and women incorporated into maquiladora work, especially those entering the money economy for the first time, develop new outlooks and rising expectations, and are often drawn into global capitalist culture. "The integration of young people into the factories has generated new businesses that profit off of their wages, note del Cit and her colleagues. "For example, catalogue companies have expanded their markets to include factory communities. Monthly catalogs circulate, offering clothing, perfumes, cosmetics and adornments. This is producing changes in the standards of beauty for both men and women. . . . At the same time, 'needs' are being created that didn't exist before. Both men and women worry about keeping up with the latest fashion. . . . Gradual indebtedness is a new economic reality, more among young women, because they spend a good part of their salaries on clothing and adornments" (ibid.:30).

FTZs and Maquiladoras in South America

Beyond Mexico and Central America, different types of FTZs are spreading throughout Latin America, ranging from the export assembly enclaves of the maquiladoras, to open border areas created by governments for the production of goods in domestic markets—such as the Brazilian Manaus FTZ—and duty and tax free commercial districts such as the Ciudad del Leste Free Zone in Paraguay, and the famous Zona Libre de Colon in Panama, a global logistic and financial center responsible for some $12 billion in imports and re-exports in the early twenty-first century (Braga, 2002:1). Together with the Dominican Republic, Haiti and Jamaica are the major centers in the Caribbean for export processing, although most of the Caribbean islands have at least one EPZ. The maquiladoras and EPZs as the archetypical symbol of the global factory have spread from the Greater Caribbean Basin into South America. In the early twenty-first century, Argentina, Brazil, Peru, Colombia, Ecuador, and Bolivia all set up EPZs. The pattern seems to be the establishment of industrial and commercial FTZs in the Southern Cone countries, where wages are higher and less attractive for TNC investment in maquiladoras, and the establishment of the traditional labor-intensive maquiladoras in the poorer Andean countries. In the Southern Cone, the largest FTZ is Brazil's Manaus. More than 300 industries in the zone employ about 50,000 workers producing industrial goods for sale in the Brazilian domestic market (Braga, 2002:1). Chile has one EPZ oriented toward assembly for export and another FTZ intended to sell to the domestic market. In these cases, TNCs are attracted to FTZs less to take advantage of cheap labor than as a logistic and tax/duty-free gateway to local markets. A number of FTZs have been established in the Andean countries. Already by 1998 there were also some 40 EPZs there, where wages were often as low as in the Caribbean Basin, including 15 in Bolivia, 12 in Colombia, 6 in Ecuador, 4 in Peru, and 3 in Venezuela (Braga, 2002:2). In 2001 Paraguay implemented an EPZ arrangement similar to those in the Caribbean and several hundred TNCs signaled their intent to set up plants.

The agency of the TCC and its Latin American contingents are apparent in the FTZs and the EPZs. Latin American entrepreneurs are organized into the *Comite de Zonas Francas de las Americas*, a trade association aimed at promoting FTZs and EPZs, affiliated with the World Economic Processing Zones Association (WEPZA), which has served as the chief transnational corporate vehicle for lobbying within the WTO for this form of globalized economic organization (Braga, 2002:3). "There is a close working relationship among the Latin American free trade zones," explained one consultant to the *Comite*. "We usually meet together in regional meetings we organize on a regular basis, especially under the auspices of the WEPZA" (Braga, 2002:4). Moreover, offshore assembling also involves more small and middle-sized firms that previously, which has opened up space for local investors to integrate into transnational production chains.

Transnational Services and the New Global Tourism

Latin America has experienced a steady "tercerization" of the political economy—an expansion of the service (terciary) sector, both formal and informal—relative to the agriculture (primary) and industrial (secondary) sectors. This is part of a broader trend characteristic of the global economy as a whole, brought about, among other factors, by the transition from peasant to capitalist agriculture, escalating productivity in both agricultural and industrial production, and the explosion of service-based accumulation made possible by information capitalism. Table 3.9 indicates the steady shift over time in Latin America in the relative weight of each sector toward services, which by the turn of the twenty-first century represented nearly 60 percent of all employment, although we must remember that much informal sector work is service-related. Most countries in Latin America now participate in a host of transnational services activities, among them, banking and related financial services, global data entry and processing, software production, call centers, and tourism.

What the business literature refers to now as offshore teleworking (transnational data entry, processing, multimedia, call centers, etc.) has spread rapidly

TABLE 3.9

*The Sectoral Distribution of Employment in Latin America,
1950–1990 (percent distribution)*

Year	Agriculture	Industry	Services
1950	54	19	27
1970	42	22	36
1990	25	24	51
2000	22	21	57

Sources: ILO, 2005, p. 111, "KILM4. Employment by Sector," Nov. 21,
available at www.ILO.org.; "World Employment Report, 2004–05:
Employment, Productivity, and Poverty Reduction" (Geneva, 2005). For
2000: ECLAC, *Statistical Yearbook for Latin America and the Caribbean,*
2005, table 1.2.5, p. 42.

in many Latin American countries. By the early twenty-first century, TNCs and local subcontractors employed millions of workers in offshore teleworking in the region, with call centers leading the way (see, inter alia, Di Martino, 2004; Datamonitor, 2004). The number of call centers in the region had reached 5,100 by 2003 and was expected to climb as high as 12,000 centers by 2008 (Di Martino, 2004:7). Argentina, Brazil, Chile, Colombia, Mexico, and several Caribbean nations led the way, although no country seemed to be left out of the call center boom. Wages in call centers in Argentina were in 2003 about one-tenth of what they were in the United States. Call centers in Brazil employed in 2003 some 500,000 agents, largely women from 16 to 24 years of age whose average monthly earnings were between $120 and $200 (Di Martino, 2004:15). Far from high-end informational jobs that much of the business literature projects, most telework in Latin America would more accurately be characterized as *informational maquiladoras:* low wages, long hours, Taylorist discipline, and a hostile anti-union environment (Braga, 2007; Di Martino, 2004). Given the increasing centrality of call centers and informational work more generally to Latin America's political economy it is worth citing Ruy Braga (2007), who has conducted ethnographic research at call centers in Brazil:

There is an average of one supervisor to every 15 or 20 Call Center operators at the workplace. This high rate of supervisors is explained by the need to maximize control of the workers, which prevents workers from leaving the information flow and gives them no moment to relax. This is a type of work that illustrates as no other the Taylorization of intellectual work and of the service sector: disciplined communications coerced under information flows and limited by the instrumental character of the script imposed by the company on the operator. The objectives are clear: to multiply transactions and to decrease their cost through the reduction of all communications to simple tools, devoid of meaning and devoid of all humanity. With the Taylorization of the service relationship and the automation of the Call Center operator job, productivity earnings are attained through marked increases in part-time labor agreements, but also in workers' physical fatigue, automated and repetitive actions, indifference regarding the function of tasks, vertigo caused by the multiplicity of calls, and Repetitive Stress Injuries (RSIs).

Meanwhile, the tourism and hospitality industry is one of the most dynamic components of transnational service sector activity inserting Latin America into the global economy. Tourism in the social science literature is not limited to leisure travel and may include international travel for reasons of business, government activity, professional work, and so on. English provides the conventional sociological definition that I follow here: "A Tourist is any person visiting, for at least 24 hours, a country other than that in which he or she usually resides, for any reason other than following an occupation remunerated from within the country visited. The purpose of this visit can be thus be classified under one the following headings: leisure, (recreation, holidays, health, study, religion and sports); or business, family, mission, meetings" (English, 1986:3). The more accurate phrase that captures the phenomenon explored in this section is therefore *tourism, hospitality, and travel,* although for the sake of simplicity I will here use the term "tourism."

The dramatic rise in tourist flows worldwide since the 1960s is a phenomenon of the global economy *par excellence,* a product both of the technical economic changes involved in capitalist globalization and, perhaps principally, its social implications (see, inter alia, Borocz, 1996; Mowforth and Munt, 1998; English, 1986; Harrison, 2001; Thank-Dam, 1990; *New Internationalist,* 1993). Technological developments in air transport, particularly the jet plane and cheaper and more efficient air transport systems, communications networks, computerized travel coordination, and so on, have advanced time-space compression to the point that the whole world has been brought into the purview of tourism and has made technically possible the explosion of this global service industry. New information and media technologies have globalized images and the possibilities of projecting them for tourist marketing purposes. The transnationalization of services, including banking, accommodation, transportation, along with the standardization of these services, provides any destination in the world with access to global markets for tourists and for industrial and service inputs that tourism requires.

Tourism also represents globalization in a very direct sense in that increasing global integration and interdependence involve a heightened flow of people (beyond leisure tourism) in the form of investors, workers (see next section), transnational professionals, and so forth, who move through different circuits in the global tourist, travel and hospitality infrastructure. Tourism thus became by the late twentieth century a central activity in the global economy, reportedly the largest and fastest growing industry in the world, having surpassed the oil business in the 1980s (although oil likely overtook tourism again in the wake of price hikes after 2001). Economic reactivation, trade openings, massive inflow of mobile transnational capital, and the rise of transnationally oriented elites and middle classes have given a tremendous impetus to the tourism, travel and hospitality industry. Tourism accounted in 2005 directly and indirectly for some 10.6 percent of the world GDP and for 214 million jobs, or some 8 percent of global employment, according to the World Travel and Tourism Council (WTTC), a peak industry organization (WTTC, 2005a).[3] Global tourist flows grew phenomenally from the 1960s into the twenty-first century, as shown in Table 3.10. In the early twenty-first century industry revenue had surpassed the half-a-trillion-dollar mark. It has become the fastest-growing economic activity, and even the mainstay, of many Third World nations, playing a major role in the economies of 125 of the world's 170 countries (Honey, 1999:8–9).

The tourist industry is organized as a complex and multitiered global service commodity chain connecting activities and groups from the most local and isolated tourist sites to TNC headquarters in global cities. The chain links together travel agencies and tour operators, often based in rich countries, with trans national airline, hotel, cruise line, car rental, credit card, public relations, advertising firms, along with the global media. It also brings in state and private tourism bureaus in both sending and host countries and a host of "inbound" agents, including tour operators, ground transporters, guides, accommodation and meeting facilities, national and private parks and other recreational sites, cultural and craft centers, and so on. The neo-liberal program of removing national barriers to the free movement of capital has facilitated the increasing transnationalization of local tourist and travel activity and heightened overall

---

[3] The WTTC refers to two figures in calculating the economic impact of the travel, tourism, and hospitality industry. The first is the "travel and tourism *industry*" and encompasses transportation, accommodation, catering, recreation, and services for visitors. The second is the "travel and tourism *economy*" and includes as well public and private construction, manufacturing, inputs and services provided to the industry or in order to promote the industry.

TABLE 3.10

Growth in International Tourist Arrivals and Receipts since 1950

Year	Arrivals ($million)	Receipts ($billion, constant 2004)
1950	23.3	2.1
1960	69.3	6.9
1970	165.8	17.9
1980	278.2	106.5
1985	320.2	120.8
1990	441.0	273.2
1995	538.1	411.3
2000	680.6	479.2
2002	700.4	481.6
2004	763.2	622.7
2010	940.0*	

Source: World Tourism Organization, *Tourism Market Trends*, 2005.
*Estimated.

TNC control (deregulation for instance has thrown open national air spaces to the transnational airline companies). These TNCs operate at all levels of the industry, which exhibits considerable vertical and horizontal integration and increasing concentration. The largest global hotel chains (e.g., Holiday Inns, Sheraton, Hilton International, Inter-Continental, Club Mediterranee, Hyatt International, Marriott, and so on) as well as multi-service and financial corporations often participate in car rental, tour operating, air travel, and other activities, and are themselves interpenetrated with global banking, telecommunications, food and beverage, and shipping TNCs.

The take off of the global tourist industry is not a spontaneous phenomenon or the result of uncontrolled demand. A powerful and well-organized lobby of industry representatives and transnational state institutions that are increasingly reliant on information technology and global marketing techniques have been aggressively promoting tourism since the 1960s. It has unfolded "under the impetus of a powerful tourist promotion mechanism, supported at the highest international level: the World Tourism Organization, the International Monetary Fund, the United Nations, the World Bank, UNESCO, etc.," notes Lanfant. "An intensive propaganda campaign was directed at the less developed countries, which were enjoined to place the tourist sector high on the list of priorities for their economies, to open their frontiers to tourists, to welcome foreign capital for investment in the tourist domain, and to concede tax advantages and guarantees to it" (1980:15). The industry has engaged in systematic corporate and transnational state planning aimed at producing the conditions, including induced demand, for this activity worldwide. "The tourism industry is a structure of economic institutions which strive for increasing control over space on a global scale, providing flexibility to adjust to seasonal and other variations in such increasingly valuable resources as climate, environmental conditions, and labor costs," observers Jozsef Borocz. "The tourism industry is unique . . . in the sense that the product which it markets is the very geographical, spatial, climatic, and cultural diversity of the global economy itself" (1996:13).

But the rise of a global tourist industry is above all a phenomenon of the social consequences of global capitalism, a major dimension of the relationship between the rich and the poor in global society. Tourism is a labor-intensive industry, attracted by cheap, relatively unskilled labor as chambermaids, waiters, drivers, clerks, porters, and so on, and made possible by the expansion of labor pools of the unemployed and marginalized worldwide. Under the new "global social apartheid," the structure of global production, distribution and consumption increasingly reflects a skewed income pattern, whereby since the early 1970s the income of 20 percent of world population has risen simultaneous to a decline in income among the remaining 80 percent. The expansion of the middle classes worldwide, and the integration of these middle classes into the global economy as consuming strata, has provided a tremendous impetus to global tourism. Worldwide growth should be seen as a result of the tendency toward social polarization inherent in global capitalism, and the new opportunities for accumulation that *this particular* structure of world income and demand generates. Tourism as it is practiced in global society takes for granted this division between the rich and the poor and the "right" of the wealthy to be pampered and waited on by the poor, whether their travel activities are for leisure or business. One person's leisure is another person's work, and these relations are not reciprocal.

The rise of a global tourist industry has involved the opening up of vast tracts of the Third World to international travelers. While all regions of the world experienced growth in international tourism arrivals from the 1980s into the new century, there was a redistribution of arrivals among regions, with the share of arrivals to developing countries increasing relative to developed countries, and with some regions exhibiting marked increases over others. Although Europe and the United States still account for the majority of tourist activity, the relative participation of developing countries in the industry has been increasing since the 1980s. Eight percent of all tourists in the mid-1970s were from the developed countries traveling to Third World countries. This figure had jumped to 17 percent by the mid-1980s, to 20 percent by the mid-1990s, and to some 25 percent by the new century.

The once established "pleasure periphery" that surrounded wealthy industrialized zones as nearby tourist locations, such as the Mediterranean for Northern Europe, the Caribbean and Mexico for the United States, South East Asia for Japan, and so on, has given way to more globalized forms of tourism and the opening up of more "exotic" and "risky" environments. Increasingly, high- and even middle-income strata from the developed countries have sought out these new destinations as the world becomes their playground. If the old mass tourism characterized by pre-packaged holidays to the pleasure periphery was associated with standardized Fordist accumulation, what Mowforth and Munt term the "new tourism" is situated within the transition to post-Fordist flexible modes of accumulation. Global tourism now involves "niche" or segmented markets catering to different income and "lifestyle" groups worldwide, including new middle and professional strata from the service and information sectors. These groups, disposing of increased leisure time, more flexible lifestyles, and seeking to accumulate "cultural capital," search out, in Waters's words, "the last morsels of authentic and exotic culture or of pristine environment" (1995:154). New middle-class tourist niches have been filled by new age travelers, ecotourists, trekkers, adventure tourists, small-group tourism, and other forms of "alternative tourism" (ibid.).

Moreover, the evidence suggests an increasing segmentation of, and participation in, the world tourist market in ways much more complex than a simple North-South divide. Most international tourists are still from the rich countries, but there has also been a steady if less conspicuous increase in global tourism among the rising middle classes of the Third World, as well as the rise of domestic tourist industries in all countries of the world catering to new and established high-consumption groups. Outbound tourism from Latin America to other regions of the world has increased steadily in the past few decades and surpassed 20 million tourists annually in the late 1990s, according to the World Tourism Organization, with some $20 billion in international expenditures. This underscores the increasing *transnational* character of the global tourist industry.

Tourism becomes a key conduit for the diffusion of "global culture." Whatever else, tourism, with its demonstration effects, ostentatious consumption, and association with mass advertising, diffuses the global culture of consumerism and individualism and contributes to cultural homogenization processes, in the regions of tourist origin and destination. Indeed, tourism extends the consumer culture in a literal way by redefining human cultures and practices and the physical environment as commodities. Tourism, it should be recalled, need not be a *capitalist* activity. The "social tourism" that predominated in the former Soviet-bloc countries, for instance, was not a commodified activity (see, e.g., Borocz, 1996). It is not tourism per se that converts cultures, peoples, and the environment into commodities, but *capitalist* tourism.

Tourism is an "axial product," meaning that it is the core of a wide range of related industries, goods, and services so that spin-offs can involve complex webs of economic activity and stimulate major social transformation. Unlike the maquiladora enclaves, tourism can become well integrated into local economies. But this does not mean that it necessarily makes a contribution to integrated development. The industry tends to deplete the very hard currency earnings it brings in by its high import dependence on goods and services (leakages in the Caribbean, for instance, are estimated at between 50 and 70 percent [Pattullo, 2005:51–52]). As I discuss below, the potential for linkages to local agriculture, industry and services is undercut by neoliberal programs that make it easier and cheaper to import from global supply chains than to search for local inputs. Tourism generates mostly low-skill, often menial and low-wage seasonal employment and is dependent on highly elastic and unstable demand over which host countries have very little control. The global tourist industry is highly competitive. Its contribution is unpredictable and subject to market saturation, fluctuations in supply and demand in tourism, changes in cultural fads, and so on. Elasticity and instability in tourist receipts make it impossible to assure a return on fixed investment in the industry and pit each Latin American country against the others and in competition as well with other regions in the world. A world economic downturn could quickly snuff out international demand. Tourism is also extremely vulnerable to external shocks; relative to most traded goods, it is highly vulnerable to political and other disturbances—as seen in the sudden drop after the September 2001 attacks on the World Trade Center in New York.

Tourism and Hospitality in Latin America

It is in the above-described context that Latin America has opened up to global tourism, especially since the 1990s. Broad opportunities to expand tourist infrastructure as an outlet for global investment became available with the opening of economies, macroeconomic stabilization, pacification, and transitions to "democracy." Tourist revenues are not technically an export. But tourism links the region to the global economy through numerous circuits and generates foreign exchange in the same way as exports do. Tourism should be analyzed in relation to the external sector as a quintessential example of the region's reintegration into global society. The region's pre-Colombian ruins and Spanish colonial districts, pristine Atlantic and Pacific Ocean beaches, remarkable ecological diversity, ranging from lush rain forests and aquatic systems to spectacular desert and mountain environments and volcanic landscapes, and the rich and diverse cultures and ethnicities, all make Latin America an attractive destination for international tourism. Droves of international tourists had become routine in hundreds of sites throughout the region, from the famed Incan lost city of Machu Picchu and other Inca ruins in the Andean zone, the "Ruta Maya" in Central America, Mexico's Riviera Maya, and indigenous handicraft villages, such as Otavalo in Ecuador. There is as well the more sordid side, including the rapid spread of casinos, drug trafficking, money laundering, and sex tourism. What ultimately makes the region most attractive for investors and affluent sectors of global society, however, is the availability of a cheap, servile labor force alienated from the region's abundant natural and historical endowments and from their own cultural patrimony.

As with other new transnational accumulation activities, the Latin American states have actively promoted tourism in collaboration with the local private sector and transnational capitalists. State measures have included immigration policies, infrastructure development, deregulation (such as the adoption of region-wide "open skies" policies), broad incentives for investors, international public relations campaigns, negotiating international credits for tourist projects, and so on. Most Latin American countries have established either a ministry of tourism or an official government tourist institute. Hundreds if not thousands of government, NGO, IGO, and private sector web sites promoting tourism in Latin America inundate the Internet. Table 3.11 gives an idea of the impact of the tourist, hospitality, and travel industry in Latin America. The 60 million international tourist arrivals to Latin America in 2004 surpassed the previous record of 57.6 million in 2000. The $45 billion the region generated in tourist revenue in 2004 represented 12 percent foreign exchange earnings from exports and much more for several countries and sub-regions.

Latin American tourist destinations show some of the highest growth rates in the world for tourist arrivals. Central America has proportionally experienced the most explosive growth in tourism, relative to other sub-regions. As Table 3.12 also shows, other Latin American tourist destinations have also experienced rapid growth, including Argentina, Brazil, Peru, Cuba and several other Caribbean countries. Tourist receipts also represent a very high proportion of foreign exchange earnings for Central America and a number of Caribbean

TABLE 3.11
International Tourism Arrivals and Receipts in Latin America, 2004

Sub-Region	Arrivals (in $million)	Receipts (in $billion)	Value Receipts (% exports)*
Mexico	20.6	10.7	7
Caribbean	18.2	19.1	12
Central America	5.8	3.9	35
South America	16.0	10.6	6
Total for Latin America	60.6	44.3	12
Select Individual Countries			
Argentina	3.4	2.6	9
Brazil	4.7	3.2	4
Costa Rica	1.5	1.4	20
Colombia	0.8	1.0	8
Dominican Republic	3.5	3.2	35
Cuba	2.0	1.9	33
Ecuador	0.8	0.4	7
El Salvador	1.0	0.3	25
Guatemala	1.2	0.8	31
Honduras	0.7	0.4	40
Jamaica	1.4	1.4	36
Nicaragua	0.6	0.2	33
Peru	1.2	1.1	12
Trinidad Tobago	0.4	2.5	66**

Source: World Tourism Organization, *Tourism Market Trends*, 2005.
  *Calculated on basis of ECLAC data, *Anuario Estadístico*, 2005.
  **Figures for 2003.

countries, and a rapidly expanding proportion of such revenues in Peru, Ecuador, and even Colombia, despite that country's armed conflict. The impact of the tourist industry in Latin America is hard to understate. In 2005 the sector accounted directly and indirectly (see footnote 3 above) for $104 billion or 7.6 percent of the region's total GDP, according to the WTTC (2005a). More than 12 million people were employed in the sector (nearly 5 million directly), representing some 7.3 percent of total employment, or one in every 13 jobs. It also accounted for 10.4 percent of total regional capital investment and nearly 3 percent of all government expenditures.

Mexico is the top tourist destination in Latin America (and the eighth-largest worldwide), with over 20 million arrivals in 2004, abut a third of the 60.5 million total visitors to the region, while the Caribbean drew in the highest amount of tourist revenues in that year, $19.1 billion, or 43 percent of the regional total. Mexico, Brazil, the Dominican Republic, and Argentina are the top four national markets in terms of tourism receipts. In relative terms, however, Central America and the Caribbean are the most highly impacted by the industry. I will take a brief look here at these two regions and at some of the other countries where the industry has a growing impact.

TABLE 3.12
Average Annual Growth (%) of Tourist Receipts and Arrivals, Latin America, 1990–2000, Latin America, Sub-Regions and Select Countries, and in World

	Arrivals		Receipts	
	1990–95	1995–2000	1990–95	1995–2000
Sub-Regions				
Mexico	3.3	0.4	2.3	6.1
Caribbean	4.2	4.0	7.0	7.0
Central America	6.1	10.7	15.7	14.7
South America	8.7	5.4	7.6	5.3
Select Countries				
Argentina	3.5	4.9	14.5	5.5
Brazil	21.8	21,7	–8.2	13.2
Chile	10.3	2.5	11.0	–2.1
Colombia	11.5	–16.8	10.1	9.4
Costa Rica	12.5	6.7	19.9	13.8
Cuba	17.8	18.6	31.7	12.5
Ecuador	4.0	7.3	6.3	9.5
El Salvador	3.9	27.6	36.4	20.6
Guatemala	2.0	8.0	5.2	17.5
Honduras	–1.3	11.6	22.5	26.6
Nicaragua	21.5	11.6	33.0	20.9
Peru	7.0	12.4	14.6	16.3
World	4.1	4.8	n/a	n/a

Source: World Trade Organization, *Tourism Market Trends,* 2005.

CENTRAL AMERICA

As the 1980s Central America military and political upheavals wound down in the early 1990s, local and transnational elites turned their attention to economic reconstruction. They proposed the expansion of tourism as a chief activity that could provide new opportunities for economic growth and insertion into global markets (see, e.g., World Tourism Organization, 1988). Ecotourism in particular made the region a new "hot spot." The strategy called for carving out a special niche within the global tourist market for the region by promoting its impressive pre-Colombian archeological sites and present day indigenous cultures and ecological preserves, along with the more routine attractions of tropical beaches, forests, and rivers. By the early 1990s the IFIs and other international agencies were providing diverse support for the establishment of the tourist industry, ranging from loans, to technical support and training programs, feasibility studies, and so on (Barrera Pérez, 1998).

As noted earlier, tourism is not limited to leisure travel, which may be the less important of the different travel categories subsumed under the definition. The more profound connection between tourism and globalization has often been missed by tourism researchers, and has to do with the tremendous increase in cross-border social intercourse and worldwide travel that the process of economic globalization itself generates. In Central America, reconstruction in wake of the regional conflict gave rise to a tremendous surge in the tourism, hospitality, and travel industry as a necessary infrastructure for economic reactivation, and this would have been the case even if leisure tourism had not been promoted. The region became inundated with foreign investors and business people, participants at peace conferences, professionals arriving to network, officials from the IFIs, United Nations and other agencies, development workers, bureaucrats from NGOs, and so on. These conditions of reactivation and integration into the newly globalized economy created a huge demand for expansion of the industry. Recognizing that international tourism requires peace and security, the five governments launched an international public relations campaign to transform the region's image from one of a zone of war and conflict to one of beaches, archeological ruins, lush tropical preserves, and hospitable meeting facilities (Robinson, 2003).

By 2004 regional tourism receipts surpassed the $3 billion mark, up from just $1 billion ten years earlier. Tourism employed directly some 574,000 salaried workers and indirectly over one million, or over 8 percent of the regional workforce. Tourism displaced bananas in 1994 as Costa Rica's principal source of foreign exchange receipts and became in the 1990s the second most important source in Guatemala, and the third in Nicaragua and Honduras (Robinson, 2003). The following advertisement on an industry website is indicative of the "branding" of the Isthmus as an exotic and wild place waiting to be discovered:

DISCOVER CENTRAL AMERICA: Central America is the backpacker's ultimate fantasy and ultimate challenge. The nascent tourist industry leaves room for exploring the road less traveled, and therein lies the catch—getting from place to place becomes an adventure in and of itself. Central America's seven countries are only a quarter of Mexico's size, but the diverse topography, culture, ecology, and activities coexist nowhere else in the world. Within the narrow isthmus, rainforest, volcanoes, coral reefs, and beaches await alongside Maya ruins. Largely marginalized and somewhat feared by travelers in past decades, Central American countries are finally emerging from years of violent political instability into a relatively peaceful period. All have democratic governments, and the wounds left by the once-prevalent civil wars are slowly healing. Once the destination only of bold (or foolhardy) adventurers, today's Central America—inexpensive and compact—is the budget traveler's new frontier. (*Let's Go*, 2006)

As a regional pacesetter, Costa Rica provides a good illustration of tourism within the globalization process. In the 1980s, the government began to invest seriously in tourism as part of its export diversification policies. The government offered tax, import, exchange, credit and other incentives for large national and foreign investors, complemented by a $15 million publicity campaign to attract foreign tourists and the construction of an international airport in the northern city of Liberia to shuttle visitors directly from abroad to tourist sites. The industry soon overtook agro-exports as the primary foreign exchange earner. The country boasted of 79 "ecolodges" and many smaller preserves, hostels, and attractions catering to "ecotourists" (Honey, 1999:131). But the government's policies also included a campaign to attract foreign investment in luxury resort projects, most notable, the Pacific coast Papagayo megaresort project, undertaken by Mexican, Costa Rica, and other international investors and billed as the Cancun of Central America. By the twenty-first century, beach resorts lined Costa Rica's coasts, many of them owned by transnational firms. In contrast to large investors, small-scale entrepreneurs were not eligible for state incentives, with the result that a two-tiered industry structure emerged, with small-scale tourist operations catering to less affluent visitors and passing on most profit to national and transnational tour operators and other service providers.

All five Central American countries in the 1990s were engaged in major tourist expansion projects. For instance, thirty-eight new tourist projects were under way in Nicaragua in 1997 alone (Barrera Pérez, 1998:51). Guatemala underwent a boom in hotel construction as the industry took off following the signing of the peace accords in December 1996. The Hyatt Regency opened in Guatemala its first hotel in Central America late that year, followed by Inter-Continental, Radisson, Choice Hotel International, Quinta Real, and Holiday Inn, among others, along with a $7 million International Meeting and Convention Center built by Camino Real (ibid.). Guatemala teamed up with El Salvador, Honduras, Mexico, and Belize to develop the "Ruta Maya" (Mayan Route), an international tourist circuit of ecological and archeological attractions centered on the ancient Mayan city of Tikal, in Guatemala's northern Peten jungle. Honduras, too, was investing in the development of the Coban archeological site and in the Caribbean coastline. Although El Salvador trailed behind, the number of visitors jumped by 50 percent in the early 1990s and the government expected that its Pacific beaches, considered to be some of the best surfing in the Americas, would be a major selling point for the industry's expansion.

The international financial and development agencies have long argued that tourism is an industry "without chimneys" that requires relatively low initial capital investment. But many studies have shown that the capacity for tourism to contribute to development is linked to the twin issues of its multiplier effect or "linkages" and of "leakages." Underdevelopment theory has pointed out that the more industrialized and diversified a country or region is to begin with, the more it will be able to supply within its borders the diverse inputs into the tourist sectors, thereby generating multiplier effects on the economy as a whole, including expanding employment opportunities outside of the tourist sector itself. Low levels of prior development, by contrast, minimize the multiplier effects and generate "leakages" whereby tourist dollars will tend to go toward imports to sustain the tourist industry and satisfy tourist demand and to other factor payments abroad, such as profit remittances and fees, so that the major portion of tourist earnings will end up being captured by transnational capital or going to the TNCs that control air travel and the tour operators and travel agents who organize and coordinate the global tourist traffic.

It would be a mistake, however, to characterize these arrangements, in Latin America or elsewhere in the Third World, along the old dependency theory lines of metropolitan capital dominating local economies with the support of comprador groups. The problem of leakages, for instance, takes on a distinct meaning once we move beyond the nation-state centrism of traditional underdevelopment theory. The wealth generated in the global economy is not "leaked" back to the metropolitan country but appropriated by transnational capital, which may circulate it anywhere around the world. The majority of international hotel services in the Third World, for instance, are now linked to the TNC hotel chains: 75 percent in the Middle East, 72 percent in Africa, 60 percent in Asia, and 47 percent in Latin America (Honey, 1999:38). But the TNC hotel chains rarely engage in direct ownership and management. Rather, most arrangements involve local investors who sign some combination of management contracts or leasing, franchise, or technical service agreement. These are precisely the same mechanisms applied by a TNC chain to exercise control over local groups when it sets up a hotel in any First World country. The local groups occupy the same structural location within the chain: they are subject to the same TNC control and must levy a tribute to the TNC irrespective of whether they are located in the First of the Third World (on the major contractual mechanisms used by the chains, see Mowforth and Munt, 1998:192, Box).

Moreover, large-scale transnational and national capital is not the only industry investor. Historical and cultural centers, such as the indigenous towns of

Atitlán and Quetzaltenango in Guatemala, the famed Inca/Quechua city of Cuzco in Peru, the colonial city of Granada and ocean community of San Juan del Sur in Nicaragua, and San Pedro de Atacama in Chile, among others, attract urban entrepreneurs anxious to invest in their country's expanding tourist sectors. They also attract foreigners and assorted travelers-cum-expatriates with limited investment capital enamored with what they perceive as quaint and exotic localities. Alongside transnational capital, these groups buy up storefronts and main streets, converting them into "tourist ghettos" of handicraft outlets, boutiques, Internet cafés, on-site tour operators, bars and restaurants. Some locals acquire their own establishments as well and join the ranks of the local entrepreneurial group even as many are displaced. Those displaced become workers in the local tourist trade, home-based suppliers of "authentic" handicraft, ambulant street vendors, scavengers, or transnational migrants (see next section and Chapter 4).

Tourism reorganizes and transnationalizes social structure in ways that redefine the relationships between different groups spanning both "host" and "sender" countries. New productive activities and social relations may bring gains to some groups caught up in changing structures and disadvantages to others. Even for the least developed countries discussed in England's notable study on tourism and North-South relations, money spent by tourists for goods and services supplied in these recipient countries remained to remunerate local labor, landowners, and capitalists, suggesting that tourism may generate substantial benefits for some local groups. The notion popularized in the underdevelopment literature of tourism as a form of colonialism is valid insofar as it refers to the colonization—for the purpose of providing services and making profits—of some social groups in global society by others, but not some nations by others. Global tourism reflects the domination of the rich over the poor in global society. But it is increasingly inaccurate to characterize this in nation-state centric terms as the domination of an imperialist core over the periphery (on such depictions of tourism as colonialism, see Britton, 1982; Nash, 1989). As with NTAEs and the maquiladoras, tourism reshapes local social structure in ways that generate local winners and losers. It contributes to the overall process of social stratification among groups as defined by their relationship to the global economy and society. The tourist industry in each region is part of the larger structures of a globalized economy whose salient social contradiction, I have argued, is polarization between groups within a transnational environment.

Applying these observations to Central America, there is much evidence to suggest that a good portion of the transnational tourist industry in the Isthmus involves substantial participation by local capitalist groups. In Guatemala four of five new luxury hotels built by transnational firms in the mid-1990s were franchised out to local investors, many of them new entrants into the industry (Austin, 1996). Much hotel and resort construction in Nicaragua in the 1990s was in the hands of local entrepreneurs who invited the participation of transnational capital (Spritzer, 1994). In addition, "outbound" tour operators often located abroad subcontract with "inbound" operators in host countries to handle a wide array of services. Such subcontracting arrangements are becoming more diverse and widespread as the new tourism spreads and the industry becomes more flexible and decentralized. These instances foment the formation of transnational groups at the local level. Affinities of interests develop that transcend national boundaries. In Central America—indicative of the region as a whole— the tourist industry has generated benefits for established local investors and new entrepreneurial groups as well as for professionals, middle strata, and some enterprising poor people, who have set up throughout Central America Spanish language schools, interpreting, translation, and personalized consulting firms, guest houses, cultural centers, commercial outlets for local arts and crafts and other cultural products, local tour packages, and so on, to cater to the legions of leisure tourists, business callers, and related international visitors. These groups are not lackeys of imperial capital but agents of new economic opportunities opened up by the integration of Central America into the global economy and the elevated cross border flow of human beings it brings.

As tourism spreads around the world it opens up new regions to commercial exploitation and draws local communities into expanding market relations. The industry is incorporating hitherto isolated or at least more autonomous communities into the global market and bringing far more of the items these communities produce into that market. As physical environments and human communities are brought into market relations they are transformed. Peasant and indigenous lands in Central America, the Peruvian highlands around Cuzco-Machu Picchu-Sacred Valley circuit, the desert communities of Atacama in Chile, and so on, are commodified. "Ecotourist," archeological, and aesthetic sites become commercial properties. Local art, crafts, and other cultural products are mass produced as tourist art. Local producers are proletarianized, converted into workers in new hotels, restaurants, resorts, transportation systems, security and consulting firms, and tour companies. Local communities and indigenous populations in particular are objectified as tropical curiosities in what often amounts to a socio-cultural colonialism (see, e.g., UNEP, 2002). This particular model of local social polarization, collective degradation and cultural alienation is not always the case. Some communities may be able to gain greater control over the local tourist trade and reap more equitably distributed benefits, as I will discuss in the next chapter. But it does hold for dozens of localities I visited throughout the Andes, Central America and parts of Mexico while conducting research for this book between 2004 and 2006.

Tourism foments land speculation, with its predictable consequences, among them the commodification of peasant and community lands and a rise in land values. These effects are acute because most tourist sites are developed not in established zones of agro-export production but in areas previously marginalized economically, such as agricultural frontiers and less accessible or populated backwaters that served as outlets for displaced rural populations. For example, in order to promote tourism along Honduras's North Atlantic coastal area, a major regional attraction due to its lush beaches, tropical coral reefs, and inland Mayan ruins, the government in 1999 lifted constitutional provisions that prohibited the sale to foreigners of land along the country's borders and coasts. The changes opened the way for developers and speculators to grab up lands along the coast. The militant protests by indigenous and Afro-Caribbean groups threatened with a loss of their lands were met by government repression (LADB, 1999).

In Nicaragua, places such as San Juan del Sur, a humble fishing and farming community that saw few foreigners when I frequented its pristine beaches in the 1980s, has been converted into a major international tourist attraction by foreign and local investor groups, including Sandinistas-cum-capitalists. As luxury hotels, vacation homes and gated condominium complexes sprouted up, the place became a favorite destination for North American retirees and tourist adventurers, a haven for light-skinned surfers, and a regional golfing and spa mecca in the making. Local property values doubled from 2003 to 2006 alone as transnational real estate companies such as Century 21, Coldwell Banker, and REMAX set up shop (Kurtz-Phelan, 2006). Predictably, much of the local population has been displaced, converted into troupes of workers for the tourist industry, farm hands, maids, gardeners, vagrants and unemployed.

ECOTOURISM: SUSTAINABLE DEVELOPMENT OR "GREENWASH"?

"Ecotourism" became a buzzword in the 1990s—the most rapidly expanding sector of world tourism. The industry advertised Central America's famed biodiversity in order to market the region as a major global site for green tourism. Costa Rica during the 1980s went from a low-key destination for tourists seeking natural preserves and quiet beaches to the foremost ecotourist destination in the Americas. The other Central American countries followed suit and jumped on the bandwagon in the 1990s. Ecotourism is billed as a component of "sustainable development," a highly contested concept that has been the focal point of political and ideological struggles in the globalization process (see Robinson, 2003, chapter 6). It is sold as a means to protect and preserve the environment while at the same time empowering poor communities. By the 1990s, environmental organizations had joined the tourist industry and international financial and development agencies in heralding ecotourism as the panacea that would conserve fragile ecosystems, benefit rural communities, instill environmental awareness, and promote development. The Ecotourism Society has defined ecotourism as: "Responsible travel to natural areas that conserves the environment and improves the well-being of local people" (as cited in Honey, 1999:6). There is no reason why in the abstract tourism and protection of the environment cannot operate in tandem. Historic sites and buildings, such as Mayan ruins in Guatemala and Honduras and colonial districts in Nicaraguan cities, have been rehabilitated as tourist attractions, and increased public awareness of environmental issues have come about as a result of ecotourism and the broader concept of sustainable development.

However, TNS functionaries have situated ecotourism within the larger strategy of capitalist globalization, emphasizing the central role of the private sector in developing ecotourism projects, the privatization of public tourist facilities, and policies to attract transnational investment capital into local projects. These functionaries and industry representatives claim that by making the environment a commodity the self-interest of the tourist industry would assure that its "assets" did not decline and would prompt a sustainable approach to environmental resources. They also claimed that it would save land and culture by offering income-earning opportunities to local communities who would otherwise engage in depredation of local resources through misuse or expansion of the agricultural frontier into virgin areas. But this claim ignores that depredation of the environment and the expansion of the agricultural frontier is the result of capitalist development itself, which converts nature into an exchange value, displaces local communities, and shifts resources from them to new capitalist enterprises that tend to deploy environmentally destructive production systems and externalize the costs.

Ecotourism in actual practice has provided a convenient "green" cover for practices that result in further degradation both of fragile ecosystems and of the conditions of poor and marginalized human communities (for critiques of ecotourism, see McLaren, 2003; Honey, 1999; Mowforth and Munt, 1998; Pattullo,

2005, chapter 5). Much "green" tourism, moreover, in reality is little more than a crude marketing ploy, what Honey has euphemistically termed "ecotourism Lite" or "greenwash." For instance, hotels and tour operators sell as "ecotourism" token measures that may be pleasing to "new age travelers" seeking to reconcile their pursuit of pleasure and cultural capital with concern over the environment. These measures may include a brief walk through a rain forest, not changing hotel guests' sheets and towels every day, using recycled-paper menus in restaurants or biodegradable soap in bathrooms, placing recycling bins in lobbies, and so on. Tourism in Central America and Mexico has been billed as "ecotourism" simply because it is related to nature and distinct from the "Four S's" of conventional tourism (sun, sea, sand, and sex), from excursions in Nicaragua into forests or lakes, to a glass-bottom boat ride over coral reefs off Honduras's Caribbean coast, white-water rafting in Costa Rica, and visits in Guatemala and Mexico to archeological ruins in the countryside, irrespective of the social or environmental impact of this activity and the broader principles of ecotourism (for examples, see Honey, 1999; McLaren, 2003; Pattullo, 2005). At its worst, ecotourism becomes a mere cover for expanding the transnational tourist industry into areas previously outside its purview and bringing previously undeveloped areas into the global market.

The creation of preserves in Central America, Mexico, the Amazonian lowlands along the Andean zone, and elsewhere, often means the removal, sometimes forcible, of people from their lands, followed by the turning over of these preserves to private capitalists to be developed and converted into profit-making ventures. In Costa Rica, Chile, Peru, Mexico and elsewhere, the number of private reserves created by wealthy foreigners rose sharply, numbering hundreds by the end of the 1990s. In Belize, promoted as one of the foremost ecotourist destinations worldwide, an estimated 90 percent of all coastal developments were bought up by foreigners in the 1980s and 1990s (Pattullo, 2005:152). Private reserves held by foreign individuals and TNCs in Costa Rica cover an estimated 5 percent of the country's territory (see Honey, 1999; McLaren, 2003). As is typical with the spread of tourism more generally, land prices have shot up in the areas surrounding these reserves with the frequent result that small landowners have been forced to sell. Stonich and her colleagues, studying the costs and benefits of eco and other forms of tourist development on Honduras's Caribbean coast, found similar results: increased social differentiation, reduced access for local people to land and other resources, escalating prices and land speculation, and a deterioration of the local ecosystem (Stonich et al., 1995). The same results have also been found in numerous studies on the Mayan communities in Guatemala and Mexico, and indigenous communities the Peruvian highlands, who take no part, beyond low-cost labor, in the development of a tourist circuit whose principal local contribution seems to be the degradation of indigenous villages that it brings. (see, e.g., Mowforth and Munt, 1998:239–242).

THE CARIBBEAN

The tourist trade has nearly become a way of life for the some 40 million people who live on the islands of two archipelagos that mark off the Caribbean as a 2,000-mile arch stretching from Florida to the Venezuelan coast, since the decline of the region's traditional plantation economies in the wake of World War II and independence from colonial masters. Mass tourism dates back to the early 1960s with the arrival of long-haul, non-stop international jet services. But the industry has expanded dramatically since the 1980s, promoted by the World Bank and other agencies of the TNS as the solution to the crisis that began the previous decade. In just ten years, from 1990 to 2000, over 100,000 rooms were added to the Caribbean hotel capacity, a 66 percent increase (WTTC, 2005a, 2005b country reports). Along with this land-based tourism the Caribbean cruise business has boomed: passenger arrivals increased from 7.8 million in 1990 to over 20 million in 2004 as the handful of giant cruise companies that dominate the industry introduced a new generation of megaships (Pattullo, 2005:195). The tourist economy in the Caribbean by 2004 had come to generate an astounding 2.4 million jobs directly and indirectly. It accounted for 15.5 percent of total employment in the area and nearly 15 percent of the regional GDP and absorbed almost 22 percent of all capital investments (WTTC, 2005a, 2005b country reports).

The most significant trend has been the rise of the so-called Hispanic Caribbean—Cuba, the Dominican Republic, and Puerto Rico—as major players in the industry. The two most populace islands in the Caribbean, Cuba and the Dominican Republic—with a population of 11 million and 8.5 million, respectively—accounted for nearly 25 percent of all tourists to the region by the early twenty-first century. For Cuba, international tourism represents one of the nodal points for a strategy of regulated integration into the global economy, along with sugar and nickel exports and more recent biotechnology, medical, and pharmaceutical services. The explosive development of the tourist industry led to a tripling of the number of hotel rooms in Cuba in the ten years from 1990 to 2000 as arrivals jumped from a negligible amount to 2 million in 2004 (Pattullo, 2005:33). Similarly, the Dominican Republic's transformation from a sugar export economy to one based on maquiladora manufacturing, NTAEs, and tourism has been nothing less than spectacular. Arrivals grew from 63,000 in 1970 to 3.5 million in 2004. The north coast of the Dominican Republic has become a tourist mecca with the opening of a state-of the-art international airport in nearby Puerto Plata in 1983.

This heightened intrusion of tourism has resulted in the predictable uprooting of local Caribbean communities whose residents are converted into new global proletarians, either working for the tourist economy or transnational immigrant workers in North America, Europe, or more prosperous Latin American countries. There is "a certain irony in the fact that tourists began to arrive in the Caribbean in greater numbers just as the poor of the Caribbean began their own more onerous journey, in the opposite direction, to find work," observes Pattullo. "For those who stayed, the chosen alternative was to turn primarily agricultural economies into pastures for pleasuring the leisured" (2005:8). And just as predictably, the booms in residential developments of villas and apartments for sale and rent brought by tourism affects the availability and the price of land, "not only putting it out of the reach of local people, but also reducing the pool of land for agriculture and other uses" (2005:42–43):

> In one generation the coming of tourism has changed the pattern of employment and the structure of communities for ever. Peasant economies have been molded into service sectors where cane-cutters become bellhops and fishermen are turned into "watersport officers." The slide away from agriculture into the service sector . . . looks dramatic. Rural communities, first dislocated by migration, now find that the young move to the tourism-dominated coastal areas looking for casual work in the way that in other parts of the world they drift to the cities. Traditional life patterns are altered as women become wage earners, often for the first time, in the hotel sector where the demand for domestic work is high. Economic interests become more stratified with the higher-class locals identifying with the tourist interests and better able to exploit the opportunities offered by foreign capital and personnel than the unskilled majority. (Pattullo, 2005:66)

It is impossible to talk about tourism in the Caribbean separate from the context of race, colonialism and the legacy of slavery that is etched into Caribbean society. The great anti-colonial essayist, Martinique-born Frantz Fanon, observed in his classic *The Wretched of the Earth* that tourism recreated the labor relations of slavery and the colonial situation. The Trinidadian-born Nobel Laureate V. S. Naipaul argued in *The Middle Passage*, "Every poor country accepts tourism as an unavoidable degradation. None has gone as far as some of these

West Indian islands, which, in the name of tourism, are selling themselves into a new slavery" (2002:210). The racialized nature of tourism in the Caribbean is overlaid with class and is reflected, beyond mostly light-skinned tourists served by Afro-Caribbeans, in a distribution of benefits from the industry that go disproportionately to lighter-skinned elites and industry workers and professionals. However, the image of a racial metropolitan domination of Caribbean colonies does not capture the global capitalist relations of race and class at play in the industry. Transnational investors from beyond Europe and North America are deeply involved in Caribbean tourism as are local investors, including several large groups with a regional and even a global reach. The Iranian businessman Pascal Mahvi is one of the larger foreign investors in the region, through his Swiss-based M Group Corporation, while Sandals and Super Clubs, both founded and run by Jamaican capitalists, control major tourist interests throughout the region, market their facilities around the world, and have collaborative arrangements with TNCs (Pattullo, 2005). Moreover, while most tourists are still light-skinned peoples of European descent an increasing number of tourists arrive from elsewhere in Latin America and the world and from Caribbean countries themselves (ibid.).

Perhaps the most alarming example of racialization processes at work in the Caribbean tourist industry comes from Cuba, where the revolutionary government had previously made major advances at overcoming the legacy of 500 years of slavery and racial inequality and in creating an egalitarian and color blind society (for works on race in revolutionary Cuba, see, inter–alia, De la Fuente, 2001; Sawyer, 2005). Despite these advances, race has continued to shape social relations and cultural processes, in part because the Cuban government itself suppressed critical debate on the issue after the early post-revolutionary years in the name of national unity against external (U.S.) aggression (ibid.). With the collapse of the former socialist bloc and the country's inexorable entrance into the global capitalist economy the government developed a number of policies to cope with the crisis that ensued, including austerity, the opening of a parallel dollar economy, the introduction, however limited, of a market (value) logic, and the creation of a commercial tourist sector for international visitors. There is widespread and convincing evidence, observes De la Fuente (2000, 2001), that these policies resulted in racially differentiated effects, especially in tourism. Many Afro-Cubans worked in tourism before it became reoriented from the internal to the world market but blacks and mulattos are abysmally underrepresented in new tourist sector jobs—which involve direct contact with (often light-skinned) foreigners and in which the opportunities for supplemental income via tips and gifts are greater. "Cubans explain blacks' low presence in tourist jobs using various arguments, all of which more or less openly imply that Afro-Cubans are unattractive, dirty, prone to critical activities, inefficient or lack proper manners and education," observes De la Fuente. "The most frequent argument revolves around the concept of a 'pleasant aspect' (*buena presencia*), a racialized construct that claims that blacks cannot be hired for these jobs due to aesthetic considerations and to the alleged preferences of the tourists" (2001:32). De la Fuente cites testimonies compiled by Cuban researchers Rafael Duharte and Elsa Santos. "The absence of blacks in tourism is . . . an aesthetic question, even though this is not the most important factor," states one informant. "The main thing is that they are entertaining white tourists. . . . These white tourists may or may not be racist. Then, why risk anything, if this is business? You employ only whites and there is no problem." Another acknowledges that "there is an aesthetic criterion in the selection . . . which favors whites. In my company, out of 60 workers three are black." The manager of one tourist company concedes that they only employ five blacks in a labor force of 500; "there is no explicit policy stating that one has to be white to work in tourism, but it is regulated that people must have a pleasant aspect, and blacks do not have it" (as cited in De la Fuente, 2001:33). The denial of access by blacks to tourist jobs means, in turn, that this social group has less access to the dollar economy and the goods and services it offers, thus generated new forms of material inequality and accompanying social and cultural discrimination.

More broadly, the reemerging tourist industry in Cuba practiced a virtual economic and social apartheid, as Pattullo (2005) has charged, barring Cubans from restaurants, bars, nightclubs, hotels and 'dollar' shops, unless accompanied by foreigners. But perhaps the most blatant form of dispossession in the tourist trade are the so-called all-inclusives: resorts in which air and ground transport, accommodation, food, drink, and entertainment are all packaged and prepaid, often in the tourist's home country. All-inclusives are spreading throughout many countries in Latin America as they gobble up privatized prime lands, beaches, and nature sites. Resort security at facilities bar the entrance to all but paid guests, identified with a plastic wristband. Non-guests must buy a prohibitively expensive day pass to access the premises. Whole areas, their natural and cultural attractions and commercial facilities such as restaurants, shops, and entertainments spots are off-limits to local populations who become unwelcome strangers in their own land. As one popular St. Lucian calypso puts it: "All-inclusive tax elusives / And truth is / They're sucking up we juices / Buying up every strip of beach / Every treasured spot they reach / Like an alien / In we own land / What's the point of progress / Is it really success / If we gain ten billion / But lose the land we live on" (as cited in Pattullo, 2005:101–102).

Peru, Mexico, Other Issues

These patterns of transnational tourism in the Caribbean and Central America are replicated throughout the region. Transnational tourism has been one of the leading activities integrating Peru into the global economy since the defeat of the Shining Path guerrilla insurgency and the introduction of the neoliberal program in the early 1990s. From 386,000 international tourist arrivals in 1994, the country received 1.2 million just ten years later. Tourism became in 2005 the largest single earner of foreign exchange, generating close to 800,000 jobs or 7.6 percent of total employment and $6 billion in economic activity. There has been a sustained wave of investment in the tourism sector: by 2005 capital investment reached $1.5 billion, or 10.6 percent of total investment that year (WTTC, 2005b, Peru country report). Transnational hotel chains came to dot the skyline in upscale Lima neighborhoods such as San Isidro and Miraflores. As elsewhere, much of this investment brought together local and foreign capitalists. London-based Orient Express Hotels, Ltd, for instance, one of the biggest investors in the country's tourist sector, entered into partnership with Peruval, a consortium of local tourist industry groups to buy up and renovate hotel properties and lodges in Lima, Cuzco, Machu Picchu and other sites (Palic, 2002). Another major investor is the Peruvian company Inka Terra, S.A.C. With World Bank backing, it has acquired hotels and tourist infrastructure around the country, ranging from the Cuzco-Machu Picchu zone to the Madre de Dios rain forest in the Amazonia and the Lake Titicaca area in the Andes (IFC, 2000). And the state sold its tourist train rails to a consortia of local and international investors who set up PeruRail as a joint undertaking. The tourist boom resulted in over one million visitors to Machu Picchu and surrounding sites in 2005 yet few benefits reached local communities, which remain some of the poorest in Peru (Peru's Challenge, 2005).[4]

---

[4] The degradation and alienation brought by the tourist trade was apparent to me during a 2004 visit through Peru's transnational tourist circuits (see also UNEP, 2002). As troops of light-skinned tourists descended upon Machu Picchu—a UNESCO World Heritage site—they feasted on $20 per person lunch buffets offered in the Sanctuary Lodge just outside the ruins and owned by Oriente Express Hotels. Everywhere, tourists were surrounded by ubiquitous Peruvian indigenous attendants (drivers, waiters, tour escorts, porters, shoe shiners) and accosted by droves of street vendors pedaling handicrafts, desperate for a single sale. The ride in the PeruRail line from Machu Picchu featured an almost surreal fashion show by the mestizo train attendants who modeled European designer clothes and paraded up and down the aisles to the tune of European fusion music and then offered these

Mexico's opening to the global economy from the late 1980s and on facilitated a massive wave of investments, both local and foreign, in the tourist industry and a sharp increase in tourist arrivals and revenues, this latter figure nearly doubling from 1990 to 2004. In the same period the number of four- and five-star hotel rooms available increased by two-thirds, from 383,000 to 638,000 (Secretaria de Turismo, 2005). Travel and tourism in Mexico generated in 2005 over one trillion dollars in economic activity, accounting for 14.5 percent of GDP and 4.1 million jobs, or over 14 percent of total employment (WTTC, 2005b, Mexico country report). In 2003 tourism overtook oil as a source of foreign exchange earnings, although this relationship reversed in 2005 as oil prices climbed. A glimpse of what the tourist trade means for Mexico's poor and indigenous is provided by sociologist Molly Talcott, who was based in southern Mexico when Hurricane Wilma hit the Cancun Caribbean coastal resort in late 2005:

> The social geography of the pre-Wilma Cancun was one of near apartheid-like conditions: the only Mexicans to be found on the *zona hotelera* beaches were those serving the cold margaritas and cervezas the flight attendant promised us. In fact, this form of segregation in the name of "economic development" was pointed out by many protesting Mexicanos at the Cancun 2003 World Trade Organization meetings. In the post-Wilma space of Cancun, such vastly unequal social relations are evident in an even more drastic contrast: the tourists whose Caribbean vacations were interrupted—the tourists who went from lounging in five-star luxury beachfront hotels to being holed up in public shelters—will soon head home and probably will not return for some time. Yet, fully one million Cancun residents have been rendered homeless. Ninety percent of the city's building has been damaged. In the meantime, *La Jornada* [a leading Mexican daily, October 23, 2005, p. 37, as referenced by Talcott, 2005] reports that shelter residents have been grouped into two categories and treated accordingly: the "five-star" class of tourists are receiving three meals a day and blankets, while the largely Mayan indigenous locals are being given water and crackers. (Talcott, 2005)

Gender relations form part of the larger social relations and practices embodied in tourism. As Kinnaird and her colleagues remind us, tourism practices as power relations are gendered in their construction, presentation, and consumption (Kinnaird and Hall, 1994). Men and women have different access

---

upscale clothing items for sale, as the train chugged along through a region in which 80 percent of the population, largely Quechua, faces poverty, malnutrition, and rampant unemployment.

to the employment opportunities opened up by tourism, which are often gender specific and are based on existing and new sexual divisions of labor. Recent studies have shown that women are generally confined to less stable, unskilled, and low-paid work, such as kitchen staff, chambermaids, and cleaners, a finding entirely consistent with the patterns exhibited in the maquiladora industry and in the NTAE and other new globalized sectors. Other studies indicate that as countries have increased efforts to promote tourism, sex tourism has risen proportionally (Hannum, 2002). While sex tourism is increasing worldwide (Thank-Dam, 1990) it has experienced the most rapid growth in Latin America in step with the promotion of tourism as a development strategy and encouraged by the way that the tourist industry has commercialized and gendered sexual images. Sex tourism has become a multi-billion dollar industry that supports an international workforce estimated to number in the millions (Hannum, 2002), symbolic of the globalization of a sex market generated by the extreme inequalities of income and power in global society, as poverty and vulnerability force people into sex work.

Brazil has long been seen as the region's leader, but as Hannum (2002) reports, Central America emerged in the early twenty-first century as the most significant magnet for sex tourism. This type of tourism has taken off in tandem with the influx of tens of thousands of U.S. and Canadian men, "sex-pats," or expatriates who have retired to the region—especially Costa Rica—not just for tax breaks, the climate and the good life, but for easy access to sexual objects. More alarming is the spread of child sex tourism: again, particularly in Central America. The End Pornography and Trafficking of Children for Sexual Purposes (ECPAT), an international NGO working to end child prostitution, estimates that more than one million children worldwide enter the sex trade annually, many of them from Latin American countries (as cited in Hannum, 2002). The ECPAT estimates that some 500,000 children in Brazil may be involved in the sex trade, and thousands in Colombia, Costa Rica, the Dominican Republic, Honduras, Guatemala, and elsewhere. Sex tourism is rising sharply in a number of Caribbean countries, among them the Dominican Republic, Cuba, and Jamaica (Kempadoo, 1999; Brennan, 2002). Increasingly prevalent as well in the Caribbean is male sex tourism and "holiday romances" with local poor men on the ply for more affluent First World women who in turn are able to exercise power in a sexual liaison in a way they are unable to back home (Kempadoo, 1999; Pattullo, 2005).

Tourism is to a considerable extent marketed based on image and the management of fantasy pitched to the psychological and cultural proclivities of the potential tourist market. Middle-class tourists are interested in arms-length representation, aestheticized poverty and contrived authenticity that filter out the real world of human rights violations, violent inequalities, deeply rooted racism and intense class and political conflict in Latin America. Tourists often have little or no knowledge of, or interest in, local cultures and history, much less the socioeconomic plight or collective aspirations of local populations. Some of these bring with them a contemptuous sense of entitlement and an arrogance of privilege.[5] The social and cultural relations between visitors and hosts reflect the larger global relations of inequality and domination into which they are inserted, highly gendered and often racialized, as wealth and poverty are brought into direct proximity. Workers in the typical tourist resort in Latin America that earn $1,200 to $3,000 annually, observes one United Nations report, attend to guests whose yearly income is in excess of $80,000. Even though these tourist workers generally earn higher wages that the national average their entire annual salary would not likely be enough to spend two weeks as a guest in the very resorts where they work (UNEP, 2002). These inequalities generate a heightened sense of relative deprivation at a time when global communications have etched the reality of poverty amidst plenty into mass consciousness everywhere. Under these conditions tourism invites heightened social control systems, including the appearance of special "tourist police" in many Latin American countries and gated facilitates to cordon off the tourist from the local population.

The Export of Labor and Import of Remittances

The age of globalization is also an age of unprecedented transnational migration (see, inter alia, Castles and Miller, 2003; Stalker, 2000; Cohen, 1988; Harris, 1995; Potts, 1990). The corollary to the rise of an integrated global economy is the rise of a truly global—although highly segmented—labor market. It is a global labor market because, despite formal nation-state restrictions on the free worldwide movement of labor, surplus labor in any part of the world is now recruited and redeployed through numerous mechanisms to

[5] One survey of adult tourists in the Caribbean found 48 percent "completely apathetic" and another 22 percent "generally unconscious about ethical issues" and just wanted to enjoy their holidays (as cited in Pattullo, 2005:173). "The typical tourist's image of Caribbeans are of "happy, carefree, fun-loving men and women, colorful in language and behavior, whose life is one of daytime indolence beneath the palms and a nighttime of pleasure through music, dance, and sex," observes Pattullo. "[Tourist] fantasies mock the history of the Caribbean: from the almost complete annihilation of the Amerindians, through slavery and the plantation system, to migration, the difficulties of nationhood and the forging of new identities and economic strategies" (ibid.:177).

where capital is in need of it and because workers themselves undertake worldwide migration even in the face of adverse migratory conditions. Just as capital and labor are migratory so, too, are wages. The flip side of the intense upsurge in transnational migration is the reverse flow of remittances by migrant workers in the global economy to their country and region of origin. Officially recorded international remittances increased astonishingly, from a mere $57 million in 1970 to $216 billion in 2005 (see Table 3.13). The actual number, however, is likely much higher. When unrecorded remittances are included, according to the World Bank, the total is conservatively estimated to have exceeded $250 billion in 2005 (Bourdreaux, 2006:A12). This amount was higher than capital market flows and official development assistance combined, and nearly equally the total amount of world FDI in 2004 (Ratha, 2004:22–23). Worldwide remittance flows dwarf most other sectors in the global economy, with the possible exception of oil/energy, and apart from the global financial system itself.

Remittances clearly crossed a threshold in the 1990s in terms both of magnitude and significance. Close to a billion people, or one in every six on the planet, may receive some support from the global flow of remittances, according to senior World Bank Economist Dilip Ratha. "The scale is huge, maybe bigger than we think, and potentially transforming" (Bourdreaux, 2006:A12). Remittances have become vital to dozens of Third World countries, and for an increasing number of countries they are the most important source of foreign exchange income, among them, Egypt, the Philippines, Albania, Jamaica, Bangladesh, and many Latin American countries (Stalker, 2000:75–92). In addition, India, China, Turkey, Morocco, Spain, Nigeria, Greece, Jordan and Yemen are all major remittance recipients. Most of the world's regions, including Africa, Asia, Latin America, and Southern and Eastern Europe all report major remittance inflows. Remittance income is growing fastest in Eastern Europe, in the wake of the EU's 2004 eastward expansion (Bourdreaux, 2006:A12). Over one-third of world remittances are sent from the United States, followed by some 15 percent from Saudi Arabia, 10 percent from Germany and from Switzerland, and smaller amounts from France, Italy, Spain, Belgium and a number of Asian countries (Ratha, 2004:25, figure 1.6).

With the participation of most countries of the world in transnational migration processes, either as exporters or importers of labor, or as both, remittances become a vital flow in the global economy. Just as capital does not stay put in the place it accumulates, neither do wages stay put. Remittances redistribute income worldwide in a literal or geographic sense but not in the actual sense of

TABLE 3.13
Worldwide Worker Remittances, 1970–2004 (in $billion)

Year	All Developing Countries	Latin America**
1970	57	.05
1980	17.7	1.7
1990	30.4	5.05
1997	70.9	14.5
1998	68.0	15.9
1999	71.9	17.7
2000	75.6	20.2
2001	83.8	24.2
2002	98.2	28.1
2003	115.9	34.4
2004	125.8	36.9
2005	($216*)	53.6

Source: World Bank, Global Development Finance, 2005 report,
Statistical Appendix, table 1.19, and Country Tables; 2005 from IDB,
2006, 11.
    *High-end 2004 estimate, Ozden and Schiff, 2006, p. 1.
    **Does not include Cuba.

redistribution, meaning a transfer of some added portion of the surplus from capital to labor, since it constitutes not additional earnings but the separation of the site where wages are earned from the site of wage-generated consumption. What is taking place is a historically unprecedented separation of the point of production from the point of social reproduction. The former can take place in one part of the world and generate the value—then remitted—for social reproduction of labor in another part of the world. This is an emergent structural feature of the global system, whereby the site of labor power and its reproduction is transnationally dispersed.

Remittances are a major mechanism of global integration yet are relatively neglected in the globalization and migration literatures, perhaps because of their novelty and difficulties in researching the complexities of this transnational social-economic process. We are only beginning to fathom the significance of remittances and its relation to globalized production and reproduction, to global social integration and the rise of truly transnational social structure. The old nation-state/inter-state framework for labor and migration studies and the social science theories they draw on is simply inadequate for proper conceptualization of the new flows of transnational migration, reverse flows of remittances, and the transnational social structures these flows engender. Yet the remittance is itself but the inverse consequence of the export of labor to the global economy. In turn, the export of labor points to the rise of a new global labor market to service the global economy in which labor is increasingly available and disposable irrespective of traditional geography and notwithstanding juridical barriers to labor's free movement across national borders. These barriers are often held up by analysts skeptical of the claims of globalization theories, yet, as Prakash and Hart have observed, despite nation-state restrictions, cross border labor mobility "is a fact of life" (2000:105).

New and rapidly expanding transnational networks have emerged from the consolidation of migration ties. These migration networks, based on household-to-household relationships now constitute a major mechanism of social and economic integration into the global economy and society. The transnational processes bound up with migration link micro and macro-social dynamics and range from multidirectional economic flows, the cross-border extension of social networks, cultural practices, political participation, state- to-state and multilateral policy coordination, and the establishment of transnational households—defined as groups that maintain relationships and connections with home and host societies. In Orozco's construct, these transnational migration patterns involve money transfers, tourism, transportation, telecommunications, and nostalgic trade (nostalgic trade refers to the import and export of goods by and for migrants with their countries of origin, such as traditional spices, foodstuffs, liquors, handicrafts, and clothing), and are known together as the "Five Ts" (Orozco, 2005:208). Orozco's survey research shows that a full 60 percent of Latino immigrants send remittances each month, one-third of them travel home once a year, 65 percent call home weekly, and 68 percent buy home-country goods (2005:309).

Remittances are tapped as a major source of investment capital. Remittances sent by Central American workers abroad, for instance, have become a major source of investment capital tapped by investors in the region, as Segovia (2006) has shown. In effect, Central American workers abroad finance the investment that allows for expanded reproduction. However, studies show that those who receive remittances use them primarily not for investment but for consumption, including food, clothing, consumer goods, housing, social services such as health and education, and social purposes, (such as weddings), while a smaller portion go to local, often family-level and informal sector, productive and service activities (Stalker, 2000:81; Meyers, 1998:7; Orozco, 2005:325). Remittances have a multiplier effect, augmenting local demand and employment and therefore generating demand for goods from the global factory and allowing the unemployed and marginalized to participate, however limited, in global consumption. Money remittances thus circulate back into the global economy, including into the country or region from which the wage originated. By contributing to economic stabilization and easing, however slightly, political tensions, remittances may help maintain social stability. Remittances make an important contribution to transnational social integration and constitute a significant factor in the reproduction of the global system.

The flows of transnational migration and remittances act as powerful mechanisms for the further transformation and integration of national and regional economic and social structures into global ones. As Kyle notes, in reference to Ecuador: "Transnational migration distorts local economies in ways that make them conform to its transnational reality, as nonmigrants must conform to the direct or indirect consequences of this new transnational dimension" (2000:102). Among the many effects, Kyle observes that the influx of dollars has helped to "dollarize" the Ecuadorian economy, that is, to gradually substitute Ecuadorian sucres with U.S. dollars as the medium of domestic exchange. Indeed, the Ecuadorian government decided in 2000 to do away with the sucre altogether and make dollars the official currency.

Economist Manuel Orozco, one of the leading researchers of these phenomena, observes (2002) that family remittances have constituted a major factor in integrating societies into the global context economically and socially. Beyond the quite limited image of international NGOs constituting a transnational civil society, the synthesis in globally integrated space of transnational labor migration, remittance of wages, and social reproduction, along with a host of social, cultural and political ties that develop around these structures, as I will discuss below and in the next chapter, represents a truly organic transnationalization of civil society. I will analyze in further detail the export of labor, transnational migration, and the rise of transnational communities of Latinos in Chapter 4. Here I will focus specifically on remittances.

Latin America is the main remittance receiving area in the world, receiving some 30 percent of all official flows. The single most important "commodity" that Latin America now supplies to the global economy is labor. The surge in labor exports from Latin American deepens dramatically the region's integration into the global economy and the remittances that emigrant workers send home becomes a vital source a major mechanism of social reproduction in the new transnational model. Latin American labor has become available not only for national and regional labor markets but for the *global* labor market, exported to North America, Europe, and as far away as East Asia, the Middle East, Australia and New Zealand.

The progressive alienation of the Latin American peasantry, artisans, and other sectors in the post–World War II period of capitalist expansion, together with the upheavals of military and political conflict in the turbulent 1960s–1980s, produced a huge pool of surplus labor available to transnational capital for a new round of accumulation under globalization. These surplus labor pools appeared in the age of renewed global labor flows, when labor has become a commodity that is itself "marketed" worldwide. Remittances start to play a major role following the wave of out-migration from Latin America to the United States and elsewhere in the 1970s and 1980s of a portion of this surplus labor, particularly from Mexico, Central America, and the Caribbean. In the 1990s, neoliberalism, free trade agreements, and economic crises further heightened alienation, mass displacement, and consequent out-migration pressures. Argentina, for instance, experienced a surge in emigration following the crisis that exploded in 2001/02, with more than 250,000 emigrating in the subsequent three years (IDB, 2006:19), particularly to Spain, Italy, and the United States. The IDB notes that for the first time "remittances inflows have surpassed outflows of remittances from migrants currently in Argentina" and are now "a significant source of hard currency" for the country (IDB, 2006:19). By 2005 remittances even for Brazil—one of the largest national economies in the world and the South American powerhouse—had come to account for over 5 percent of exports and over 1 percent of GDP. Several million Brazilians sent $6.4 billion back home after living in Japan, the United States, Europe, and elsewhere (IDB, 2006:22). In the first five years of the twenty-first century, almost a million Colombians moved to the United States, Spain, and elsewhere, sending back billions of dollars in remittances and making them the second-largest source of foreign exchange, after oil (IDB, 2006:23).

Table 3.14 shows the phenomenal growth of remittances to Latin America at the turn of the century and Table 3.15 indicates their extraordinary economic—and therefore social and political—impact.

Remittances were in 2005 the number one source of foreign exchange for the Dominican Republic, El Salvador, Guatemala, Guyana, Haiti, Honduras, Jamaica, and Nicaragua, and the second-most important source for Belize, Bolivia, Colombia, Ecuador, Paraguay, and Suriname. At least 2 million Dominican-born adults now live outside their country and the $2.7 billion they sent back in 2005 dwarfed the value of the main export, amounting to 625 percent of exports of ferro-nickel and 45 percent of total exports (IDB, 2006:25). Remittances from Ecuador by 2005 had overtaken bananas and tourism as a source of income from abroad, surpassed only by oil exports (IDB, 2006:26). In Central America, the export of labor from the five republics, largely to the United States, skyrocketed in the 1980s with the cycle of revolution, counter-revolution and U.S. intervention. Emigration, however, did not decline with the end of the regional conflagration; it increased as poverty and unemployment spread under the ravages of neoliberalism and as transnational social networks among migrant families facilitated ongoing out-migration. Even emigration from Costa Rica—the most developed and most stable country in the region—increased by 20 percent between 2000 and 2004, with an estimated 100,000 Costa Ricans leaving for abroad. Regional remittances rose between 1980 and 1990 by 727 percent, from $77 million to $560 million. But then from 1990 to 2005 as the regional conflict wound down remittances ballooned to $8.8 billion, an increase of 1,571 percent, or twice the rate of growth in the first period. Hence transnational migration and remittances became institutionalized even after the original conditions that gave rise to them subsided, and as, in Orozco's words, the Central American and Caribbean countries "gradually transformed themselves from agroexporting economies to labor-exporting nations" (2002:1).

In El Salvador remittances have become the country's lifeline. By 2005 their value had reached 80 percent of the total of all other exports and represented a full 17.1 percent of the GDP. For 100 years the Salvadoran economy and society was dominated by coffee. It was the coffee-based oligarchy that ushered in the liberal revolution, later on propped up and rotated dictators, and financed the death squads. There was no better symbol of the country's transformation through globalization than the rise of labor export and remittances, so that by 2005 they had climbed to 1,700 percent the value of coffee exports! In Guatemala—another "coffee republic"—remittances also became the principal source of foreign currency, equal in 2005 to 202 percent of apparel exports, 344 percent of tourism income, and 645 percent of coffee exports (for these figures on Central America, see IDB, 2006:24–28, 31, 34). And the $2 billion that Brazilian immigrants in Japan sent home outstripped the earnings from coffee exports in 2005. In the classical so-called banana republic (in reference to its historic dependence on the export of that fruit), Honduras, remittances in 2005 surpassed 700 percent of the value of banana exports. By 2005 the $20 billion sent back by an estimated 10 million Mexicans in the United States was more than the country's tourism receipts and surpassed only by oil and maquiladoras exports. Some 75 percent of Latin American remittances were sent in 2005 from the United States ($40 billion). Another 15 percent was sent from Western

TABLE 3.14

Officially Recorded Latin American Emigrant Remittances, Select Years 1970–2005, Regional and Select Countries (in US$ million)

	1970	1980	1990	1997	1998	1999	2000	2001	2002	2003	2005
Argentina	0	0	0	66	69	64	86	190	187	253	780
Brazil	n/a	n/a	n/a	2,000	1,600	1,900	1,600	1,800	2,400	2,800	6,411
Bolivia	0	1	5	85	88	96	127	135	113	126	860
Colombia	26	106	495	774	4	1,312	1,610	2,056	2,480	3,076	4,126
Costa Rica	0	4	12	130	128	126	136	198	251	321	362
Dominican Republic	25	183	315	1,142	1,406	1,631	1,839	1,982	2,194	2,325	2,682
Ecuador	0	0	51	648	799	1,090	1,322	1,421	1,438	1,545	2,005
El Salvador	0	49	366	1,199	1,340	1,387	1,765	1,926	1,954	2,122	2,830
Guatemala	0	26	119	408	457	466	596	634	1,600	2,147	2,993
Guyana	0	0	0	15	15	20	27	22	51	64	270
Haiti	0	106	61	256	327	422	578	624	676	811	1,077
Honduras	0	2	63	190	225	328	416	540	718	867	1,763
Jamaica	0	96	229	730	758	790	892	1,058	1,260	1,398	1,651
Mexico	0	1,039	3,098	5,546	6,501	6,649	7,596	9,918	11,029	14,595	20,034
Nicaragua	0	0	0	150	200	300	320	336	377	439	850
Peru	0	0	87	636	647	670	718	753	705	860	2,495

Source: World Bank, Global Development Finance, Country Tables, 2005 report; data for 2005 from IDB, 2006.

Europe, particularly, Spain, Italy, Portugal, and the United Kingdom (IDB, 2006:12). Other large flows came from Japan to Brazil and Peru, and from Canada to Jamaica and Haiti.

It should be stressed that the figures in tables 3.13, 3.14, and 3.15 are based on officially recorded remittances and probably significant underestimates because they fail to capture transfers that take place through informal channels, including the traditional method of hand-delivery through courier (Meyers, 1998:4). Studies in a number of countries indicate that only about half, or even less, of all remittances may travel through official channels (see, e.g., Stalker, 2000:80). Moreover, official data does not register direct deposits that many Latin American immigrants make in their home countries (Orozco, 2003:3). Officially recorded remittances for Nicaragua, for instance, were only $150 million in 1997. But other estimates placed the amount of remittances sent into Nicaragua through formal *and* informal channels at about $800 million in 1998, which was well in excess of annual export income (*Envío*, 1999:10). And in Guyana, to take another example, the diaspora is likely as large—or even larger—than the country's population. According to the IDB, there are some 700,000 Guyanese in Guyana and between half a million and one million living abroad who sent home remittances accounting for an astonishing 34.3 percent of GDP (IDB, 2006:29). Yet World Bank figures barely acknowledged $64 million in transfers for 2003.

Remittances allow millions of Latin American families to survive by purchasing goods either imported from the world market or produced locally or by transnational capital. They allow for family survival at a time of crisis and adjustment, especially for the poorest sectors—safety nets that replace governments and fixed employment in the provision of economic security. Remittances expand and integrate regional markets, allowing millions of Latin American families to survive by purchasing goods either imported from the world market or produced locally or by transnational capital. The money sent to the region through these flows enters both the formal and informal local economies, as do their bearers, as consumers and as small-scale producers. It provides a vital source of small-scale capital for micro-enterprises in the informal sector. By way of example, studies for El Salvador found that by the late 1990s some one-third of all Salvadoran households received remittances as did 40 percent of all households living in poverty (Meyers, 1998:4; *Envío*, 1999:54), and that they made up a full 47 percent of the total income of Salvadoran families who received them (as cited in Lungo, 1996:105; Roberto and Seligson, 1991). In neighboring Guatemala, a United Nations report estimated that already by the early

1990s remittances constituted up to 30 percent of income for poor families (see Orozco et al., 1997: 53), while in nearby Dominican Republic one third of all families receive some remittances (Meyers, 1998:10). Researcher Peggy Levitt found that in one Dominican Republic community, Miraflores, 60 percent of all households received remittances from family members in the United States and for nearly 40 percent of those households the remittance constituted between 75 and 100 percent of their income (2001:52). The remittance is more than an economic flow that sustains national macroeconomic equilibrium and facilitates family social reproduction. It is also an agent of social, cultural, political, and ideological transformation—or what Levitt terms social remittances. Remittances act as a mechanism of global cultural diffusion, and as I will discuss in the next chapter, transnational migration brings about new forms of transnational social structure.

Emigration and remittances serve the political objective of pacification. As Latin American emigration to the United States dramatically expanded from the 1980s and on it helped dissipate social tensions and undermine labor and political opposition to prevailing regimes and institutions. They help offset the decline of other sectors and income sources, such as traditional agriculture; reduce macroeconomic imbalances; close balance of payments gaps; and, in some cases, avert economic collapse (see, e.g., Orozco, de la Garza and Barahona, 1997:54–55). In sum, by the 1990s remittances had become a critical stabilizing factor in the Latin American economy. It is not likely that macroeconomic stability—touted as the fundamental achievement of neoliberal policies—could have been achieved, or maintained, without them. Remittances therefore shore up the political conditions for an environment congenial to transnational capital. Table 3.15 places the economic weight of remittances in relative perspective.

If the export of labor generates the reverse flow of remittances, the global circulation of Latino wages via remittance flows is made possible by the rise of a global financial system: the deregulation of national financial systems, the lifting of currency and exchange controls, the transnationalization of banking, the rise of computerized electronic transfers, and so forth. In turn, the control over remittance transfers has become a multibillion-dollar industry increasingly dominated by transnational commercial banks and financial companies. Private financial institutions have seen in remittances an opportunity to capture a major source of revenues—to have senders and receivers move their funds through these private institutions—and they have pursued strategies to "bank the unbanked" (see, e.g., Maimbo and Passas, 2005). The typical Latin

TABLE 3.15
*Officially Recorded Remittances as a Percentage of Exports
and GNP, 2005, Select Latin American Countries*

	Exports	GDP
Argentina	2.0	0.4
Brazil	5.0	1.1
Bolivia	33	8.5
Colombia	19	4.1
Costa Rica	5	1.8
Dominican Republic	45	9.1
Ecuador	20	6.4
El Salvador	80	17.1
Guatemala	77	9.3
Guyana	49	34.3
Haiti	224	20.7
Honduras	69	21.2
Jamaica	104	19
Mexico	10	2.8
Nicaragua	55	16.9
Paraguay	20	7.2
Peru	15	3.2
Average 11 countries	62	11

Source: IDB, *Remittances 2005: Promoting Financial Democracy*, 2006.

American worker in the United States sends home $200 to $300 per month. The profits to be made on 10 to 15 million Latin Americans in the United States sending remittances are enormous, considering an average transaction fee of some 6–15 percent of the sending amount and additional service charges, such as door-to-door delivery, and manipulation of exchange rates (Orozco, 2002:5; Ratha, 2004). The IDB has recorded some 200 million separate remittance financial transactions a year from Latin Americans living outside their country of origin (IDB, 2006:12). But in addition to the charge on the transfer, control over the money sending market by transnational financial institutions means that these enormous quantities of currency enter the global financial system, where they may be tapped through numerous channels by transnational capital.

In the early twenty-first century Western Union controlled some one-fourth of the global money transfer market, although its relative market share was in decline. Other big players were Thomas Cook and MoneyGram (Orozco, 2003:6). Together with private banks that entered the money transfer market in the 1990s the big companies have increasingly squeezed out informal and local businesses, often in the hands of Latino small merchants and shop owners from the same country as money senders (Orozco, 2003:6). By late 2002 some fifty commercial banks based in the United States offered transfers to Mexico, some also offering ATM cards to recipients in Mexico at low cost (Orozco, 2003:10).

As remittances have been leveraged by banking and other business sectors, this expanding market has typically involved a transnational fusion of business groups in diverse countries. In Mexico, the U.S. Postal Service teamed up with the Mexican bank Bancomer in 1997 to set up a transnational remittance service, as did Wells Fargo and Banamex, and U.S. Bank and Banca Serfín (Meyers, 1998:4). Moreover, the Mexican retail chain Elektra, linked to Woolworth Mexicana and several private banks, set up a business to provide the remittance in local currency transfer operations in association with Western Union and began to expand into Central America in the late 1990s (Meyers, 1998:18). In the Dominican Republic, remittances have become a booming industry for investors who created the Association of Dominican Foreign Exchange Remittance Enterprises and that in turn has teamed up in partnerships with a number of U.S. business and financial groups (Meyers, 1998:4). In Colombia the local market is controlled by consortia of Western Union and several Colombian companies (IDB, 2006:23). The Chilean-based worldwide transfer company, AFEX, handles remittances from the United States to Mexico and other Caribbean Basin countries. The most powerful Salvadoran banking houses—Banco Agrícola, Banco del Comercio, Banco Cuscatlán, and Banco Saladoreño—have all opened branches in the United States (IDB, 2006:27). Commercial banks from Guatemala, Honduras, Jamaica, Mexico, Colombia, and elsewhere are heavily invested in the money transfer market and have opened up branches in many U.S. cities (ibid.). Companies such as Gigante Express, Pronto Envío, Mateo Express, Vimenca, and Dinero Seguro are household names in the respective countries in which they operate. The labor of Latin American emigrant workers and the money they send back to family members at home therefore opens up new possibilities for the transnationalization of private banking groups in Latin America, specifically, their integration into the global financial system, and into the ranks of the TCC.

Latin American governments have sought to by incorporate migration and remittances into their economic and political strategies and to develop mechanisms for leveraging (Lowell and De la Garza, 2000). Soon after assuming office in 1989, for instance, the ARENA government in El Salvador promoted the legalization of *casas de cambio* (exchange houses), which encouraged remittances by giving Salvadorans a way to legally change dollars at near the black market rate. These new houses had the double effect of channeling dollars into the formal financial system where they could be used to finance imports (Murray, 1995:89). The Nicaraguan and Guatemalan governments took similar steps in the early 1990s. The Salvadoran government's decision in 2000 to dollarize its economy, eliminating its own currency, the colon, and making U.S. dollars its legal tender, was closely related to the country's over-whelming reliance on remittances as its source of foreign exchange (Orozco, 2002:9). As Orozco observes, transnational migration and the reverse flow of foreign currency also takes place through the sharp increase in the return of nationals to their home countries as visitors, which as well brings in significant amounts of foreign exchange and spurs the tourist industry and its earnings (Orozco, 2002:9). The Mexican government began formal outreach programs such as Paisano and Program for Mexican Communities Living Abroad (PCMLA) to encourage Mexican immigrants in the United States to raise funds on behalf of their home towns. The PCMLA operates officially through the network of 42 consulates and 23 institutes or Mexican cultural centers in the United States (Orozco, 2002:8). The governments of Mexico, Central America and the Caribbean, and more recently the Andean countries, have individually and collectively lobbied U.S. authorities on behalf of Latin American immigrants and protested deportations and repressive immigration legislation.

Latin American migrants residing abroad also constitute a significant—and in some cases, primary—source of tourism for Latin American countries. This is especially so for Central America and for some of the Caribbean countries. For instance, Central American immigrants in the United States generate much of the demand for air travel to the region; their telephone calls to relatives account for a majority of U.S.–Central American telecommunications; they transferred over $8 billion in remittances in 2005; and their nostalgic commerce has grown steadily. Orozco reports that JFK International Airport alone carries nearly 140,000 people annually between New York and Santo Domingo, the majority of them Dominican tourists and businesspeople engaged in the Dominican Republic. Similarly, the Central American airline, Grupo Taca, flies 21 times a day from the United States to El Salvador and at least 70 percent of its passengers to the region are Central Americans. One-third of Latin American immigrants in the United States travel home at least once a year and spend an average of $1,000 to $2,000 per visit in their home country. Telecommunications have also contributed to the transnational relations. The volume of calls to Central America and the Caribbean has increased tremendously as connectivity has improved, leading to a major expansion of business investment in land lines, cell phone services, the Internet, and cable transmissions. This expansion has catered as much to grassroots transnational communities as to transnational capitalist investors. Migrants abroad have also become a major new ethnic market for exports from their home countries, especially of nostalgic goods (more than 70 percent of Latino immigrants in the United States surveyed by Orozco reported that they purchased goods from their home countries). In the extreme case of El Salvador, these products are estimated to represent a least 10 percent of the country's total exports (for these details and discussion, see Orozco, 2005:310–314).

Remittances have been exalted in recent years by such TNS agencies as the World Bank and the Inter-American Development Bank as "the new development finance" and an innovative solution for "high level human development" (Elton, 2006:1; IDB, 2006; see also Ratha, 2004; Maimbo and Ratha, 2005). These enthusiasts claim that remittances are a stable source of finance that goes straight to the most needy sectors, are immune to the whims of global capital, and even have the unique quality of increasing in times of economic crisis back home (Elton, 2006:1). Yet remittances represent the *failure* of the transnational development model. As Elton observes, these enthusiasts tend to come from the same international institutions that have promoted the neo-liberal policies that have in the first placed triggered unprecedented displacement, unemployment, impoverishment, and out-migration. Remittances are often spent overwhelmingly on consumption with little multiplier effect and leave the country as quickly as they enter. They often generate inequalities in receiving communities among those families receiving remittances and those that do not (Meyers, 1998:9). And despite the claims that they are a solution to poverty, a study commissioned by the World Bank concluded that remittances typically reduce the severity of poverty—particularly among the lowest decile income group, which may receive up to 50–60 percent of total income from remittances—but do not significantly reduce overall poverty levels in recipient countries (Ozden and Schiff, 2006:3).[6] It is therefore clearly a palliative and not a cure for poverty. Elton describes a Remittances Disease as a "first cousin of the better-known Dutch Disease," whereby a large inflow of remittances appreciates the local currency, rendering exports less competitive, distorting the local labor market and the allocation of productive resources (2006:3). To the extent that remittances are a virtual life-support system for some nations, asks Elton, "do they prolong

---

[6] Adams (2006:79), for instance, calculated that international remittances to Guatemala reduced the level of poverty in that country by a mere 1.6 percent, despite the fact that these flows amount to a full 9 percent of Guatemala's GDP.

the lives of moribund economies, postponing the implementation of new policies or the election of new leaders? . . . The danger is not that remittances will make a difference but that they are becoming a smokescreen to hide the pressing need to address the structural causes of unemployment and poverty in migrant sending nations" (2006:3).

CHAPTER FOUR

Transnational Processes in Latin America

Class, State, and Migration

The transformation of Latin America's political economy that we reviewed in the previous chapter constitutes the backdrop to sweeping social, political, cultural, ideological, and institutional changes in the region as it has integrated into global capitalism. I refer to such changes as *transnational processes:* the diverse changes associated with each country's and each region's incorporation into emergent global society (Robinson, 2003). These range from the transnationalization of classes, the state, and civil society, to the reorganization of political systems and authority structures, the appearance of new social agents and movements, and novel cultural and discursive practices. This chapter focuses on some of the more pronounced changes in the social structure in Latin America as the region has globalized, highlighting class relations, the state, labor, and migration.

Transnational Class Formation in Latin America

Transnational class formation is a major dimension of capitalist globalization. As global capitalism penetrates new spheres and subjects them to the logic of transnational accumulation, pre-globalization classes (such as peasantries and artisans) tend to disappear, replaced by new dominant and subordinate class groups linked to the global economy. The transnationalization of the class structure in Latin America can be summarized as follows:

- The rise of new dominant groups and capitalist fractions tied to the global economy;
- The downward mobility, or proletarianization, of older middle classes and professional strata and the rise of new middle and professional strata;
- Proletarianization of peasants and artisans and the rise of new working-class constituencies;
- The working class itself becoming flexibilized and informalized;
- The appearance of an expanding mass of supernumeraries or marginalized.

What was the composition of the class structure in Latin America in the early twenty-first century? The size of the capitalist class has not fluctuated significantly in recent decades and constitutes between 1 and 2 percent of the economically active population (EAP) in every country, according to ECLAC data analyzed by Portes and Hoffman (2003:44). Senior executives and managers in the public and private sectors make up an upper strata that comprises between 1 and 5 percent of the EAP, while professionals, defined by Portes and Hoffman as university-trained elite workers employed by private firms and public institutions, comprise another 5 percent of the EAP in most countries. The dominant classes in Latin America are thus made up jointly of large and medium-sized employers, senior executives and professionals, and comprise some 10 percent of the population. The subordinate classes comprise the remaining 90 percent, although these percentages vary from one country to another. Among the subordinate classes are a petty bourgeoisie, made up, in Portes and Hoffman's words, of "own-account professionals and technicians, and micro-entrepreneurs with personally supervised staff" (2003, table 1). I would be more inclined to characterize much of what Portes and Hoffman term the petty bourgeoisie and "self-employed" as informalized and casualized workers displaced from public sector employment by adjustment policies and whose labor power is incorporated in new ways into capitalist accumulation. I would characterize, moreover, as petty-bourgeois—or as middle strata—portions of those groups that Portes and Hoffman place in the dominant classes.

The working class, as construed by Portes and Hoffman, is divided into the non-manual–labor formal proletariat, the manual-labor formal proletariat, and the informal proletariat. Informal workers—defined by unregulated, irregular income and nonmonetary forms of compensation—are by far the largest group everywhere, accounting for approximately 46 percent of the labor force. That group is followed by the non-manual–labor proletariat, defined by wages subject to legal regulation, with approximately 24 percent, and the non-manual–labor formal proletariat, or those technicians and white collar workers whose salaries are subject to legal regulation, standing at some 12 percent (2003, table 1, note: these figures do not add up to 100 because they are approximations and vary significantly from country to country).

Portes and Hoffman do not recognize a new axis of class fractionation among both dominant and subordinate classes. New transnational capitalists and transnationally oriented elites have emerged in Latin America around globalized circuits of accumulation as have new transnational working classes who labor in these dynamic circuits. Dominant groups have fractionated between nationally and transnationally oriented fractions as capitalist globalization has progressed, with major political implications. The working class as well can be divided into a declining group of those who labor in older nationally oriented circuits of accumulation and those who have shifted to transnationally oriented circuits. The decline of import-substitution industrialization (ISI) industries and domestic market enterprises disorganized and reduced the old working class that tended to labor under Fordist arrangements, including unionization and corporatist relations with the state and employers. This fractionation often has political implications, as the declining group is more likely to belong to trade unions, to be influenced by a corporatist legacy, and to agitate for the preservation or restoration of the old labor regime and its benefits. It is also more likely to be male. The new workers faced a flexible and informalized labor regime. There has been a contraction of middle classes and professional strata that had developed through public sector employment and government civil service in the face of the dismantling of public sectors, privatizations, and the downsizing of states. At the same time, restructuring involves the rise of new middle and professional strata, whose members may have the opportunity to participate in global consumption patterns, frequent modern shopping malls, communicate through cells phones, visit Internet cafés, and so on. These strata may form a social base for neoliberal regimes and become incorporated into the global capitalist bloc.

The penetration of capitalism into the countryside results in an ongoing and massive displacement of the peasantry. A major story of globalization—worldwide—is the agonizing death of the peasantry. Where have the peasants, the displaced workers, and the middle classes gone? First, they have turned to transnational migration. Second, they constitute the new labor force for new agribusiness farms, factories, and service sectors of the global economy. Third, they have shifted en masse to the informal sector. There is an explosive growth of supernumeraries, of the marginalized and excluded population, a phenomenon tied both to transnational migration and to the growth of informality. The informal sector has always been functionally linked to the formal sector, yet under globalization the lines between formality and informality become ever more blurred. In particular, the nature of flexible accumulation networks and employment, chains of subcontracting and outsourcing, creates conditions for new types of relations among economic agents that lend themselves to informality.

In simplified terms, class conflict and politics in Latin America as the region has globalized involve two sets of intertwined dynamics:

1. struggles between descendant nationally oriented and ascendant transnationally oriented elites. When we cut through the fog of ideological discourse we find that political competition among elites in the late twentieth and early twenty-first century often broke down along this fault line; and

2. struggles waged by popular sectors against global capitalism and neoliberal restructuring. Earlier struggles against dictatorship and for an extension of the Keynesian or developmental state have given way to new mass struggles against neoliberalism, or have been combined with them, and are often led by emergent subjects (the indigenous, women, etc.).

The first few decades of globalization involved a change in the correlation of class forces worldwide away from nationally organized popular classes and toward the transnational capitalist class (TCC) and local economic and political elites tied to transnational capital. Under globalization, the domestic market has been eliminated as a strategic factor in accumulation, with important implications for class relations and social movements. By removing the domestic market and popular class consumption from the accumulation imperative, restructuring helped bring about the demise of the populist class alliances between broad majorities and nationally based ruling classes that characterized the pre-globalization model of accumulation. Later on, popular classes—themselves caught up in a process of reconfiguration and transnationalization—stepped up their resistance, and the hegemony of the transnational elite began to crack. I will return later to this resistance. First I focus on the dominant classes.

The principal contradiction within dominant blocs worldwide under globalization has been between national-based fractions of capital and transnational fractions. These transnational fractions are distinct from old landed oligarchies and from the old nationally oriented elites who were oriented toward domestic markets that emerged during the period of nation-state capitalism. The contradiction between these two groups became politicized in many countries of Latin America. The opposing interests and projects of these two groups often underlie the surface political battles among ruling classes and states. As the logic of national accumulation became subordinated to that of global accumulation, transnationalized fractions of local dominant groups in Latin America gained control over states and capitalist institutions in their respective countries. These groups, in-country agents of global capitalism, become integrated organically as local contingents into the transnational elite. Capitalist globalization could not have unfolded in Latin America without such agents who could undertake structural adjustment and oversee an institutional transformation. These new transnationally oriented economic groups and political elites captured state power in country after country during 1980s and 1990s, and used that power to integrate their countries into the emerging global economy and society. They are the manifest agents of capitalist globalization in Latin America.

The Transnational Capitalist Class in Latin America

In late May 2005, some thirty of the richest men (along with one woman) in Latin America gathered at the exclusive Mexican port resort of Ixtapa at the invitation of multibillionaire Carlos Slim, the single-richest man in Latin America and at the time of the 2005 meeting, the third-richest man in the world, who made his fortune through the privatization of Mexican telecommunications. The attendees represented the upper echelons of the Latin American contingent of the TCC. Among them were the Venezuelan magnate Gustavo Cisneros, the principal stockholder of the Univisión television network; Cisneros's Mexican counterpart Emilio Azcárraga, the majority shareholder of Televisa, the biggest television network in Latin America; Álvaro Noboa, one of the largest banana producers in the world and the richest man in Ecuador; Julio Mario Santo Domingo, the richest man in Colombia and overlord of a vast empire that spans four continents and ranges from beverages, airlines, and telecommunications, to banks, petrochemicals, and agro-industries; the Chilean Andrónico Lucsik, owner of a major portion of the food and beverage industry in that country; Lorenzo Zambrano, the president of Cementos de Mexico (Cemex), the largest cement producer in the world; and so on (Reyes, 2003). The gathering was convened to analyze deepening poverty in Latin America and the potential threat it represented to the neoliberal order that facilitated the rise of those present to the heights of the global capitalist economy.

Beyond this upper-most echelon of billionaires, an increasing number of capitalist groups in Latin America have joined the ranks of the TCC. A dynamic new breed of transnationally oriented entrepreneurs emerged with the opening to the global economy. It is not possible here to undertake a systematic study of the TCC in Latin America. Nonetheless, the general pattern with regard to the rise of this class group appears to be as follows: (1) it is concentrated in finances, telecommunications, retail, commercial, and other services, along with nontraditional export activity, precisely those sectors most associated with the global economy; (2) the new transnational capitalist groups are not self-made. The leading TCC family networks date their fortunes and class status to the late nineteenth and early twentieth century as capitalism developed in Latin America. But they underwent a qualitative transformation in the 1980s and 1990s, experiencing an unprecedented windfall in the amassing of wealth and power, propelled by privatizations and other opportunities opened up by neoliberal globalization, including new types of access to the world market and forms of association with extra-regional transnational capital. The transnational fractions of the capitalist class and the state bureaucracies that have risen to power in Latin America and elsewhere in the South are not the comprador class of the dependency theorists, who were seen as well-paid junior partners of imperialist capital. They are local contingents of a TCC and other strata whose economic interests and social advancement reside less in the development of national capitalism than in the global capitalist system that they participate in and defend.

Reflecting broader trends in the global economy, the private sector in Latin America has increasingly been characterized by the emergence of large conglomerates and of *grupos,* the latter defined by Rettberg as "networks of legally independent firms, affiliated with one another through mutual shareholding or by direct family ownership under a common group name" (Rettberg, 2005:38). Whereas conglomerates consist of formally integrated companies, the *grupos* are companies that are largely independent of one another yet function under the coordination of a central entity. These conglomerates and *grupos* have increasingly organized into a new breed of TNC in Latin America, known in the business literature as *multilatinas.* These corporations may originate in a particular country but have been in the process of aggressive transnational expansion in Latin America and beyond, often in diverse forms of association with transnational capital from outside the region (Fernández Jilberto and Hogenboom, 2004).

Common to the conglomerates and *grupos* is that they span a variety of economic sectors. Many of the Latin American conglomerates and *grupos* originated in the earlier period of ISI, and some were partially or wholly state owned before the process of privatization in the 1990s. Indeed, groups of investors came together specifically to capture enterprises through the privatization process. Thus privatization not just fomented the process of capitalist class formation but also resulted in the transnationalization of economic groups. The conglomerates and grupos have become interlinked with transnational capital from outside the region in a variety of ways, involving them in globally integrated production processes. What emerges from this integration of local domestic and regional capitals is not a new Latin American dependency but the transformation of Latin American capitalists into regional components of the transnational capitalist class. Fernández Jilberto and Hogenboom observe the transformation of the relationship between Latin American companies and TNCs from outside the region:

> The massive penetration of FDI in the 1990s involved new forms of channeling investment, linking foreign and local producers. Whereas most foreign investment had been previously done through branches of multinationals that were directly controlled by the headquarters, many multinationals started to operate in association or through joint ventures with local economic groups. These alliances appeared as a result of the privatization process and/or on the basis of investment funds. There are also cases in which branches of transnational companies have become associated to other multinational's branches, to new or old local economic groups, or to foreign banks, in order to maximize their share in privatizations. (2004:166)

The outcome of neoliberal restructuring and regional integration processes "is a structural framework that is favorable to the expansion of large private companies at the national and regional level," observe Fernández Jilberto and Hogenboom:

> Latin American conglomerates have profited substantially from these circumstances. Among Latin America's current corporate giants are both old and new companies, a large share of which takes the shape of economic groups and conglomerates. . . . through exports, financial markets, and mergers and joint ventures, Latin America's large companies are increasingly linked to global capital and the global economy at large. (2004:150)

A few, such as Mexican Telmex and Cemex, have joined the ranks of the top global corporations. Slim, for instance, became in 2007 the richest person in the world, displacing Bill Gates and Warren Buffet from first and second place, with an estimated fortune of $53 billion (AFP, 2007), launched his Grupo Carso conglomerate, following the 1990 privatization of the Mexican phone system. Apart from its Latin America-wide mobile telephone empire (Telemex inside Mexico and América Móvil in the rest of Latin America), Grupo Carso controls hundreds of industrial, financial, and service firms and has, among other holdings outside the region, a 9 percent stake in the telecommunication TNC Global Crossing Ltd. and in the CompUSA consumer electronic chain (Dickerson, 2006a), as well as major holdings in Saks Fifth Avenue, Circuit City, among others (Reyes, 2003). A growing number of other TNCs have become competitive well beyond the Americas. Brazilian-based Gerdau, for instance, a steel conglomerate, and Embraer, a maker of small passenger jets, have acquired or built manufacturing assets in the United States, Europe, and Asia (Martínez, Souza, and Liu, 2003:3). The family dynasty of Ecuadorian Álvaro Noboa owns some 120 enterprises throughout South America, Europe, the United States, New Zealand, and Japan (Reyes, 2003). Gustavo Cisneros heads the Cisneros Group, a vast empire of 67 enterprises in over 100 countries, and is considered "the most influential businessman in Latin America" (Reyes, 2003:56), with close ties to the Rockefeller and Bush families. Grupo Mexico, a Mexican-based mining conglomerate that emerged through the privatization of the mining industry in the late twentieth century, owns numerous holdings on both sides of the U.S.–Mexico border, including the American Smelting and Refining Company (Bacon, 2006), so that, if anything, its U.S. partners are subordinate juniors. One leading *multilatina* executive estimated that in 2005 there were some 70 companies in the region that are capable of competing worldwide in the global economy, and that they had been pursuing a strategy of establishing strategic alliances, partnerships, and other collaborative arrangements with the leading extra-regional TNCs so as to become globally competitive (Souza, 2005).

The transnationalization of Latin American capitalist groups has been spurred by global competition. Between 1991 and 2001, the ownership of the 500 largest companies in Latin America experienced a shift, with nonregional TNC ownership growing from 27 percent to 39 percent, largely as a result of outside participation in the privatization process, as the percent of these 500 largest companies that were state owned dropped by almost the same amount, from 20 percent to 9 percent of the total (Martínez, Souza, and Liu, 2003:3). This rising foreign competition pressured national Latin American companies, which historically served only their home country markets, to consolidate and expand into other Latin American countries and beyond, transforming themselves into *multilatinas* (Martínez, Souza, and Liu, 2003:3). Parallel to the transnational expansion of Latin American capital there has been a dramatic concentration of capitals within each country and in the region as a whole, with merger waves and the acquisition by larger firms of smaller ones. Global competition has spurred not only the transnationalization of national firms but also the transnational interpenetration of Latin American capitals. "In the face of globalization and the fear of being invaded in their own back yards by the giant multinationals," writes Gerardo Reyes, a journalist who has interviewed many of the leading capitalist families in Latin America and studied their networks,

> almost all of the conglomerates are in a process of worldwide expansion. In this race they compete amongst themselves but they also align with each other and join ranks. Slim is a partner of Azcárraga, while in turn Azcárraga has partnered with Cisneros and Cisneros is a partner of Santo Domingo. At the same time they have forged alliances with European and U.S. firms that arrived in the heyday of the [privatization] bonanza. (Reyes, 2003:11)

By the early twenty-first century, leading *multilatinas* were competing successfully among TNCs for markets and influence. Mexico's Bimbo, the Argentine-based food company Grupo Arcor, the Colombian-based Compañía Nacionál de Chocolates and Inver-Alimenticias Noel SA were all competing with Kraft and Nestlé for food markets throughout the region. Similarly, leading banks in Brazil were competing with the world's largest global banks (Martínez, Souza, and Liu, 2003:6–7). In 2000, non-Latin American TNCs accounted for more than 80 percent of mergers and acquisitions in the region, whereas by 2003 the *multilatinas* accounted for 63 percent of this activity, spending $6.5 billion dollars in such acquisitions (Martínez, Souza, and Liu, 2003:7), and in 2005 more than 50 percent of all mergers and acquisitions in Latin America were driven by local firms (Santiso, 2006).

Alongside the sharp rise in foreign direct investment into Latin America there was a burst of Latin American investments to other Latin American countries and cross-border mergers of firms within the region. In 1997 alone, for instance, Latin American investors committed $8.4 billion dollars in privatization deals and other purchases of local companies in several countries of the region. Fifty-eight percent of this was accounted for by privatizations and the remaining 42 percent by the purchase of private sector assets (ECLAC, as cited in Bull, 2004:2). Chilean firms invested in other countries of the Southern Cone (representing 38 percent of the total), Mexican firms invested in Central America and some South American countries (representing 27 percent), and Argentine companies invested in the Southern Cone (24 percent) [ECLAC, as cited in Bull, 2004:2]. The flagship Chilean department store Falabella expanded into neighboring countries in the early twenty-first century through a series of acquisitions, so that by 2004 it was the second-largest company in the retail sector in Latin America, surpassed only by Wal-Mart Mexico (ECLAC, as cited in Bull, 2004:3). There has also been significant cross-border investment by Brazilian firms and integration between businesses originating in smaller countries. Mexican business groups have established joint ventures and strategic alliances with TNCs, integrated their capital into the global financial system, and undertaken direct foreign investment abroad, including in North America, Central America, and the Caribbean. If the North American Free Trade Agreement (NAFTA) allowed TNCs unrestricted access to Mexico it also opened the North America market to Mexican investors. Mexico's América Móvil, a cell phone division of Teléfonos de Mexico, had by 2004 accumulated more than 40 million clients in Mexico, Brazil, Argentina, Venezuela, Colombia, Ecuador, and the Central American countries (ECLAC, as cited in Bull, 2004:3). In Central America, numerous companies have expanded throughout the region, among them, the Grupo Gutiérrez in Guatemala, which owned several large food chains, the Salvadoran Grupo Poma, with investments in tourism and hotels, and the regional airlines, Grupo Taca (Bull, 2004:3). More generally, stock markets throughout the region have integrated, facilitating the melding of "national" and "foreign" property holdings into simply transnational ownership of the region's capitalist assets (Robinson, 2003).

The transnationalization of local capitalist classes is also reflected in, and facilitated by, the expansion of Latin American stock markets in the 1990s and on. The top 100 of the largest publicly traded companies in 2002 in Latin America (ranked by net sales) included both local and foreign giants (Fernández Jilberto and Hogenboom, 2004:155). Some of the largest on this list include Brazilian-based Petrobras; Mexican-based Telmex, Telcom, Carso Global, Wal-Mart–Mexico, the beverage producer Grupo Model, retailer Grupo Sanborns, and Cemex; the Chilean aviation producer Lanchile; and Telefónica del Peru. Mexican and Brazilian-based companies account for 78 among the 100 (Fernández Jilberto and Hogenboom, 2004:155). Of course these and other Latin America-based TNCs are in no way "national," given the transnationalization of their operations, ownership, and associations. "A significant share of these groups nowadays not only export goods but also capital by means of direct foreign investments, creating new companies, buying existing companies, establishing strategic alliances with counterparts, and of course through mergers," observe Fernández Jilberto and Hogenboom. "Therefore, the term 'local' economic group or large company nowadays sounds somewhat awkward as the majority have passed the phase of national production and investment" (2004:157).

The ranks of the Latin American contingent of the TCC are drawn disproportionately from the bigger countries, in particular, Mexico, Argentina, and Brazil. Nonetheless, the transnationalization of capitalist classes has taken place in the smaller countries as well. Central America is an eye-opening example. In his excellent research on the rise of new business groups in Central America, Alex Segovia (2006) shows how there has been an increasing cross-border integration of Central American economic groups since 1990, and especially within the highly globalized financial, commercial and service sectors, along with the growing association of these groups with transnational capital from around the world. What were previously the leading national economic groups, and that vigorously defended their national markets from outside competition, began to internationalize and interpenetrate from 1990 and on, expanding operations in conjunction with the liberalization of trade and investment in the region and a new cycle of investment by TNCs in local phases of transnationally integrated production and service systems. Reflecting this regional capital integration, intra-regional trade among the five republics grew from $671 million in 1990 to nearly $3.5 billion in 2004 (Segovia, 2006:9).

As elsewhere in Latin America, transnational capitalist groups in Latin America consolidated their position through a combination of privatization and association with transnational investors from outside the region. Between 1990 and 2004 nearly $24 billion in foreign direct investment (FDI)—which includes groups from one country investing in other countries of the region— poured into Central America. Much of this went into buying up privatized telecommunications, electrical energy and other utilities, banks, and other service and financial enterprises, along with investment in maquiladoras, retail, tourism and other nontraditional export activities. TNCs previously developed a significant presence in Central America in the decades after World War II, and especially in the 1960s through the Central American Common Market. But this earlier cycle of FDI was aimed at setting up production within the protected regional market in order to supply that market. The previous ISI/agro-export model in Central America depended on the surpluses and foreign exchange generated by the traditional agro-export sector, a structural arrangement that favored traditional agrarian elites and national oligarchies. But as the source of foreign exchange and surpluses have increasingly shifted to new accumulation activities, to services and commerce, and to new forms of transnational financing, such as remittances and association with TNCs, the new economic groups have been able to break their earlier dependence on the old agro-export oligarchy and shift the balance of class forces within the dominant groups further in their favor.

The new Central American economic groups, as Segovia shows, have expanded their operations beyond the Isthmus, to Mexico, the United States, the

Caribbean, and in some cases, to Europe and South Africa, and are truly inserted as dynamic players into globalized circuits of accumulation. The scope of accumulation for these groups that were nationally based a few decades earlier has expanded to the region as a whole and increasingly to other areas of the global economy. Some of the largest new economic groups in Central America include the El Salvador–based Grupo Poma and Grupo TACA, the Guatemalan Paiz family empire, Grupo Fragua, as well as the Guatemala-based Grupo Pantaleón, Grupo Gutiérrez-Bosch, and Grupo Castillo, the Pellas-family group in Nicaragua, among others. At the same time as these Central American groups have transnationalized regionally they have also developed strategic alliances and associations amongst themselves, with extra-regional TNCs, and with economic groups from other countries. For instance, Grupo La Fragua is associated with the Costa Rican–based retail trade holding company CSU and with Wal-Mart; the Grupo Pellas with General Electric and IBM; the Salvadoran-based Cuscatlán Bank with Grupo Financiero Popular of Puerto Rico; and Grupo Poma with the powerful Grupo Carso of Mexico, among many others (Segovia, 2006:60). The Salvadoran-based beverage, hotel, and agro-industrial conglomerate, Agrisal, controlled by the Meza Ayau family, established in 2005 a strategic alliance with the South African beer consortium SABMiller; the two set up a regional venture, Grupo Bevco, that brings them together with the Honduran-based Grupo La Constancia and the new Nicaraguan firm, Industrial Cervecera de Nicaragua. The Castillo family group in Guatemala has a similar alliance with AmBev of Brazil; through their joint venture Cervecería Rio they have linked with firms in Honduras, Guatemala, Nicaragua, and El Salvador. One of the most powerful Honduran capitalist families, the Facuse group, associated in 2000 with Unilever and in 2003 with Standard Fruit Company. And these are just a few examples (for further details, see Segovia, 2006, table 8:62–70).

The TCC in Latin America as a Political Agent

The Latin American contingents of the TCC have increasingly developed a political action capacity and used it to extend their influence over political systems and state policies. As they have integrated into TNC networks they have been at the center of the push for regional liberalization, trade integration, and privatization (Fernández Jilberto and Hogenboom, 2004). Capitalists and technocratic elites established new institutional bases from which to develop programs and assemble teams, largely constituted by new private sector associations and elite foundations. These business associations have been key vehicles for organizing, politicizing, and bringing to power transnational fractions. A study of these business associations shows them to have been actively engaged in policy development, liaising with local states in promotion of neoliberal restructuring and new economic activities associated with the transnational model, and lobbying for regional and global integration. They provided leadership to increasingly coherent transnational fractions among local private sectors, helping these fractions to shape state policies, and furnishing a platform for advancing the globalization of Latin America. These umbrella organizations played a significant role everywhere in neo-liberal reform and in lobbying for free trade agreements, in many cases negotiating these agreements in consort with, or even on behalf of, state managers (see, e.g., Schneider, 2001).

Rettberg found that in Colombia newer transnationally oriented conglomerates and *grupos* have weakened the traditional political influence of older business associations identified with the previous economic model (Rettberg, 2005). In Ecuador, the Ecuadoran Federation of Exporters (FEDEXPORT), with the assistance of the AID, set up the Corporation for the Promotion of Nontraditional Agro-Exports (PROEXTANT), which played a pivotal role in promoting floriculture and other new economic activities tied to the global economy (Sawer, 2005:49). In Central America, dynamic new transnationally oriented elites formed new private sector associations in every Central American country in the 1980s and 1990s that set out to compete with earlier associations oriented toward protected domestic markets. These new associations were major players in the region's neoliberal structuring and integration into global capitalism, and in the introduction of a host of new export activities, such as the spread of maquiladoras and nontraditional agricultural exports (Robinson, 2003). They joined forces to form the Federation of Private Sector Entities of Central America and Panama (Fedepricap) for the purpose of developing a single Central American private sector platform on economic policies and political issues and coordinating initiatives regarding the region and its relationship to the global system. In 1998, Fedepricap drafted a comprehensive position paper endorsing liberalization and calling for the dismantling of remaining regional barriers to integration into the global economy (Robinson, 2003:221). Similarly, private sector groups in Central America, in partnership with transnational capital from outside the region, were pivotal in pushing for the reform and privatization of telecommunications (Bull, 2004, 2005).

The local contingent of the TCC in Central America has drawn on the classical mechanisms of capitalist class influence in the political process to shape state policies in favor of globalization. Among these mechanisms are widespread financing of political parties and also placement of its members in strategic positions within these parties, control over the media, the establishment of policy-planning institutes and think-tanks that develop proposals and programs which are then presented to the media (which the economic groups control), political parties, civil society groups, and state managers, and the placement of its representatives directly in state institutions, especially in ministries related to economic policy. The most powerful economic groups in the region constitute an informal club that enjoy "doorknob rights" (*derecho de picaporto*), as one leader of the Guatemalan business sector, who was also a high level state official, told Segovia in an interview—meaning that their economic power gave them the right to knock on the door and converse informally with the highest authorities in government at any time and under any circumstances (Segovia, 2006:90).

The TCC in Central America increasingly engages politically as a unified group. The major economic groups hold periodic informal meetings to discuss problems in the region and possible solutions, to plan collective political initiatives, and to host international meetings in which high-level government officials are often in attendance. Contingents from the five republics operate as a regional bloc vis-à-vis political process. The Pelas Group in Nicaragua, for instance, contributed half a million dollars to the neoliberal Nicaraguan presidential candidate, Enrique Bolaños, in 2000 while at the same time he was one of the major contributors to the 2001 electoral campaign of the right-wing presidential candidate, Abel Pacheco, in neighboring Costa Rica. The other major contributors to Pacheco's campaign were the Grupo Banistmo, based in Panama, and the Salvadoran-based Grupo Cuscatlán. Meanwhile, the major economic groups from El Salvador, Guatemala, and Honduras financed the presidential campaign of Antonio Saca in El Salvador in 2003/4 and that of Óscar Berger in Guatemala in 2003, while Salvadoran groups were major financers of the 2001 campaign of Ricardo Maduro in Honduras. All of these neoliberal candidates triumphed in elections so that in the early twenty-first century every Central American country had a government placed in power, in part, by the TCC and responsive to its interests—and in the inverse, hostile to the interests of the popular classes (for these details, see Segovia, 2006:92–93, 96–98).

In Mexico, dynamic transnational capitalist sectors were the driving force behind the rise to power of the National Action Party (PAN) and its neoliberal program in the 1990s. These sectors joined TNCs with which they are associated, such as Wal-Mart, PepsiCo, Halliburton, Bechtel, and Citigroup, to provide critical backing in the 2006 fraud-tainted presidential elections for the PAN candidate, Felipe Calderón. Several of the largest corporate political action groups, among them the Grupo Mexico and the Grupo Villacero, bankrolled Calderón's candidacy and campaigned openly through commercials and the use of media groups they control against the leftist candidate, Andrés Manuel López Obrador (Bacon, 2006). The open and brazen support given by Mexico-based Televisa, the largest network in Latin America, to the right-wing candidacy of Felipe Calderón was considered crucial in influencing the outcome of the 2006 elections (the flipside of this support was a blackout of the political activities of the leftist candidate, López Obrador, and his supporters).

Capitalist groups from Mexico, Central America, and the Caribbean formed the Network of Businesspeople (Red de Empresarios) in 2001 to push forward the Plan Puebla Panama (PPP), a vast plan to stimulate investment in the region by expanding infrastructure (Bull, 2004:6). NAFTA was promoted by a well-organized lobby of Mexican capitalist groups oriented toward the global economy, while in the South American Common Market (Mercosur) countries peak business associations from each member country formed the Mercosur Industrial Council (CIM) to push for integration. These business organizations often organized and led the states in the process. As Schneider shows, the private sector, led by two umbrella organizations, was responsible for the inclusion of Chile in Mercosur in the early 1990s. The story of the central role of the private sector in liberalization in Chile is well known (see, e.g., Silva, 1996). The private sector was a major backer of the 1973 coup that overthrew socialist president Salvador Allende and a consistent supporter of the dictatorship of General Pinochet. The key years in which Chilean capital came out fully in support of neoliberalism and began itself to transnationalize was following the 1982–1983 economic crisis when the military government turned to the main business organizations to develop joint policy initiatives. As Silva (1996) shows, the largest firms usually belonged to conglomerates with the financial capacity to expand into the more dynamic emerging sectors of the economy, such as nontraditional exports and financial activities that involved a major transnational thrust. The losers were both small and medium-sized firms, and more importantly, those that were unable or unwilling to set their sights beyond the domestic market.

Control over the media in Latin America has also afforded the TCC with a decisive means of political influence. Television is controlled by four giant groups: Televisa of Mexico; Globo of Brazil; the Cisneros group in Venezuela; and the Clarín group in Argentina (Reyes, 2003:14). As Reyes and his colleagues show:

A large portion of the news produced in the region is processed [in these four] mass communication fiefdoms, which in turn feeds back into the accumulation of fortunes and of power: the media is used to promote the products produced by the economic empires that own the media, including political candidates. From their apartments in Paris or New York, or even directly from the editorial rooms, the Latin magnates also manage national politics. Their whims have produced presidents and courting their bad favor has buried candidates. They are the primary contributors to political campaigns. They have supported democracies and dictatorships and they have the privilege of soliciting or of ignoring the advice and supplications of governments. (Reyes, 2003:14–15)

Through all kinds of formal and informal processes state managers, technocrats, and private sector representatives have developed policy networks (Teichman, 2001) that liaise with representatives from TNS institutions in the formulation of policies and strategies of global capitalist development in the region. In the case of Mexico, "privatization in combination with other policies geared to stimulate manufacturing export activities has strengthened the country's most powerful financial and industrial conglomerates and their transnational allies" (Teichman, 1995:2001). Neoliberal policies have been developed through informal ties among key ministries such as Commerce and Industrial Development, representatives of transnationally oriented capitalist groups in Mexico, and TNS institutions. Similar overlapping policy clusters that often bypass the formal policy-making apparatus have been identified in Central America (Robinson, 2003) and elsewhere. These clusters in turn liaise with each other across the region and in international forums in transnational policy networks that illustrate the transnational elite in action.

We must also single out the role of new professional and technocratic strata whose members may or may not also belong to the capitalist class yet who play a key role as organic intellectuals for local fractions of the transnational elite. There has been a proliferation of studies in recent years on the role of technocrats (see, inter alia, Centeno, 1994; Centeno and Silva, 1997; Domínguez, 1997; Montecinos and Markoff, 2001; Carter, 1997). The analysis of technocratic elites is a part of the established literature in development and political economy. They are identified as bureaucratic groups with a cosmopolitan outlook and international professional standards who apply capitalist rationality to state policies. But the transnational technocratic elite is a new breed, thrown up by the political and economic dynamics of globalization and transition, and it has risen to prominence in countries and regions around the world. Technocrats apply a capitalist rationality in place of rentier state activities, patronage net-works, clientalism, corporatist structures, crony capitalism, and like forms of economic organization. The transnational technocratic elite, in turn, applies the rationality of the global economy over the logic of nation-state capitalism. Jorge Domínguez and his colleagues (1997) have coined a new term for the fore-most individuals among this new technocratic elite, *technopols*. As the term implies (techno=technocrats; pols=politicians), technopols combine "the intro-spection of the thinker with the sociability of the politician" (Feinberg, in Domínguez, 1997:9). Beyond mere technocrats, they are political organizers and leaders who are able to build legitimacy within local political systems for the program of integration into global capitalism. The new technocratic elite who emerged from among transnationally oriented groups became strategically placed in new private-sector associations, in political parties, educational insti-tutions, and in local states, playing major roles in the design and implementa-tion of the transnational agenda.

The Transnational State in Latin America

The crisis of oligarchic rule and the popular and revolutionary struggles of the first few decades of the twentieth century opened the way for an era of develop-mentalist capitalism and populist political projects that brought the popular classes into the state, often through corporatist arrangements. These classes were not able to achieve hegemony over the state apparatus, with the exception of certain momentary revolutionary experiences. Nonetheless, they were able to contest state policies, push for the expansion of public sectors, and shift some social priorities in favor of workers and the poor. This Latin American variant of the "class compromise" of the Fordist-Keynesian era broke down with the onset of globalization. As transnational capital achieved hegemony, the new transna-tionally oriented dominant groups (1) achieved a more direct control over the state; (2) expelled popular classes from ruling coalitions as the doors of the neo-liberal state slammed shut; (3) reoriented the state from developmentalist to neoliberal; and (4) shifted its function from promoting previous national mod-els to promoting the transnational model of accumulation.

The transnationalization of the state, therefore, did not entail a roll back as much as a reorientation, as state services were redirected away from the popular and working classes and toward private capital, and within private capital, from national to transnational fractions. The state had to be restructured along neolib-eral lines in order for it to implement the policies of adjustment and integration into the global economy, and in turn these policies favored the development of transnational fractions at the expense of the old national fractions of the elite. In distinction to the previous ISI-populist development model, the neoliberal state in Latin America created through liberalization, deregulation, and integration generated the conditions for the transnationalization of domestic and regional capitalist groups at the same time that it created the conditions for the influx of capital from outside the region and the association of local (national and regional) and global capitals. By stimulating transnational capital flows, Latin American states have acted as components of the TNS.

There has been a transformation of the linkages between the state and the private sector, a more direct instrumentalization of the former by the latter in relation to the earlier period and a reversal of the tendency in state-capital relations toward state dominance in the earlier period of capitalist development (Robinson, 2003). On the one hand, the structural power of the global economy, and especially of global financial markets, instills new forms of discipline on national states. On the other hand, transnationally oriented capitalist, technocrats, and other elites instrumentalize the state in news ways, ranging from a more direct placement of their representatives in government agencies to influence wielded by new business associations, and direct pressures by the IFIs and other international agencies. Bull (2004:11) refers to the "privatization of politics," whereby transnationally oriented private sector groups achieve privileged access to the policy-making process at the same time as major policy decisions are taken out of the public sphere. She cites an extreme case of neoliberal reforms giving new transnational capitalist groups privileged access to politicians and high-level technocrats: in Honduras it was reported that cabinet meetings in the Flores government (1998–2002) were held in the board room of one of the country's largest banks, of which the Minister of Governance was the director (Bull, 2004:12).

The particular circumstances through which transnational fractions came to command a neoliberal state have varied from country to country. In my study of Central America (Robinson, 2003), I show how in each of the five republics emergent transnationally oriented business groups tied to local maquiladora operations, nontraditional agricultural exports, transnational tourism, and new globally integrated banking and commercial circuits formed dynamic new associations that played a major role in the 1990s in promoting neoliberal restructuring and in bringing to power candidates and parties that represented their interests. Rettberg (2005) similarly found in for Colombia that new grupos that emerged in the 1980s and 1990s with economic diversification and the neoliberal opening wrestled influence over the political process away from the country's more traditional business associations. In a comparative study of Chile, Argentina, and Mexico, Teichman finds:

> Probably the most striking similarity among the three cases is the access of the owners/executives of very powerful conglomerates to the economic policy process—an access and influence unmatched by any other social group. . . . [They] were in the best position to take advantage of the opportunities afforded by the new economic model, particularly in the areas of export promotion and the opportunity to purchase state companies. Moreover, as policy makers opened up channels of communication to the private sector, powerful private sector interests seized the opportunity to influence policy. (2001:199)

The case of Mexico is particularly illustrative. The new transnationally oriented state managers were all Ph.D.-educated with degrees from Harvard Business School and other elite universities. They introduced the neoliberal dogma into the Mexican policy-making apparatus and into civil society through private universities, the media, business, and civic associations. At the apex of the Mexican transnational capitalist groups was a politicized leadership that rose to the fore, the so-called compact group, representing the upper echelons of Mexican business allied with the three neoliberal presidents who ruled from 1988 to 2006, Carlos Salinas de Gortari (1988–1994), Ernesto Zedillo (1994–2000), and Vicente Fox (2000–2006) [Saxe-Fernández, 2002:117–118]. This compact group became the inner circle of Mexican TCC members on the heels of the privatization of some 200 state firms under the Salinas de Gortari government.

In the process of its transnationalization, the state has been penetrated by two new social forces, one from within and the other from without. From within, transnationalized fractions vied for, and gained control over local states in the 1980s. From without, diverse transnational actors representing an emergent transnational state (TNS) apparatus, among them the IFIs, bilateral agencies, multilateral political entities and informal organizations of the transnational elite, penetrated local states, liaised with transnationalized fractions therein, and helped design and guide local policies. Through these processes, macroeconomic policymaking and enforcement shifts to a transnational policy arena. A policy apparatus is carved out within the national state that is insulated from mass pressure, on the one hand, and from elite groups and their rivalries, on the other. The transnational bloc that replaced the developmentalist bloc within the state came to devise overall economic guidelines and strategies, monitor progress, and link national state economic policy making to TNS policy making. This bloc, in effect, colonized the state, gaining control over key branches linking each country to the global economy and society, such as ministries of foreign affairs, finances, economic development, and Central Banks. Central Banks often gained an autonomy, which shielded them from the pressures of the government apparatus, such as social ministries and legislatures, and from the larger political system (on the trend toward Central Bank autonomy, see *The Economist*, 1998b). These branches of the neoliberal state become functional parts of a TNS, gateways between the local and the global. States become engulfed in sets of larger global class relations. They do not become representatives of some other nation-state (e.g., of U.S. imperialism), as nation-state theories suggest, but of transnational capital and the transnational elite.

Throughout Latin America the struggle between descendant national fractions of dominant groups and ascendant transnational fractions was often the backdrop to surface political dynamics and ideological processes in the late twentieth century. Battles were played out in numerous sites, from electoral contests, to disputes for leadership among national business associations, to sometimes bloody infighting among ruling parties. In Mexico, for instance, the clash between the two fractions was behind the bloody power struggles of the 1990s within the Institutional Revolutionary Party (PRI) that had ruled the country for six decades. The "dinosaurs" in the power struggle represented the old bourgeoisie and state bureaucrats whose interests centered firmly in Mexico's corporatist-ISI version of national capitalism. The new "technocrats" were the transnational fraction of the Mexican bourgeoisie that captured the party, and the state, with the election to the presidency in 1988 of Carlos Salinas de Gortari. The Salinas de Gortari government set out to dismantle the old national capitalist system and to facilitate a sweeping integration of Mexico into the global economy.

Neoliberal states have overseen sweeping privatizations. These transfers of public assets from the state to private capital have been a major mechanism for the extension of capitalist production relations, akin to what Marx called "the alienation of the state," a form of primitive accumulation that results in the commodification of formerly public spheres managed by states. The number of privatizations in the Third World expanded tenfold in the 1980s (McMichael, 1996:133). These privatizations, as McMichael notes, accomplished two radical changes: (1) they reduced the state's ability to engage in economic planning and implementation, thereby privileging private sector control; and (2) they extended the transnationalization of the ownership of assets in the Third World (on privatization more generally, see Martin, 1993). The wave of privatizations in Latin America from the 1980s into the twenty-first century included just about every aspect of the economy, from national phone and telecommunications companies, to electrical, water, gas and other public utilities, airports and seaports, sugar refineries, public banks, pensions, insurance services, tourist centers, forests, land and water, parastatal agricultural and industrial production enterprises, among others. *Government itself* has been privatized to the extent that numerous state functions have been transferred to the private sector, either directly or through outsourcing, and converted from social (public) to market (private) logic. Health, education, and other services, have become *for profit,* meaning that these activities are reorganized not in order to meet human needs but in order to make money. Privatization results in a pure market-determined distribution. Given the highly skewed structure of income distribution, the process tends to aggravate inequalities and social polarization.

Latin America accounted for the most extensive privatizations of any region from the late 1980s into the twenty-first century. According to the World Bank, 1,300 privatization transactions took place in Latin America from 1988 to 2003, generating $195 billion in revenue, or 48 percent of total privatization revenue worldwide, with Brazil ($80 billion), Argentina ($43 billion), and Mexico ($34 billion) leading the way (World Bank, 2006a). These privatizations were legitimated as necessary to reduce government spending and balance budgets, to free up resources for debt repayment, and because the private sector is "more efficient." However, the claim that private control is more efficient than public management has been belied by actual experience in Latin America (see, inter alia, Hacher, 2004; Noticen, 2004a; Smith, 2002). Privatization greatly reduced the space for popular and working classes to contest power structures and vie for redistribution and social wages through a public sector. Privatizations were a major axis of conflict as these classes struggled to preserve public sectors, as private investors tussled for the spoils, and as public officials padded their pockets through the widespread corruption that accompanied the process. This enormous influx of liquid capital through the sale of public assets contributed to state solvency and to the region's apparent economic recovery in the 1990s. But by the turn of the century privatization revenue dwindled as the stock of enterprises for sale declined, contributing to the renewal of crisis, as I will discuss in the next chapter.

The neoliberal states also deregulated financial systems at the behest of transnational elites. Transnational finance capital is the most mobile fraction of capital and is the hegemonic fraction on a world scale. Money capital has come to determine the circuits of accumulation worldwide as it acquires new methods for appropriating value from competing capitals, from working classes, and from the state. One such method that financial deregulation made available to groups that control liquid capital is currency speculation and the manipulation of devaluations. A strategy that transnational investors in Latin America, as elsewhere, have pursued has been to remove liquid capital from the country, particularly on the eve of a crisis, and then return it in the wake of a devaluation; in this way its value multiplies (of course transferring a large amount of currency out of a country can itself precipitate a crisis). Another strategy is to unload on states debt acquired by private groups.

During the 1990s transnational banks in Latin America became major buyers of government bonds and securities (see next chapter). As well, Latin American banks borrowed heavily in international capital markets that had become more accessible as a result of large-scale foreign direct investment in the region's financial systems and the integration of these systems into the global financial system. These banks then converted the foreign currency they borrowed into loans for local investors, who were themselves often associated with transnational capital. When governments respond to perceived breakdowns in transnational investor confidence, they raise interest rates and tighten monetary policy, which in turn induces local recession and economic hardship. At the same time, however, rising interest rates and recession often result in widespread defaults on bank loans, as happened in both Mexico and Argentina. In each case, the state stepped in to bail out local banking branches and to guarantee private sector debt. In this way, the state both subsidized domestic/transnational investors and then socialized private investor debt and private bank risk. This should be seen in broader class terms as a shifting of accumulation crisis from capital and upper strata to labor and popular classes as local states act as instruments of the interests of transnational capitalist groups, including their local contingents.

In Mexico, to take one example, local investors transferred abroad $25 billion from deposits, bonds, and securities in the buildup to the 1995 "peso crisis" and then brought these funds back in once the Mexican government devalued the peso by two-thirds, thus inflating their holdings by 200 percent (Saxe-Fernández, 2002:120). And in another example, local financial investors in Argentina were able to turn their Argentine pesos into dollar holdings and convert their private debts into public debt in the 1980s and 1990s. When crisis hit in 2001, these investors were in a strategic position to take advantage to multiply their capital at the expense of the mass of Argentina's working and middle classes. "In essence, during the last twenty years, the Argentine population has been subject, in sequence, to the following mechanism," observes Joseph Halevi. "The state takes upon itself the burden of the private external debt. The private sector keeps running up additional debt, while the state sells out its public activities through privatization policies, thereby generating profits (rents) for the private corporations whether national or international. The state then unloads the burden of debt onto the whole population, especially the working population." To this must be added, he goes on to note, "the export of capital engaged in by the Argentine capital-possessing classes. . . . The class based connection between international and local finance capital can be seen from the fact that the entire adjustment of the external debt burden was imposed on the real economy, while capital was enticed with promises of easy gains through privatizations, monopolistic rates indexed to the dollar in the event of devaluation (in utilities for example), and the freedom to exit the country quickly" (Halevi, 2002:18, 21).

What do these examples this tell us? As they have become integrated into global circuits, capitalists in Argentina, Mexico, and elsewhere join the ranks of the TCC. They become deterritorialized. Crises in these countries represented enormous opportunities for these investor groups who could move their capital and themselves about without regard to national borders and state regulation. Latin American and other transnational investors, as they become integrated into globalized circuits, appropriate surpluses generated by Latin American workers and by workers elsewhere in the global economy, from those in Los Angeles to Tokyo, to those in Milan, London, Johannesburg, and elsewhere. Numerous nodes allow transnational class groups to appropriate the wealth that flows through global financial circuits. The physical existence of these groups in a particular territory is less important than their deterritorialized class-relational existence in the global capitalist system. How is this related, in turn, to the state? Class groups collude or struggle over state policies and practices. But more than an arena of contestation, we should recall, the state is itself a class relation that institutionalizes historical constellations of class forces embedded in social relations of production and in civil society. A state is a "moment" of these class power relations congealed in a set of political institutions (Robinson, 2004a). Capitalist globalization has brought about a "recongealment" of the state around a new constellation of class and social forces brought about by capitalist globalization. However, the whole process is highly fluid and contested. The neoliberal states that took shape in the late twentieth century, and the TNS more broadly, were by the turn of the century in crisis, as I will discuss later.

Class, Consumption, and the Wal-Martization
of Commerce in Latin America

While early research into the global economy focused on the phenomenon of "runaway factories" and industrial export processing zones an equally important globalization of national retail sectors was taking place. If the first stage in the "retail revolution" was the emergence of large-volume discount stores, such as Wal-Mart, created in 1962, the second stage, from the 1980s and on, was the shift by the retail chains from national to global sourcing, scouring the world for the cheapest suppliers and lowest cost labor—the so-called China price. The third stage, the transnationalization of the retail chains themselves, took off in the 1990s. Gereffi and Korzeniewicz (1994) refer to buyer-driven commodity chains as global *production* chains that are shaped and controlled by giant retailers or end purchasers that subcontract production abroad. But what is now taking place is novel, the rise of global *retail* chains, whereby the retailers and other TNCs at the pinnacle of production chains seek to close the circle by capturing the retail distribution in new regions, such as Latin America, and new market segments, such as working classes and the poor. More theoretically speaking, the sphere of *distribution* is becoming globalized on the heels of the globalization of the spheres of *production* and *circulation*.

During the 1990s Latin American transnational consumer goods companies and supermarket chains expanded aggressively in the region with the neoliberal opening, at the same time as these national and regional chains linked up with global retail chains such as Royal Ahold, Wal-Mart, K-Mart, Target, and Carrefour. The resultant transnational supermarkets and retail conglomerates have rapidly taken over the retail sector in Latin America, transforming consumer markets as well as the circuits of production and distribution that supply retailing. They increased their percentage of the Latin American retail market from 10 percent to 20 percent in 1990 to 60 percent by 2000 (Reardon and Berdegue, 2002:371). By the twenty-first century, supermarkets, "hypermarkets," large chain stores, and warehouse and membership clubs, were the dominant players in the region's agri-food economy. "In one globalizing decade [the 1990s]," observe Reardon and Berdegue, "Latin American retailing made the change which took the U.S. retail sector 50 years" (2002:371). These TNC supermarket and mega-retail chains have pushed to expand from the middle- and upper-income consumer markets they were able to saturate as a result of trade liberalization in the 1980s and 1990s, into new low-income commercial market segments. In the 1990s TNC strategists set out to study the consumption patterns of low-income groups in the region whom they had previously written off or simply saw as a labor pool but not as potential retail customers. They concluded that these groups could be converted into consumers through an aggressive expansion out of their high-income niches. The business literature began referring to the poor as emerging consumers.

"Selling consumer products to Latin America's 250 million low-income consumers—men and women who constitute 50 to 60 percent of the region's population and wield some $120 billion in annual purchasing power—[has become] a necessity" for further expansion in the region, according to one Harvard Business School report (D'Andrea, Stengel, and Goebel-Krstelj, 2004:1). These emerging consumers among the poor spend from 50 to 100 percent of their disposable income on consumer products, compared with 35 percent or less for the well off (D'Andrea, Stengel, and Goebel-Krstelj, 2004:2). The goal of capturing local markets and redirecting the consumption of millions of emerging consumers away from traditional community retailers, local shops, and street vendors could be achieved through the advantages of "global scale and local focus" and via new strategies of targeting sub-segments of emerging consumers in specific geographic areas, acquisitions and mergers, and localized business models that could be replicated in extended networks of stores (D'Andrea, Stengel, and Goebel-Krstelj, 2004:2, 11).

There are two sets of class relations behind the rise of global retailing in Latin America I wish to highlight here. First, while global retailers control the commanding heights of this emerging corporate empire it would be a mistake to see the process as a "foreign" takeover of "domestic" capital. Rather, local supermarket chains have typically merged with these TNCs in holding companies, joint ventures, acquisitions, and other forms of association. The Costa Rican supermarket chain CSU, for instance, merged in 2003 with La Fragua, a Guatemalan chain, and with the Netherlands based Royal Ahold, creating the Central American Retail Holding Company (CARHCO), with 322 stores and $2 billion in sales throughout Central America (Dugger, 2004). When Wal-Mart achieved a controlling 51 percent stake in the holding company, local CARHCO investors became shareholders of Wal-Mart and CARHCO's Corporate Affairs Director Aquileo Sanchez became the chief Wal-Mart executive for Central America (*Noticen*, 2006b). Similar processes were under way in South America in the 1990s, where transnational supermarket chains bringing together regional and extra-regional investors went from controlling 10 to 20 percent of the agri-food market to dominating it, especially in the larger countries, such as Brazil, Argentina, and Chile (Dugger, 2004). Wal-Mart has expanded into Latin

America in partnership with regional retail chains, such as Cifra in Mexico, the CARHCO in Central America, and the Bompreco retail chain in Brazil. While Wal-Mart gains access to vast new markets in these countries its partners acquire a whole new set of opportunities through unprecedented access to global consumer markets (Petrovic and Hamilton, 2006:130).

Moreover, while extra regional capital does play a major role, the dynamic involved as much TNC penetration from outside the region as it did the domestic and cross-border expansion of Latin American retailers. The Uruguayan-Argentine chain, Disco, for instance, became larger by acquiring other Argentine firms, while the Chilean Santa Isabel spread into Peru and Ecuador. In the 1990s both Disco and Santa Isabel entered into a joint ventures with Royal Ahold of the Netherlands, the largest food retailer in the world, thus giving them both a greatly enhanced presence toward the end of the 1990s in much of South America (Reardon and Berdegue, 2002:375). In sum, the Wal-Martization of commerce in Latin America does not pit TNCs against domestic capitalists as much as it converts groups of local capitalists into affiliates of the TCC.

The second set of class relations is between the transnational retailers, on the one hand, and popular class sectors, on the other, among them, workers, small-scale retailers and producers, and poor communities. The disappearance of artisans, local merchants, and small producers—the "old" middle classes or petty bourgeoisie—is a classic story of capitalist penetration into new spheres. As Reardon and Berdegue show, up until the 1980s most Latin American countries had a few capital city supermarkets while the rest of commerce was in the hands of small-scale grocery stores, traditional plaza markets, and local discount and specialized stores, alongside independent kiosks, small stands serving neighborhood and pavement traffic, and so on. Starting in the late 1980s, national and multinational supermarket chains moved out of their niche in upper-class neighborhoods, spilling into middle- and working-class neighborhoods in the big cities, and from there to intermediate cities and smaller towns. At the same time these chains were spreading from richer and larger countries to poorer and smaller countries throughout the region (2002:375). The "big fish eating smaller fish" process is, of course, a telltale pattern of capitalist development, including centralization and concentration. The takeover by transnational corporate retailers has thrown tens of thousands of small traditional shops, "mom and pop stores," and neighborhood outlets out of business and also brought about a decline in plaza markets, contributing to the process of displacement and proletarianization among traditional middle sectors. In Argentina, for example, 65,000 small shops went out of business between 1984 and 1993, while 5,000 closed their shops in Chile from 1991 to 1995 (Reardon and Berdegue, 2002:374).The shift from traditional neighborhood shops, community markets, and street vendors to corporate food retailing brings a corresponding shift in supply chains from local farmers and smallholder communities to transnational agribusiness and commercial outsourcing networks of the global economy. Small farmers find themselves shut out, forced to retreat to shrinking rural markets or proletarianized. Buyer-driven supermarket chains link backward to large and medium-sized producers, and transnational agribusiness and commercial capital push out small producers and peasant communities that previously linked forward with local and traditional retail businesses. In Guatemala, for instance, the Association of Mini-Irrigation Users of Palencia, a group of individual producers who pooled production inputs and marketed their goods cooperatively, began to see their products passed over in the wake of the consolidation of the big retailers into the CARHCO holding company. CARHCO's Fragua informed them that their produce did not meet company specifications of uniform size, color, and weight. Unable to acquire the greenhouses and other resources to meet the new specifications, the Association dissolved; many of its members left the countryside to migrate to Guatemalan cities and to the United States (*Noticen*, 2006b).

The spread of Wal-Mart is emblematic of these relations. Wal-Mart is the largest corporation in the world. In 2003 it operated more than 5,000 huge stores worldwide and employed more than 1.5 million people, making it the largest private employer in Mexico, Canada, and the United States (Lichtenstein, 2006:3). If in the mid-twentieth century General Motors symbolized bureaucratic management, mass production, the social incorporation, and political enfranchisement of a unionized blue collar workforce, Wal-Mart, with its notoriously oppressive labor conditions, low paid, flexibilized, feminized workers, outsourcing and union-busting practices, is in Lichtenstein's words, "the template business setting the standards for a new stage in the history of world capitalism" (Lichtenstein, 2006:4). Wal-Mart entered the Mexican market in 1991 through a partnership with Cifra, Mexico's leading retail company. By the new century it was the biggest retailer in the country, with 710 stores and fast-food restaurants in the country, more than $13 billion in annual sales, and the largest private employer, with over 100,000 workers and 49 percent of all supermarket sales (Cevallos, 2005; Tilly, 2006:189).

The feminization of retail is particularly striking in Mexico, where over 50 percent of all workers in the sector are women. Although Wal-Mart pays slightly more than most retail employers in that country, it nonetheless pays below average wages; and its workers put in an average of 51-hour weeks (Tilly, 2006:192). In neighboring Central America, Wal-Mart was already importing over $350 million in goods from the region, including fruits and vegetables, garments and other goods produced in the region's export processing zones prior to its purchase of a stake in CARHCO. Already notorious for its low wages and exploitation of a largely female workforce in the Isthmus, the company sent James Lynn to Central America in 2002 to report on abusive labor practices in the maquiladoras. But when Lynn returned and presented a report documenting widespread abuses, such as factories with fire doors padlocked from the outside, a lack of potable drinking water in factories, and women workers dismissed when they became pregnant, he himself was fired as an undesirable whistleblower (Noticen, 2006b).

In late 2004 Wal-Mart opened one of its superstores less than two miles from the ancient Teotihuacan pyramids in Mexico despite protest from local social movements and small businesses. In 2005 the chain sparked fierce protests from indigenous communities in Pátzcuaro, Michoacán, and Juchitán, Oaxaca, after it announced plans to open stores in both those heavily indigenous communities. More generally, such transnational corporate penetration of food markets as Wal-Mart has achieved brings cultural shifts and contributes to a change in dietary patterns and lifestyles. In Mexico, for instance, the consumption of beans—a highly nutritious staple for millennia—dropped by more than half between 1995 and 2005 as the market became flooded with processed and prepackaged Ramen instant noodles, a dish loaded with fats, carbohydrates, and sodium. The invasion of processed and fast-foods has resulted in soaring levels of obesity, diabetes, and heart disease, particularly among the poor (Dickerson, 2005).

The arrival of the global supermarket and commercial chains in Latin America forces us to reconsider the North-South framework of analysis, according to which the North exploits the South through an international division of labor in which the latter sends foods and other raw materials produced with cheap labor to the North. While this pattern still holds, in part, and certainly remains part of the story, the larger picture is one in which (1) the North also sends to the South foods and other raw materials produced with cheap labor and advanced technology and yields, so that California "factories-in-the-field" and agro-industry market output in Latin America through globalized commercial networks; (2) the new agro-industrial complexes in the South, especially NTAEs, are "Californized," that is, based on the same combination of cheap labor and advanced technology and yields; and (3) the output of these complexes is marketed globally through the very same globalized retail networks as information technologies and the logistics revolution allow mega-retail chains to set up distribution centers, sourcing networks and joint-venture operations to both supply local stores and export products to the global market.[1]

Meanwhile, the transnationalization of commerce and retail networks in Latin America would not be possible without the plethora of regional, hemispheric, and global integration processes that have taken place, the topic to which I now turn.

Integration: Creating Regional Platforms of Global Capitalism

How do we understand regional integration processes? Some observers consider such regional blocs as the NAFTA in North America, the EU in Europe, or the APEC in Asia to be attempts by each region to create buffers against competition from other regions (see, e.g., entries in Rosamond, 2002; Shaw and Soderbaum, 2003). In my view, however, most trade and integration agreements worldwide are stepping-stones for a more expansive global integration. The type of regionalism that has unfolded in Latin America since the 1980s is an "open regionalism" (CEPAL, 1994; Bulmer-Thomas, 2001; Fernández Jilberto and Hogenboom, 2004). This open regionalism is distinct from earlier integration schemes. A central objective of the regional integration that took place after World War II was to support the ISI model of development by expanding markets and allowing for economies of scale while protecting regional markets behind high external tariffs. It was thus an inward-looking integration, whereas open regionalism is outward-oriented. New models of regional integration are an integral part of Latin America's neoliberal transformation and globalization. Governments and business groups have used regional integration models in order to coordinate the timing and intensity of the region's further articulation to the process of globalization. Regional integration has allowed Latin American firms and business associations to expand

---

[1] In Guatemala, the number of supermarkets doubled in that decade and captured 35 percent of the retail food market. "At La Fragua's immense distribution center in Guatemala City, trucks back into loading docks, where electric forklifts unload apples from Washington State, pineapples from Chile, potatoes from Idaho, and avocados from Mexico," according to one report. "The produce is trucked from here to the chain's supermarkets, which now span the country" (Dugger, 2004:1). CARHCO in Central America draws on supply chains and sourcing networks throughout Central America to supply supermarkets in the Isthmus and in the United States. Carrefour uses its global sourcing network to contract melon producers in northeast Brazil to supply its 67 stores in Brazil as well as Carrefour distribution centers in 21 countries around the world (Reardon and Berdegue, 2002:381).

cross-nationally within the region and also provided them with new avenues of access to the global economy.

The strategy of open regionalism combined three formal types of economic integration: agreements for sub-regional integration; bilateral accords for trade liberalization; and agreements liberalizing trade between groups of countries. Between the mid-1980s and the late 1990s, Latin America unilaterally reduced its average external tariff from over 40 percent to 12 percent (Devlin and Estevadeordal, 2001:17). The region also actively participated in the Uruguay round of the GATT negotiations, and all countries except the Bahamas and Cuba joined the WTO when it was created to replace the GATT in 1995. At the same time there was a parallel wave of new regional reciprocal free trade and integration agreements, an astonishing twenty in all between 1989 and 2000 and many more under negotiation.[2] Among the more notable agreements were the following: the creation in 1990 of the Mercosur by Brazil, Argentina, Uruguay, and Paraguay, with Chile and Bolivia as associate members; the Andean Community, established in 1995 by Colombia, Ecuador, and Venezuela; the revival of the Caribbean Economic Community (CARICOM); NAFTA, which went into effect in 1994 and brings together Mexico, the United States, and Canada; and the Central America Free Trade Agreement (CAFTA), negotiated since 2003 and finally approved in 2007 by all five Central American republics, the Dominican Republic, and the United States. These treaties paved the way for rapid growth in intra-regional imports and exports alongside the growth of extra-regional trade (notwithstanding a decline in the late 1990s, reflecting the regional recession). (See Table 4.1.) Intra-regional trade rose from 13 percent of total trade in 1990 to 20 percent toward the end of that decade (Devlin and Estevadeordal, 2001:17).

Local elites and TNS agents also drew up program to reconfigure geographies along new transnational lines throughout Latin America via cross-border

[2.] These included Andean Community (1998); Caribbean Community (CARICOM, 1989); Central American Common Market (1990); Chile-Mexico (1991); Southern Cone Common Market (MERCOSUR, 1991); CARICOM-Venezuela (1992); North American Free Trade Agreement (NAFTA, 1992); Chile-Venezuela (1993); Colombia-Chile (1993); Costa Rica-Mexico (1994); Group of Three (Mexico, Colombia, Venezuela, 1994); Bolivia-Mexico (1994); Chile-Ecuador (1994); Chile-MECOSUR (1996); Chile-Canada (1996); Bolivia-Mexico, 1996); Mexico-Nicaragua (1997); CACM-Dominican Republic (1998); CACM-Chile (1999); Mexico-EU (2000); Mexico-Israel (2000). Those under negotiation included: Free Trade Area of the Americas (FTAA); Canada-Costa Rica; Mexico-Panama; CACM-Panama; Northern Triangle [El Salvador, Guatemala, Honduras]-Andean Community; Chile-USA (approved in 1994); Central American Free Trade Agreement (CAFTA); MERCOSUR-EU (approved 2005); Chile-South Korea (approved 2004); APEC-Mexico-Japan. Source: Bulmer-Thomas, 2001:296, table A.1.

TABLE 4.1
ALADI* Intra-Regional Exports, 1990–2000 (in
$billion)

Year	Amount
1990	12.17
1991	15.11
1992	19.41
1993	23.69
1994	28.56
1995	35.81
1996	38.31
1997	45.65
1998	43.23
1999	34.79
2000	44.18

Source: Bulmer-Thomas, 2001, tables A-2 and A-3, pp. 297–298.
*ALADI: Asociacion Latinoamericana de Integration (Latin
American Integration Association, membership includes
Argentina, Bolivia, Brazil, Chile, Colombia, Ecuador, Mexico,
Paraguay, Uruguay, and Venezuela. Cuba joined in 2000).

infrastructural projects, among them the Plan Puebla Panama (PPP), Plan Colombia, Vision 2019, and the Initiative for Regional South American Integration (IIRSA). The PPP sought to carve a vast integrated area in Meso-America out of the five southern-most states of Mexico, the five Central American republics, Belize, and Panama and in this way to make the entire zone readily available to transnational corporate exploitation of its land, labor, and natural resources. The IIRSA, launched in 2000 by the Brazilian government with financing from the Inter-American Development Bank, set out to create production, export, and service corridors in South America as nodal points for regional integration. Similar to the PPP, the Initiative proposed investments in energy, transportation and telecommunications and the establishment of corridors running East-West across South America so as to link the Atlantic and Pacific and provided Brazil with a more efficient outlet to Asian markets. The most important of these corridors would run through Bolivia and would open up that country to Brazilian and Argentine-based TNCs anxious to expand regionally.

If integration in Central America in the 1960s was driven by governments and aimed at creating a protected regional market, since 1990 the process has been oriented toward inserting the region as single unit into the global economy and has been driven less by governments than by investor groups and by local communities attempting to find a workable insertion into the global economy (Segovia, 2006). Intra-regional trade in Central America increased 500 percent from 1990 to 2004 (Segovia, 2006:9) as integration facilitated the rise of a single regional labor, capital, and consumer market. As the Isthmus became a unitary platform for global capitalism a new form of territorial integration was taking shape among several border zones, among them, the San Juan River Valley between Nicaragua and Costa Rica, the tri-state triangle where El Salvador, Honduras, and Guatemala share a border, and the Gulf of Fonseca between El Salvador, Nicaragua, and Honduras. These border areas began to resemble what Dicken has called "transborder clusters and corridors" (1998:6067), or dynamic zones of concentrated globalized economic activity. The San Juan River Valley produces a variety of NTAEs and agro-industry and hosts expanding transnational tourism, while the Gulf of Fonseca is dotted with shrimp farms that supply the global market and agro-industry has spread to the western tri-country El Salvador-Guatemala-Honduras border region. The region, in effect, is becoming sliced up and integrated into the global economy without respect to traditional borders and based on the mobilization and flexible deployment throughout the region of capital, labor, and natural resources. Labor supply to these areas forms part of the regionally integrated system. Nicaraguans and Hondurans migrate in increasing numbers to El Salvador's eastern zone, while Salvadorans and Guatemalans have migrated back and forth between the two countries in accordance with the ebb and flow of the local demand for labor (Segovia, 2006:11).

At a South American presidential summit in 1994 the Mercosur and Andean Community countries formed the South American Community of Nations as a continental political and economic forum modeled after the European Union. The presidents agreed to create a continent-wide free trade zone by 2014, to establish a South American Bank, and to develop a common currency, parliament, and passport by 2019. In that same year, the presidents from thirty-four nations in the hemisphere (all except Cuba) met at the first Summit of the Americas in Miami. There, under U.S. leadership, they proposed a Free Trade Area of the Americas to integrate the entire region, from Alaska to Tierra del Fuego, into a single free trade area. Between 1994 and 2005 there were four additional summits and eight trade ministerial meetings. The process, however, reached an impasse in 2005 in the face of Venezuelan, Brazilian, and Argentine opposition to the U.S.-led integration project. The virtual collapse of negotiations did not signal regional resistance to integrating into global capitalism as much as differences over the terms of that integration and over the political leadership through which it would proceed. It is difficult to imagine a return to the nation-state order, in Latin America or elsewhere in global society. Instead, diverse social and political forces are locked in battle over what type of transnational structures will predominate into the twenty-first century. Early in the century, the Venezuelan government began to promote an alternative program of regional integration, the Bolivarian Alternative for the Americas, known by its Spanish acronym, ALBA. The ALBA sought an integration based on a configuration of class and social forces less dominated by transnational capital and its agents, as I will discuss in Chapter 5.

From International to Transnational Relations: Latin America and China

In the ten years from 1994 to 2004 trade between China and Latin America quintupled to $40 billion annually (Kraul, 2006). The sharp expansion of Latin American exports to China (particularly of raw materials), of imports from China, and of Chinese-origin investment in the region, led some to conclude that China and the United States were locked in a struggle over hegemonic influence in Latin America (see, inter alia, Petras, 2001). In this outdated nation-state and interstate framework of analysis, competition takes the form of rival national capitals or struggles for control between "domestic" and "foreign" capital, and interstate conflict is driven by rivalry among core powers for hegemony over the periphery. A global capitalism framework offers a more satisfying explanation: as China and Latin America have both entered the global economy their external relations are meshing in a larger web of transnational relations.

China has become the industrial workhouse of the world as an increasing portion of world industrial production shifts to that country. This not a story of capital from outside of China competing against capital inside of China; this is the workhouse of transnational capital. Transnational capital is just that—*transnational*. Investors operating in China are of Chinese, U.S., German, Japanese, Brazilian, South Africa, Thai, Indian, and Kuwaiti nationality, among many others. Capitalist groups from all over the world concentrate accumulation inside China for well-known reasons: massive abundant cheap labor that is also educated, one of the largest agglomeration economies in the world, a state responsive to the conditions necessary for globalized accumulation, and so forth. How are we therefore to interpret the effort by Chinese-based enterprises and the Chinese state as it tries to expand its world markets for those goods pouring out of the global China workhouse? This is not an instance of Chinese competing against U.S., French, Japanese, and other national elites, each competing with one another trying to develop new markets in Latin America. As I have argued previously (Robinson, 2007b), this classical image belongs to an earlier moment in world capitalism and mystifies the underlying transnational dynamic at play.

The "Chinese" expansion into Latin America that began in the 1990s is one particular form in which the diverse agents of transnational capital have attempted to expand markets globally, to sustain an accumulation process in which the principal class contradictions are not national but transnational, and in which the fiercest capitalist competition is not between national capitalist groups but between national and transnational fractions of capital and among transnational conglomerates. The new global capitalism has a territorial expression particular to it because global capitalism lands, so to speak, or "zones in on" particular transnationalized territories, such as China's coast, to undertake component circuits of global accumulation. The view that U.S., Chinese, and Latin American relations can be explained as a tussle between a declining U.S. hegemony trying to preserve its domination in Latin America and to ward off expanding Chinese influence confuses surface dynamics with underlying essence and misses the point.

As Latin America has globalized it has increased its supply of raw materials to the workhouse of the world, exporting to the Chinese coastal zones vast quantities of soy, copper, oil, aluminum, wood pulp, and so on (Dickerson, 2006a). A commodities boom took place in Latin America in the early years of the twenty-first century, fueled in large part by ballooning demand in China for raw materials, and accounting in large measure for the economic recovery that the region experienced following a prolonged recession from 1999 to 2002. When copper goes from Chile to China or oil from Venezuela to China it goes to feed not "Chinese" capitalism but global capitalism in China, to fuel transnational accumulation taking place in Chinese territory. These are not nation-state relations; they are global capitalist relations. If we want to understand Latin America's transnational relations, its relationship to political processes and power structures worldwide, we need to develop a global capitalist and not a nation-state–centric framework of analysis.

While I cannot pursue the issue further, two examples will suffice. The first is Chile–Chinese integration. Trade between these two countries increased from $680 million in 1998 to $7 billion in 2004 as China became Chile's second-largest trading partner (Dickerson, 2006b). Chilean copper, wood pulp, wine, and fresh foods have poured into China, and a reverse flow of manufacturers supplied an increasing portion of the Chilean consumer goods market. Industrial manufacturers that previously supplied the domestic market have gone out of business as new commercial and elites and other producers tied to the global economy have flourished (see Chapter 2). Paradigmatic is the case of José Ramón de Camino, who gave up his domestic textile business to import footwear made in China that he markets through a chain of Payless retail shops in Santiago, franchised with the U.S.-based company, and by wholesale distribution to local stores in the provinces. These arrangements bring together TNCs producing footwear in China with the U.S.-based Payless franchise and distinct commercial agents in Chile.

National and regional particularities are not irrelevant, yet Latin America's complex and multidimensional relations with the world simply cannot be understood through an outdated nation-state–centric lens. Nationally oriented capitalists in Chile are perhaps the weakest in Latin America relative to transnationally oriented groups due to the country's earlier and sweeping integration into global capitalism following the overthrow of Allende in 1973. While transnational fractions of the elite came to power in nearly all countries of Latin America in the 1980s and 1990s, the relative strength of nationally and transnationally oriented groups varied among sub-regions and from country-to-country. Mexico and Central America, for instance, were not as successful as South American countries in developing export markets in China for their raw materials at the same time as export processing zones in China offered cheaper labor and therefore competed with the Greater Caribbean Basin in attracting TNC investment (see Chapter 3).

The second example is that of China's multibillion-dollar investment in Latin American oil and natural gas industries and in related infrastructural projects. In the early twenty-first century China signed a series of energy deals in the Western Hemisphere amounting to tens of billions of dollars, ranging from tar sands in Canada to natural gas fields in Argentina and Bolivia and oil fields in Venezuela and Ecuador (Kraul, 2006). In 2005 the U.S. Congress held hearings to determine whether U.S. interests were threatened as a result of this expanding Chinese presence in the Western Hemisphere energy sector and concluded on the basis of reports and testimonies that those interests were not at risk (Kraul, 2006). Rather than competition between the United States and China over energy resources the Chinese expansion was creating a larger global pool of available energy needed to keep fueling a voracious global capitalist economy and to keep the Chinese work-house in operation.

Meanwhile, if the notion of transnational relations applies to states, inter- and supra-national institutions, and transnationally oriented social groups, it does as well to those individuals and communities who become transnational by virtue of their own cross-border movement. I now turn to the topics of trans-national migration and communities.

Latin America and Transnational Migration

The Global Circulation of Immigrant Labor

The latter decades of the twentieth century began a period of massive new mi-grations worldwide. Migration stems from the very dynamics of capitalist devel-opment. Lydia Potts has shown that mass labor migrations historically are generated by (1) the expansion of capitalism into new areas; (2) the industrial-ization of areas already brought into the world capitalist system; (3) intensive new booms in capital accumulation; and (4) labor imports providing a means of reproducing capital's dominance in specific conjunctures (Potts, 1990). All four of these instances have come together under globalization. A low-end estimate by the United Nations placed the number of immigrant workers in 2005 at some 200 million by the new century (Orozco, 2003), double the number from twenty-five years earlier. Some of the largest labor flows were from Southern Europe and North Africa to Western Europe, from the Caribbean Basin and South-East Asia to the United States, and from the Middle East and South Asia into the Arab oil-exporting countries.

In one sense, the South penetrates the North with the dramatic expansion of immigrant labor. But transnational migratory flows are not unidirectional from South to North, and the phenomenon is best seen in global capitalist rather than North-South terms. Labor-short Middle Eastern countries, for instance, have programs for the importation (and careful control) of labor from throughout South and East Asia and North Africa. The Philippine state has become a veritable labor recruitment agency for the global economy, or-ganizing the export of its citizens to over a hundred countries in Asia, the Middle East, Europe, North America, and elsewhere. Indeed, the Philippines biggest export, by far, is labor, as measured in remittances, which dwarf all other export earnings. Greeks migrate to Germany and the United States while Albanians migrate to Greece. South Africans move to Australia and

England, while Malawians, Mozambicans, and Zimbabweans work in South African mines and the service industry. Malaysia imports Indonesian labor, while Thailand imports workers from Laos and Myanmar and in turn sends labor to Malaysia, Singapore, Japan, and elsewhere. In Latin America, Costa Rica is a major importer of Nicaraguan labor, Venezuela has historically imported large amounts of Colombian labor, the Southern Cone draws on several million emigrant Andean workers, and an estimated 500,000 to 800,000 Haitians live in the Dominican republic (IDB, 2006:36), where they cut sugar cane, harvest crops, and work in the maquiladoras under the same labor market segmentation, political disenfranchisement, and repression that immigrant workers face in the United States and in most labor importing countries.

What is the importance of this transnational migration to the global system? Central to capitalism is securing a politically and economically suitable labor supply, and at the core of all class societies is the control over labor and disposal of the products of labor. But the linkage between securing labor and territoriality is changing under globalization. As labor becomes "free" in every corner of the globe, capital has vast new opportunities for mobilizing labor power where and when required. National labor pools are merging into a single global labor pool that services global capitalism. The transnational circulation of capital induces the transnational circulation of labor. The global economy absorbs local labor surpluses so that transnational migration functions as an adjustment mechanism of local and national labor markets through the supranational redistribution of that labor. This global circulation of labor becomes incorporated into the process of restructuring the world economy, providing a world-level labor supply system for global production chains.

Migrant workers are becoming a general category of super-exploitable labor drawn from globally dispersed labor reserves into similarly globally dispersed nodes of intensive or specialized accumulation. The emerging geographic pattern is one in which zones of accumulation in the global economy may be localized, such as Costa Rica's central mesa, the southern coastal regions of China, the greater Buenos Aires area, and so forth, or they may be transborder, such as stretches of the U.S.-Mexico border, the Costa Rica-Nicaragua border, or parts of the Thai-Indonesia border, among others. Here the core constitutes intense nodes of accumulation that are not coterminous with nations or global regions while the periphery are other localized zones that supply labor, raw materials, or other inputs. Thus southern and central Mexico provides labor to regional northern and Mexico City economies, the interior of China supplies labor to the coast, and Nicaraguans are mobilized from diverse points toward maquiladoras in Managua, to Costa Rica-Nicaragua border zones, or to the Costa Rican central mesa. However, even this adjusted analysis is misleading since, in the end, these central and peripheral characteristics may be present within the same locale—and increasingly are. Flexible accumulation and a new global division of labor have resulted in an increased heterogeneity of labor markets in each locale. The ghettos of Los Angeles and Mexico City are just as much peripheral labor reserves for accumulation in those cities as is the south and central Mexican countryside, as the global cities and other literature on urban political economy have shown. Here again we need to reconceive core and periphery not in terms of territory or fixed geographies but in terms of social groups in a shifting transnational environment.

In an *apparent* contradiction, capital and goods move freely across national borders in the new global economy; labor, however, cannot move this way, and its movement is subject to heightened state controls. The global labor supply is, in the main, no longer coerced (subject to extra-economic compulsion) due to the ability of the universalized market to exercise strictly economic discipline, but its movement is juridically controlled. This control is a central determinant in the worldwide correlation of forces between global capital and global labor. A *free* flow of labor would exert an equalizing influence on wages across borders while state controls help reproduce such differentials. Eliminating the wage differential between regions would cancel the advantages that capital accrues from disposing of labor pools worldwide subject to different wage levels and would strengthen labor worldwide in relation to capital. In addition, the use of immigrant labor allows employers in receiving countries to separate reproduction and maintenance of labor, and therefore to "externalize" the costs of social reproduction. The new transnational migration, therefore, helps capital to dispose with the need to pay for the reproduction of labor power. Hence, state controls are often intended *not to prevent* but to *control* the transnational movement of labor. As global labor markets replace national labor markets, states, with their coercive capacities and national borders, shift from organizing and regulating national labor markets to managing super-exploited and super-controlled labor pools. The inter-state system thus acts as a condition for the structural power of globally mobile transnational capital over labor that is transnational in actual content and character but subjected to different institutional arrangements under the direct control of national states.

The division of the global labor force into immigrants and citizens is a major new axis of inequality worldwide. The maintenance and strengthening of state controls over transnational labor creates the conditions for "immigrant labor" as a distinct category of labor in relation to capital. The creation of these distinct categories becomes central to the global capitalist economy, replacing earlier direct colonial and racial caste controls over labor worldwide. Most transnational immigrant workers become inserted into segmented labor markets as low-paid, low-status laborers under unstable and precarious work conditions without the political or labor rights accorded to citizens. They are racialized to the extent that cultural and physical markers can be used—or constructed—to demarcate these workers. Class and race and national borders all come together to generated explosive relations of exploitation and oppression, as well as resistance, that I will discuss in more detail in Chapter 6 in a case study of Latino and Latina immigrants in the United States.[3]

The "Age of Migration" in Latin America

Latin America has been swept up in this new "age of migration" (Castles and Miller, 2003). The wave of out-migration from socially and economically devastated regions began in the 1980s and accelerated in the 1990s and into the new century. The 20 million Latin American immigrants in the United States in the early twenty-first century (IDB, 2006) included some 10 million Mexicans, 5 million Central Americans, and several million more from Colombia, the Dominican Republic, Haiti, Peru, and elsewhere. These figures do not include U.S.-born Latinos, Cubans, or Brazilians. Several million more migrants had migrated to Spain, Portugal, the United Kingdom, other parts of Europe, Japan, Australia, Canada, and elsewhere; and another 3 to 5 million migrants worked in neighboring countries in Latin America (IDB, 2006:13). Over 10 percent of the Dominican population has migrated to the United States. A quarter to a third of Nicaragua's 5 million people reside in either Costa Rica or the United States. Up to 20 percent of all Haitians are in the United States and the Dominican

[3] Connecting labor with capital in the global economy, as Kyle (2000) notes, is now a multibillion-dollar industry. Globally organized networks of "migration merchants," or usurious middlemen, provide a full range of legal and illegal services needed for migration, including the supply of passports, visas, work permits, cash advances, safe houses, above ground and clandestine transport, border crossing by *coyotes*, and employment opportunities in countries of destination—all for fees that can add up to tens of thousands of dollars and may place the transnational migrant in a situation of indentured servitude for many years.

Republic. Up to 33 percent of El Salvador's 7 million people were living abroad in 2005, as were 15–20 percent of all Mexicans (ibid.; Bourdreaux, 2006:A12). Such a mass movement of people, moreover, integrated tens if not hundreds of millions more who remained at home into transnational social structures, as I will discuss below.

Social scientists generally identify "push" factors as those that repel people outward and "pull" factors as those that draw people in, while neoclassical economics emphasizes the forces of supply and demand for labor. On the one hand, capitalist globalization—structural adjustment, free trade agreements, privatizations, the contraction of public employment and credits, the breakup of communal lands, and so forth, along with the political crises these measures have generated—has *imploded* thousands of communities in Latin America and unleashed a wave of migration, from rural to urban areas and to other countries, that can only be analogous to the mass uprooting and migration that generally takes place in the wake of wars. This mass transnational migration has functioned as a major political safety value diverting what may otherwise have been much more severe political and social conflict. In a sense this is a coerced or forced migration, since capitalist globalization has exerted a structural coercion over whole populations. On the other hand, transnational migration and wage remittances as a new family-survival strategy at the micro-level is made possible and necessary by globalization: *possible* by demand from global labor markets and transportation, communications, and other technologies that facilitate transnational labor mobility; and *necessary* because of neoliberal restructuring and the collapse of national economies. The mass migrations out of Ecuador, Central America, Mexico, and elsewhere in Latin America starting in the 1980s coincided with the collapse of the previous model of development and the onset of globalization. With the collapse of national economies internal migration became less viable as a survival strategy. Global cities and other zones of intensive accumulation within and outside of Latin America became vacuums sucking in this immigration. The upheavals and displacement of restructuring and global integration have made it difficult if not impossible to reproduce existing family and community structures. These structures are becoming replaced by new social formations, among them, by transnational communities and transnational families.

The Pew Hispanic Center concluded after analyzing this mass migration that emigration and the return flow of remittances were emblematic of *crisis response* throughout Latin America. Emigration is "not merely the result of economic problems experienced by an individual or family but rather was a response to a nation's economic crisis. Thus, the closure of banks, rapid currency depreciation, commercial bankruptcies and the overall atmosphere of financial instability were cited as causes of migration [in focus groups] beyond unemployment and other personal economic losses" (2003:14). In the first four years of the twenty-first century, for example, an estimated 1 million Ecuadorians—nearly 10 percent of the population—left their country, half of them to Spain and most of the rest to the United States (IDB, 2006:26). This mass migration was closely tied to the economic, political, and environmental crises that shook the country from the 1990s and on. In turn, the report noted, the Ecuadorian case and evidence elsewhere show that "the ability to establish a monetary flow from abroad quickly and of sufficient size to ensure a family's economic survival" is now a ready means of dealing with crisis and instability in much of Latin America. Similarly, in Central America "crises responses have become normalcy," in the sense that the initial wave of out-migration in the 1980s may have been induced by the political and military upheaval but once transnational social networks of migrants and remittance flows were established, further emigration became a "normal" response to ongoing crises conditions, including calamities such as Hurricane Mitch, bouts of political protest and instability, continued high rates of unemployment, and other economic difficulties (2003:15–16). Argentina, Colombia, Venezuela, and Haiti, among other countries, have also experienced surges in migration as a response to crises.

Emigration and Depopulation in Mexico and Central America

Mass migration describes a "local social milieu characterized by a metaphorical 'migration fever,' " according to Kyle (2000:30), induced by structural pressures that build up to such a point that individual reasons for migrating become "superfluous to broader social forces" (Kyle, 2000:30). Net migration flows from Mexico grew from an average annual of 220,000 between 1980 and 1984, to 370,000 between 1990 and 1994, and then to 575,000 between 2000 and 2004 (Pew Hispanic Center, as cited in Binford, 2005:32). By the 1990s Mexicans were migrating in large numbers beyond the historic sending areas of West Central Mexico (Michoacan, Guanajuato, Jalisco, and Zacatecas), streaming out of the southern states of Puebla, Oacaca, Guerrero, Veracruz, and Chiapas as well as the northern states. Virtually every corner of Mexican territory has been impacted by mass migration to the United

States—96.2 percent of all municipal regions in Mexico, according to the government's National Population Council (as cited in Delgado-Wise and Cypher, 2005:26; see also www.conapo.gob.mx). Emigration exceeded outflows from China and India as Mexico became the number one labor-exporting country in the world proportional to its population (United Nations World Economic and Social Survey, 2004, as cited in Delgado-Wise and Cypher, 2005:25). Between 1990 and 2004 the Mexican-born population with residence in the United States doubled, from 5.4 million to 10.2 million, bringing the number of residents of Mexican origin in the United States to an estimated 27 million (ibid.:25).

Neoliberalism in Mexico during this time (1) opened the country to the global economy; (2) generated a global reserve army of labor uprooted and available to work in the global production system, whether in the maquiladoras or as emigrants; (3) lowered the relative and real cost of labor as productivity actually rose; and (4) shifted the correlation of class and social forces away from popular classes and nationally oriented economic groups and toward global capital and transnationally oriented elites. Delgado-Wise and Cypher argue that the Mexican economy has become a labor export–led model after NAFTA went into effect in 1994, driven by the export of Mexican labor to the United States together with the use of cheap and largely poorly trained labor in the maquiladora industry (while emigration represents the direct export of labor the use of cheap labor in the maquiladora sector constitutes its "indirect" export since this labor becomes embodied in maquiladora sector's export products).[4]

> At the very moment when NAFTA's proponents had touted the growth in manufacturing exports a darker association was ignored—the explosive growth of emigrants to the degree that Mexico has now become the principal country of emigrants in the world. Further, NAFTA was conceived as the very antidote to emigration, with proponents asserting that the workings of the 'free trade' ar-

[4] Delgado-Wise and Cypher argue that this arrangement represents a subordinate integration of the Mexican economy into the U.S. economy for the benefit of the latter in its competition with rival national economies and regions in Europe and Asia. Such nation-state centric analysis is misinformed. The provision of cheap Mexican labor is not for the "U.S." economy but for the *global* economy. The maquiladora workers are global economy workers. What used to be Mexican domestic industry has been externally reoriented and integrated not into the "U.S." economy but as component processes of global production chains and circuits of accumulation. And all this has been in the interests not of "the United States" or "U.S." capital but of global capital. This much should be clear by Delgado-Wise and Cypher's recognition (2005:9–10) that NAFTA has been a losing proposition not only for Mexican workers, peasants, and small and medium-sized businesses but also for the working class and portions of the middle class and some sectors of business in the United States at the same time as it has benefited TNCs on both sides of the border and the powerful Mexican economic *grupos* that have prospered under NAFTA and neoliberalism.

rangement would lead to Mexico specializing in labor-intensive activities that would absorb the idle and underutilized labor force. Instead, few jobs in formal sector, and even fewer jobs of a permanent nature, have been created, forcing as many as three fourths of the annual new entrants into a 'free to choose' scenario wherein the options consist of entering the informal sector as a house servant, a street vendor or something similar or emigrating to the U.S. Indeed, emigration has become such a powerful current that 31 percent of the municipalities in the country are now suffering from depopulation. (Delgado-Wise and Cypher, 2005:10)

Despite the hardening of immigration policies in the United States following the September 2001 attack on the World Trade Center and the Pentagon, out-migration from Mexico to the United States actually intensified in the new century. This immigration has as much to do with economic and social restructuring in the United States as it does with conditions in Mexico. The U.S. economy, as I will discuss in Chapter 6, is increasingly dependent on immigrant labor—indeed, the United States is the nation with the highest levels of immigration in the world, absorbing 20 percent of all migrants. As a result of such controls there has been a shift from a circular Mexican migratory pattern toward one in which the dominant form of immigration is to establish residence, and this has been accompanied by widespread immigration of Mexican women and even entire families (Delgado-Wide and Cypher, 2005:29). Heightened U.S. state controls have also inflated the cost of migration. The fees paid to *coyotes,* or professional people smugglers, along the U.S. Mexico border—the principal point of entry for the majority of Latino immigrants to the United States—was between $200 and $400 for the Mexico–Los Angeles route in the late 1990s but increased sharply following the 2001 attacks on the World Trade Center and heightened militarization along the border (Ratha, 2004:41), climbing into the thousands of dollars, depending on the services.

In Central America, until the late 1970s most migration took place within the nations of the region or as intra-regional movements of workers between neighboring countries, from zones of subsistence production to the agro-export plantations and agricultural frontier, or to expanding urban centers (Castillo, 1996). The regional political-military upheaval in the 1980s, however, triggered a veritable exodus. The low-end estimates place the number of Central Americans who emigrated to the United States in the 1980s at 3 million people, or 15 percent of the total Isthmanian population at the time of 20 million, mostly from El

Salvador, Nicaragua, and Guatemala (additionally, more than 1 million people emigrated to other countries within the region and another 1 million were internally displaced) [Robinson, 1993; Castillo, 1996; U.S. Bureau of the Census, 1997).[5]

Pacification in the 1990s did not bring an end to outmigration. Migrants were no longer political and war refugees; the inducement now became socioeconomic ravages of neoliberalism: unemployment, informalization, landlessness, and poverty (Robinson, 2003). Transnational social networks established during the 1980s became a durable structure exerting a steady pull on migration as extended family members sought reunification abroad and whole communities organized the emigration of their members. Migration flows, once established, as Portes and Borocz observe, tend to continue with relative autonomy as contacts across space, social channels, "family chains," and new information and interests which they promote, sustain migrations even when the original economic or political inducements have disappeared (1990:612–613).

Intra-Latin American Migrations

While Latin American immigration to the United States has received much attention the intensification of transnational labor flows within Latin America has been no less dramatic. Millions of Colombians migrated to Venezuela in the 1980s and 1990s, for instance, where they worked as seasonal labor for the coffee crop, in other agricultural labor, and in construction and services. This flow continued in the 1990s but tapered off in the new century, although by that time up to 4 million immigrants, largely Colombians, were in the country (Castles and Miller, 2003:147); this figure represented between 10 percent and 20 percent of the country's population. The Argentine Secretary of State Guido di Tella anticipated in 2001 that by the year 2020 Bolivian and Paraguayan immigrant workers would make up 20 percent of the Argentinean population, concentrated in construction, textile, agricultural, domestic, and street-related jobs (Grimson, 2001). One report estimate the number of Bolivian immigrant workers in Argentina's northern strip and in Buenos Aires at between 1 million

---

[5] However, the real figure was probably much higher. U.S. government figures are generally assumed to be *much* lower than the real figure, as they only count those who come in contact with U.S. authorities. Just the figure for Guatemala immigrants, for instance, estimated at between one and 1.2 million in the United States (over 10 percent of the Guatemalan population), is close to the official U.S. government figure for *all* Central Americans in the United States (Rincon, Jonas, and Rodriguez, 1999). In fact, Central American countries accounted for four of the top nine countries sending undocumented immigrants to the United States (Stalker, 2000:28) and by the early 1990s more than 100,000 Central Americans were being deported from the United States each year.

and 2 million (Peredo Leigue, 2006), while another placed the number of Paraguayans at 300,000 (IDB, 2006:36). Just as day laborers (*jornaleros*) can be found in major U.S. cities, Bolivian and other immigrants can be seen congregated in working-class Buenos Aires neighborhoods for employers to come and hire them for one or a few days. These workers lacked political rights and legal recourse and faced subhuman work conditions, discrimination, prejudice and xenophobia (Grimson, 2001; Peredo Leigue, 2006). In one highly publicized incident in March 2006 a deadly fire swept through a Buenos Aires sweatshop, killing six Bolivians trapped inside, among them four children. The blaze illuminated the existence of a network of clandestine factories where thousands of undocumented workers toiled in conditions that government officials characterized as "virtual slavery" (Notisur, 2006a).

Chile experienced a sharp increase in immigration starting in the second half of the 1990s, largely of Peruvians, as well as Bolivians and Ecuadorians, who have become concentrated in domestic work and other informal services, construction, and industry, particularly in the capital city of Santiago (Pizarro, 2003; Stefoni, 2003). This "new immigration" brought the foreign-born population in the country to some 200,000 by 2002—an all-time high for Chile—some 33 percent of them from Andean countries (ibid.). Peruvian female immigrants in particular have been relegated to domestic work as nannies and maids in affluent neighborhoods in Santiago; 43 percent of all Peruvian immigrants in Chile are domestic workers as are more than 70 percent of Peruvian immigrant women (Pizarro, 2003:44). The feminization of Peruvian migration and the preference of Chilean employers for Peruvian nannies are becoming institutionalized, according to Pizarro, as upper- and middle-class Chilean families increasingly prefer these immigrant domestic workers because they have little choice but to become live-ins. In this way they can be more easily controlled during their employment and disposed of when their services are no longer required (Pizarro, 2003). More generally, the Andean immigrant community in Chile has faced increasing negative cultural stereotyping, discrimination, and intolerance (Pizarro, 2003; Stefoni, 2003).

While small-scale emigration of Nicaraguans to Costa Rica has occurred for decades, the massive transfer is a more recent phenomenon bound up with transnational processes (Morales and Castro, 1999; Morales, 1997; Venutelo, 1997; Sandoval, 2004).[6] By the late 1990s Nicaraguan immigrants in Costa

[6] Moreover, labor shortages have emerged in some zones of Central America resulting from the mass out-migration to the United States. This has produced new patterns of intra-regional migration. Nicaraguans and Hondurans, for instance, have migrated in increasing numbers to El Salvador's

Rica were estimated at an astonishing 500,000 to 700,000, representing between 12 percent and 18 percent of the Nicaraguan population, and just as astonishing, equaling an estimated 16 percent of the Costa Rican population and up to 30 percent of the EAP (Morales and Castro 1999:31). The immediate cause of this migration on the "push" side was the saturation of both formal and informal employment opportunities in Nicaragua in the 1980s in the face of economic crisis and military conflict; on the "pull" side, the transformation of Costa Rica's productive apparatus resulted in a massive shift of Costa Rican workers out of traditional activities in agriculture resulting in labor shortages. De-peasantization of the Costa Rican countryside left both old and new agro-export activities without a workforce, which was replenished by Nicaraguans. As Costa Rican smallholders lost their lands to transnational corporations and Costa Rican capitalists who proceeded to reorient production toward the global economy there was a switch from Costa Rican to Nicaraguan labor precisely at these new or reorganized production sites, in the same way as employers in the United States have switched from white and black to Latino immigrant labor. "The immigrant workforce has become a key factor in the development of a series of new productive activities promoted by the Costa Rican state since the mid-1980s as part of the new export-oriented model" (Morales and Castro, 1999:54).

Beyond agriculture, Nicaraguans in Costa Rica are concentrated in unskilled, poorly paid, and precarious jobs, generally manual labor, although they show up in almost every sector of the economy. Traditional agro-exports (especially banana, but also coffee), several NTAE industries (particularly melons), the construction industries, maquiladora factory work, domestic service and other service sector activities have become major "absorption niches" for Nicaraguan laborers. Nicaraguans predominate among security guards, restaurant workers, porters, shoe repair, electronic repair, janitors and cleaners, as hair salon assistants, and so on, in a pattern remarkably similar to Latino immigrant employment in the United States. The massive entry of Nicaraguans into the Costa Rican labor market has coincided with the development of new forms of "flexible" employment associated with the new capital-labor relation, especially temporary, part-time, seasonal, and contract work, and a drop in the general wage level in these categories, so that much work done by Nicaraguans is precarious and provides no benefits or security.

---

eastern zone, while Salvadorans and Guatemalans have migrated back and forth between the two countries in accordance with the ebb and flow of the local demand for labor (Segovia, 2006:11).

The Nicaraguan population in Costa Rica exhibit all the classical sociological signs of a minority group, including systematic subordination within
stratification structures on the basis of ethnic identification, the construction of social and cultural barriers that reinforce this subordination, humiliation in the hands of the majority group, social demarcation by characteristics
singled out or constructed by the majority group, residential segregation,
and an increasing sense of ethnic self-identity and solidarity (Venutelo,
1997; Sandoval, 2004). Nicaraguan minority group formation in Costa Rica
is a process fomented by the state, which has taken a series of measures to
create and sustain a juridical category of immigrant workers from Nicaragua
and to structure labor market segmentation along these lines. One such
measure was the 1995 decision to oblige all Nicaraguans to obtain a seasonal
work card issued by the government. Each card was valid for only six months
at a time, which in effect made it impossible for Nicaraguans to legally obtain stable or long-term employment in better-off jobs. The measure therefore helped to sanction the ethnic segmentation of the labor market,
contributed to the casualization of labor, at least in the bottom rungs of the
segmented structure, and provided the state with a powerful instrument of
control over the Nicaraguan immigrant workforce (synchronized with the
repressive practices of Costa Rican police and immigration authorities).
Scapegoating and anti-Nicaraguan sentiment has gained ground among
Costa Rican popular sectors as social polarization and the insecurities that
adhere to the transnational model have been felt in the same way that
anti-Latino racism has spread through white working-class sectors in the
United States.

In all of these cases—Bolivians in Argentina, Peruvians in Chile, Colombians in Venezuela, Nicaraguans in Costa Rica, Haitians in the Dominican Republic, Mexicans, Central Americans, and other Latinos/as in the United
States—we find a telltale pattern of racialization of immigrant labor pools. Such
racialization becomes a mechanism that legitimates the inferior status of immigrants in segmented labor markets, facilitates greater social control over immigrant workers, and justifies the scapegoating of immigrant communities in
the face of insecurities and tensions generated by economic restructuring and
globalization. But immigrant workers and their families are not passive victims.
They exercise a collective agency in interaction with other transnational agents
that propels the dynamics of global capitalism. In the next chapter I will look at
the immigrant rights movement in the United States, spearheaded by the 30
million Latin American immigrants in that country. I now turn to another

dimension of their agency, the creation of transnational communities as a form of "globalization from below."

Transnational Latin American Communities

Transnationalism and Transnationality

The concepts of transnationalism and transnationality first became popular in the social sciences in the 1990s to denote a range of practices and processes brought about by the sheer increase in social connectivity across borders and that cannot be defined through the traditional reference point of nation-states (see, inter alia, Basch et al., 1994; Smith and Guarnizo, 1998; Schiller and Fourton, 2001; Domínguez, 1998; Kearney, 1995; Rouse 1991; McNeill, 1996; Vertovec, 1999:447). Within the field of immigration studies, transnationalism came to refer to the activities of immigrants to forge and sustain multi-stranded social relations that link their societies of origin and settlement as a single unified field of social action (Basch et al., 1994:7). While most scholars agree that transnational networks were maintained to a greater degree in earlier waves of immigration than was previously thought (Schiller, 1999), there is simply no historic precedent to the quantity and character of transnational links in the era of globalization. The same social and economic forces unleashed by globalization that give capital transnational mobility have also allowed immigrant groups to become transnational. Global communications, transportation networks, and financial infrastructures allow immigrants to maintain ongoing exchanges between their home country and their country (or countries) of immigration. These communities find that they are able to create "transnational spaces" to a degree previously unknown and live simultaneously in two or more worlds (Levitt, 2001; Portes, 1995, 1996; Portes et al., 1999).

Recognizing this new reality, the scholarly literature undertook a paradigm shift from international to transnational migration, and began to refer to these communities as transnational communities (see, inter alia, Portes, 1995; 1996). Long-standing concepts of immigrant experience are inadequate to capture new realities on the global, national, community, and individual levels. Migration is no longer a one-way street, with immigrants adapting, as assimilation theory would suggest, to new ways of life in host countries. Hybrid cultural and political processes develop through the extension and institutionalization of transnational immigrant networks challenging seemingly dichotomous and mutually exclusive categories, such as external vs. internal, national vs. international, sending vs. receiving countries, sojourner vs. settler, or citizen vs. noncitizen.

Portes, one of the pioneering scholars of transnational communities, has emphasized the agency of small-scale entrepreneurs in the formation of such communities (1995; 1996). Different immigrant groups have found economic niches in countries of destination, such as marketing indigenous goods from back home, contracting for outsourcing phases of global production chains, setting up enterprises to meet local demand for goods and services among their ethnic kin (which may involve small-scale importing from back home), and so on. These economic activities are themselves a result of flexible global production and commerce, which opens up diverse new niches around the world. As these mobile immigrant groups institutionalize these networks they come to constitute transnational communities that maintain social, cultural, political, and economic ties in both countries, living between the two, and as intermediaries between communities in different countries. "As the members of these communities travel back and forth, they carry cultural and political currents in both directions," notes Portes. "Their emergence complicates our understanding not only of global trade but also of immigration and national identity." The result of this process, according to Portes, is "the transformation of the original pioneering economic ventures into transnational communities that include an increasing number of people who lead dual lives. Members are at least bilingual, move easily between different cultures, frequently maintain homes in two countries, and pursue economic, political, and cultural interests that require a simultaneous presence in both" (1996:76–77).

Portes and other researchers, such as Peréz Saínz and Andrade-Eekhoff (2003), see transnational practices as increasing the autonomy and power of the migrants and non-migrants engaged in them. However, transnationality is in my view a contradictory condition and certainly not a uniform experience. It is constructed upon the class, as well as gender, racial, and other social relations of global capitalism. Most members of transnational communities are not successful entrepreneurs but migrant workers. Moreover, the politics of transnational communities are nuanced and may range from reactionary to revolutionary. They can be can be fomented by states and elites in the interests of transnational capital as much as they can be driven by popular struggles. The Mexican government, for instance, created in 1990 the Program for Mexican Communities Abroad to facilitate projects co-sponsored by the government and transnational communities, with the goals of getting NAFTA passed, pursuing U.S.–Mexico economic integration, and dampening support among Mexican immigrant groups for the opposition Party of the Democratic Revolution (see, e.g., Smith, 1998). Transnationalism may have "the potential to break down borders and traditions and create new cultures and hybrid ways of life," observes Yen Le Espiritu, "but also to fortify traditional hierarchies, homogenize diverse cultural practices, and obscure intra-group differences and differential relationships" (2003:214).

The study of transnational communities requires a theoretical and methodological focus on transnational social networks (see, inter alia, Massey et al., 1998; Basch, Schiller, and Blanc, 1994; Portes, 1997; Portes and Borocz, 1990). Such networks get started as "pioneering" migrants make initial contacts and open paths that are used by subsequent and expanding streams of migrants. Eventually a "chain migration" sets in as kin and community-based migration produce a snowball effect. These networks become self-reinforcing transnational social structures, a mezo or intermediate level that mediates between micro-processes, such as family decisions to send migrants, and macro-level structural processes, such the collapse of local economies. "More than movement from one place to another in search of higher wages, labor migration should be conceptualized as a process of progressive network building," argue Portes and Borocz. "Networks constructed by the movements and contact of people across space are at the core of the microstructures which sustain migration over time. More than individualistic calculations of gain, it is the insertion of people into such networks which helps explain differential proclivities to move and the enduring character of migrant flows" (Portes and Borocz, 1990:612).

Dominican and Mexican Transnational Communities

The new transnational migrants often engage in circular migration—having left home countries often "not to start a new life but to better the one they already have back home" (Kyle, 2000:xi)—by keeping households in two countries. In many Mexican, Central American, and Andean communities that send labor abroad it is common to see housing construction at different stages of development, satellite dishes, electronic appliances, teens dressed in the latest world fashions, and other symbols of global consumption fueled by remittances. In her study of one "transnational village" that links the Dominican community of Miraflores with emigrants from that community to the

Boston area in the United States, Levitt observes, "over the years migrants from the Dominican Republic and friends and families left behind have sustained such strong contact with one another [it is] as if village life has two settings." Life becomes transformed for both emigrants and those who remain behind through "a continuous circular flow of goods, news, and information" between Boston and the island. Miraflores migrants "do not shift their loyalties and participatory energies from one country to another. Instead, they are integrated to varying degrees, into the countries that receive them, at the same time that they remain connected to the countries they leave behind" (2001:5). Levitt refers to the transformative effects of transnational migration on home communities as social remittances: that is, influences beyond monetary remittances that penetrate and reorient the local social, political, and cultural fabric. Transnational villages emerge and endure, in her view, particularly because of these social remittances as "the ideas, behaviors, and social capital that flow from receiving to sending communities" and act as "tools with which ordinary individuals create global culture at the local level" (2001:11).

But with this transnationalization of social structure come heightened relations of dependence on global capitalism. Dominican emigrants in the United States, as Levitt points out by way of example, find that they can no longer return to their home communities because so many family members and friends from those communities are dependent for survival on their support from abroad. "Immigrant life yields ambiguous rewards," she observes. "On the weekends, they go to the mall, where they can choose from a range of products so vast it is almost unimaginable. But work consumes them. They leave at five o'clock in the morning, return at two, eat, bathe, and then work again until ten at night. Their jobs give them little besides a paycheck. Many live near the bottom of the socioeconomic ladder. . . . They watch the Anglo world from its margins, now knowing how to negotiate their way in. . . . Those who regret their choices find it difficult to turn back because so many family members and friends depend on their support" (2001:200).

Transnational migrants often become involved in the political systems of both countries. The political culture of transnational communities is itself transnational, a synthesis of multiple national and regional political cultures, so that transnational migrants develop new identities that are neither those of their points of origin or destination. In fact, the governments of the Dominican Republic, Mexico, Venezuela, Brazil, and Ecuador amended their constitutions in recent years to accommodate this new transnational reality and include migrants as official members of more than one political community. These measures include allowing for dual citizenship, for voting abroad, and for bi- and multi-national political organizing. In Trinidad and Tobago, as in Colombia and Brazil, nationals can vote at polling sites set up by their consulates. Colombians living abroad have their own special elected "expatriate" representative in the Colombian legislature. If Jesus Galvis, a travel agent in New Jersey who ran for the Colombian senate in 1997, had been elected, observes Levitt (2001:19), he planned to hold office simultaneously in Bogotá and in Hackensack, where he was a city councilor. By the late 1990s New York City was home to the largest concentration of Dominican voters outside of Santo Domingo, and candidates in island elections routinely incorporated into their electoral strategies campaigning in New York, Boston, and other U.S. cities. Indeed, several U.S.-based Dominicans served in that decade in the Dominican Congress (Levitt, 2001:142).

Family remittances are a key form of linkage among emigrant Latinos and Latin America. Many immigrants in the United States have formed transnational migrant organizations to maintain relationships with their countries of origin and, more specifically, with their particular communities or origin. Among these are Hometown Associations (HTA), formed among communities of remittance senders to coordinate support not only for relatives but also for their hometowns at the same time as they retain a sense of community and identity in the United States (Lowell and De la Garza, 2000; Orozco, 2002; Mahler, 1998a, 1998b; Roberts et al., 1999; Levitt, 2001). These HTAs often finance charitable activities in their hometowns, infrastructural improvements, assistance for education and health needs of the hometown population, capital investment for income-generating projects, and so forth. By the late 1990s more than 400 of these emigrant clubs were operating among Mexican immigrants in the United States (Orozco, 2002:8). Clearly the activities of these HTAs are located in the interstices of global capitalist development, but they nonetheless point to bottom-up forms of globalization—a point emphasized by Smith and Guarnizo in their oft-cited 1998 study.

However, HTAs are not just a Mexican phenomenon. Most Latin American immigrant communities in the United States, reports Orozco, have organized into HTAs (Orozco, 2005:322), including those from Ecuador, Central America, Peru, Colombia, and other countries. The international activities of HTAs can be described in terms of four features (Orozco 2002, 2005). First and second, their orientation ranges from charitable aid to investment, respectively. From a balance-of-payments perspective, these activities are like remittances in that they are unrequited and unilateral private donations, albeit carried out on a community basis. Charitable work includes the donation of clothes, construction material for the town church, or small cash amounts to purchase goods for local religious festivities. Infrastructural improvements include raising money to pave the hometown streets, create parks, build sewage treatment and water-filtration plants, buy or maintain cemetery plots, or build health care facilities. A third group of activities is oriented toward "human development," the daily educational and health needs of the townspeople. These activities include funds for scholarships, library books, health supplies and medicine, and sports facilities. A fourth type of activity involves capital investment for income-generation projects managed by local community members and often supervised by immigrants.

Marketing Ethnic Identity in the Global Bazaar

One of the most celebrated examples of the new transnationalism in Latin America is that of the Otavalans. The Quichua indigenous communities of the Otavalo valley in the Ecuadoran Altiplano, some 100 kilometers north of Quito, has become a showcase of "globalization from below," driven by migrants who have created a transnational ethnic economy. The Otavaleños have historically produced native handicraft and specialty textiles that, starting in the 1980s and 1990s, were exported and sold in ethnic markets around the world. The Otavaleños also export street musicians who can be seen in major cities around the world playing folkloric Andean music at intersections, shopping malls, bars, and metro stations. A number of Latin American localities have become world renowned in recent years for the marketing of native handicraft, such as the Mexican city of Oaxaca or the village of El Arenal in El Salvador. But Otavalo stands out as the model case study. In contrast to other forms of global marketing, the world trade in these Otavalan cultural commodities is controlled not by transnational capital but by members of the indigenous community who have shifted their sights (and sites) from local to global markets. These merchants move back and forth from Ecuador to the dozens of countries and hundreds of cities through which they have been able to draw on social and cultural capital to establish "colonies" in foreign cities and carve out a networked niche in the global economy. Some merchants were traveling to as many as twenty-four countries and then returning to Ecuador in the same year (Kyle, 2000:202). In essence, Otavaleños have been able to construct a cultural identity as an "exotic Other" that can be marketed globally.

The Otavalan case may be a clever use—or production—of ethnic identity as a marketing device in the global bazaar, but it also highlights the crass nature of global cultural commodification. As the Otavalan merchant-weavers increased their influence in the late twentieth century they began to buy and sell not only their own products but also indigenous textiles and crafts in countries such as Bolivia, Peru, and Panama; they marketed the products as their own to unsuspecting tourists back at home in Otavalo or during selling trips abroad (Kyle, 2000:144). "Otavalans are rapidly becoming the principal brokers of native crafts from Latin America—even supplying handicrafts to tourist destinations lacking colorful indigenous populations," observes Kyle. "Hence, we have the basic cultural irony of [the] economic base of the region—an Andean indigenous group running a global export economy and incorporating the material culture of other native groups into their marketing arsenal, while remaining confident in their own 'authentic; cultural identity . . . the distinction between local and extralocal is blurred. . . . [T]he Otavalans' handicrafts are authentically inauthentic" (2000:144). Moreover, by coming to control the indigenous handicraft market in other Latin American countries, the Otavalan merchants are middlemen who not only reap the exchange value of foreign-made crafts but also add to its value by their association with it as "authentic Indians" (Kyle, 2000:147). In this way Latin American indigenous cultural images become global products, as the Other and "authenticity" are commodified and marketed.

The success of some Otavaleños as transnational entrepreneurs should not be romanticized as a viable alternative to the depredations of global capitalism. For one, millions of other Ecuadorians have taken up transnational migration in the face of displacement, unemployment, and economic crisis in the more customary form as low-paid immigrant labor. The vast majority of Ecuadorians migrate transnationally to sell not handicrafts but their labor. There were several hundred thousand Ecuadorian immigrants in this category in New York City alone by the late 1990s. Moreover, the saturation of overseas handicraft markets—in the late 1990s no fewer than 40 Otavalan stalls were set up in the annual "running of the bulls" festival in Pamplona, Spain (Kyle, 2000:187)—points to the limits of entrepreneurial globalization from below. Such entrepreneurialism is in the end, at best, an interstice of capitalist globalization from above.

Second, whether the migrants leave as merchants or as low-wage workers, the families and communities of Ecuadorian transnational migrants suffer the effects of ruptured family life, absent parents, and other traumas of separation.

The transnational dispersal of production and reproduction tasks may strengthen transnational communities and families in an analytical or conceptual sense and may present families with a survival option not previously available. Nonetheless, we would do well to remember the high cost transnational households involve in terms of family and individual well-being. Ehrenreich, Hochschild, and their colleagues (2004), to cite one study, have documented the psychological and social devastation suffered by families forced to become transnational as a survival imperative. In the emerging "international division of reproductive labor," poorer regions export to wealthier ones "reproductive" labor in the form of millions of nannies and maids who take over the reproductive household work of middle- and even working-class families in expanding, and often highly racialized, transnational class relations in which care-giving has become a globally mobile commodity. Women forced to sell their reproductive services abroad are deprived of the opportunity to raise their own children while those children suffer the lifelong traumas of prolonged, even permanent, separation from their mothers.[7]

And third, as Kyle (2000) documents, the rise of a new Otavalan transnational merchant class is one dimension of a larger dialectic of growing class distinctions and internal stratification within Otavalan communities. Some of these merchants, for instance, set up maquiladora-style handicraft workshops in Otavalo that employ Otavalan labor displaced from the land or traditional employment as the whole region has become swept up in neoliberal restructuring and globalization. The merchants have also been able to dominate the supply of handicraft to the national tourist market as transnational tourism has taken off in the country (see Chapter 2), especially with the opening of Poncho Plaza in Otavalo, which has become a major international tourist attraction, and the construction of a major highway from Quito to Otavalo.

It was no surprise that the Otavalan merchant-weavers were not supportive of the 1990 indigenous uprising (see next chapter). While their ethnic demarcation may have been a source of oppression for a majority of Ecuadorian indigenous, it had become (for the new Otavalan elite) cultural capital in the global economy.

---

[7] More generally, gender relations are also transformed in multiple ways by transnational migration that defies the generalization of any one pattern. In Ecuador men are more likely to emigrate while those women who stay behind may experience increased autonomy in their household and community relations. Levitt (2001) found that women in the Dominican Republic, who constitute a significant portion of out-migrants, enjoyed improved status relative to male partners when they migrated to the United States and in their communities of origin. In both cases, however, women who stayed behind and female relatives in extended (and transnationalized) households assumed a greater burden of social reproduction and faced new hardships.

Militant indigenous mobilization represents a potentially destabilizing threat to the Otavalan elite's class interests.

More generally, while many transnational migrants suffer discrimination and super-exploitation abroad, their migrant-sending families and communities experience a connection to the global economy that may become a source of heightened status and social power locally, a portal for the penetration of powerful transnational social processes. The flows of transnational migration and remittances often generate new forms of inequality among migrant-sending communities, with returning migrants and recipients of remittances able not only to consume but also to accumulate local economic and status advantages. Kyle points to the sharp rise in land prices and regional inflation that fueled social polarization in Otavalo and other sending regions in Ecuador. This is connected, in turn, to the demise of semi-independent household economies, the private purchase and concentration of what were collective holdings, the spread of wage labor among nonimmigrant households, polarization between a rising merchant-weaver class and a class of increasingly dispossessed wage laborers, and growing relative deprivation.

Latin American Communities in Globalization

A central proposition of this book is that there are few, if any, remaining localities in Latin America that remain pre-capitalist. The global handicraft trade represents a point of entry for a more thorough penetration of capitalist relations into Otavalan communities. These transnational processes, in Kyle's words, "connect even the most remote, illiterate weavers with foreign consumers and wholesalers, [so] that the entire region has become vertically integrated, reinforcing internal hierarchies in a group unified by a common culture and language" (2000:14). More generally, while transnational migration may only involve directly a minority of the population of a particular country its effects are all-pervasive and transform the country as a whole. In Otavalo the social relations of global capitalism are penetrating and transforming the Valley in ways that are indicative of countless local communities in Latin America. Cid Aguayo (2006) refers to rural districts such as Otavalo that have become fully integrated into the economic, political, and cultural circuits of global capitalism as "global ruralities." As ruralities integrate in new ways into the global system they give new meaning to the classical term "global village," now less the idea of a world shrunk by global communications than small settlements in rural districts that are full participants in the globalization process, as distinct from earlier images of rural zones as pre-modern reserves and pre-capitalist residues.

If Otavalo and Oaxaca are examples of global ruralities in Latin America integrated into global capitalism through the worldwide handicraft trade, another for Cid Aguayo is Chile's Central Valley (see Chapter 2), integrated through transnational food chains, and yet a third is Chiapas, in Mexico, which represents another kind of counter-hegemonic integration based on the articulation of the Zapatista movement to worldwide resistance movements, including the organization of three international meetings in Chiapas itself that brought together global justice activists from around the world. The Zapatistas, in Cid Aguayo's view, "constitute a movement that operates both locally and globally, articulating their local demands with the global demands of the Global Justice Movement," so that San Cristobal de las Casas (the capital of Chiapas), the Lacandona jungle, and the small town of La Realidad that hosted the international meetings, "constitute highly cosmopolitan places" (2006:21).

To what extent the majority in these global ruralities, or what Pérez Saínz and Andrade-Eekhoff (2003) refer to as communities in globalization, experience an improvement in their life chances or become empowered through integration into global capitalism is a matter of debate. Cid Aguayo concedes that Chile's Central Valley has become a "neo-liberal village" yet claims that there are "some exceptional places," such as Otavalo, "that have managed to obtain some kind of leverage vis-à-vis global processes, actually advancing themselves as spaces of material, cultural, and ideological production for the world" (2006:4). But to speak of places "advancing themselves" is to shift the analytical focus from social groups and their relations in particular spaces to these spaces themselves and to reify space in the process. As we have seen in the case of Otavalo, global integration has produced winners and losers within the same global rurality as local class and power relations become reconfigured.

The globalization debate often centers on how to conceptualize scalar dimensions of the process and in particular on the relationship of the local to the global. Pérez Saínz and Andrade-Eekhoff argue that the new geography of globalization is best captured by a focus on the neighborhood community as the most important socio-territory for the global South. The challenge for local communities is to draw on their socio-cultural and political peculiarities so as to minimize the risks and maximize the opportunities of globalization. They reach such conclusions after examining the experience of three Central

American communities that have achieved an insertion into global commodity chains. La Fortuna, a town in Costa Rica, has become a supplier of services such as hotels, restaurants, and local tour operators for international tourists coming to visit the nearby active volcano, El Arenal. La Palma in northern El Salvador has specialized in the production of handicrafts for local and global tourist markets. And San Pedro Sacatepequez, a largely indigenous municipality located just outside of Guatemala City, has become an important center for apparel manufacturing subcontracting. These three communities, they assert, illustrate successful modes of insertion into global markets through the provision of distinctive locally produced goods and services.

The argument that communities may benefit *as communities* from global integration seems to me to ignore the underlying structural constraints in the global political economy that originate from without and confront local communities, and how these constraints shape class and power relations both at the local level and between the local and the global. Indeed, the three case studies put forward by Pérez Saínz and Andrade-Eekhoff appear to contradict their propositions. They find La Fortuna to be the most successful insertion of the kind they are advocating. Yet this success, they conclude, is based less on collective community action than on the higher level of prior development in Costa Rica than in the other two countries. Decreased poverty levels in La Palma are associated not with local production for global commodity chains but with remittances from Salvadorans who have migrated abroad. And the authors themselves describe San Pedro Sacatepequez as an instance of submaquilas that supply maquiladoras in Guatemala City, which are in turn subcontracted by transnational firms. Local subcontractors harness in this way an indigenous labor force that remains mired in poverty and social marginality despite the insertion of their labor into global commodity chains. This would seem less a community insertion into global production for the purpose of local development than a capitalist decentralization that opens up opportunities for local entrepreneurial elites.

Pérez Saínz and Andrade-Eekhoff concede as well that all three communities face potential instability—maybe even ruin—as globalization advances: in La Fortuna transnational hotel chains could buy up local properties; in La Palma foreign buyers have threatened to open up a mass production factory to replace local workshops; and in San Pedro Sacatepequéz local submaquilas lost work contracts with Van Heusen's Guatemala City subcontractors when the transnational firm pulled out of the country after workers unionized. Clearly there is an underlying process in which local communities become subordinated to transnational capital and to intermediaries who appropriate much of locally produced values. In the end, globalization produces winners and losers and generates new social hierarchies at the local level; it is best to shift our focus altogether in analyzing winners and losers in the process from territorially defined spaces to social groups in the global system.

CHAPTER FIVE

The Antinomies of Global Capitalism
and the Twilight of Neoliberalism

Global capitalism faces an expanding crisis that began in the early twenty-first century and involves three interrelated dimensions (Robinson, 2004a).[1] First is a *crisis of social polarization*. The system cannot meet the needs of a majority of humanity or even ensure minimal social reproduction. Second is a *structural crisis of overaccumulation*. The system cannot expand because the marginalization of a significant portion of humanity from direct productive participation, the downward pressure on wages and popular consumption reduces the ability of the world market to absorb world output. The problem of surplus absorption makes state-driven military spending and the growth of military-industrial complexes an outlet for surplus and gives the current global order a built-in war drive. Third is a *crisis of state legitimacy and political authority*. The legitimacy of the system has increasingly been called into question by millions, perhaps even billions, of people around the world and is facing expanded counter-hegemonic challenges.

Overaccumulation and the "Realization Problem"

As capitalism produces vast amounts of wealth it also generates, as part of the very way the system functions, polarization and crisis—not as a result of bad policies but because of something built into the nature of the system. Investors only make a profit by selling the goods and services produced in the market. Yet workers by definition cannot purchase the entire amount of goods and services they produce, since their wages must be less than the value of those goods and services or else there would be no profit and the capitalist production process would grind to a halt. So long as new markets and sources of profitable investment are constantly opened up, the process of capital accumulation

---

[1] There is a fourth dimension to the crisis that I cannot take up here, that of sustainability. It is not clear that ecological holocaust can yet be averted.

continues. But at some point capitalists as a group, or some among them, are left with surplus that cannot be unloaded. At that point what is known in crisis theory as the "realization problem" sets in, meaning that wealth generated through investment cannot be marketed or reinvested and hence profits cannot be made. This is the point at which, typically, economic recession sets in or new mechanisms for sustaining accumulation, such as credit or financial speculation, come into play.

Capitalists around the world institutionalized their newfound structural and relative power over global labor brought about by the changed correlation of forces under globalization to forge the new capital-labor relationship, to reduce relative wages, and to generate novel profit-making opportunities. To the extent that capitalists achieved these things they saw their profits rise. Also, the shift in income from working and poor people to capital and to new high-consumption middle, professional, and bureaucratic strata provided a global market segment that fueled growth in new areas. Yet these processes only made more acute the underlying realization problem. Seen in a broader historic perspective, two processes germane to capitalist development have intensified through globalization. One is the secular process by which the spread of capitalism uproots pre-capitalist classes such as peasantries and converts them into members of the working class. The accelerated incursion of capitalist production into the countryside around the world in the second half of the twentieth century uprooted hundreds of millions of peasants and threw them into the capitalist labor market, often as unemployed or underemployed workers. The other is the cyclical process by which capitalists, in an effort to reduce labor costs and thereby increase profits, continuously replace human labor by labor-saving and productivity-raising machines and technology. This process accelerated dramatically in the closing decades of the twentieth century as a result of new globalizing technologies made available for rationalization and automation of the labor process. Hundreds of millions of workers became replaced by robots, computers, automated bank tellers and phone operators, and so forth.[2]

The result of these twin processes was an astonishing expansion of the ranks of the unemployed and the underemployed worldwide. The International

---

[2] This holds true for both high- and low-wage zones. As Overholt (2006) explains: "Scholarly studies show that most job losses in the United States are attributable to domestic causes such as increased domestic productivity. A few years ago it took 40 hours of labor to produce a car. Now it takes 15. That translates into a need for fewer workers. Protectionists who blame China for such job losses are being intellectually dishonest. In fact, both China and the U.S. have lost manufacturing jobs due to rising productivity, but China has lost ten times more—a decline of about 25 million Chinese jobs from over 54 million in 1994 to under 30 million ten years later."

Labor Organization reported that by the end of 1998, some one billion workers—or one third of the world's labor force—was either unemployed or underemployed (ILO, 1998). A third of the economically active population out of work represented an employment crisis that rivaled the Great Depression of the 1930s and underscored the inability of a good portion of humanity to engage in consumption in the global economy. On the one hand, this "superfluous" or "redundant" pool of labor could not consume, and on the other, it represented a potentially destabilizing threat to the system. In any event, this situation only aggravated the dual problem of overproduction and underconsumption.

Under the emergent global social structure of accumulation the social reproduction of labor in each country becomes less important for accumulation as the output of each nation and region is exported to the global level. At the aggregate level of the world economy this means an overall system-wide contraction in demand simultaneous to a system-wide expansion of supply. Global neoliberalism aggravates the tendencies inherent in capitalism toward overaccumulation by further polarizing income and therefore contracting the system's absorption capacity. This classic realization problem is now manifested in novel ways under global capitalism. Zones of high absorption become the pillars of the system, or the "markets of last resort," in times of economic difficulty, such as the United States in the mid, and especially the late, 1990s, following the 1997 Asian financial crisis (the U.S. current accounts deficit increased from $47.7 billion in 1992 to $420 billion by the end of 2000 ([Clairmont, 2001, 46]). Markets of last resort may help fuel world economic growth even as many regions experience stagnation and crisis. An excess of accumulated capital coupled with vast new opportunities for investment and profit making around the world as a result of the opening up of new markets and new regions for capitalist investment led in the 1980s and 1990s to a major expansion of world productive capacity and helped revert, temporarily, the crisis of stagnation and declining profit-making opportunities of the 1970s. But at the *systemic* level, the reproduction of capital remains dependent on that of labor, and this represents a contradiction internal to the global capitalist system. Hence, the contradictions that present themselves now in any one zone of the global system, such as in Latin America, are internal to (global) capitalism rather than between capitalism and atavistic elements. The most fundamental social contradiction in Latin America *and* in global society is this: the model of polarized (flexible) accumulation does not and cannot resolve these contradictions of capitalism and, moreover, tends to aggravate them.

Overaccumulation has led global investors in recent years to engage in an unprecedented wave of speculative investments in what has come to be known as the "casino economy" or "casino capitalism" (Strange, 1986), although there were also more long term structural processes at play that explained financial speculation (see, e.g., Arrighi, 1994). Trillions of dollars, for instance, were invested in stock markets and real estate in the downtown districts of such global cities as New York, London, and Tokyo, as well as in newly emerging areas of high growth, such as in the metropoles of Southeast Asia, driving up stocks and real estate values in a fictitious process of value creation (i.e., the process did not necessarily involve the creation of new tangible wealth but simply the inflation of the value, or price, of existing assets). This "financial bubble" resulted in the stagnation of the Japanese economy, scattered recessions throughout the 1980s and 1990s, the periodic bursting of stock market and real estate bubbles, several Wall Street and dot.com crashes, and finally, the Asian financial meltdown of 1997–1998, which in the view of many precipitated the worldwide economic downturn of the early twenty-first century and signaled the beginning of a deeper structural crisis in the global economy (see, e.g., Brenner, 2002). Below I will discuss further this financialization of the global economy and its significance for Latin America. Here let us observe that the breakdown of nation-state-based redistributional projects restored growth and profitability but also aggravated the tendencies inherent in capitalism toward overaccumulation by further polarizing income and heightening inequalities worldwide.

Global Polarization and the Crisis of Social Reproduction

One of the ideological constructs of the global capitalist system is to treat the existence of poverty and inequality as if it were a problem of a scarcity of resources or insufficient growth. The problem is not a lack of resources or growth but *how* resources are allocated and distributed and *who*—what social groups and classes—exercises control over resources and how they are put to use. In past epochs of capitalism the problems of overaccumulation and social polarization were offset, in part, through two processes. One was classical imperialism, or the forcible opening up of new territories and markets by the centers of power in the world capitalist system through military force and wars of conquest. The imperialist bounty allowed for rising standards of living and offset the tendency toward polarization in the metropolitan heartlands of the world colonial system even as it exacerbated the crisis for the victims of colonialism. The other was diverse redistributive mechanisms developed in the framework of nation-state capitalism, culminating in the post World War II system of Keynesian demand creation. Keynesian absorption mechanisms such as credit creation and redistribution through taxation and social spending offset overaccumulation crises. Many if not all of these recurrent crises were mediated by the nation-state. There are no longer any new frontiers to colonize in the epoch of globalization and the old nation-state redistributive systems are less viable. The result has been a process of rapid global social polarization and an expanding crisis of social reproduction.

There has been much debate on how to measure global inequality. One major point of debate is whether inter-national or intra-national inequalities are the more important of global trends. Korzeniewicz and Moran (1997) find rising cross-national inequalities and a more mixed picture within countries, while Goesling (2001) and Firebaugh (2003) find that the late twentieth century was characterized by the diminishing significance of between-nation income differences relative to intra-national (or global) inequalities. What is clear is that inequality continues to rise *within and between* countries; the growth of inequality itself is not seriously disputed, nor is its linkage to globalization (see, inter alia, Chossudovsky, 1997; Cornia and Court, 2001; Nederveen-Pieterse, 2002; Reddy and Pogge, 2002; Galbraith, 2002; Korzeniewicz and Moran, 1997; Firebaugh, 2003; Goesling, 2001; Milanovic, 2002). In most countries, the average number of people who have been integrated into the global marketplace and are becoming global consumers has increased in recent decades. However the absolute number of the impoverished—of the destitute and near destitute—has also been increasing and the gap between the rich and the poor in global society has been widening since the 1970s (Tables 5.1 and 5.2 draw on distinct sources to indicate the widening gap).

Broad swaths of humanity have experienced absolute downward mobility. Even the IMF was forced to admit in a 2000 report that "in the recent decades

TABLE 5.1
Shares of World Income, 1965–1990

Population	Percent of Total World Income			
	1965	1970	1980	1990
Poorest 20%	2.3	2.2	1.7	1.4
Second 20%	2.9	2.8	2.2	1.8
Third 20%	4.2	3.9	3.5	2.1
Fourth 20%	21.2	21.3	18.3	11.3
Richest 20%	69.5	70.0	75.4	83.4

Source: Korzeniewicz and Moran, 1997.

TABLE 5.2
Global Income Distribution, 1988 and 1993

Population	Percentage of World Income		
	1988	1993	Difference 1988–1993
Top 1%	9.3	9.5	0.2
Top 5%	31.2	33.7	2.5
Top 10%	46.9	50.8	3.9
Bottom 10%	0.9	0.8	−0.1
Bottom 20%	2.3	2.0	−0.3
Bottom 50%	9.6	8.5	−1.1
Bottom 75%	25.9	22.3	−3.6
Bottom 85%	41.0	37.1	−3.9

Source: Milanovic, 1999.

[*sic*], nearly one-fifth of the world population has regressed. This is arguably one of the greatest economic failures of the 20th century" (IMF, 2000, as cited in Palast, 2003:152). While global per capita income tripled over the period 1960–1994, there were over a hundred countries in the 1990s with per capita incomes lower than in the 1980s, or in some cases, lower than in the 1970s and 1960s (UNDP, as cited in Stalker, 2000:139). In 1980, 118 million people lived in nine countries where income per capita was declining; in 1998, there were sixty such countries and 1.3 billion such people (Freeman, 2002:1). While the rate of growth in world GDP has declined in each decade since 1970, the growth rate for per capita GDP actually became negative in the 1990–2000 decade (Table 5.3).

At the end of the twentieth century the richest 20 percent of humanity received 85 percent of the world's wealth while the remaining 80 percent of humanity had access to 15 percent of the world's riches and the poorest 20 percent received only 1.0 percent, according to the UNDP. The result of globalization "is a grotesque and dangerous polarization between the people and countries that have benefited from the system," asserted the 2000 report, "and those who are mere passive receivers of its effect" (UNDP, 2000). In this new *global social*

TABLE 5.3
Percent Growth Rate of World GDP and GDP per Capita,
1970–1990 (in constant 1995 dollars)

	World GDP	Per Capita GDP
1970–1980	5.51	3.76
1980–1990	2.27	0.69
1990–2000	1.09	−0.19

Source: Freeman, 2002, appendix of tables.

apartheid, the gap between the global rich and the global poor is growing at a
rate unprecedented in modern human history.

Legitimacy Crises and the Problematic Nature
of Transnational Hegemony

The functions of the neoliberal state are contradictory. As globalization proceeds, internal social cohesion declines along with national economic integration. The neoliberal state retains essential powers to facilitate globalization, but
it loses the ability to harmonize conflicting social interests within a country, to
realize the historic function of sustaining the internal unity of a nationally conceived social formation, and to achieve legitimacy. This helps explain the collapse of the social fabric in country after country and outbreaks of spontaneous
protest among marginalized and disenfranchised sectors as governments
around the world faced mounting crises of legitimacy and political authority.
The economic quandaries of the global system generate endemic social instability, political tension, and military conflict. "The market is literally tearing the
world apart; it is beginning to render large tracts of it ungovernable," notes Freeman. "As its economic mechanisms become increasingly incapable of resolving
the social contradictions they create, the nations and societies through which it
is mediated are being plunged into increasingly open political conflict. The endemic crises, armed conflicts and governmental instability of the Middle East,
of Central Asia, of the Balkans, of Central and Northern Africa, of Central and
Southern America, and of South-East Asia, each has its own specificity. But the
basic driving force behind all of them is the same: the crushing weight of two
decades of accelerating economic stagnation, accompanied by universally growing inequality" (Freeman, 2002:4).

If one dimension to the crises of authority among dominant groups worldwide is objective—the inability to attenuate polarization tendencies inherent in
capitalism and aggravated by new global modes of accumulation—another is
subjective and has to do with the challenge to global capitalist hegemony posed
by diverse oppositional and subaltern forces, not all of them progressive. Under
these twin conditions a crisis of political authority tends to become a more
expansive crisis of hegemony. Gramsci developed the concept of hegemony to
refer to the attainment by ruling groups of stable forms of rule based on "consensual" domination of subordinate groups. Gramsci's notion of hegemony
posits distinct forms, or relations of domination, in brief: *coercive domination*
and *consensual domination*. Hegemony may be seen as a relationship between

classes or groups in which one class or group exercises leadership over other classes and groups by gaining their active consent. It involves the internalization on the part of the subordinate classes of the moral and cultural values, the codes of practical conduct, and the worldview of the dominant classes or groups: in sum, the internalization of the *social logic* of the system of domination itself.

No emergent ruling class can construct an historic bloc without developing diverse mechanisms of legitimation and securing a social base—a combination of the consensual integration through material reward for some, and the coercive exclusion of others that the system is unwilling or unable to co-opt. Emergent transnational elites set about in the 1980s and 1990s to construct a global capitalist historic bloc in the Gramscian sense as a social ensemble involving dominant strata and a social base beyond the ruling group, and in which one group exercised leadership (the TCC) and imposes its project through the consent of those drawn into the bloc. Hegemony requires a material base—what some social scientists have called a moral economy, or the material conditions, institutions, and concomitant norms that allow for the social reproduction of subordinate groups (see, e.g., Scott, 1976). To the extent that neoliberalism has done away with a "moral economy" it undermines the material base for a transnational hegemonic project.

To the extent that an historic bloc must rely on more direct domination or coercion as opposed to consent in securing its rule its hegemony will be increasingly problematic if not impossible. Global elites may have achieved in the 1980s and 1990s—at best—a certain "restricted" as opposed to "expansive" hegemony in global society, less through the internalization by popular classes worldwide of the neoliberal worldview than through the disorganization of these classes in the wake of the juggernaut of capitalist globalization. But since the late 1990s they have been unable to reproduce even this restricted hegemony and have had to resort to direct coercion to maintain control. Even at that, achieving either consensual integration or effective coercive exclusion has been increasingly difficult, given the extent of social polarization and of resistance worldwide. The global capitalist order is not viable for a majority of humanity and it can only function to the extent that it is able to maintain and defend worldwide structures of inequality and domination. The problem of social control has become ever more acute.

The political coherence of ruling groups always frays when faced with structural and/or legitimacy crises as different groups push distinct strategies and tactics or turn to the more immediate pursuit of sectoral interests. The more politically astute among global elites have clamored in recent years to promote a post–Washington consensus project of reform, a so-called globalization with a human face, in the interests of saving the system itself (see, e.g., Stiglitz, 2002). But there were others from within and outside of the bloc that called for more radical responses. When prevailing social structures are threatened, whether in perception or in actuality, ruling groups become desperate and unpredictable. The principal political agents of global capitalism—especially U.S. state authorities—appeared in the early twenty-first century to respond to the tensions and contradictions of global capitalism with a political radicalization, with a drive toward the institutionalization of the new forms of coercive authority, with a worldwide war mobilization as the global system seemed to descend into chaos.

A Global War Economy?

If neoliberalism was able to "peacefully" force open new areas for global capital in the 1980s and the 1990s this was often accomplished through economic co-ercion alone, made possible by the structural power of the global economy over individual countries. But this structural power became less effective in the face of the three-pronged crisis mentioned above. Opportunities for both intensive and extensive expansion began to dry up as privatizations ran their course, the "socialist" countries became integrated, the consumption of high-income sec-tors worldwide reached ceilings, spending through private credit expansion could not be sustained, and so on. The space for "peaceful" expansion, both in-tensive and extensive, became ever more restricted. Military aggression became an instrument for prying open new sectors and regions, for the forcible restruc-turing of space in order to further accumulation. The train of neoliberalism became latched on to military intervention and the threat of coercive sanctions as a locomotive for pulling the moribund neoliberal program forward. The "war on terrorism" achieved a number of objectives for a global capitalism beset by structural, political, and ideological crises. It provides a seemingly endless mili-tary outlet for surplus capital, generated a colossal deficit that justifies the ever-deeper dismantling of the Keynesian welfare state and locks neoliberal austerity in place, and legitimates the creation of a police state to repress politi-cal dissent in the name of security.

Yet global capitalism will continue to be unstable and crisis-ridden. Global inequalities, wherever their social dynamics are operative, lead to new social control systems and a politics of exclusion. The "war on terrorism" provided a convenient cover for the transnational elite to extend its drive to consolidate and defend the project of capitalist globalization with a new and terrifying coercive dimension. The powers that be in the global capitalist order seemed intent on organizing and institutionalizing a global police state following the September 2001 attack on the World Trade Center. Could we witness the rise of a global fascism, a *new war order,* founded on military spending and wars to contain the downtrodden and the un-repented and to seize new territories, resources, and labor pools? Conflict in global society is prone to occur at multiple levels: between transnationally oriented elites and those with a more local, national or regional orientation; between agents of global capitalism and popular forces; among competing groups within the globalist bloc who may foment inter-state conflicts in pursuit of their particular interests; and so on. The picture is further complicated by the instability wrought by the breakdown of social order and the collapse of national state authority in many regions. In particular, challenges to the global capitalist bloc may come from subordinate groups in transnational civil society or from specific nation-states when these states are captured by subordinate groups, such as in the case of Venezuela under the leadership of Hugo Chávez, as well as from dominant groups who are less integrated into (or even opposed to) global capitalism, such as, for example, the Baath Party/Iraq state elite prior to the 2003 U.S. invasion, sectors among the Russian oligarchy, or Chinese economic and political elites.

The U.S. government under the George W. Bush presidency militarized social and economic contradictions, launching a permanent war mobilization to try to stabilize the system through direct coercion. U.S. interventionism and militarized globalization constituted less a campaign for U.S. hegemony than a contradictory political response to the explosive crisis of global capitalism—to economic stagnation, legitimation problems, and the rise of counter-hegemonic forces. The U.S. state has attempted to play a leadership role *on behalf of* transnational capitalist interests, to act as guarantor of global capitalism, both materially and symbolically, by deploying force and threatening to apply coercion and sanctions against those who would transgress property rights, close off any territory to transnational investors, or threaten to withdraw from the system.

The U.S. state has undertaken an unprecedented role in creating profit-making opportunities for transnational capital and pushing forward an accumulation process that left to its own devices (the "free market") would likely ground to a halt. A Pentagon budget of nearly $630 billion in 2007—the highest annual amount since World War II (Rosen, 2007)—an invasion and occupation of Iraq with a price tag of nearly half a trillion dollars by 2007 and a proposed multi-billion dollar space program that would rest on a marriage of

NASA, the military, and an array of private corporate interests must be seen in this light. Some have seen the $500 billion invested by the U.S. state in the first four years of its Iraq invasion and occupation as evidence that the U.S. intervention benefits "U.S. capital" to the detriment of other national—e.g., "EU"—capitals. However, Bechtel, the Carlyle Group, and Halliburton are themselves transnational capital conglomerates (Briody, 2003). It is true that military, oil, and engineering/construction companies, many of them head-quartered in the United States, managed to secure their particular sectoral interests through brazen instrumentalization of the U.S. state under the Bush presidency. However, these companies are themselves transnational and their interests are those not of "U.S. capital" in rivalry with other countries but of particular transnational clusters in the global economy. Transnational capital-ists are themselves aware of the role of the U.S. state in opening up new pos-sibilities for unloading of surplus and created new investment opportunities. "We're looking for places to invest around the world," explained one former executive of a Dutch-based oil exploration and engineering company, and then "you know, along comes Iraq" (as cited in *Monthly Review*, 2004:64).

The "creative destruction" of war and natural and humanitarian disasters generates new cycles of accumulation through "reconstruction." The complex consisting of military, energy, engineering, and construction constitutes one of those sectors of global capital that most benefits from the creative destruc-tion of crises, wars, and natural and humanitarian disasters. Klein has char-acterized this new mechanism of accumulation as "disaster capitalism" (2005b), while Bello observes that "post-disaster and post-conflict reconstruc-tion planning and implementation are increasingly influenced by neo-liberal market economics" and that the same set of actors are "now dominant in both arenas: the U.S. military-political command, the World Bank, corporate con-tractors and humanitarian and development NGOs" (Bello, 2006b:281). In 2004 the U.S. government created the "Office of the Coordinator for Re-construction and Stabilization." The idea was to utilize post-conflict and post-disaster reconstruction to transform "the very social fabric of a nation" along neoliberal lines, explained one official (Klein, 2005b). "The rise of a predatory form of disaster capitalism," in Klein's words, "uses the desperation and fear created by catastrophe to engage in radical social and economic engi-neering" (Klein, 2005b). In a sense the U.S. state became rentier insofar as the main dominant groups became increasingly dependent on the extraction of rents through the conversion of public into private resources. These groups aggressively turned to the state to convert public resources into private profits by way of disaster capitalism and publicly funded but privately contracted reconstruction.

But more importantly, the U.S. state mobilized the resources through war and disaster capitalism to generate new outlets for surplus and sustain global accumulation. The $607 billion invested by the U.S. state in war and "reconstruction" in Iraq between 2002 and 2007 (Rosen, J., 2007) went to a vast array of investors and subcontractors that spanned the globe (Phinney, 2005). Kuwaiti Trading and Contracting, Alargan Trading of Kuwait, Gulf Catering and Saudi Trading and Construction Company were just some of the Middle East-based companies that shared in the bonanza, along with companies and investor groups as far away as South Africa, Bosnia, the Philippines, and India (ibid.). The picture that emerges is one in which the U.S. state mobilizes the resources to feed a vast transnational network of profit making that passes through countless layers of outsourcing, subcontracting, alliances and collaborative relations, benefiting transnationally oriented capitalists from many parts of the globe. The U.S. state is the pivotal gear in a TNS machinery dedicated to reproducing global capitalism.

Suffice it to conclude here with the observation that the empire of global capital has barely emerged and yet already faces deep crisis. Globalization resolved some problems for capital but the underlying laws of capitalism remain in place and continually assert themselves. The unfolding crisis in the world economy may turn out to be neither a recurring business cycle nor the opening salvos of a new restructuring crisis. Hardly had the neoliberal model triumphed in the 1980s and 1990s than it began to appear as moribund. The struggle for what will take its place is now underway and is the backdrop to the political upheavals that began to rock Latin America in the early twenty-first century. Neoliberalism may prove to be a parenthesis between old nation-state accumulation models and a new global social structure of accumulation whose contours are not yet clear. The global crisis is experienced in different forms in distinct countries and regions. Let us now examine in broad strokes how it has been manifest in Latin America.

Social Crisis in Latin America: Inequality, Immiseration, Marginality

Capitalist globalization through the neoliberal model has not only failed dismally to resolve the historic plight of poverty and deprivation among the majority in Latin America; it has *aggravated* that plight. While poverty and inequality are long-standing and tenacious in the region, globalization has brought new dimensions to these phenomena. To understand these we need first to look at how capital-labor relations have been restructured.

Global Capital-Labor Relations in Latin America

Neoliberal programs in Latin America have sought to create an optimal environment for private transnational capital to operate as the putative motor of development and social welfare. As transnational elites in Latin America set about to integrate their countries into the global economy they came to base "development" on the virtually exclusive criteria of achieving maximum internal profitability as the condition sine qua non for attracting transnational capital: what Korzeniewicz and Smith (2000) call the low road to globalization. Profitability in this regard rested above all on the provision of cheap labor along with access (often state subsidized) to the region's copious natural resources and fertile lands. New capital-labor relations have developed out of a logic of accumulation based on the provision to the global economy of an abundant supply of cheap, flexible, and disciplined labor as a "comparative advantage." In turn, the availability of a vast reserve army of cheap labor impedes growth in productivity and reinforces these particular conditions of profitability.

For neoliberal elites, successful integration into the global economy became predicated on the erosion of labor's income, the withdrawal of the social wage, the transfer of the costs of social reproduction from the public sector to individual families, a weakening of trade unions and workers movements, and the suppression of popular political demands. Hence, in the logic of global capitalism, the cheapening of labor and its social disenfranchisement by the neoliberal state became conditions for "development." The very drive by local elites to create conditions to attract transnational capital has been what thrusts Latin American majorities into poverty and inequality. The contraction of domestic markets, the growth of the informal economy, and austerity programs, among other components and effects of capitalist globalization, have resulted in the informalization of the work force, mass under- and unemployment, a compression of real wages and a transfer of income from labor to capital.

I will look here briefly at four related aspects of global capital-labor relations in Latin America: deregulation, informalization, marginalization, and feminization of labor. It is important to remember that these new relations did not simply fall into place. They were imposed on Latin American workers and popular sectors in the face of mass resistance and prolonged struggles and are fundamentally unstable arrangements. Under these new class relations of global capitalism the elements of reciprocity and redistribution historically embedded in social/collective labor tend to disappear. The emergence of new post-Fordist flexible regimes of accumulation require "flexible" and "just in time"—that is, casualized, feminized, deunionized, and contingent—labor. Flexibility means that capital abandons reciprocal obligations to labor in the employment contract while states, with their transmutation from developmentalist to neoliberal, roll back public obligations to poor and working majorities.

Deregulation

TNS agencies have relentlessly pushed for the deregulation of labor markets. According to a 1993 World Bank report (as quoted in Thomas, 1996:79–80):

> Most policy discussions on the mechanics of structural adjustment and market-oriented reforms ignore labor market deregulation. And yet, labor markets in many countries are highly distorted, introducing efficiency costs and making adjustment more difficult. A dynamic and flexible labor market is an important part of market-oriented policies. It helps reallocate resources and allows the economy to respond rapidly to new challenges from increased foreign competition. Moreover, freeing the labor market of distortions improves the distribution of income because it encourages employment expansion and wage increases in the poorest segments of society.

For the World Bank, labor market inflexibility or "rigidity" includes the high costs of dismissing workers, restrictions on hiring temporary workers, high levels of fringe benefits, and so on (World Bank, as cited in Thomas, 1996:91). Neoliberal labor market reform has included: legislation to reduce the power of trade unions; a sharp reduction in public employment (in part as a result of privatizations and in part a result of downsizing); and a revision of labor codes so as to make the work force flexible. Neoliberal governments in just about every Latin American country revised labor laws in the late twentieth century. While these reforms varied from country to country, in general they made it easier for employers to dismiss workers and to do so without due compensation; authorized temporary, part-time, and contract labor in place of permanent employment; allowed the establishment of private employment and temp agencies; extended probationary periods from weeks to months, and in some cases to years; reduced or eliminated requirements for health, unemployment, vacation, and other work benefits; weakened minimum wage and overtime stipulations; introduced sub-minimum wage "youth employment" programs; extended the legal workday; curtailed employer severance pay obligations; and encumbered unionization and sometimes banned it outright, as in the FTZs.

These measures eroded the power of trade unions and helped shift the correlation of class forces in favor of capital during the 1980s and 1990s. "Unions lost members (although not necessarily combativeness) in the public service sector and state enterprises, i.e., in the sectors most seriously affected by the adjustment process and where the most committed activists were to be found," observes Bronstein. "The power of unions in the private sector was also eroded, as companies in hitherto-protected industries disappeared, and as those companies which did survive sought to replace a relatively stable labor force, which enjoyed the protection of labor legislation and where there was a reasonably high level of unionization, with a different sort of worker who was less inclined to join unions and could be hired on a less secure basis. In short, the unions lost their political constituency, as power shifted away from the ministries with social responsibilities—to which union leaders had traditionally enjoyed access—to ministries of finance or economics" (1997:10).

The deregulation of labor markets is justified with the claim that the incentive of low wages and flexible workers will lead to an increase in jobs. The data actually shows, however, a general trend in Latin America toward rising unemployment. Open urban unemployment for Latin America as a whole increased steadily in the 1990s—a decade of "recovery" from the 1980s recession—from 5.7 percent in 1991 to 10.7 percent by the end of the decade, reached 10.8 percent in 2002 and did not drop below 10 percent between then and 2005 (ECLAC, cited in Ruesga and Fujii, 2006:5). Equally as important as data on unemployment is the changing nature of employment—particularly, the spread of flexible labor and the capital-labor relations associated with global capitalism. Even if the transnational model has generated increased employment in some cases, global economy jobs in Latin America—in the maquiladoras, transnational services, NTAEs—are largely precarious and unstable employment, including low wages, short-duration contracts, long work days, irregular hours, and degrading and dangerous work conditions. The ILO has calculated that of every ten new jobs created in the 1990s, eight were low-quality positions in the informal sector (Lander, 2005:25). Despite neoliberal claims that wages would improve through the deregulation of labor markets the typical outcome of reform has been a fall in wages in both the formal and informal sectors and a transfer of income from labor to capital (Thomas, 1996:86–87).

Predictably, the first country to reform its laws was Chile, during 1978 and 1979, followed by Colombia in 1990, Peru in 1991, Argentina in 1991 and 1995, Panama in 1995, and so on, as almost every Latin American country followed suit (Bronstein, 1997). Mexico was interestingly the one country that by 2007 had still not revised its labor laws even as flexible and unprotected employment became the most frequent work arrangement. Under the leadership of Carlos Abascal, a leading transnational capitalist and secretary of labor from 2001 to 2006, the Mexican government attempted repeatedly to reform the country's labor laws. The effort was to retain the corrupt and clientalist business unionism of the twentieth century Mexican corporatist system while at the same time eliminating the worker rights and protections that came with that system. The campaign to implement what was called *Plan Abascál*—drawn up by Abascal and the World Bank and presented in 2001 (LaBotz and Alexander, 2005:18)— met the widespread resistance of independent trade unions and social movement coalitions fighting simultaneously to democratize the country's powerful but corrupt and collaborationist unions and to prevent neoliberal reforms. Independent unions, including the combative Authentic Labor Front (FAT), formed the National Union of Workers (UNT) in 1997, while other unions and popular organizations formed the Mexican Union Front (FSM) as an attempt to create "an alternative unified, democratic, working-class, anti-capitalist unionism" (cited in LaBotz and Alexander, 2005:20). These federations joined forces with a broad array of popular organizations and social movements to successfully resist the *Plan Abascál*. Nonetheless, by the twenty-first century casualized work relations were spreading quickly in Mexico in the face of informalization and the widespread replacement of fixed with contingent workers in privatized enterprises.

Informalization

Informality has received increasing scholarly attention in recent years. Studies on development have long noted that underdeveloped countries are characterized by a bloated informal sector, attributed to the insufficient ability of industry and formal services to absorb those displaced by the extension of capitalist relations. The informal sector is generally defined as the self- employed, casual workers, those who work in enterprises employing four persons or fewer, and those who work in unregulated conditions in terms of labor legislation, taxes, social security, and so forth. If earlier literature characterized the informal sector as a pre-capitalist vestige more recent research showed that the informal economy is functionally integrated into the formal economy (Castells and Portes, 1989) and has been integral to capitalist development (for overviews, see Fernández-Kelly 2006, in Fernández-Kelly and Shefner, 2006; Cortes, 2001).

However, globalization requires us to take the analysis a step further. The widespread transition from a regime of Fordist to flexible employment relations, subcontracting and outsourcing arrangements, an array of new forms of capitalist association and flexible organization all link formal and informal activities and blur the boundaries between formality and informality. Those located in the expanding informal economy are networked through a myriad of mechanisms and relationships into global production and service chains. As TNCs outsource specific production and service tasks to local subcontractors, for instance, the labor they continue to employ is subject to casualization while subcontractors draw on labor from the informal economy. Moreover, as the cost of reproduction is expunged from the capitalist sector it is absorbed by the informal sector, which replenishes the pool of labor. Informalization becomes immanent to the production relations of global capitalism, a mechanism for the appropriation of surplus in new ways by capital. Ultimately capital comes to dominate a vast army of workers *and* "independent" producers laboring in various degrees of formality and informality and drawn through numerous channels directly or indirectly into the global economy as the distinction between what Marx referred to as the *formal* and the *real* subsumption of labor to capital becomes blurred.

The previous ISI-populist model in Latin America involved a segmentation of urban labor markets into a protected (formal and regulated) sector and an unprotected (informal and unregulated) sector. Formal employment grew steadily during the ISI era, whereas in the neoliberal era formal employment has contracted inverse to the expansion of informal work. There has been a double movement as the region has globalized toward the deregulation of this protected sector and an increasing informalization of previously formal work. The vast majority of labor in microenterprises is informal, while at the same time large and medium firms and governments increasingly downsize and rely on casualized labor by contracting temporary or part time workers, hiring them off the books and without written contracts, and outsourcing and subcontracting operations to smaller enterprises where the bulk of work is casualized.

The majority of the urban labor force worked in the formal sector in the previous developmentalist epoch. In 1950, 69.2 percent or urban workers in Latin America worked in the formal sector. This figure increased to 70.2 percent in

1970 (PREALC, as reported by Thomas, 1996:85, table 1). The percentage in individual countries ranged from a high of 80.9 in Argentina to low of 42.1 in Ecuador. By the 1980s, the percentage of the urban labor force working in the formal sector had decline to 59.8. By 1985 it had dropped to 53.1, by 1992 to 45.7, and by 1998 to just 42.1 percent (PREALC, as reported by Thomas, 1996:88, table 2; 1998 from ILO, as cited in Portes and Hoffman, 2003:50). The drop in Argentina was from the 1970s high of 80.9 percent to 50.4 percent in 1992 while the other large economies experience similar declines. Brazil went from 72.1 percent to 45.8 percent and Mexico from 65.1 percent to 44 percent (PREALC, in Thomas, 1996:88, table 2). Table 5.4 shows the informal sector share of employment and rates of unemployment for select countries in 2004.

At the same time employment in small firms and self employment increased sharply throughout the region, indicating both the shift from formal sector employment to scratching out a living as self-employed in the informal sector and the increasing reliance of large firms on outsourcing and subcontracting to small enterprises that generally operate under informal conditions. Of a working population of 105 million in 1992, observes Thomas, those self-employed and employed in small firms had risen to 50 million, while 32 million worked in large firms, 16 million in public sectors, and 7 million as domestic servants. While all categories grew in absolute terms, the increase in self-employment and employment in small firms represented nearly four times the combined growth of those employed in large firms and in the public sector. "Hence, Latin America has seen a major re-alignment in the distribution of labor across categories," observes Thomas (1996:89).

TABLE 5.4

Latin America: Informal Sector Employment and Open Unemployment Rate, Select Countries, Percentages, 2004

Country	Informal Sector	Unemployment Rate
Argentina	44.3	12.1
Colombia	59.9	15.5
Costa Rica	41.8	6.7
Dominican Republic	49.5	18.4
Ecuador	57.6	8.6
Panama	41.6	14.0
Paraguay	62.9	10.0
Peru	58.0	10.5
Uruguay	37.7	13.1
Venezuela	52.2	13.5

Source: ILO, 2005, table 3.27.

There has been an explosion of people who scratch out a living through the provision of whatever service they are able to market since the informal sector has been the only avenue of survival for millions of people thrown out of work by contraction of formal sector employment and by the uprooting of remaining peasant communities by the incursion of capitalist agriculture. Because anyone can enter the informal sector, even if to sell chewing gum, shine shoes, or clean windshields at traffic intersections, the actual figures for unemployment in Latin America in recent decades are considerably lower than the social crisis generated by neoliberalism would lead one to expect. National and international data collection agencies reports those in the informal sector as "employed," despite the highly irregular and unregulated nature of the informal sector, characterized by low levels of productivity, below-poverty (and below legal minimum wage) earnings, and instability, usually amounting to underemployment. The key category of *under*employment includes those who wish to work more in a given activity and are unable to do so as well as those who work at jobs that generate insufficient productivity and income. In Thomas' view underemployment is a major form of labor market adjustment in Latin America. Household surveys from Lima, for example, showed that unemployment increased between 1987 and 1993 from 4.8 to 9.9 percent but the rate of underemployment rose from 34.9 to 77.4 percent during this time.

Are Microenterprises Entrepreneurialism or Marginality?

If the growth of the informal sector has been in part the natural outcome of restructuring and globalization, it has also been spread through AID and IFI programs and polices to promote what has come to be known in the new development discourse as "microenterprises," or petty businesses. The AID's Private Enterprise Initiative, for instance, a program initiated in the 1980s that sought to bolster private sectors around the world, called for funding microenterprise projects as part of the policy of expanding assistance to private business (Robinson, 2003:268). The promotion of micro-enterprises through government and IFI programs such as small scale credit, technical training, and the provision of market information, has been extolled as a progressive attempt to democratize the economy by distributing more equitably the assistance usually only provided to large-scale capitalists and TNCs, and to address the problem of poverty and marginality among the millions of people who labor in the informal sector.

Such a strategy was made popular by Hernando de Soto's 1987 book, *El Otro Sendero: La Revolution Informal* (The Other Path: the Informal Revolution), which achieved somewhat of a cult status among neoliberal ideologues and policy makers. In *El Otro Sendero*, De Soto argued that legal and administrative barriers placed on poor people by government regulation of their informal economic activity impede their "entrepreneurial energies" and that market deregulation could overcome poverty and marginalization. The microenterprise strategy has also become popular among First World liberals following the experience of the Grameen Bank in Bangladesh, which has gained worldwide attention with its policies of making loans to poor women. While the issue cannot be explored here, the Grameen Bank does not deserve its reputation as a democratic and progressive form of liberation for the poor, and especially women, in that country, and has actually become an ideological bonanza for the transnational elite, including the World Bank and several TNCs that support the Grameen Bank (among them, Monsanto). The loan program serves to depoliticize the most oppressed sector of Bangladesh society, to fragment communities and draw them into, and subordinate them to, a web of market relations, according to Blackstock (1999; see also Bello, 2006a).

Some microenterprises in Latin America have become "successful" small firms within the precarious parameters of informality. As new structures of flexible accumulation take hold, for instance, local and transnational firms shed ancillary operations through subcontracting and outsourcing, which allow microenterprises to provide highly localized and small-scale services, and this can constitute a niche for new groups (Pérez Saínz, 2002). Promoting microenterprises thus becomes a way of establishing functional and organizational links between the formal and informal sectors, with small and microenterprises linked vertically to the large capitalist firms and TNCs. Guatemalan researchers Escoto and Marroquín, who studied AID programs for microenterprises in that country, found that the aim of AID programs was to articulate them vertically to the expanding export production (agro-exports, NTAEs, maquiladoras, etc.) of large scale enterprises and TNCs, through the provision of localized services. "In the end, the AID was seeking the 'formalization' of microenterprises, not as an end in itself, but as a means for the firms in the formal sector to take advantage of the potential services [microenterprises] could offer them" (Escoto and Marroquín, 1992:86). The lower one moves down in these vertical structures, the more likely it is that informal employment, or self-based (or family-based) employment, will predominate.

The spread of these tiny "enterprises" is largely identified with the growth of self-employment as subsistence activity. As thousands of people employed in the public sector were dismissed in the 1990s through privatization and other adjustment policies they were encouraged through diverse programs to establish their own microenterprises and become "entrepreneurs" as a way of binding to the market sectors of the population recently disrupted from stable socioeconomic arrangements by restructuring. The logic that dictates microenterprises is one of simple reproduction, or subsistence. But the flexible organization of production in the transnational model also provides new opportunities and allows certain strata to integrate into the global economy as developed (or at least as better off) social clusters. Hence the heterogeneity of transnationalized labor markets spans the formal and informal sectors. The segmentation of labor markets in Latin America is similar to that taking place throughout global society. Most new employment opportunities entail unskilled labor-intensive activities, such as new agricultural and maquila work or petty commerce and self-employment in the informal economy. But there is also the creation of skilled employment, such as tourist workers who must be bilingual or administer facilities, or those who are successful at setting up a small firm in the informal sector. These jobs may bring to the worker or professional the consumption and technological- cultural benefits that global society has to offer.

If the microenterprise movement does not actually alleviate poverty and marginalization, it does become a mechanism for imbuing the popular classes, especially the excluded, with a market ideology, and for exercising some influence over a sector prone to social unrest. People who are involved in micro-business come under not only the material domination of large business but also under its ideological sway. The logic is one of how to "make the market work" for the poor rather than how to overcome the impoverishing effects of the market itself. The existing structures, with their extant distribution of property and social resources, are legitimated by an ideology of individual rewards and individual responsibilities. There is a tendency for the transnational model to fragment the popular classes and therefore thwart their collective political protagonism. However, as informality has become the predominant social form the locus of popular mobilization has increasingly spread from the workplace to communities and from more formal class to other identities. In some cases, as Fernández-Kelly, Shefner, and their colleagues have shown, the informal economy becomes an important site of political action and contestation (2006), certainly to the extent that it becomes articulated to new resistance politics and counter-hegemonic movements, as I will discuss later.

Feminization

There is a huge and rapidly growing literature on the gendered nature of globalization (Moghadam, 2005), and a consensus that the process affects men and women differently and entails contradictory social-gender effects. Gender has played an important role for many researchers of globalization for two reasons. First, much of the debate in 1970s and 1980s on the "new international division of labor" (NIDL) emphasized the phenomenon of young women working for transnational corporations in export-processing enclaves (see, e.g., Nash and Fernández-Kelly, 1983; Joekes, 1987; Fernández-Kelly, 1983; Tiano, 1994), in the context of the well-documented massive entrance of women into the global workforce in recent decades. Women, we should recall, do two-thirds of the world's work, receive one-tenth of the world's income, and possess less than one one-hundredth of the world's property. When we speak of female entrance into the labor force we mean specifically their shift from unpaid to paid or market- based work. Around the world women's share of total industrial labor rarely exceeds 30 to 40 percent, for instance, but the proportion of women workers in EPZ factories producing textiles and electronics components is as high as 90 percent (Moghadam, 2005:53). Second, the "feminization of poverty" thesis has pointed out that the worldwide rise in poverty in the late twentieth and early twenty-first centuries associated with global economic restructuring and neoliberalism has affected women disproportionately, and that the new poor are disproportionately women (and children).

The feminization of labor refers to female proletarianization and the influx of women into relatively low-paying and often sex-segregated jobs, although it *also* refers to the growth of part-time and temporary work among men (Moghadam, 2005). The transnational model in Latin America, as Joekes (1987:81) puts it in reference to the global economy as a whole, is as much *female* led as *export* led. The entrance of women into labor markets is most pronounced among new economic activities linked to the global economy. "The 1980s might be labeled the decade of labor deregulation. It has also marked a renewed surge of feminization of labor activity," notes Guy Standing in his oft-cited study, *Global Feminization through Flexible Labor*. "The types of work, labor relations, income, and insecurity associated with 'women's work' have been spreading, resulting not only in a notable rise in female labor force participation, but in a fall in men's employment, as well as a transformation—or feminization—of many jobs traditionally held by men" (Standing, 1989:1077).

There is an increasingly female face to the working class in Latin America (see Table 5.5 and Piras, 2004). A major portion, often an outright majority, of workers in the new transnationally integrated circuits in Latin America are women. However, women disproportionately bloat the ranks of the informal sector and disproportionately suffer unemployment (ILO, 2005, table 2-A:86). The crisis of peasant agriculture, as we saw previously, has led to male unemployment and out-migration toward cities (and abroad) and forced rural women to search for paid employment as a survival strategy. On the other hand, employers often prefer female over male workers because preexisting patriarchal structures provide capital with extra leverage over women workers. Patriarchal relations are not eliminated but grafted onto expanding capitalist relations, intensifying unequal power relations between men and women.

Structural adjustment has disproportionately affected women, whose workload increases as family incomes decline and as social services are scaled back. Women seeking paid employment face fewer options than men, principally domestic service for middle and upper classes, the restaurant industry, itinerant trading in the informal sector, or maquiladora work (see Table 5.6). Women account for fully 70 percent of all new jobs in the informal sector and face an intensified "double burden" of production and reproduction: as they enter the paid workforce they are still largely responsible for reproduction in the household (see, inter alia, Benería and Feldman, 1992; Safa, 1995a; Moghadam, 2005).

The feminization of labor is a contradictory process, illustrated in the debate over women and work in the NTAE sector. The experience of women in NTAEs

TABLE 5.5
Entrance of Women in Labor Force, as a Percentage of Females in EAP in Paid Workforce, Latin America and Select Countries, 1980–2010

	1980	1985	1990	1995	2000	2005	2010*
Latin America	27.9	30.1	32.2	34.5	36.9	39.3	41.5
Argentina	24.1	29.9	35.4	36.7	38.7	39.6	41.0
Bolivia	23.3	26.0	30.6	33.0	35.3	37.6	40.3
Brazil	33.9	35.6	36.7	38.5	40.7	43.0	44.7
Costa Rica	18.9	20.6	23.9	26.8	29.8	33.2	36.6
Ecuador	16.9	20.7	24.4	27.4	30.4	33.5	36.4
Guatemala	11.8	14.5	17.1	20.1	24.1	27.9	31.9
Honduras	15.7	18.4	21.0	24.0	27.1	30.2	33.5
Mexico	24.7	25.6	27.0	30.4	33.4	36.3	39.2
Peru	29.5	31.6	33.5	35.6	38.1	40.4	42.7
Uruguay	32.4	38.3	39.9	42.3	44.0	45.4	46.9
Venezuela	22.0	25.3	28.3	31.4	34.5	37.7	40.6

Source: ECLAC, *Statistical Yearbook,* 2005, table 1.2.2.
    *Estimated.

TABLE 5.6
Women in the Urban Informal Economy in Latin America, 1990–2003

	1990	1995	2000	2002	2003
Total (% female EAP in informal sector)	47.7	51.0	50.3	49.4	51.0
Independent/Self-Employed	23.2	24.1	23.7	22.8	24.1
Domestic Service	13.8	17.0	15.4	15.2	15.4
Microenterprise*	10.4	9.9	11.2	11.3	11.5

Source: ILO, 2005 Labor Overview for Latin America and the Caribbean, table 6-A.
*Includes workers in establishments employing up to five workers.

in Latin America is consistent with what Mies (1999) has observed as a pattern in the Third World when subsistence agriculture is subsumed under cash crops for exportation. Women's labor is either invisible as a part of the subsistence labor force or women are forced to migrate in search of waged employment (Mies, 1999). Once they enter the labor market, women are channeled into "feminine," and often the most labor intensive, tasks such as fruit and vegetable picking (Deere and Leon de Leal, 1987). On the other hand, Bee and Vogel argue that women who were previously marginalized as unpaid family labor in peasant households have found new opportunities to rework household relations as a result of their entrance into the paid workforce. Controlling a substantial portion of the household income may increase women's influence over the decision-making process in the household and raise their sense of self-worth (Bee and Vogel, 1997). Others, such as Korovkin, observe an increase in stress as rural women workers face an intensified "double shift" and are forced to withdraw from community life (Korovkin, 2003).

In my view, to ask if the entrance of women into the global economy is helpful or harmful is to mistakenly frame the issue (for varied discussion, see, inter alia, Safa, 1995b; Korovkin, 2003; McClenaghan, 1997). It is clear that class (and often ethnic) differentiation among women has heightened through globalization, so that middle and upper class women have advanced even as poor women have faced new hardships, challenges, and family-based stresses. Formal employment or greater juridical equality may have improved women's status in some senses without necessarily challenging patriarchal relations. Female flexible labor in the capitalist centers of production permits the system to reinforce women's subordination in the household centers of reproduction. The empowerment of working and poor women would involve overcoming the sexual division of labor in both family and society while valuating and socializing reproductive labor. While women may gain certain benefits from their massive incorporation into the new farms, factors, and service sectors of the global economy in Latin America, the overall effect of flexible labor, gender-segmentation in the workplace, and domination by transnational capital is new forms of control and subordination.

A New "Pauperization" of Labor

Globalization in Latin America has been associated with a dramatic sharpening of social inequalities, increased polarization, and the persistence of widespread poverty (Roberts, 2002; Hoffman and Centeno, 2003; Korzeniewicz and Smith, 2000; Portes and Hoffman, 2003; Green, 1995; Reygadas, 2006; Damian and Boltvinik, 2006), reflecting the broader pattern of global social polarization. There has been a pauperization of labor as average income for the working population either stagnated or declined, and in some cases, plummeted. Average incomes for workers fell by 40 percent in Venezuela, by 30 percent in Buenos Aires, and by 21 percent in Brazil in the 1980s and early 1990s. In Argentina the 1990 minimum wage was 40 percent of that in 1980 and in Peru it was 23 percent (Hoffman and Centeno, 2003:370). The decline of wages is a worldwide trend but it would seem that the descent into the working poor has been more precipitous in Latin America than elsewhere. Portes and Hoffman note that three-fourths of the employed population in Latin America, "corresponding approximately to the sum of the formal and informal proletariats, does not generate enough income from their jobs to surpass the poverty level. This implies that with few national exceptions, to be a worker in Latin America means to be poor" (2003:59). Portes and Hoffman conclude:

> In synthesis, results of our analysis show that: (a) with the exception of Chile, the average incomes of the Latin American urban workforce stagnated or declined in real terms during the years of neo-liberal adjustment; (b) the average incomes of all the subordinate classes, including the urban petty bourgeoisie, declined as well; (c) the incomes of the dominant classes increased faster than average in all countries, with the exception of Panama, but including Chile; (d) as a result, the ratio of income received by these classes relative to the various proletarian classes increased during this period, exacerbating what already was a gulf in the economic condition and life chances of the wealth and the poor. More than ever, the fact was reaffirmed that, in Latin America, it is not necessary to be unemployed in order to be poor. (2003:65)

As Table 5.7 shows, poverty increased in the 1980s, from 40.5 percent in 1980 to nearly half the subcontinent's population in 1990, then declined somewhat in the late 1990s but began to rise again in the new century, reaching 44 percent in 2002 as the region experienced renewed recession. Poverty levels vary significantly among Latin American countries, with a high of 77 percent in Honduras in 2002, a low in Uruguay of 15 percent, and a wide range in between: 21 percent in Chile; 40 percent in Mexico, 20 percent in Costa Rica; 49 percent in El Salvador, 63 percent in Bolivia, 55 percent in Peru, 45 in the Dominican Republic, and so on (ECLAC, as cited in Damian and Boltvinik, 2006:146–147). But no country escaped a rise in poverty from the 1970s into the twenty-first century.

How poverty is measured remains highly contentious (for discussion, see Damian and Boltvinik, 2006). Traditionally it has been conceived as insufficient income and simply measured on a per capita basis.[3] Later definitions have included access to public services and the creation of such compound indexes as the United Nations Development Program's Human Development Index (HDI, which combines per capital income with literacy and life expectancy levels) as well as quality of life conceptions focusing on health, nutrition, and infrastructure. The measurement of income poverty and income inequality used by the IFIs is a particularly partial and skewed method that conceals the full extent of both deprivation and of social inequality, as Boltvinik (see Damian and Boltvinik, 2006), among others, has shown. In any event, the slight reduction of poverty in the 1990s took place, we should recall, in the wake of the unprecedented expansion of poverty in the 1980s. In the 1960s and 1970s, after all, the poverty rate hovered around 35 percent of the population (CEPAL, 2000)—still well below what it was in 2005!

Figures for the poverty *rate*, moreover, conceal the sharp rise in the absolute number of the poor, which increased by 84 million people during this period, from 136 million in 1980 to 220 million in 2002, an increase of 61.8 percent (ECLAC data, as cited in Damian and Boltvinik, 2006:145). Most telling is the steady rise in the number of poor people during the 1990s, since by the end of the 1980s Latin America had resumed growth rates and attracted a net inflow of capital following the stagnation and decline during much of the decade. In the early 1990s, officials from the IFIs began to speak of "recovery," by which they meant that growth (accumulation) had in most countries resumed. The pattern

---

[3] We should recall the extremely misleading nature of the standard measurement used by the World Bank and other IFIs: indigence is simply measured as earnings of less than one dollar per day and poverty simply as earnings of less than two dollars per day. Therefore, if someone's annual earnings increases from, say $344 to $371 she is considered to have risen above indigence, and if a person's earnings goes from $720 to $810 he has been lifted out of poverty.

TABLE 5.7
Poverty and Extreme Poverty in Latin America, 1980–2002,
as a Percentage of Total Population

Year	Below Poverty Line			Below Extreme Poverty Line		
	Total	Rural	Urban	Total	Rural	Urban
1980	40.5	29.8	59.9	18.6	10.6	32.7
1990	48.3	41.4	65.4	22.5	15.3	40.4
2000	42.5	35.9	62.5	18.1	11.7	37.8
2002	44.0	37.8	61.8	19.4	13.5	27.9

Source: ECLAC, *Panorama Social de America Latina,* 2001 and 2003, as compiled in Damian and Boltvinik, 2006, figure 7.1, p. 146.

under globalization is not merely growth without redistribution but the simultaneous growth of wealth and of poverty as two sides of the same coin. We should recall that poverty and inequality are social relations of unequal power between the dominant and the subordinate. What poverty really means is the inability to make choices, to control one's life circumstances, to dispose of one's own labor and its fruits. Poverty is less an inert state than a social relationship of power and powerlessness. The essence of poverty is a class relationship between the poor and the rich.

Latin America remained in the twenty-first century the most unequal region in the world, "defying description and belief," in Hoffman and Centeno's words (2003:365). Indeed, the evidence indicates that a significant portion of the misery for a large part of the population does not necessarily stem from poverty in and of itself but from the consequences of radically asymmetrical distribution (Hoffman and Centeno, 2003; Korzeniewicz and Smith, 2000). During the developmentalist era some sectors of the economically active population experienced upward mobility but in the globalization era every country with the exception of Colombia in the 1980s has experienced an increase in the concentration of income and wealth (Hoffman and Centeno, 2006:367). The Gini coefficient, which measures income inequality (0 is perfect equality and 1 is perfect inequality) rose from 0.45 in 1980 to 0.50 in 1989 (World Bank, 1997a), and then to 0.53 by the late 1990s (Reygadas, 2006:121), and then to 0.58 in 2002 (UNDP, 2004:43), compared to a world average in the 1990s of average of 0.38 and 0.34 for the developed countries. Moreover, the richest 10 percent of the urban population increased its share of income from: 30 to 36 percent of the total in Argentina from 1980 to 1997; from 39 to 44 percent in Brazil (1979–1996); from 35 to 40 percent in Colombia (1990–1997); from 23 to 27 percent in Costa Rica (1981–1997); from 26 to 34 percent in Mexico (1984–1996);

from 29 to 37 percent in Panama (1979–1997); and from 29 to 33 percent in Paraguay (1981–1997) (ECLAC, 1998b, table 17). In 1990, the richest ten percent of Latin Americans had 25.4 times the income of the poorest ten percent; in 2002 the correlation was 40 times (UNDP, 2004:43).

Income-measured poverty and inequality are only one dimension, and often not the most important, of social inequality and deprivation. Added to income polarization is the dramatic deterioration in social conditions as a result of austerity measures that have drastically reduced and privatized health, education, and other social programs. Popular classes whose social reproduction is dependent on a social wage (public sector) have faced a social crisis, while privileged middle and upper classes become exclusive consumers of social services channeled through private networks. Here we see the need to reconceive development in transnational social rather than geographic terms. Global capitalism generates downward mobility for most at the same time that it opens up new opportunities for some middle class and professional strata as the redistributive role of the nation-state recedes and global market forces become less mediated by state structures as they mold the prospects for downward and upward mobility.

The escalation of deprivation indicators in Brazil, Mexico, and Argentina, which together account for some three-fifths of Latin America's 500 million inhabitants, reveals the process of immiseration that most Latin Americans experienced under global capitalism. Between 1985 and 1990, the rate of child malnutrition in Brazil increased from 12.7 to 30.7 percent of all children (World Bank, 1997). In Sao Paulo, 1.1 percent of the population lived in the *favelas* in 1970, but by 1993 nearly 20 percent lived in the sprawling poverty of these notorious shantytowns (Hoffman and Centeno, 2003:368). In Mexico the purchasing power of the minimum wage dropped 66 percent between 1982 and 1991. It was calculated that in the mid-1990s it took 4.8 minimum wages for a family of four to meet essential needs, yet 80 percent of households earned 2.5 minimum wages or less. As a result malnutrition has spread among the urban and rural poor (Barkin, Ortiz, and Rosen, 1997). In Argentina, meanwhile, unemployment rose steadily in the 1980s and 1990s from 3 percent in 1980 to 20 percent in 2001, the number of people in extreme poverty from 200,000 to 5 million and in poverty from one million to 14 million, illiteracy increased from 2 to 12 percent and functional illiteracy from 5 to 32 percent during this period (Gabetta, 2002). In fact, the HDI actually *decreased* for many Latin American countries in the 1990s. With 1.0 the highest score and zero the lowest, the index decreased for the following countries in the 1990s: Argentina,

Chile, Uruguay, Costa Rica, Mexico, Panama, Venezuela, Colombia, Brazil, Peru, Nicaragua, Ecuador, El Salvador, Honduras, Bolivia, and Guatemala (UNDP, 2002, 7, table 1).

Neoliberalism and Stagnation

During Latin America's "lost decade" of the 1980s, other regions, particularly East Asia, North America, and Europe, became the most attractive outlets for accumulated capital stocks. Latin American stagnated in absolute terms and experienced backward movement when seen in relation to other regions in the world economy. The region experienced a contraction of income and economic activity. Its share of world trade dropped by half from 1980 to 1990, from about 6 percent to about 3 percent (Wilkie, 1995, vol. 3). In the 1980s it became the region with the slowest growth in per-capita income, behind other Third World regions and behind the world as a whole, as indicated in Table 5.8. While such nation-state indicators need to be approached with caution, they underscore the depth of the crisis that accompanied the breakdown of the ISI model and the region's troubled integration into the emergent global economy.

While there was a resumption of growth in the first part of the 1990s, the much-touted recovery was accompanied by increased poverty and inequality. What is most notable about Table 5.9 is that GDP per capita declined in the "lost decade," by 0.9 percent, from 1980 to 1990, and then barely recovered in the "growth years" of the 1990s, growing by 1.5 percent from 1991 to 2000 and by 1.4 percent from 2001 to 2006. Table 5.9 also contrasts the stagnation of the neoliberal era to the robust growth from 1960 to 1980 in the preceding era. Aggregate per capita income increased 82 percent from 1960 to 1980 but then grew only 14 percent from 1980 to 2005 (Weisbrot, 2006).

TABLE 5.8
Comparison of Growth by Regions (% average annual growth rate)

	1965–1980	1980–1989	1990–2000
World	4.1	3.1	2.6
Latin America	6.1	1.6	3.3
Sub-Sahara Africa	4.2	2.1	2.4
East Asia	7.3	7.9	7.2
South Asia	3.7	5.1	5.6
OECD members	3.8	3.0	2.4

Source: World Bank, *World Development Report*, 1991, 1992, 2001, 2002.

TABLE 5.9
Latin America: Annual Growth Rates, GDP and
GDP per capita, Region and Select Countries and Years

	GDP	GDP per Capita
Latin America		
1960–1980	5.5	4.0
1980–1990	1.2	−0.9
1991–2000	3.3	1.5
2001–2006	2.9	1.4
Argentina		
1981–1990	−0.7	−2.1
1991–2000	4.2	2.9
1998–2000	0.2	−1.1
2001–2006	3.7	2.7
Brazil		
1981–1990	1.6	−0.4
1991–2000	2.6	1.2
1998–2000	1.7	0.4
2001–2006	2.9	0.8
Colombia		
1981–1999	3.7	1.6
1991–2000	2.6	0.6
1998–2000	−0.3	−2.1
2001–2006	3.9	2.2
Ecuador		
1981–1990	1.7	0.9
1991–2000	1.7	−0.4
1998–2000	−1.6	−3.5
2001–2006	5.1	3.6
Mexico		
1981–1990	1.9	−0.2
1991–2000	3.5	1.7
1998–2000	5.2	3.6
2001–2006	2.4	0.9
Venezuela		
1981–1990	−0.7	−3.2
1991–2000	2.0	−0.2
1998–2000	−0.8	−2.8
2001–2006	4.0	2.2

Source: Compiled from ECLAC, *Statistical Yearbook for Latin America and the Caribbean,* various years.

The next two tables indicate two additional patterns. First, Table 5.10 suggests that the region's stagnation coincided with a deeper integration into the global economy. The region produced ever-greater amounts of wealth for the world capitalist system as the volume of its exports to the world increased significantly throughout the 1980s and 1990s. Between 1983 and 2000, the volume of the region's exports *rose* by an annual average of 15.1 percent, yet the value of these same exports actually *decreased* by an annual average of 0.1 percent.

TABLE 5.10
*Volume and Unit of Value of Latin American Exports
(average annual % growth, in batch years)*

	Volume	Unit Value
1983–85	16.2	−9.9
1986–88	17.7	−5.9
1989–91	13.7	5.2
1992–94	22.3	3.3
1995–97	11.5	8.4
1998–2000	8.9	−0.7
1983–2000	15.1	0.1
(average annual change)		

Source: Compiled from ECLAC, 1983, 1998a, 1999.

Second, Latin America continued to generate wealth that fueled the world capitalist economy even as the region stagnated. Latin America exported over the period from 1980 to 2006 an annual average of $42 billion in profits and interests (Table 5.11). "Growth," therefore, represented the creation of tribute to transnational finance capital. Latin Americans have worked harder and harder to increase the wealth they have produced for the global economy yet the income they have received from that work has decreased as they have become more impoverished and exploited. Global capitalism has not represented in Latin America a major new round of expansion: it has represented a shift in wealth and class power. The social crisis in Latin America is not as much a crisis of production as it is of distribution. If inequality is a social relation of unequal power between the dominant and the subordinate, it is, more specifically, the power of the rich locally and globally to dispose of the social product.

TABLE 5.11
*Net Capital Flows, Net Payment on Profits and Interest, and Net Resource Transfer
(in $billion)*

	Net Capital Inflows	Net Payments Profit/Interest	Net Transfer
1980–1990	167	−297	−129
1991–1998	488	−313	175
1999	49	−51	−3
2000	54	−54	0.4
2001	51	−54	−3
2002	11	−53	−48
2003	20	−58	−37
2004	0	−67	−67
2005	−0.4	−77	−77
2006	−13	−90	−102

Source: ECLAC, Preliminary Overview of the Economies of Latin America and the Caribbean, 2006.
    Note: All figures rounded to nearest decimal; total of columns one and two may not equal column three.

The steady deterioration of the terms of trade indicated in Table 5.11 is a consequence, in part, of Latin America's continued overall dependence on commodity exports. Venezuela and Ecuador remain highly depend on oil exports, Chile still depends on copper prices, Brazil and Argentina on a variety of low-tech and basic agricultural exports, Peru on its mining sector, and so on. And when Latin America recovered from the recession of 1999–2002 it was, in part, a result of sharp price increases for primary sector exports, which in turn was closely tied to an expansion of exports to China (ILO, 2005:18; see also previous chapter). This continued dependence on commodity exports is a structural asymmetry that has developed over centuries. But it should not be overstated. First, exports of primary products relative to the total value of the export of goods actually decreased sharply for the region as a whole, from 67 to 44 percent, between 1990 and 2003. And during this same period the percentage of total Latin American exports represented by its ten leading products dropped from 43 to 33 percent, indicating the rapid pace of export diversification (ECLAC, *Statistical Yearbook for Latin America and the Caribbean*, 2004, tables 68 and 70). Second, while globalization has not done away with this structural asymmetry it does compel us to reinterpret its meaning. The value generated by Latin America's participation in global accumulation is appropriated and re-circulated in the global system in new ways by groups that are better understood in terms of transnational class than nation-state or North-South relations. What this situation does present is a worsening of the development (or social) crisis for the poor majority in Latin America and should not be confused with the region's contribution to global capital accumulation nor with the participation of transnationally oriented elites in that accumulation. The ultimate cause of Latin America's stagnation is to be found in the larger crisis of global capitalism that we have already analyzed, and in particular, in the "financialization" of the global economy and the volatility generated by dependence on global capital markets.

Financial Globalization and Latin America

It is important here to recall the central role of financial expansion in the emergence of the global economy. The deregulation and transformation of the global financial system is considered by many to be at the very heart of the globalization process. Financial deregulation, the rise of hyper-mobile transnational finance capital as the hegemonic fraction of capital on a world scale, the apparent decoupling of financial from productive activity, and the frenzied global speculative bustle of "casino capitalism" are often linked to technological changes and the possibilities opened up by information and communications technologies. But they clearly related to rising debt of all types—state, consumer, corporate—which means a rise in interest payments to money capital and a shift in profits from production to financial transactions. They also clearly have more structural roots, in particular in the Kondratieff cycles, in that the end of long swings (e.g., of the boom during the decades after World War II) is characterized by an abundance of capital savings and accumulated surplus values expressed in the hegemony of money capital and financial speculation (Arrighi, 1994).

This "financialization" of the world economy has been well researched. Since the 1970s cross-border bank lending has skyrocketed. It rose between 1980 and 1990 from $324 billion to $7.5 trillion (Robinson, 2004a:26). By the early twenty-first century, several trillion dollars were being traded in currency speculation and other financial operations around the world each day. As early as 1994, daily turnover at the ten largest stock markets was estimated at one trillion dollars, compared to the daily world trade in goods that year of ten billion dollars, so that real trade in actual goods and services was only one percent of fictitious trade (Pettman, 1996:158). As the volume, intensity, and complexity of such global financial transactions have increased many times over, finance has in effect become decoupled from production. This financial globalization dates to the early 1970s, when the U.S. government suspended the dollar's gold convertibility in 1971 and then in 1973 abandoned the fixed exchange rate system, thereby effectively doing away with the Bretton Woods system that had been set up three decades earlier. The decision reflected the buildup that had been taking place in the preceding years in dollar accounts outside of the United States as a result of the increasing internationalization of production. As multinational corporate activity spread in the post-War years these firms, regardless of their nationality, accumulated dollars around the world and deposited them in accounts outside of the United States, thus giving rise to what became known as Euromarkets.

These offshore financial markets signaled the end of autonomous national financial systems and were one of the chief structural pressures that lay beneath the U.S. decision to end the Bretton Woods arrangements. The floating exchange rate system that replaced it meant that the forces of supply and demand would henceforth determine the exchange rate for national currencies. The lifting of gold's convertibility with the dollar and subsequent financial deregulation unleashed an unprecedented wave of financialization of the world economy, including a sharp rise in international bank lending, the cross-border movement of currencies in search of interest rate advantages, and a torrent of global financial speculation, especially currency speculation, that was now possible since the end of gold convertibility meant the end of fixed exchange rates. In turn, this opened the floodgate for broad new forms of transnational financial accumulation.

Financial globalization accelerated in the 1980s and 1990s as governments around the world deregulated their banking systems and financial and stock markets as part of the reorientation of state policies in favor of an open and expansive global economy. Equally as important, one of the mechanisms that has allowed for this global financialization is the creation of new financial instruments known as derivatives. A financial derivative is a way of converting money into instruments that can be traded as a commodity, such as stocks and bonds in international equities markets, institutional investment (e.g., insurance companies, pension funds, investment managers, trust banks), syndicated finance in syndicated loan markets, and other forms of the "securitization" of finance. Securitization means that different forms of debt (e.g., mortgages, government debts) can be transformed into tradable (i.e., profit-making) instruments. These varied instruments can be considered non-bank financial activities in that they are not supplied by banks but by new financial institutions, such as brokerage houses, that have proliferated with the rise of the global economy. Any concentrated pile of money becomes attractive to traders, whether it is negative (debt) or positive (a pension fund).

This is one of the major accomplishments of innovations in finance in the 1980s. It allows transnational investors, if they cannot or do not wish to invest in new material production such as a factory or commercial establishment, to invest their money in the financial sector. This can and often does involve currency speculation but more often than not it involves investment in financial derivatives, which burst on the global economic scene starting in the late 1970s and has boomed ever since. New financial institutions set up to make a profit out of managing the global circulation and accumulation of money in turn supply these financial derivatives. In this way, there is a vast new infrastructure for recycling and further accumulating the vast quantities of money circulating through the global economy—new forms of financial profit making associated with global capitalism. In effect money capital replaces productive capital as the regulator of global circuits of accumulation. Under globalization the relationship between financial investors and material production has been redefined. Tendencies associated with financial globalization such as the global mobility of money, new forms of financial commodification (derivatives, etc.), the hegemony that money capital has achieved over investment capital in recent decades, and so on, have facilitated the appropriation by money irrespective of geography of value produced through material production. Globally mobile money can snatch up material surpluses with much greater ease, and value acquired in this way becomes totally mobile (see, e.g., Hoogvelt 1997).

What interests us here is the increasing reliance of governments on global financial markets for balance of payments and more generally for access to liquid capital, and the consequent discipline that these markets are able to impose in the form of imposing adjustment and integration into global capitalism. Concretely, the majority of capital inflows in Latin America since the 1970s have been in the form of finance capital, first as international bank loans in the 1970s and early 1980s, and then since then, as diverse forms of portfolio financial investment—in stocks, bonds, swaps for privatizing enterprises, currency speculation, and so forth. If governments hope to attract transnational investment, particular from global financial markets, they must in the first instance stabilize the internal macroeconomic environment, which means adopting the package of neoliberal stabilization measures, and in the second, open up to the global economy, which means structural adjustment programs.

The debt crisis of the 1970s and 1980s was the critical variable in Latin America's late twentieth-century turn to globalization and financialization. The autonomous nature of national finances in the Keynesian era generally assured few short-term debt flows to the Third World. But all this began to change in the 1970s with the collapse of the Bretton Woods system and the sharp rise in world oil prices. On the one hand, many Latin American and other Third World countries faced spiraling balance of payments deficits in the face of rising oil import prices and the cost of maintaining imports for ISI industries. On the other hand, "petrodollars" were recycled from OPEC producers to the international banks that recycled these funds as loans to Third World governments. Financial deregulation and the lifting of capital controls further aggravated the debt spiral. Latin America's debt climbed from some $50 billion in 1974 to over $300 billion in 1981 and to more than $410 billion in 1987. The massive borrowing spree corresponded in immediate terms to balance-of-payments crises associated with the exhaustion of the ISI model. But structurally it was rooted in long-term movements in the world economy, particularly the emergence of transnational finance capital as the hegemonic fraction in the global economy. This massive infusion of capital into Latin America, linked to the concentration of economic power in transnational finance capital in the global system at large, had profound effects on existing groups and class con-stellations. The need to earn foreign exchange to pay back the debt requires that nations restructure their economies toward the production of exports in accordance with the changing structure of demand on the world market. Over an extended period, debt contraction and subsequent restructuring had the con-sequence of strengthening those sectors with external linkage, redistributing quotas of accumulated political and economic power toward emergent transna-tionally oriented fraction, and especially toward those associated with transna-tional finance capital.

If in an earlier era imperialist powers applied gunboat diplomacy to collect on Latin America's foreign debt, following World War II the Bretton Woods in-stitutions came to mediate debt. Although the debt steadily climbed in the 1970s it remained manageable until 1979, when the U.S. Federal Reserve sharply raised interest rates to deal with inflationary pressures. Since most Latin American loans were tied to this de facto interest rate, debtor country in-terest and principal payments skyrocketed almost overnight. The possibility that billions of dollars lent to Latin America would turn into bad debts threat-ened the stability of creditor banks, and with them, of the entire international financial system. It was at this time that the IMF and the other Bretton Woods institutions came to take on new collection and surveillance functions on be-half of transnational banking interests, at the same time as the latter organized collective action, encouraging the formation of the Paris Club of creditor coun-tries and the London Club of private creditors, among other forums. In 1982 Mexico announced that it could no longer service its debt, and all the other Latin American nations, except Colombia, followed on its heels. The debt crisis was under way. Between then and 1984, twenty-four Third World countries were forced to reschedule and to refinance their loans. However, none of the Latin American governments officially repudiated their debts in the 1980s, de-spite considerable popular pressure to do so. On the other hand, Latin Ameri-can exporters and emerging financial and commercial interests lobbied heavily against defaulting (Weaver, 2000:177).

Debt repayment became the mechanism for imposing neoliberal struc-tural adjustment on Latin America. By the mid-1980s private banks began to curtail their lending and by the 1990s the new forms of non-bank money capital that had burst on the scene—portfolio investors in bonds, insurance companies, pension and mutual funds, and so forth—replaced bank loans as the major source of capital inflows. Debtor countries now began to open up their capital accounts, thereby allowing the free inflow and outflow of both short and long-term finance, which meant submitting to the exigencies of global financial markets. Financialization and debt increased the power of transnational capital over debtor countries but it also increased the relative power and influence of groups within the debtor country tied to transnational circuits. The image of the IMF and the other IFIs against the debtor or adjusted nation is misleading. Globalization has definite agents in Latin America—new financial, commercial, and service groups oriented toward the global economy, those with substantial holdings in foreign currencies, exporters more generally, and select middle and professional strata.

Foreign investment flows in Latin America prior to globalization involved three previous waves. The first was in the latter half of the nineteenth century and included portfolio investment (loans and mostly government bonds) that went mostly for railroad construction, ports, public utilities and other types of public works (Marichal, 1989:68–170; Stallings, 1987). The second was foreign *direct* investment as distinct from lending in the early twentieth century and went into railroads and other infrastructural works that supported export production. The third took place largely after World War II and involved multinational corporate investment in the region's industrialization. The fourth wave of foreign investment began with escalating bank lending of the 1970s and early 1980s and subsequently involved a massive inflow of transnational capital, primarily in financial speculation and portfolio investment. Latin American states fundamentally altered prior policies toward foreign direct investment developed during the previous epoch of nation-state developmentalist capitalism. The opening to the global economy has included a dismantling of almost all legal arrangements of the previous Keynesian era that regulated, limited, and selectively subordinated the participation of FDI in state-led development programs. The liberalization and deregulation of capital markets and banking systems, along with the process of privatizations, were major determinants in the massive surge of transnational capital into Latin America in the 1980s and especially the 1990s (see Table 5.12), as the region once again became an attractive outlet for investors.

However, the vast majority of the inflow of capital was a consequence not of direct productive—that is, greenfield—foreign investment as much as from diverse portfolio and financial ventures, such as new loans, the purchase of stock in privatized companies, and speculative investment in financial services, such as equities, mutual funds, pensions, and insurance (Fitzgerald, 1998; Marichal, 1997; Veltmeyer, 1997). For example, of $91 billion that flowed into Mexico between 1990 and 1993, $61 billion was in such financial portfolio investment and only $16.6 billion was in direct investment (Marichal (1997:28). Table 5.12 gives an indication of just how central the purchase of stock in privatized enterprises and speculative finance capital has been to the inflow of resources in the 1990s.

Financialization and Crisis

Given this dependence on global capital markets the threat of capital flight now became the major mechanism through which transnational capital exercised structural power over local states and populations. Portfolio equity (financial investment in companies, government bonds, etc.) can be altered or withdrawn with the mere click of a mouse. The integration of world capital markets means that capital has no fixed resting place. Where it alights for the time being depends on the assurance that it will bring returns with minimal risk. The ability to withdraw and withhold credit quickly gives transnational financial actors an enormous new capacity to shape policy making at the national level. Countries compete with each other for transnational capital flows. Signaling creditworthiness and demonstrating the investment potential have become the overriding preoccupation of state managers and local investor communities.[4]

Moody's Investor Service and Standard and Poor's Rating Group, two leading private rating and risk assessment agencies, had no analysts outside the United States in 1983, yet ten years later they each had about a hundred in Europe, Japan, and Australia (Sassen, 1996). These agencies exercise distinct "gatekeeper functions," in that a low rating can assure that transnational investors stay away from a particular country and a high rating facilitates capital inflow. As Schwartzman observes, "transparency" has been coupled with liberalization as a prerequisite for capital mobility. "Once investors have access to emerging markets, what matters most is knowledge about risk. Liberalism without transparency is treacherous" (2006:282). Global financial investment corridors "have requirements not necessarily identical to trade and direct foreign investment corridors," she notes. "New transformations were of crucial importance in rendering recipient countries worthy of investment flows from the developed nations. The emerging markets required two crucial reforms: (1)

---

[4] The dependence of national states on transnational finance capital should not be seen in the classical dependency perspective of core and peripheral countries. It is enough to observe the United States had become just as or even more "dependent" than Latin America in the 1980s and 1990s on the inflow of FDI and the purchase by foreign investors of treasury bonds to balance its fiscal and trade accounts, and by doing so, to keep the U.S. economy and the global economy afloat.

TABLE 5.12

Net Foreign Investment, International Bond Issues, and Proceeds from Sale of Public Enterprises, Latin America and Select Countries, 1991–2000 (in $million)

	1991	1992	1993	1994	1995	1996	1997	1998	1999	2000
Latin America										
Net FDI	11,066	12,506	10,363	23,706	24,799	39,387	55,580	61,596	77,047	57,410
Intl. Bond Issues	7,192	12,577	28,794	17,941	23,071	46,915	52,003	39,511	38,707	35,816
Proceeds from Privatization	16,702	14,866	10,179	8,529	3,433	11,458	24,408	42,461	N/A	N/A
Argentina										
Net FDI	2,439	3,218	2,059	2,480	3,756	4,937	4,924	4,175	21,958	5,000
Intl. Bond Issues	795	1,570	6,308	5,319	6,254	14,070	14,622	15,615	14,183	13,045
Proceeds from Privatization	1,896	5,312	4,589	1,411	1,340	1,033	969	598	N/A	N/A
Brazil										
Net FDI	89	1,924	801	2,035	3,475	11,666	18,608	29,192	28,612	30,000
Intl. Bond Issues	1,837	3,655	6,465	3,998	7,041	11,545,	14,940	9,190	8,586	10,955
Proceeds from Privatization	1,564	2,451	2,621	1,972	910	3,752	17,400	36,600	N/A	N/A
Colombia										
Net FDI	433	679	719	1,297	712	2,795	4,894	2,432	1,135	985
Intl. Bond Issues	—	—	567	955	1,083	1,867	1,000	1,389	1,676	1,451

Proceeds from Privatization	105	27	4	681	138	1,476	3,180	470	N/A	N/A

Mexico

Net FDI	4,742	4,393	4,389	10,973	9,526	9,186	12,830	11,311	11,568	13,500
Intl. Bond Issues	3,782	6,100	11,339	6,949	7,646	16,353	15,567	8,444	9,854	7,547
Proceeds from Privatization	10,716	6,799	2,507	771	—	—	84	581	N/A	N/A

Peru

Net FDI	–7	150	687	3,108	2,048	3,242	1,702	1,860	1,969	1,185
Intl. Bond Issues	—	—	30	100	—	—	250	150	—	—
Proceeds from Privatization	—	3	208	317	2,578	946	2,460	421	462	7,395

Venezuela

Net FDI	1,728	472	–514	136	686	1,676	5,036	4,168	1,998	3,480
Intl. Bond Issues	578	932	3,438	—	356	765	2,015	2,660	1,215	489
Proceeds from Privatization	2,276	30	32	15	21	2,090	1,506	174	N/A	N/A

Source: Compiled from ECLAC (1998–1999, table III.1, 50; 2000–2001, 99, table A-13 & 100, A-14).
FDI: foreign direct investment.

unlimited access to investment opportunities, and (2) detailed information regarding those opportunities. While privatization, deregulation, and liberalization facilitate the entry (and guarantee the exit) of outside investors, transparency gives investors information about the potential security/risk of their investments" (2006:281).

Perhaps the most notorious case of the power of global capital markets over local states and political agents took place during the 2002 elections in Brazil. Prior to the election, the Workers Party (PT) under the leadership of presidential candidate Luis Ignacio da Silva ("Lula") campaigned on an anti-neoliberal platform and called for a major redistribution of land, expanded social programs, in part by redirecting funds earmarked for debt repayment, and popular democracy. But in the lead up to the election, private rating agencies and global investors signaled their fear of a PT victory by pulling out billions of dollars from the country. Merrill Lynch and Morgan Stanley Dean Witter shifted their recommendations against Brazil, Brazilian Brady bonds dropped sharply, and Goldman Sachs created a "Lula-meter" to evaluate the risks of a Lula victory (Schwartzman, 2006:299). In the lead up to the actual vote Citigroup cut its Brazilian exposure by selling off equity, as did Bank of America. The global financier George Soros was reported to have said, "in Rome, only the Romans voted, in modern global capitalism, only Americans vote, Brazilians don't vote," and to predict that if Lula won financial markets would retreat and Brazil would drown in chaos (Schwartzman, 2006:299). As Brazil moved toward the abyss of crisis Lula and his team turned to allaying the fears of global capital markets. In August, two months before the vote, he gave his blessing to a $30 billion IMF loan negotiated by the outgoing government that committed him, if he were to be elected, to maintaining adjustment policies and not defaulting on the country's foreign debt.

The influx of transnational finance capital into Latin America facilitated macroeconomic stabilization, fueled consumption, and helped finance growth, leading the transnational elite to believe it had "resolved" the debt crisis in the 1980s by making the debt serviceable and removing the issue from the political agenda. But the region-wide external debt in fact continued to grow throughout the late 1980s and 1990s, from $230 billion in 1980 to $533 billion in 1994, to over $761 billion in 2004, although the total declined to $633 billion in 2006 (ECLAC, 2006, table A-18). Argentina's debt climbed from $27 billion in 1980 to $63 billion in 1990, and then steadily upward to $144 billion by 1998. In this same period, Brazil's debt climbed from $71 billion to $232 billion, and Mexico's from $57 billion to $160 billion. Colombia, Ecuador, Peru, Venezuela, and the

Central American republics were also heavily indebted relative to their economic size. For Argentina, payment *on the interest alone* ate up 35.4 percent of export earnings in 1998. For Brazil, the figure was 26.7 percent; for Colombia, 19.7 percent; for Ecuador, 21.2 percent; for Nicaragua, 19.3 percent; for Peru, 23.7 percent; and for Venezuela, 15.3 percent (ECLAC, 1998a, p. 114, table VII.11). In addition, region-wide revenues from privatizations, a major attraction for foreign investors, peaked at $38 billion in 1998 and then dropped precipitously to $12 billion in 2000 and to just $410 million in 2003 (World Bank, 2006a). Net FDI also peaked in 1999, at $77 billion, and then slid downward, to $63 billion in 2001, $35 billion in 2003, and $33 billion in 2006 (ECLAC, *Preliminary Balance of the Latin American and Caribbean Economy*, 2006, table A-16).

What were the class relations behind this deepening financialization? Latin American banks borrowed in international capital markets made more accessible by their integration through banking FDI and then converted their foreign currency borrowing into loans for local investors, themselves often associated with transnational capital (Bose, 2005). When crisis has hit in the form of large-scale capital flight, such as in 1995 in Mexico (the "peso crisis"), when investors pulled tens of billions of dollars from deposits, bonds and securities and transferred them abroad, or the similar 2000–2001 Argentine financial crisis, precarious stability collapsed. Moreover, the deregulation of capital markets and the transnationalization of national banking systems mean that the flow of capital that begins with runs on deposits by large institutional investors passes effortlessly out of the country and into global financial circuits. In Latin America, local investors joined foreign capital in appropriating public assets as they were privatized while states have engaged in a pattern of assuming the burden of private sector debt, in effect socializing on an ongoing basis the debt accumulated by private capital. Numerous nodes allow transnational class groups to appropriate the wealth that flows through global financial circuits.

One of the many mechanisms in which value shifts from local economic agents and popular classes to transnational capital is through maintaining artificially high exchange rates. This allows speculators to buy cheap dollars with local currency and then to pull these dollars out of the country when crisis threatens. In order to sustain these exchange rates states must continually attract foreign capital through high interest rates on bond issues (which places tremendous burdens on small and medium producers), by pumping foreign exchange reserves into the local financial system as investors convert local currencies to dollars, and through other mechanisms that create an environment of extreme liquidity or high volatility, in short, a crisis-prone environment. The most notorious case was in Argentina, where the neoliberal governments of Carlos Menem and de la Rua in the 1980s and 1990s maintained a policy of peso-to-dollar convertibility. The crisis finally broke in December 2001 when the government sequestered bank accounts and devalued the peso by 200 percent, a mechanism known as the "corralito." Workers, the middle classes, and small businesses saw the value of their savings and salaries plummet overnight, leading to mass mobilizations that forced the resignation of several presidents over the course of a few weeks.

Cracks in the Neoliberal Monolith

Financial crises present those associated with transnational finance capital to expropriate values from states, workers, small and medium-sized businesses, and other sectors. As transnational investors cash in on their speculative profits and move on, we find that those who pull their capital out of one region, or shift it instantaneously from one to another, are nationals of numerous countries. Indeed, as the analysis of "cashing in on speculative profits," or "cutting losses and moving on" shows in the case of Argentina, Mexico, or any other recent example, the nationals from the self same country (that is, Argentine, Mexican, or elsewhere) often participate in this transnational capital movement, since they are themselves transnational investors. But as recurrent crises that favor some groups and hurt the majority accumulate they blow over into social explosions and political upheavals that threaten the social order. The illusion of neoliberal invincibility was shattered by the Argentine crisis that exploded in December 2001 and cracked the Washington consensus beyond repair. The first cracks in the neoliberal monolith had come in the Mexico peso crisis of 1995 on the heels of the Zapatista uprising and the "Tequila shock" that reverberated throughout the region. This was followed by the 1998 Brazilian crisis. But it was the Argentine crisis of 2001–2002 that most signaled the beginning of the end of neoliberalism.

Argentina was the paragon of neoliberal success until the government entered into default on its debt in late 2001—the largest default in history—thrusting the issue of the Third World debt back into the world limelight (Soederberg, 2006). The Argentine government could keep the economy buoyed so long as there were state assets to sell off or as long as it could sustain the conditions for attracting mobile capital from global institutional and portfolio investors. Governments respond to perceived breakdowns in transnational investor confidence by raising interest rates and tightening monetary policy, which in turn induces local recession and economic hardship. At the same time, however, rising interest rates and recession often result in widespread defaults on bank loans, as happened in both Mexico and Argentina. Once there is no quick money to be made, capital flight can—and has—plunged countries into overnight recession. Latin America began a downturn in 1998 and although the region as a whole showed positive growth again in the new century this was accounted for by high growth rates in a handful of countries while many stagnated and experienced bouts of negative growth. Table 5.11 shows that Latin America was a net exporter of $219 billion in capital surplus to the world economy during the "lost decade" of 1982 to 1990, and then became a net importer from 1991 through to 1998. But starting in 1999 the region reverted once again to an exporter of capital and continued to export capital through to 2006.

If servicing the debt and assuring an attractive environment for global financial markets has had deleterious effects on the living conditions of popular classes and placed Latin America in ever increasing hock to transnational finance capital it also cemented the power of the emergent transnational bloc in the region. But once debt-repayment pressures reach the point in which default becomes a possibility or a government can longer contain pressure for it to meet even minimal social obligations the spiral of crisis begins. Local states are caught between the withdrawal of transnational investors and mounting unrest from poor majorities who can no longer bear any further austerity. The slide into crisis began at the turn of the century when the net outflow of resources once again came to surpass the net inflow. Neoliberal states shift accumulation crises from capital and upper strata to labor and popular classes but they also must perform the contradictory role of social control of popular majorities who bear the brunt of crisis, which generates mounting legitimacy problems for these states. The slide into crisis was also the turning point in which neoliberal elites moved from the offensive to the defensive as popular forces became once again ascendant.

Stepping back in perspective, the problem of stagnation in Latin America is ultimately the same as that of social polarization and overaccumulation in the global economy. Sustaining dynamic capitalist growth, beyond reining in global financial markets and shifting from speculative to productive investment, would require a redistribution of income and wealth to generate an expanding demand of the popular majority. This is a very old problem that has been debated for decades within and outside of the region: how to create effective demand that could fuel capitalist growth. The ISI model was unable to achieve this on the basis of protected national and regional markets; the neoliberal model has been unable to achieve this on the basis of insertion into global markets. Seen from the logic of global capitalism the problem leads to political quagmire: how to bring about a renewed redistributive component without affecting the class interests of the dominant groups, or how to do so through the political apparatuses of national states whose direct power has diminished considerably relative to the structural power of transnational capital. This is a dilemma for the global system as a whole.

The pressures to bring about a shift in the structure of distribution—both of income and of property—and the need for a more interventionist state to bring this about, is one side of the equation in the constellation of social and political forces that seemed to be coming together in the early twenty-first century to contest the neoliberal order. Political, economic, and academic elites began to look for an alternative formula to pull the region out of its stagnation and at the same time to prevent—or at least better manage—social and political unrest. These regional efforts paralleled calls by the transnational elite elsewhere for a limited reform of the global system. Prominent left of center parties and leaders, for instance, including Cuahutemoc Cardenas of the Party of the Democratic Revolution in Mexico, Ricardo Lagos of the Socialist Party in Chile, Lula of the Workers Party in Brazil, Carlos Álvarez of the FREPASO in Brazil, and Jorge Castañeda from Mexico, drew up the Buenos Aires Consensus in 1998 that called for a renewed social democracy in the region. While the document called for "growth with equity" and a greater role for the state in assistance to the poor it was explicit that the logic of the market must not be challenged and nor should an open integration into global capitalism (Korzeniewicz and Smith, 2000). A number of these groups—such as Lagos in Chile and Lula in Brazil—subsequently came to power. If these elites represented one part of the social and political forces that could bring about a rupture in the neoliberal bloc the other were the popular classes and their escalating struggles.

Legitimacy Crisis of the Neoliberal State

The United Nations released a report on democracy in Latin America in 2004 that warned: "The increasing frustration with the lack of opportunities, combined with high levels of inequality, poverty and social exclusion, has resulted in instability, a loss of confidence in the political system, radical action and crises of governance, all of which threaten the stability of the democratic system itself" (UNDP, 2004:25). The report referred to a "crisis of politics," evident in the low credibility and prestige of political parties and of confidence in governments, and in "deficits of citizenship: in particular, issues concerning civil and social rights" (UNDP, 2004:51). According to the Santiago-based Latinobarametro, which conducts annual polls on the state of public opinion in the region, most people believe that the rich always or almost always manage to have their rights respected while similar majorities are of the opinion that the poor, immigrants, and indigenous peoples suffer severe legal disadvantages (2004, 2006). Since the Latinobarometro began publishing its annual reports in 1996 it has found that approximately 80 percent of the population in the 18 countries in which it conducts polls have "little or no" confidence in political parties, while some 75 percent have little or no confidence in legislatures, and about 60 to 70 percent, varying from country to country and from year to year, have little or no confidence in presidents, the armed forces, private enterprise, banks, the police, and the judicial system (2006:30). A broad majority also believed that their countries were headed in the wrong direction (2004:37).

The Latinobarometro reports found that some 90 percent of the population considered the economic situation in their countries to be "bad" or "very bad" during the 1996–2005 decade, some 80 percent viewed their family economic situation in the same terms, and 70 to 75 percent said they were worried about becoming unemployed (2006:36, 37, 50). Over half believed that the state should assure the welfare of the population (2006:52) and 75 percent felt that their country's powerful social and economic groups controlled the state for their own interests (2006:66). Only 20 percent said they were satisfied with the market economy and only 20 percent agreed with the privatization of public services (2004:38, 41). At the same time, some 60 percent of those interviewed in the region preferred democracy to any other kind of regime but only 35 percent expressed satisfaction with their political systems (with many countries scoring considerably lower) and some 45 percent said they would be willing to support an authoritarian government if it could solve the country's economic problems (2004 and 2006). (Importantly, also, as I will discuss in the next chapter, Venezuelans in 2006 viewed their democracy more favorably [57 percent satisfaction] than any other Latin American country, except Uruguay, and 59 percent viewed their economic situation in that year as "better" or "much better" than previously, the highest score in the region [2006:35]).

Latinobarometro, a conservative pro-neoliberal polling company funded largely by Latin American and EU governments and private corporations (see website at www.latinobarometro.org), attributes these results to citizens' lingering "statist" attitudes and to their "lack of awareness" that it is best to leave the economy to the private sector. Economic problems have made it difficult for citizens to "assimilate the neo-liberal capitalist economic mentality" (2006:53). A more satisfying interpretation, I believe, is that these and other reports underscore the spiraling crises of legitimacy that the neoliberal states of Latin America faced in the early twenty-first century and the causal role played by capitalist globalization in these crises. The failure of the economic system has helped undermine the credibility of political systems and placed mounting strains on states.

From Authoritarianism to Polyarchy

Projects of domination are always unstable.[5] The terror that the privileged few have of the dispossessed many has been expressed in diverse pathologies throughout the ages founded on fantastic and often delusional discourses aimed at rationalizing domination and inequality as part of the drive to secure social order. Earlier colonial and racial theories that naturalized social inequalities have been replaced more recently by arguments of "cultural difference" and a "clash of civilizations" that purport to explain current global stratification. It is in this context that we must see a discourse that portrays those political agents at the center of power and privilege in global society as the highest representatives of freedom and democracy in the world. Once we clear the fog of such discourse, how do we understand the transformations in political systems and institutions in Latin America in the globalization age?

During the 1960s and 1970s repressive military regimes took over in many Latin American countries, while in others, such as in Central America, civilian-military regimes had been in power since the 1930s world crisis. This authoritarianism was an instrument of local elites, acting in conjunction with international elites, and in particular, with the United States as the dominant outside power, for suppressing an upsurge in nationalist, popular, and leftist challenges to the status quo. More specifically, as the "bureaucratic authoritarian" literature of the 1970s argued, the military takeovers responded to threats to social orders resulting from the exhaustion of the ISI-populist model of capitalist development (see, e.g., O'Donnell, 1973). The military takeovers had a dual objective: (1) to crush popular and revolutionary movements through mass repression and institutionalized terror, and (2) to begin the dismantling of the old model by launching processes of economic adjustment and deeper integration into the world market in concurrence with the emergence of the global economy.

But the dictatorships and military regimes could not stabilize their domination. They could not suppress indefinitely mass popular movements that were

---

[5] This section is an abbreviation of my extensive work on this topic. See, inter alia, Robinson, 1996a, 2000, 2006b.

demanding not only democracy and human rights but also profound change in the social order. These movements threatened, beyond a mere regime change, to bring down the whole elite-based order—as happened in Nicaragua in 1979 and threatened to happen in El Salvador, Haiti, Guatemala, and elsewhere. This threat from below, combined with the inability of the authoritarian regimes to manage the dislocations and adjustments of globalization, generated intra-elite conflicts that unraveled the ruling power blocs. It became clear to dominant groups, and especially to emergent transnational elites and their organic intellectuals, that these old methods of political domination were no longer workable. Elite rule required renovation in the face of the global integration of social life and the mass mobilization of people whose way of life was becoming fundamentally altered by capitalist globalization. If neoliberalism was to make the world available to capital it was also necessary to "make the world safe for capital," that is, to develop more stable modes of political domination and social control. To reestablish authority—capitalist hegemony—would require an overhaul of cultural, ideological, and political systems around the world.

The crisis of elite rule in Latin America—and throughout the Third World— was resolved, at least momentarily, through transitions to *polyarchy* that took place in almost every country in the region during the 1980s and early 1990s, to use the term first coined by Robert Dahl (1971). Polyarchy refers to a system in which a small group actually rules, on behalf of capital, and participation in decision making by the majority is confined to choosing among competing elites in tightly controlled electoral processes. Democracy, of course, is antithetical to global capitalism, if we understand it to mean *power of the people*. Democracy is about *power*, the ability to achieve one's will even in the face of resistance by others, in the Weberian definition, or the ability to meet objective interests, to shape social structure in function of these interests. By this definition, it is an emancipatory project of both form and content: democratic participation is a tool for changing unjust social and economic structures so that a democratic political order facilitates the construction of a democratic socioeconomic order.

Such a subversive notion of democracy was incompatible with the systematic inequalities of capitalism. The concept had to be sanitized and it was. A "redefinition" of democracy took place in Western, particular, U.S. academic circles closely tied to the policy making community in the years following World War II to counter the classic definition as power or rule, *kratos*, of the people, *demos*. A new "institutional" definition built on earlier elitism theories that called for an enlightened elite to rule on behalf of ignorant and unpredictable masses. In redefining democracy away from the power of the people and toward polyarchy, these policy makers and intellectuals often cited Joseph Schumpeter in his classic 1942 study *Capitalism, Socialism, and Democracy*. Schumpeter argued for "another theory" of democracy, as an institutional arrangement for elites to acquire power by means of a competitive struggle for the people's vote. "Democracy," he said, "means only that the people have the opportunity of accepting or refusing the men who are to rule them" (1942:285). Hence polyarchy refers simply to procedure and does not involve an end to class domination or to *substantive* inequality. The polyarchic definition of democracy had come to dominate social science, political and mass public discourse. It is this conception that informed the "transitions to democracy" and the veritable cottage industry of academic literature on the subject.

U.S. and transnational elites called for a shift in policy to "promoting democracy" in the wake of the 1979 overthrow of Somoza in Nicaragua, which beyond any other single event made clear that the old forms of control were no longer viable in a rapidly changing global order. They concluded that it would be necessary to intervene *before* elite orders themselves are overthrown by mass democratization movements. The challenge became how to manage political change and preempt more fundamental social change. U.S. policy makers developed new strategies, modalities, and instruments of political intervention under the banner of promoting democracy. Polyarchy was to be promoted in order to co-opt, neutralize, and redirect mass popular democratic movements—to relieve pressure from subordinate classes for more fundamental political, social, and economic change in emergent global society. In this way, the outcome of mass movements against the brutal regimes that ruled that continent involved a change in the political system, while leaving intact fundamentally unjust socioeconomic structures. What transpired in these contested transitions to polyarchy was an effort by transnational dominant groups to reconstitute hegemony through a change in the mode of political domination, from the coercive systems of social control exercised by authoritarian and dictatorial regimes to more consensually -based (or at least consensus-seeking) systems of the new polyarchies. At stake was what type of a social order—the emergent global capitalist order or some popular alternative—would emerge in the wake of authoritarianism. Masses pushed for a deeper popular democratization while emergent transnationalized fractions of local elites in Latin America, with the structural power of the global economy behind them, as well as the direct political and military intervention of the United States, were able to gain hegemony over democratization movements and steer the breakup of authoritarianism into polyarchic outcomes. The transitions to polyarchy have not been illusions of reform; they constitute real political reform, made possible by the universal imposition of economic or "market discipline" as a mechanism of social control that substitutes extra-economic or coercive discipline. The demands, grievances and aspirations of the popular classes tend to become neutralized less through direct repression than through ideological mechanisms, political co-optation and disorganization, and the limits imposed by the global economy.

Moreover, in Latin America, as elsewhere, transitions to polyarchy became a mechanism to facilitate the rise to power of transnationally -oriented elites. Militaries, with their total control and often-parochial institutional interests, were less responsive to the needs of emerging transnational elites and neoliberalism. The neoliberal elites needed access to more direct political power and to new means of legitimating capitalist globalization. The emergence of global networks of accumulation require stable rules for economic competition that new capitalist and professional sectors are eager to construct while excluding the rest of the population from meaningful participation in economic and political life. It is logical that polyarchy has been promoted by the transnational elite as the political counterpart to neoliberalism. Transitions to polyarchy provided transnational elites the opportunity to reorganize the state and build a better institutional framework to deepen neoliberal adjustment. These transitions were in this sense adjustments of political structure to the changes in economic and class relations brought about by capitalist globalization. Polyarchy would seem to represent a more efficient, viable, and durable form for the political management of socioeconomic dictatorship in the age of global capitalism—or at least it seemed that way in the late twentieth century.

The challenge for those seeking to reconstitute capitalist hegemony was how elected regimes could push through unpopular neoliberal programs; how the wishes of the people—the electorate—could be subverted within the institutional framework of polyarchy as a system of consensual domination. A whole genre of "democratic consolidation" literature in the 1990s explored in this regard the types of "political engineering" required to assure economic reform in the face of mass opposition. Some of the literature focused on the need to build up strong executives and to weaken legislatures more susceptible to popular pressure in order to insulate governments from democratic pressure (see, e.g., Philip, 1993), while others argue that parliamentary government could best do the trick (see Linz and Valenzuela, 1994). "Governance" becomes the *ability not to meet, but to diffuse*, mass demands on the political system. What was most striking about the polyarchic systems that took shape in the 1980s and 1990s was the extent to which globalizing elites were insulated from popular pressures and demands. In most countries in Latin America the neoliberal project advanced *despite* systematic and at times well-organized mass opposition. Voting against the neoliberal program by electing to office candidates who opposed that program did little good. Globalizing elites were able to achieve social outcomes in the interests of transnational capital and against the objective interests as well as the actual subjective demands of popular classes.

Local technocratic elites began to operate increasingly through transnational networks that bypassed the formal channels of government and other social institutions subject to popular influence. John Markoff notes that "as power passes upwards to supranational structures, including financial networks . . . it is far from obvious that ordinary people have more effective control over the institutions that shape their lives" (Markoff, 1997:66; see also Conaghan and Malloy, 1994). Here we see the limits that the global system places on the ability of popular majorities to actually utilize polyarchy to have their will prevail. The "twin dimensions" of polyarchy—"political inclusiveness" (the popular vote) and "political contestation" (the ability of popular majorities to run their own candidates and to even place them in power)—do not translate into the exercise of power by popular classes understood as the ability to shape social structures in their interests.

In the 1980s and 1990s numerous Latin American polyarchic regimes, such as Alberto Fujimori's in Peru, Carlos Menem's in Argentina, Fernando Collor de Mello's in Brazil, and Carlos Ándres Pérez' in Venezuela, among others, were elected on explicit anti-neoliberal platforms only to perform U-turns on coming to power and implement sweeping austerity and adjustment. In the face of mass protest these regimes had to govern by executive fiat, violating constitutional norms and individual civil rights. As Green (1995) has pointed out, Argentina's Menem issued as many decrees during 1989–1992 as were announced by all of his civilian predecessors since 1922. In Bolivia, the elected government declared a state of siege to suppress opposition to structural adjustment. In Colombia, the government used anti-terrorist legislation to defuse opposition to privatization. In Peru, Fujimori simply dissolved the legislature and seized emergency powers in his 1992 "self-coup." In most cases, these "U-turn specialists," as Green (1995) called them, were thrown out by electorates (impeached in the cases of Perez and Collar de Mello), which then voted for new anti-neoliberal candidates who in turn repeated the U-turn.

The changed correlation of class and social forces brought about by capitalist globalization helps to explain the survival of the new polyarchies. The fragmentation and weakening of the popular classes through restructuring and marginalization, along with the neoliberal culture of individualism and consumerism, contributed to the social control of the dispersed and atomized victims of global capitalism.

If the structural power of global capitalism to impose discipline through the market (usually) makes unnecessary the all-pervasive coercive forms of political authority exercised by authoritarian regimes, the concept of coercion here is not limited to physical coercion such as military and police force. Economic coercion as the threat of deprivation and loss, the threat of poverty and hunger and so on, forces people to make certain decisions and take certain actions, such that apparently "free" choices are made by groups that have in fact been coerced by structures, and by other groups that control those structures, into making particular choices. The transnational elite demonstrated a remarkable ability to utilize the structural power of transnational capital over individual countries as a sledgehammer against popular grassroots movements for fundamental change in social structure.

Vilas notes that under prevailing conditions of socioeconomic exclusion, personal autonomy is not possible for the poor majority and "patron-client relations of domination and subordination tend to substitute for impersonal institutional loyalties" (1997:6). Subordinate groups manage their survival in nondemocratic power structures and social networks by developing direct, non-mediated political relationships with power holders. The impoverished appear to support strongmen and authoritarian solutions and also exhibit political apathy and electoral abstentionism. "Poverty is usually accompanied by a feeling of powerlessness which in turn is reinforced by the objective insecurity pervading everyday life in poor neighborhoods," notes Vilas. "In this setting, voting may harbor quite a different meaning from that discussed in conventional political theory. . . . Here, voting is an ingredient of an overall system of tradeoffs between the haves and the have-nots, an instrument to achieve specific resources like schooling, jobs, personal security, land titles, and the like" (62). Embedded in the social order are what Held (1995) terms conditions of "nautonomy" generated by the asymmetric production and distribution of life chances that negate autonomy and severely circumscribe the real possibilities of political participation. Pervasive authoritarian power relations housed within the formal structures of polyarchy, shaped by the structures of socioeconomic exclusion and class domination, help explain the electoral reproduction of neoliberal regimes.

Yet, notwithstanding polyarchy, human rights violations are still systematic and widespread in Latin America, as the annual reports by the various human rights monitoring groups make clear. The new victims are now as much the social and economic outcasts as they are political dissidents. The "social cleansing" of the poor and undesirable has involved: the infamous mass murder of street children in Guatemala, Brazil, and elsewhere by police and by death squads hired by affluent businessmen and local politicians; the death of thousands of poor people—the vast majority as they await trial—in countless prison uprisings in penitentiary systems unfit for human habitation; such periodic grizzly scandals as the round-up and execution by security forces in Colombia in 1995 of homeless individuals and their delivery to a private medical school as specimens for medical students to practice autopsies; the burning alive of an indigenous leader in Brasilia in early 1997 by upper class teenagers for apparent amusement (they were acquitted of homicide); and so on. None of these cases were anomalies: they were all manifestations of the social power of a minority wielded against the outcast in a socioeconomic system which by its very nature violates the human rights of a majority of society's members (on these cases, see Robinson, 2000).

"Democratization" literature claims that democracy rests exclusively on process and that the political sphere can and should be separated from the economic sphere, so that there is no contradiction between a "democratic" process and an anti-democratic social order punctured by sharp social inequalities and minority monopolization of society's material and cultural resources. However, a central argument in this literature, and one that directly mirrors U.S. and TNS policy, is that polyarchy requires free-market capitalism and that promoting polyarchy is complementary to and supportive of promoting free-market capitalism. In the 1989 landmark study funded by the AID, *Democracy in Developing Countries*, considered the basic primer in this literature, Diamond, Linz, and Lipset state: "We use the term democracy in this study to signify a political system, separate and apart from the economic and social system. . . . Indeed, a distinctive aspect of our approach is to insist that issues of so-called economic and social democracy be separated from the question of governmental structure" (xvi). The polyarchic definition of "democracy" thus claims to separate the political from the economic and yet it simultaneously connects the two in its actual construct, just as transnational elites insist that polyarchy must go hand-in-hand with neoliberal global capitalism—hence, the cliché "free-market democracy."

Thus, even though "democratization" theorists claim to separate the political from the socioeconomic, they do not really do so. This is a logically fatal contradiction in democratization theory. When global capitalism is the concern, the political is expected to be linked to the social and the economic and "normal society" is capitalist society (see, e.g., Diamond and Plattner, 1993). But when economic inequalities and social justice are the concern, the political is expected to be separated from the social and the economic. By making this separation, such issues as socioeconomic exclusion, who exercises power, who controls the material and cultural resources of society, and so forth, become irrelevant to the discussion of democracy. What is relevant is simply political contestation among elite factions through procedurally free elections. This separation of the socio-economic from the political sphere is an ideological construct because it appears in the mind of the intellectual and the policy maker but not in reality. This type of social science becomes to a large extent the legitimation of political practices such as promoting polyarchy and the social interests served by those practices. But this antinomy in theory reflects the antinomy in the practice itself.

The Antinomy of Capitalist Polyarchy

To the extent that states rule by consensual ("democratic") over coercive mechanisms their legitimacy rests on the hegemonic incorporation of those ruled. Yet hegemonic projects require a viable material basis; material contradictions of the social order will threaten to undermine ideological hegemony on an ongoing basis; this is the problematic nature of hegemony, which must be permanently constructed and reconstructed. Latin America seemed to reach a qualitative turning point by the turn of the century as crises accumulated, mass pressures mounted, and counter-hegemonic forces reached a critical mass. By the beginning of the twenty-first century the ideological hegemony of neoliberalism had cracked (Broad and Cavanagh, 2003). The loss of legitimacy by neoliberal states made it more and more difficult for the institutional mechanisms of polyarchic systems to contain popular pressures and defuse mass movements. It was not clear in the early twenty-first century if fragile polyarchic political systems would be able to absorb the tensions of economic and social crisis without themselves collapsing.

In Latin America, as in global society at large, inequality in the distribution of wealth and power is a form of structural violence against the poor majority. This structural violence generates collective protest which calls forth state repression. This repression transforms, on a regular ongoing basis, structural violence into direct violence. Polyarchy does not mean an end to direct coercion but a more selective application than under a dictatorship and that such repression becomes "legalized"—legitimated—by civilian authorities, elections, and a constitution. State repression organized by polyarchic regimes has been used throughout Latin America to repress protest against neoliberal structural adjustment and has claimed thousands of lives. Almost every Latin American country experienced waves of spontaneous uprisings generally triggered by austerity measures, the formation in the shantytowns of urban poor movements of political protest, and a resurgence of mass peasant movements and land invasions, all outside of the formal institutions of the political system, and almost always involving violent clashes between states and paramilitary forces and protesters (Green, 1995; Walton and Seddon, 1994). These uprisings and their violent suppression highlighted the relationship between the violation of socioeconomic rights and the violation of "traditional" human rights. Social polarization brought about by neoliberalism has generated mass conflict that the neoliberal states have not been able to control without resorting to human rights violations. In the end the imperative of social order makes itself felt in coercive domination. Hegemony, Gramsci reminds us, is consensus protected by the "armor of coercion."

Popular oppositional forces in Latin America did not articulate an alternative to capitalist globalization in the immediate post–Cold War years, whether of a democratic socialist or a redistributional character. This lack of an alternative opened up space for the dominant project. Yet there was ongoing rebellion against globalization from within civil society, struggles by popular social movements of the indigenous, women, shantytown dwellers, trade unionists, peasants, environmentalists, and so on. The dominant groups in Latin America reconstituted and consolidated their control over *political society* in the 1980s and 1990s but the new round of popular class mobilization in the 1990s and early twenty-first century pointed to their inability to establish an effective hegemony in *civil society*. The renewal of protagonism demonstrated by subordinate groups at the grassroots level has been outside of state structures and largely independent of organized left parties. Grassroots social movements flourished in civil society at a time when the organized left operating in political society was unable to articulate a counter-hegemonic alternative despite its continued vitality. The failure of the left to protagonize a process of structural change from political society helped shift the locus of conflict more fully to civil society. Latin America seemed to move in the late 1980s and 1990s to a "war of position" between contending social forces in light of subordinate groups' previous failures to win a "war of maneuver" through revolutionary upheaval and the limits to "power from above." But as crises of legitimacy, perpetual instability, and the impending breakdown of state institutions spread rapidly throughout Latin America in the early twenty-first century, conditions seemed to be opening up for a renovated war of maneuver under the novel circumstances of the global economy and society.

The problem of order and control was not resolved by transitions to polyarchy. The social and economic crisis has given way to expanding institutional quandaries, the breakdown of social control mechanisms, and transnational political-military conflict. A long period of political decay and institutional instability seemed likely. By the new century popular forces in civil society began to renew struggles over state power, as I will take up in the next chapter. But we should not lose site of the structural underpinning of expanding institutional crises and recall the fundamental incompatibility of democracy with global capitalism. The transnational model of accumulation being implemented since the 1980s does not require an inclusionary social base and is inherently polarizing. This is a fundamental structural contradiction between global capitalism and the effort to maintain polyarchic political systems that require the hegemonic incorporation of a sufficiently broad social base. Socioeconomic exclusion is immanent to the model since accumulation does not depend on a domestic market or internal social reproduction. To phrase it another way, there is a contradiction between the class function of the neoliberal states and their legitimation function. Global capitalism generates social conditions and political tensions—inequality, polarization, impoverishment, and marginality—conducive to a breakdown of polyarchy. The same market that generates an affinity between capitalism and polyarchy largely because the market replaces coercive systems of social control also creates and recreates the socioeconomic conditions that make impossible genuine democracy. In the long run the transnational elite cannot promote polyarchy in Latin America and also promote global capital accumulation and the class interests embedded therein.

The *New War Order* in Latin America

As counter-hegemonic forces renew their assaults on the neoliberal states in the new century heightened transnational conflict is likely. The *new war order* is manifest in Latin America in a general remilitarization throughout the region, a sharp increase in U.S. political-military intervention, the introduction of sophisticated new social control systems, and a new rhetoric of ant-terrorism that has legitimated mounting surveillance, policing and militarized social control, including an unprecedented militarization of the U.S.-Mexico border (see next chapter). Latin America seemed poised for a new round of U.S. political and military intervention under the guise of wars on "terrorism" and drugs. Even though Washington has attempted to promote polyarchy the need to save the state from popular and insurrectionary sectors has led it into an ever deeper alignment with local authoritarian political forces and paramilitary groups who have been strengthened by U.S. support (NACLA, 1998). The U.S.-led militarization of global capitalism discussed earlier had begun to manifest itself in the new century through an expanding set of transnational military exercises, U.S. programs, policy initiatives and proposed doctrinal shifts.

The commander of the U.S. Southern Command, General James T. Hill, declared in a June 2004 appearance before the U.S. Congress that "radical populists" in Latin America were tapping into "deep-seated frustrations of the failure of democratic reforms to deliver expected goods and services." These radical populists, said Hill, were "emerging terrorists" that, in combination with "traditional terrorists" such as drug traffickers, gangs, and guerrilla movements, represented a threat to the United States" (LADB, 2004; Isacson et al., 2004). Hill was alluding, in part, to Venezuela. U.S. hostility to the revolutionary government of Hugo Chávez in Venezuela and the political alliance for his ouster between Washington and the displaced business class is of particular significance because Chávez spearheads a new brand of radical politics in the region. But it is worth noting that one or another of the hemisphere's governments have labeled as "terrorist" the Landless Workers Movement of Brazil, the Zapatistas of Mexico, the Colombian Armed Revolutionary Forces (FARC) and the National Liberation Army (ELN) guerrilla movements of Colombia, the indigenous movement in Ecuador, the Farabundo Martí National Liberation Front in El Salvador, the Sandinistas in Nicaragua, coca growing campesinos in Bolivia setting booby traps against eradication forces, Honduran peasants blocking roads to stop over-logging, the Mapuche indigenous activists in Chile who damaged plantation property to press their land claims, and other legitimate leftist social and resistance movements. El Salvador, Argentina, Mexico, Colombia, and Chile, among other countries, passed "anti-terrorist" legislation in the years following 9/11 with provisions similar to the U.S. Patriot Act. The U.S. Central Intelligence Agency identified in 2002 as "a new challenge to internal security" the indigenous movement that had spread throughout the hemisphere and has often been at the forefront of popular mobilization (Habel, 2002).

The U.S. government inaugurated in 2003 a new doctrine, dubbed "Effective Sovereignty," which contended that security in Latin America is threatened by the inability of the region's government's to exercise control over vast "ungoverned spaces" within their borders. "Today, the threat to the countries of the region is not the military force of the adjacent neighbor or some invading foreign power," explained General Hill. "Today's foe is the terrorist, the narco-trafficker, the arms trafficker, the document forger, the international crime boss, and the money launderer. The threat is a weed that is planted, grown, and nurtured in the fertile ground of ungoverned spaces such as coastlines, rivers and unpopulated border areas" (Isacson et al., 2004:6). The spread of radical populism is "overlaid upon states in the region that are generally marked by weak institutions and struggling economies. This resulting frailty of state control can lead to ungoverned or ill-governed spaces and peoples." Several years later, in 2006, the Pentagon released its *Quadrennial Defense Review,* which called for the militarization of police work, permanent surveillance, and the maintenance of "a long-term, low-visibility presence in many areas of the world where U.S. forces do not traditionally operate" in order to allow "preventative measures" to "quell disorder before it leads to the collapse of political and social structures" and to shape "the choices of countries at strategic crossroads" (Grandin 2006a, and more generally, see Grandin 2006b).

As global capitalism has penetrated the most remote spaces in Latin America the social control and institutional administration of these spaces becomes essential to their integration. Behind the new doctrine is the need for much greater control over space that is required for the stability of global capitalism and the region and an institutional presence. In accordance with the new doctrine, the open-ended U.S. military mission is to maintain a military and surveillance presence in "stateless" areas as vast and diverse as the Amazon basin, Central America's Mosquitia, or impoverished and gang-ridden urban shantytowns in the region's sprawling cities. Such a doctrine requires a shift from a conventional concentration of military force and interventionist capacity to high-tech surveillance and overwhelming speed, mobility and flexibility. Hence an emerging transnational military infrastructure involves a string of surveillance stations, forward bases, and access agreements between the U.S. military and governments in Latin America and the Caribbean. During the 1990s and the early twenty-first century Washington established new military bases in Manta (Ecuador), Tres Isquinas and Leticia (Colombia), Iquitos (Peru), Queen Beatrix (Aruba), Hato (Curaçao), and Comalapa (El Salvador), alongside existing bases in Puerto Rico, Cuba (Guantánamo), and Honduras (Soto Cano). It also planned to establish a liaison with military facilities in Argentina (Tierra del Fuego) and Brazil (Alcantara). The Pentagon also enhanced its monitoring and surveillance mechanisms, including the SIVAN (System of Surveillance for the Amazon) project carried out by Raytheon, with the capacity to monitor 5.5 million kilometers in the Amazonia, and seventeen other radar sites, mostly in Peru and Colombia, and an International Law Enforcement Academy in El Salvador.

This expanding string of military bases and surveillance stations form a new "theater architecture" in U.S. military jargon, an interlocking web of Cooperative Security Locations (CSLs, previous known as "forward operations locations") that range from more traditional bases to smaller installations, radar stations, base access agreements, and so forth, that supports the objectives of securing access to markets, strategic resources (especially oil), controlling narcotic trafficking, and immigrant flows, as well as more traditional counterinsurgency, intelligence gathering, and possible actions against leftist governments and social movements (Lindsay-Poland, 2004). In what could be considered post-Fordist "flexible" militarization, the Pentagon has referred to this as a new "Lily Pad" strategy of small military facilities in proximity to global hotspots. The lily pad network is intended to allow U.S. and allied military forces to leapfrog troops and equipment, shifting its weight from one "pad" to another to address crises with projections of power in Latin America. The establishment of this decentralized military structure throughout Latin America allows the United States in conjunction with allied security forces to bring influence to bear on the area with fewer uniformed personnel and without casting a large shadow on the region.

While Hill called for an increase in U.S. military assistance to the region's armed forces, a remilitarization under heavy U.S. sponsorship had already been underway for several years, including a new round throughout the hemisphere of joint U.S.-Latin American military exercises and training programs (Habel, 2002). The number of Latin American personnel trained by the United States increased by nearly 100 percent between 1999 and 2003, while Hill himself made no fewer than seventy-eight trips to Latin America from August 2002 to July 2004 to consolidate transnational military ties in the hemisphere (Isacson et al., 2004). U.S. military aid to Latin America jumped in the wake of September 11, 2001, from some $400 million to nearly $1 billion dollars in 2006 (Grandin, 2006a). Moreover, during this time some 15,000 Latin American military personnel have been trained each year by U.S. military forces. These officers are then encouraged by the Pentagon upon return to their home countries to increase "cooperation among military, police, and intelligence officials" and create "an intelligence sharing network with all other governments in the region," in the words of U.S. Southern Command Gen. Craddock, and to be on guard against "anti-free trade populists" who "incite violence against their own government and their own people" (Grandin, 2006a).

Beyond the Lily Pad strategy U.S. officials have encouraged Latin American militaries and their civilian allies to rearm, enlarge, and reorient security forces toward containing "internal enemies" in the face of the erosion of polyarchic institutions and neoliberal legitimacy and the expanding challenge from popular forces. Moreover, much of the U.S. military and surveillance infrastructure is managed by or in conjunction with private TNC contractors, such as Raytheon's SIVAN, or Dyncorp, which manages the Manta base in Ecuador (Lindsay-Poland, 2004), as well as with local subcontractors (Lindsay-Poland, 2004), who then acquire a direct business interest and a local political stake in U.S. intervention.

This fusion of U.S. state and private transnational capital in organizing a gendarme for global capitalism is quite consistent with the increasing privatization of warfare, whereby wars of intervention become not only "politics by other means" but themselves profit making activities inserted into global accumulation circuits. Transnational corporate investors in Latin America are coming to rely increasingly on a U.S. military and surveillance canopy in those zones under guerrilla influence, wracked by social conflict or political violence, or where local state institutions are unable to impose authority. Here we see clearly the role of the U.S. state in seeking to assure the security and other conditions for transnational capital accumulation.

Colombia is the neurological epicenter of regional counterinsurgency, U.S. intervention, and "anti-terrorism" campaigns. U.S. intervention in Colombia's half-century-long civil war dates back decades (Stokes, 2005). The latest round began with the launching of *Plan Colombia* in the late 1990s as an alleged counter-narcotics operation and then expanded dramatically in 2002, with the launching of an offshoot, *Plan Patriota,* into a full scale counterinsurgency against that country's powerful guerrilla movements. But beyond counterinsurgency, *Plan Colombia* seeks to convert Colombia into a platform for region-wide operations against leftist governments, social movements, transnational immigrant networks, drug traffickers, youth gangs, intellectual property piracy, and other "threats" to the neoliberal order. Plan Colombia cost $4.7 billion between its launching in 2000 and 2006 and was set to increase by nearly $4 billion more between 2007 and 2009 (*Notisur,* 2007). If we add another $3 billion invested by the AID in Colombia during this time (Mondragon, 2007) the total amount set aside by the United States in Colombia during the first decade of the twenty-first century approaches some $12 billion, which gives an idea of the magnitude of the U.S.-state role and the centrality of Colombia to the global capitalist order in Latin America—and, indeed, in the world.

In addition to Colombia, another strategic site is the Tri-Border Region where Paraguay abuts Argentine and Brazilian territory. Specifically, in 2005 the Paraguayan government signed an agreement with the United States for the stationing of some fifty U.S. soldiers on an ongoing rotational basis at U.S.-built Mariscal Estigarribia air base. The Tri-Border Region, referred to by Grandin (2006a) as the "Wild West of Latin America," is a reputably lawless corner of the continent known for high levels of contraband and corruption, and has been singled out by U.S. officials as an alleged site of Islamic terrorist groups. Some 10 percent of the 150,000 inhabitants of Paraguay's legendary border city, Ciudad del Este, are of Arab descent, many of whom arrived in the

1980s in the wake of the Lebanese civil war (Ciudad del Este is a free-trade boom town that is also home to thousands of South and East Asians; see Chapter 3).

But the Paraguay case also makes clear the *function* of transnational militarization as a protective canopy for defense of the global capitalist order in the region. The authorization granted by the Paraguayan congress in 2005 for the entrance of U.S. troops followed the passage by President Nicanor Duarte of a decree permitting the country's armed forces to assume internal security functions and the training by U.S. forces of a new paramilitary rural "guard" to protector soy producers—soy, let us recall from Chapter 2, is the cutting edge of transnational accumulation in the Tri-Border Region—from land invasions and other resistance activities by the country's burgeoning peasant and landless workers movement. Since 2003 Plan Colombia resources have been used to help the Colombian army to defend an oil pipeline in Colombia owned by the Los Angeles-based Occidental Petroleum. In a similar vein, Plan Colombia, and more generally the "drug wars" in the Andean region, has accelerated integration into global capitalism (Stokes, 2005).

The expanding role of U.S. intervention in Latin America points to the increasing reliance on coercion by transnational dominant groups in the face of the crisis of legitimacy and breakdown of the political authority of neoliberal regimes. The region is being swept up in the global war order and is clearly in for a prolonged season of transnational conflict. We are approaching a crossroads, comparable to that of the late 1960s into the early 1980s. More pointedly, 1968 was a key year in that it signaled the rise of a worldwide counter-hegemony, the ideological and political turning point that led capital to conclude that it had to restructure the system. The crisis of capitalism that ensued in the early 1970s gave capital the impetus and the means to initiate that restructuring. Capital went global and unleashed neoliberalism. But in the first decade of the twenty-first century we reached another crossroads, like 1968, in which the ideological hegemony of global capitalism has cracked. We are now in the midst of the battle over how the crisis will unravel and what will take the place of neoliberalism. Latin America is on the front line of that battle.

CHAPTER SIX

A New Cycle of Resistance

The Future of Latin America and Global Society

There has always been a considerable time lag in terms of working-class response to capital restructuring (Arrighi, 1996). Globalization disorganized the working classes in the late twentieth century, acting as a centrifugal force for these classes around the world and as a centripetal force for transnationally oriented elites. Restructuring fragmented the working classes as intense competition forced on workers in each nation debilitated collective action. During earlier periods of world capitalism the popular sectors were *brought together* as inter- subjectivities and mounted collective challenges to the social order. To the extent that the old subjectivities were fragmented and dispersed and new subjectivities had not yet coalesced, capitalist globalization blunted the collective political protagonism of the popular classes. Mass social dislocation, evaporating social protection measures, declining real opportunities, and spiraling poverty that neoliberalism generated—all of this sparked widespread yet often spontaneous and unorganized resistance around the world in the 1980s and 1990s, as epitomized in "IMF food riots," 100 of which were recorded in Latin America from 1976 to 2006 (Grandin, 2006b:208). But everywhere there were also organized resistance movements. At a certain point in the 1990s popular resistance forces formed a critical mass, coalescing around an agenda for social justice, an "anti-globalization" or global justice movement. By the turn of the century the transnational elite had been put on the defensive, and a crisis of the system's legitimacy began to develop—as symbolized with the creation of the World Social Forum (WSF) in Porto Alegre, Brazil, under the banner "Another World Is Possible."

Latin America has been at the cutting edge of these worldwide struggles. The economic downturn that hit the region between 1999 and 2002 unleashed pent-up counter-hegemonic social and political forces that discredited neoliberalism and brought about a new period of popular struggle and change. The dominant groups in Latin America reconstituted and consolidated their control over *political society* in the late twentieth century, but the new round of popular class mobilization in the 1990s and early twenty-first century pointed to their inability to sustain hegemony in *civil society*. The renewal of protagonism demonstrated by subordinate groups at the grassroots level has been outside of state structures and largely independent of organized left-wing parties. Grassroots social movements have flourished in civil society at a time when the organized Left operating in political society has been unable to articulate a counter-hegemonic alternative despite its continued vitality. The failure of the Left to protagonize a process of structural change from political society helped shift the locus of conflict more fully to civil society. Latin America seemed to move in the 1990s to a "war of position" between contending social forces in light of subordinate groups' failure to win a "war of maneuver" through revolutionary upheaval and the limits to power from above. But as crises of legitimacy, perpetual instability, and impending breakdown of state institutions spread rapidly throughout Latin America in the early twenty-first century, conditions seemed to be opening up for a renovated war of maneuver under the novel circumstances of the global economy and society.

Several alternatives to the dominant model of global capitalism appear to be on the agenda in the region. A new model of revolutionary struggle and popular transformation from below is emerging, based on the Venezuelan experience, but more broadly, on mass popular struggles in Ecuador, Bolivia, and elsewhere. Yet global capital has been able to blunt some of these struggles from above, and a reformist bloc allied with global capital is competing to shape a post-neoliberal era. From 1999 through 2007 popular electoral victories in a number of countries in Latin America brought to power governments that began to forge a regional economic and political ant-neoliberal bloc. Neoliberalism, however, is but one model of global capitalism; resistance to this model is not necessarily resistance to global capitalism. Behind this turn toward the Left, or what observers called the pink tide, are competing configurations of social and class forces, ideologies, programs, and policies. There has been an ongoing realignment of social and political forces throughout Latin America the outcome of which is uncertain and open-ended. The crossroad that Latin America has reached is not about "reform versus revolution" as much as it is about what social and political forces will achieve hegemony over the anti-neoliberal struggle and what kind of project will replace the orthodox programs that have ravaged the region since the 1980s.

In this chapter I will focus on resistance to global capitalism in Latin America and the potential for counter-hegemonic movements, including an assessment of the apparent turn to the Left in the early twenty-first century. I first look briefly at the "pink tide" and then at the spread of social movements. Next, I take up three case studies in more depth: the indigenous movement, the Latino-led immigrant rights movement in the United States, and the Bolivarian revolution in Venezuela. The Venezuelan study is a launching point for further discussion on the prospects for transformative projects, the challenges these projects face, and the alternative futures for the region as well as for global society.

"Radical Populism" and the Pink Tide

Populism is the term most-often evoked to describe the turn to the Left in Latin America. "Classical populism" of the early and mid-twentieth century was based on multi-class coalitions that brought about significant structural change, redistribution, and incorporation of subordinate groups through the import-substitution industrialization (ISI) economic model and the corporatist form of state-society relations. As Laclau has observed, key distinguishing features of classical populism were the lack of specificity and the unpredictable nature of the movement (Laclau, 1977). A new radical populism in the globalization age is now said to resemble classical populism in that it seeks to mobilize subordinate groups and to bring about structural transformations short of revolutionary change, drawing on radical ("populist") discourse (see, e.g., discussion in Ellner, 2001, 2005). Yet populism is limited in its usefulness as a concept to explain the resurgence of radical politics in the early twenty-first century. As Laclau (2004) notes, it concentrates too much on style of leadership and on the force of charismatic authority than on the character of the leader's support base. At its worst, such simplistic analysis is a methodologically individualist "big man" approach to social change that depicts the oppressed as temperamental, politically naïve, and easily manipulated—unable to engage in their own self-interested collective agency.

So how do we characterize the governments brought to power through popular electoral victories in a number of countries that opposed neoliberalism, at least in discourse and at least initially? These included Hugo Chávez in Venezuela (1998); Lula and the PT in Brazil (2002); Lucío Gutiérrez in Ecuador (2002—Gutiérrez was subsequently run from office in a popular uprising in 2005); Lago and the Socialist Party in Chile (2002), followed by Michelle Bachelet (2006) of the same party; Néstor Kirchner in Argentina (2003); Evo Morales in Bolivia (2005); Tabaré Vásquez and the Broad Front in Uruguay (2004); Rafael Correa in Ecuador (2006); Daniel Ortega and the Sandinistas in Nicaragua

(2006); along with near-wins (amidst charges of electoral fraud) for the FMLN in El Salvador (2004); Andrés Manuel López Obrador in Mexico (2006); Ottón Solís in Costa Rica (2006); and Ollanta Humala in Peru (2006).

These popular electoral victories—the so-called pink tide—were interpreted by many as a decisive turn to the Left in the region. But such an interpretation is insufficient to understand the complexity of what has taken place. The "turn to the Left" has demonstrated the limits of parliamentary changes in the era of global capitalism as much as it also symbolizes the end of the reigning neoliberal order. It is important not to paint the distinct "pink tide" experiences with a single brush. The new leftist leaders all in one way or another came to power on the heels of mass popular resistance to neoliberalism, but there is more that differentiates than unifies the distinct cases. On the one hand, the case of Brazil was most indicative of mildly reformist thrust of many of the new Leftist government—and the most tragic for the popular classes. Lula, denied the presidency in three previous electoral contests but victorious in 2002, took the vote only after his wing of the PT moved sharply toward the political center. He forged a social base among middle-class voters and won over centrist and even conservative political forces that did not endorse a left-wing program yet were unwilling to tolerate further neoliberal fallout. Lula promised not to default on the country's foreign debt and to maintain the previous government's adjustment policies, thereby indicating that the real power was that of transnational financial capital. Portending what was to come, almost as soon as he took office in 2003 he slashed the budgets for health and educational in order to comply with dictates of the international monetary fund (IMF) that the government maintain a fiscal surplus.

Other pink tide governments attempted to expropriate popular power from below and undercut its transformative potential along the lines of what Gramsci (borrowing from Croce) called *transformismo* (Gramsci, 1971:58–59), whereby actual and potential leaders and sectors from the subordinate groups are incorporated into the dominant project in an effort to prevent the formation of counter-hegemony. This was the case with the presidency of Lucío Gutiérrez, brought to power in Ecuador by a coalition of indigenous and popular movements, or under the presidency in Argentina of Néstor Kirchner. Gutiérrez, a former army colonel, won the 2002 election with the support of that country's powerful indigenous and social movements after he promised to reverse the neoliberal program of his predecessors and implement popular reforms. But from the start Gutiérrez was subject to pressure from transnational capital and the Ecuadorian elite to push him in the opposite direction. Upon taking office he appointed several indigenous cabinet ministers as well as representatives of the local and transnational corporate community. Within months, Gutiérrez capitulated to these conservative political forces in the tenuous governing coalition and reverted to an open neoliberal program. In Argentina, Kirchner strongly criticized the neoliberal policies of his predecessors, yet his own program was limited to minor policy modifications to favor domestic producers and consumers—among them, low interest rates, capital controls, price controls on public services, and the restoration of some social welfare programs, alongside a clientalist co-optation of a portion of the *piqueteros* and other popular movements (see below).

In Nicaragua, Daniel Ortega and what remained of the Sandinista National Liberation Front (FSLN) dressed with a Leftist discourse what in the preneoliberal era would have been characterized as a routine attempt to establish a populist multi-class political alliance under the hegemony of capital and state elites. In the years since the 1990 electoral defeat new Sandinista economic groups developed close business and personal ties with transnationally oriented capitalist groups while the political leadership negotiated a heavily criticized pact to divide up government power with the Liberals, one of the two historically dominant bourgeois oligarchic parties. While the FSLN retained a mass, if dwindling, base among the country's peasantry and urban poor, many leading Sandinistas grouped around Ortega had become successful businessmen heavily invested in the new transnational model of accumulation, including in tourism, agro-industry, finances, importing-exporting, and subcontracting for the maquiladoras. Their class interests impeded them from challenging transnational capital or organizing a transformative project yet their legitimacy depended on sustaining a revolutionary discourse and undertaking redistributive reforms (Robinson, 2003).

In a policy document released shortly after taking office in 2007 the FSLN declared that its project rested on two planks, one political and the other economic. The first, "citizen power councils," were to incorporate local communities into the "struggle against drugs, narco-trafficking, gangs, diseases, ignorance, degradation of the environment, and the denial of human rights" (FSLN, 2007:5). Absent was any reference to these councils as politicized forums or vehicles for popular self-mobilization; they seemed to be conceived as instruments for a controlled incorporation from above of grassroots communities into the state's social control and administrative programs. The second plank, "economic associations for small and medium producers," called for "reorienting economic policies toward these sectors so as to link them up to the large-scale private sector" (ibid.): that is, to incorporate these small-scale rural and urban producers via credits and technical assistance into the dominant transnational circuits of accumulation through subcontracting and other ancillary activities. The document called for "respect for all forms of property," attracting transnational corporate investment, and an agro-industrial model of development. At the same time, however, the Sandinista program included a re-nationalization of health and educational systems, greater social spending, progressive tax policies, and a literacy campaign, among other popular welfare measures.

Hence, what emerged in these cases was an elected progressive bloc in the region committed to mild redistributive programs respectful of prevailing property relations and unwilling or simply unable to challenge the global capitalist order. This was not very different from what had informed the social democratic thinking that defined the Buenos Aires consensus. These new governments were "progressive" insofar as they introduced limited redistribution and restored a minimal role for the state, less in regulation accumulation than in administering its expansion in somewhat more inclusionary ways. When we cut through the rhetoric, a number of these governments—such as the Socialists in Chile or Kirchner and Lula—were able to push forward a new wave of capitalist globalization with greater credibility than their orthodox neoliberal predecessors. Many Leftist parties, even when they sustained an anti-neoliberal discourse, such as the PT in Brazil, the Frente Amplio (Broad Front) government of Tabaré Vásquez in Uruguay, and the Sandinistas in Nicaragua, abdicated earlier programs of fundamental structural change in the social order itself. What stood out about a number of the pink tide governments is that (1) there has been no significant redistribution of income or wealth, and indeed, inequality may still actually be increasing; and (2) there has been no shift in basic property and class relations despite changes in political blocs, discourse in favor of the popular classes, and mildly reformist or social welfare measures. In Argentina, for instance, the percentage of national income going to labor (through wages) and to the unemployed and pensioners (through social welfare subsidies and pensions) dropped from 32.5 in 2001, before the crisis exploded, to 26.7 in 2005. In Brazil the wealthy grew in number by 11.3 percent in 2005 as inequality deepened (Zibechi, 2006). Moreover, programs to subsidize the consumption of the poor and the unemployed, such as *Zero Fome* (Zero Hunger) and *Bolsa Familia* (Family Basket) programs in Brazil or social welfare payments plans in Argentina and Uruguay, were financed by taxing not capital but formal sector workers and middle classes. It was increasingly dubious whether viable redistributive strategies were possible without more fundamental changes in property relations. Would this new social democratic tide amount to better local managers of global capitalism than their orthodox neoliberal predecessors? How long could low levels of redistribution hold back the tide of rebellion? On the other hand, Venezuela was leading a radical anti-neoliberal regional bloc that would appear to include Bolivia under Evo Morales and Ecuador under Rafael Correa. Redistributive reforms have been much deeper in Venezuela than in other pink tide countries and have been linked to the goal of transformations in state structure and property relations to the end of an authentic empowerment of the popular classes, as I will discuss below. Bolivia and Ecuador seemed to be following a similar path of more radical reform although at the time of writing (mid-2007) it was too early to reach conclusions about outcomes. In all three countries there were constitutional assemblies convened by popular referendum to redraft the constitution in favor the popular classes, a reversal of the most egregious neoliberal policies, a re-nationalization of energy and other natural resources and the use of those resources for social investment. There were ongoing land redistributions in Venezuela and Bolivia and promises of such programs in Ecuador.

Casteñeda, the anti-communist, anti-Cuban, and pro-Washington former Mexican Foreign Minister and a leading social democratic critic of the socialist Left in Latin America, argued that there are "two Lefts" in the region: a "right Left" that would include Lula in Brazil, Lagos, and later Bachelet in Chile, and Vazsquez in Uruguay, and a "wrong Left" led by Chávez in Venezuela, and included, of course, Fidel Castro in Cuba, as well as Morales, López Obrador, Humala, and others. The former—"reconstructed, formerly radical"—emphasizes social policy (education, antipoverty programs, health care, housing) but within a more or less orthodox market framework. The "wrong Left," according to Casteñeda, has "proved much less responsive to modernizing influences. . . . For all these leaders, economic performance, democratic values, programmatic achievements, and good relations with the United States are not imperatives but bothersome constraints that miss the real point. They are more intent on maintaining popularity at any cost, picking as many fights as possible with Washington, and getting as much control as they can over sources of revenue, including oil, gas, and suspended foreign-debt payments" (Castañeda, 2006). Never mind the ideologically driven absurdities in Castañeda's argument: Venezuela, for instance, had the best economic performance in all of Latin America, was rated the most democratic, and boasted the most impressive programmatic achievements. The fact is that there *are* two Lefts: a reformist one that dominated the pink tide and sought to reintroduce a mild redistributive component into the global capitalist program in the region, and a more radical one that sought a more substantial transformation of social structures, class relations, and international power dynamics.

Most analyses failed to capture the dialectics of class relations and social struggles that have produced distinct dynamics among the pink tide countries, leading in some cases to more reformist and in others to more radical-oriented outcomes. Certainly in the former cases, what is emerging is a new, post neoliberal form of the national state. This new state would still form a part of the larger institutional networks of the TNS, function to facilitate an integration of local and national communities into global capitalism, generate the internal conditions necessary for globalized accumulation, and reorient national and regional economies toward global markets. But these states as the outcomes of the crisis of legitimacy of neoliberal elites may be better equipped to achieve a relegitimation, develop new mechanisms for consensual domination and hence governability, de-radicalize dissent and ameliorate social unrest by being less exclusionary than the neoliberal state in terms of the politics of redistribution.

Yet there is nothing pre-scripted about these processes; they are contingent and unpredictable. Progressive governments seeking short-term popular objectives spark both opposition from dominant groups and mobilization for more fundamental change from subordinate groups. This in turn opens up new opportunities, confrontation, and further politicization of masses. If transnational capital is able to emasculate radical programs through structural pressures exerted by the global economy, the popular electoral victories and near-victories involved as well the mobilization of new collective subjects and mass social movements that are not easily cowed by the transnational elite. The fate of the pink tide will depend considerably on the configuration of class and social forces in each country and the extent to which regional and global configurations of these forces open up new space and push such governments in distinct directions. Latin America in the early twenty-first century stands at a crossroad; it has moved into an historic conjuncture in which the struggle among social and political forces could push the new resistance politics into mildly social democratic and populist outcomes or into more fundamental, potentially revolutionary ones.

The Proliferation of Social Movements

As earlier corporatist structures have cracked with the demise of the developmentalist model new oppositional forces and forms of resistance have spread—social movements of workers, women, environmentalists, students, peasants, the indigenous, racial and ethnic minorities, community associations of the urban poor, and so on. The variety and scope of these movements have been nothing short of stunning. The list of what they have struggled over is vast: against privatizations; for agrarian reform; to reclaim urban spaces; for indigenous and black rights; against the introduction of genetically modified seeds; for wage increases and labor rights; to protect biodiversity and the environment; for women's rights; to block corporate-controlled highway and airport construction; for the destitution of corrupt government officials; for health and educational programs; for popular access to corporate-controlled media; for nationalization of natural resources, and so on. These movements spearheaded a wave of popular protest in Latin America in the early twenty-first century that brought forth the new progressive politics. Old and new social movements have supplemented to a significant degree the traditional structures of representation, in particular trade unions and populist, social democratic, and labor-based political parties.

Movements of rural workers and dispossessed peasant families were a leading edge of popular struggle. As we saw in previous chapters, the extension of capitalist agriculture and the incorporation of national agricultural systems into an integrated global agro-industrial complex resulted in the uprooting of millions of rural dwellers. One of the largest and most influential social movements in Latin America, the Landless Rural Workers Movement (MST) in Brazil, was organized to challenge these new global capitalist class relations in the countryside (Wright and Wolford, 2003). Since its founding in 1984 the MST has grown to over one million members. Over 1,000 rural activists have died as a result of confrontations with large landowners, their hired thugs, and state forces. By 2003 the movement had managed to pressure the government to enact agrarian reform that has distributed over 20 million acres of land to some 350,000 families (ibid.). The movement of the landless has spread throughout Latin America and organizations similar to the MST have flourished in Bolivia, Chile, Ecuador, Peru, Colombia, Central America, and elsewhere. Many of these local and national movements participate in the Latin America-wide Coordinating Committee of Peasant Organizations (CLOC) and in the worldwide network, Via Campesina.

While some of those displaced by capitalist globalization have migrated abroad others have filled the teeming slums of Latin America's cities where they have organized countless urban community movements, such as the Homeless Workers Movement in Brazil, whose tactics of struggle include occupying

vacant and abandoned buildings throughout the country, just as its rural counterpart, the MST, organizes land invasions. Similar movements are active in
Peru, Ecuador and Venezuela, among other countries. Relatedly, the *piqueteros*,
or picketing unemployed workers, of Argentina first grabbed the international
spotlight in the wake of the 2001 collapse of the Argentine economy and the
subsequent popular uprising. But the movement actually first emerged in the
early 1990s in the face of massive layoffs and steady increases in unemployment generated by privatization and other neoliberal measures. The most well
known of the *piqueteros* tactics are the setting up of road blocks along major in-
terurban highways and marching through city downtown streets during peak
hours. *Piquetero* struggles have been part of a more expansive movement in
Argentina of neighborhood assemblies and community organizations.

The *piqueteros* and neighborhood assemblies in Argentina have referred to
their practice of non-hierarchal grassroots organizing that is independent of
political parties and state manipulation as *autonomism*. The autonomist movement, in turn, reflects a broader orientation toward popular struggle and social
change in Latin America that has been referred to as *horizontalism*. Such horizontalism, a hallmark of the new wave of social movement struggles in the
Americas, rejects hierarchal forms of organizing and operating, emphasizes
democratic—often consensus—decision making within popular organization,
coordination among distinct sectors and movements with respect for each one's
autonomy, and rejects any form of subordination to political parties and to
states. I will return later to the matter of the relationship between social movements, political organizations, and the state. Here we can note that the possibilities opened up by a globalized "network society" make possible a new dynamism
of social movements based on distinct collectives organized into broad and overlapping networks. The new social movement struggles are grounded in local
communities that are networked into larger webs with a capacity to organize
and to convene broader collective action during key conjunctures.

The fulcrum of social movements has also shifted toward those marginalized and pushed into informality, involving a shift toward communities, from
spaces of production to spaces of reproduction. Through *piquetero* struggles, for
instance, the locus of resistance among the poor and working classes in Argentina has shifted to a large extent from the workplace and traditional workplace
unions to local communities and community-based organizations—as expressed in the *piquetero* slogan, "the new factory is the territory." The significance of this shift cannot in my view be understated. An *employed* worker,
especially one enjoying full time work and the types of labor stability associated

with the capital-labor relations of the previous epoch, could withhold his or her labor as a critical mechanism of struggle. The strike may have been the paramount symbol of the working class struggle in the previous epoch. But how do workers struggle in an epoch of public sector retrenchment and corporate downsizing, when so many of its ranks—often the majority—are unemployed or only sporadically employed as well as flexibilized, deregulated, and informalized? An unemployed worker cannot withhold his/her labor; a work stoppage has no place for this worker: hence the centrality of the *piqueteros'* shift from withholding their labor to engaging in activities to disrupt the normal functioning of the system. In this way the unemployed—although marginalized in a structural sense—are recreated as a working class political actor in the new epoch of global capitalism.

As working class struggles shift from the site of production to that of reproduction, that is, to the community from whence come and return workers, the prospects for working class struggles in the new epoch revolve around the development of a new *social movement unionism,* understood as a fusion of trade union and community struggles (see, e.g., Moody, 1997). But they also clearly revolve around organizing the unemployed, part-time, and informal workers, which would in turn hinge on a new conception of the trade union as organizations of not only employed workers but also all members of the working class. What must be placed on the agenda is organizing two key working class sectors: the unemployed/underemployed; and informal sector workers. More generally, this means developing new methods of organization and mobilization for a flexibilized working class that is now found fragmented, dispersed, and informalized. There may be some lessons to learn here from the recent experience of organizing the informal sector in Venezuela and trade union and social movements in Argentina such as the *piqueteros.*

The 1980s and 1990s also witnessed a flourishing of participation by women in diverse social movements along with a burgeoning of women's and feminist organizations. Women have mobilized to address collective problems that women, children, and poor people face, and also to address the special forms of gender oppression and inequality that they suffer as women. In their diverse forms of mobilization, women have effectively articulated the central concerns of daily life—access to housing, health care, employment, freedom from violence against women and against the poor, democracy, and environmental preservation. Women have struggled as workers in trade unions, as mothers and as citizens in human rights movements, as housewives in shantytowns, as leading organizers and spokespeople for indigenous movement, and as guerrillas in armed movements. Reinforced by global communications, internal and international migrations, rising levels of formal education for women, and increased personal autonomy and mobility, feminism has become a powerful social movement in its own right. By the 1990 hundreds of feminist organizations were operating locally, nationally, and transnationally in Latin America, linked into a powerful hemispheric network and to broader global networks (see, e.g., Jaquette, 1994; Jelin, 1990; Moghadam, 2005).

The women's movement in Latin America, and more generally, worldwide, has experienced a remarkable dynamic. By force of structural circumstance, it has engaged in a synthesis of the particular struggle against women's oppression with the struggle against the deleterious effects of capitalist globalization at each of the three levels of resistance to capitalism that van der Pijl (1997) has identified in his typology. As women have entered the workforce en masse in recent decades they have been at the vanguard of popular struggles around the process of production and exploitation (*the first level*), such as in the maquiladoras. But, in step with the essence of gender inequality and subordination, women remain locked into the sphere of reproduction even as their participation in production becomes formal. Hence women are at the forefront of battles over social reproduction that take place in the "private" (household) and "public" (community, workplace, and state) spheres (*the second level*). And women have also played a major role in struggles against the incursion of capitalism and its disruption of community and autonomy (*the third level*), as epitomized in the mass participation and leadership roles of women in the Zapatista and other revolutionary movements or in the MST of Brazil.

The Indigenous Revolt

Latin America is a place of remarkable racial and ethnic diversity. Its population is a rich and varied amalgam of peoples of pre-Conquest American, European, African, Asian, and Middle Eastern descent. The indigenous themselves are organized into hundreds, and formerly thousands, of distinct ethnic groups. By independence in 1825, the indigenous constituted some 42 percent of the population in Latin America, compared to 12 percent for blacks, 28 percent for mestizos, and 18 percent for Europeans. At the turn of the twenty-first century, the indigenous constituted officially between 5 and 10 percent of the population. The category of Indian is not stable. Not all peoples of indigenous descent maintain their identity, others do not declare their identity openly, and there are numerous problems in official censuses and some cases, such as Chile, where governments do not even include indigenous as a category. The indigenous are an outright majority in Bolivia, some 60 to 70 percent of the population, and in Guatemala, where they comprise some 60 percent of more of the total population. They form sizable minorities in Peru (40 percent or more), Mexico (12 15 percent), Chile (5 to 30 percent), Ecuador, 30 to 38 percent, and elsewhere (Yashar, 2005, table 1.1:21, except Chile). They are concentrated in two broad zones: the highland communities running from Mexico's Sierra Maestra through the Central American highlands and up and down the Andean chain in South America; and the lowland communities along Central and South America's Caribbean coast and the Amazonian region.

The colonial racial pyramid or pigmentocracy, which placed whites on top, blacks and Indians on the bottom, and diverse mestizo and mulatto identities in the interstices, gave way after independence to ongoing systems of racial and ethnic stratification that have continued into the twenty-first century. While formal (legally sanctioned) inequality may have largely disappeared, under globalization lived racial and ethnic inequalities have if anything intensified. Indigenous peoples living in the Amazon, Andes, and Mesoamerica share deep poverty and structural inequality, with estimated national poverty rates for indigenous peoples ranging from 65 to 85 percent (Psacharopoulos and Patrinos, 1994:207). Literacy requirements—one in a long historical list of restrictions on electoral and political participation—were in place until 1945 in Guatemala, 1970 in Chile, 1979 in Ecuador, 1980 in Peru, and 1985 in Brazil, effectively disenfranchising many indigenous men and most indigenous women (Lapp, 1994, cited in Yashar, 2005:37). Even after enfranchisement, the number of indigenous peoples in the lower or single chamber of the legislature in 2002 stood at a mere 0.8 percent in Peru, 3.3 percent in Ecuador, 12.4 percent in Guatemala, and 26.2 percent in Bolivia (UNDP, 2004:87). Neoliberalism and globalization have affected systems of racial and ethnic inequality in a number of ways, including (1) an "indigenization of misery," in which formal socioeconomic inequalities have grown as adjustment, austerity, and crisis have disproportionately affected indigenous (and black/Afro-Latin America) communities, highlighting the racialized nature of impacts of capitalist globalization; (2) new forms of ethnic segmentation of labor markets, so that exploitation and exclusion have spread; and (3) intensified transnational corporate appropriation of indigenous land and resources.

The indigenous have a long and well-known history of resistance to genocide, enslavement, exploitation and oppression, from wars against the Conquest, to ongoing uprisings against colonial oppression, and resistance to the first great incursions of capitalism in the late nineteenth and early twentieth centuries. Starting in the late twentieth century, the indigenous movement experienced nothing short of a spectacular renaissance as all over Latin America a new generation of indigenous leaders, both men and women, emerged to lead new forms of struggle. The Confederation of Indigenous Nationalities of Ecuador (CONAIE), the National Organization of Colombian Indigenous (ONIC), the Zapatistas and the Indigenous National Congress (CNI) of Mexico, the pan-Maya movement in Guatemala, and the mass indigenous organizations among the Aymara and Quichua in Bolivia, are at the forefront of popular struggle and resistance to global capitalism in the Americas.

The indigenous movement has developed new forms of struggle and organizational structures that are more horizontal than vertical, including horizontal coalition building and participatory congresses, assemblies, and elections. Each community organizes itself and then links horizontally to neighboring communities, giving way to regional and in the case of Ecuador, national organizations. In turn local and national indigenous organizations have organized transnationally. Often the indigenous organizations have emphasized independence from political parties and alliances with other social movements. These horizontal practices do not appear, however, to be a principle based on the horizontalist thought of the Argentine and other autonomists as much as a natural extension of collective forms that generally characterize those indigenous communities that have retained a measure of autonomy.

In June 1990 a weeklong indigenous uprising led by the recently formed CONAIE paralyzed Ecuador and launched the emerging indigenous agenda. The "revolution of the ponchos" forced the state to officially recognize the country's ethnic heterogeneity, leading to an official declaration that the Ecuador is a "pluricultural nation" and paving the way for other programs such as bilingual education. Subsequent mobilizations spearheaded by CONAIE forced the government to turn over two million acres of land to indigenous communities and toppled three governments who attempted to enact neoliberal reforms in 1997, 2000, and 2005. The continental indigenous movement then took off around the campaign against the 1992 Columbus quincentenary celebrations. In October 1991, 500 delegates meeting in Guatemala and representing 120 indigenous organizations from around the Americas, including peoples of "the Eagle" (North America), "the Condor" (South American Andes), "the Jaguar" (Amazon basin), and "the Quetzal" (Mesoamerica), launched a counter-campaign, "500 Years of Indigenous and Popular Resistance."

Barely two years later, on January 1, 1994, Mayan indigenous communities organized by the Zapatistas in the southern Mexican state of Chiapas captured world attention with a military-political uprising. In Colombia, the Indigenous Councils of Northern Cauca, representing some 110,000 Indians in that region, spearheaded 2005 campaigns against a free trade agreement with the United States (Klein, 2005), inspiring trade union, student, peasant and urban organizations to organize against the agreement. Although there is no one united organization in Bolivia, powerful regional organizations among the Aymara and Quechua Indians with a capacity to act nationally emerged in the 1980s and 1990s and have played the leading role in the country's recent political life. Their sustained mass mobilizations throughout the 1990s and early twenty-first century forced two neoliberal regimes to resign, in 2003 and 2005, and led to the election in 2005 of Evo Morales, the first indigenous president in South America since the Conquest.

Key principals that ground much contemporary indigenous organizing are cultural-political autonomy, ethnic heterogeneity in place of mestizo homogeneity, and new forms of collective identity with ethnicity and culture serving as markers for mobilization. While such ethnic-based movements have a long history of organizing, protesting, and mobilizing in Africa, Asia, and parts of Europe, there has been no comparable pattern of ethnic-based mobilization in contemporary Latin America until the recent upsurge. It is not that the indigenous have not organized in the past; it is that they have not organized until now along ethnic lines to promote an explicitly indigenous agenda. In Yashar's analysis (2005) of the rise of ethnic-based indigenous movements, changes in "citizenship regimes" associated with liberalization and structural adjustment undermined the local autonomy of indigenous communities and politicized indigenous identities. The shift from corporatist to neoliberal citizenship regimes shattered corporatism's class-based model and social rights and replaced them with a more atomized or individualized set of state-society relations that undercut indigenous local autonomy. At the same time democratization from the late 1970s and on allowed indigenous communities to mobilize, while this mobilization took advantage of transcommunity networks that had developed in previous years as a result of church, union, and non-governmental organization activities.

To this analysis we can add the decline and crisis of the pre-globalization Left and its class-based politics. As well, indigenous mobilization is linked to transformations in the global political economy. Global structural shifts form a larger backdrop to the mobilization of new subjects—such as the indigenous—in a rapidly expanding transnational civil society. Indeed, one of the remarkable aspects of the indigenous upsurge in Latin America is its *transnational* character. Local indigenous organizations, even when they have not coalesced into nationally unified movements (as in Peru) have liaised with organizations in other countries and international NGOs through transnational networking (Brysk, 2000). Indigenous peoples have formed transnational organizations such as the South American Indian Council, the International Indian Treaty Council, the Campaign for 500 Years of Indigenous, Black, and Popular Resistance, and the Amazonian Coalition. Their transnational mobilization resulted in the drafting by the United Nations of a declaration of indigenous rights and the declaration of 1993 as the Year of Indigenous people. The indigenous struggle illustrates how the local and the global have become organically linked in new forms of resistance in Latin America, in discourse, analysis, demands, strategies of resistance, and transnational forms of organization.

Some have seen the newfound emphasis on indigenous—as distinct from class (such as peasant)—identity as a new identity politics and even as a "postmodern" turn among the indigenous and other Fourth World peoples. There is indeed a newfound indigenous identity and struggles around such cultural rights as bilingual education and recognition of "pluricultural nationality," or the right to maintain ethnonational identities distinct from, although formative of, multinational states. Indigenous struggles have forced discussion on constitutional amendments in Ecuador, Bolivia, Mexico, Guatemala, Peru, Columbia, and elsewhere to recognize the multiethnic and pluricultural makeup of each country as a new view of the nation and the state emerges. These assessments of a postmodern turn, however, are misleading, insofar as alongside cultural rights the resurgent indigenous struggles have revolved around militant sets of social, material, and political demands that go well beyond multiculturalism and challenge the very logic of global capitalism. By the twenty-first century it had become clear to a new generation of indigenous leaders that indigenous discourse and organization proved to be a powerful way to advance political and material struggles than other forms of class-based organizing. All of the major indigenous struggles in Latin America, including those in Mexico, Ecuador, Bolivia, and Guatemala, have emphasized the links their between resurgent struggle and broader resistance to neoliberalism and capitalist globalization. Central to the new indigenous struggles are demands for political autonomy from the neoliberal state and for land and territory. Crucially, this demand is not *just* for *land* but for *territory;* the right to continue collective forms of land ownership and in this way challenging head-on the capitalist form of property and the neoliberal logic of the spread of markets in land. They have also demanded as part of political autonomy and territorial control, control over resources, such as land, lumber, and mining (as in the case of the Mapuche in Chile), oil and natural gas, as in Bolivia and Ecuador, and so forth. In putting forward these demands they have clashed head-on with capitalist globalization and its agents, including transnational energy, mining, and agribusiness corporations and constitute a frontal challenge to transnational corporate plunder in Latin America.[1]

Indigenous struggles spearhead popular class demands; these are *struggles against (transnational) capital* and for a transformation of property relations. Ethnicity and class have fused in the new round of indigenous resistance, which has become a—perhaps *the*—leading edge of popular class mobilization.[2] The indigenous movement represents a threat to transnational capital because indigenous communities block access to land and natural resources under indigenous custodianship. Collective ownership of land and administration of collective resources, participatory democracy within indigenous communities, a cosmology and value system that is socialist—indeed, "primitive" communist—in essence, are anti-theses of global capitalism. The fundamental indigenous notion of *mother earth* as something that cannot be "owned," much less privatized, and which must be respected and sustained, is diametrically opposed to global capitalism's drive to commodify and plunder nature. Transnational capital seeks integrate indigenous into the global market as dependent workers and consumers, to convert their lands into private property, and make

---

[1] In Guatemalan, indigenous groups and their supporters have waged pitched battles against a veritable invasion of transnational companies that seek, with World Bank backing, to open vast new gold, nickel, and other mining operations in their communities (Witte, 2005; Tamayo, 2006b). Amazonian indigenous groups in Ecuador, Peru, and Colombia face expropriation and state repression as they resist the new TNC incursions into their territories to exploit oil and natural gas deposits. Highland as well as Amazonian indigenous communities in Peru and Ecuador have as well experienced what could only be described as a wholesale invasion of transnational mining companies attempting to get at vast deposits of gold, cobalt, zinc, copper, and other mineral deposits discovered in recent years (Tamayo, 2006b).

[2] A 2004 report by the U.S. National Intelligence Council, an advisory group to the CIA, the NSC, and the Pentagon fretted that indigenous movements, such as those protesting in Bolivia over transnational corporate control of gas reserves, could "evolve into more radical expressions" and converge "with some non-indigenous but radicalized movements, such as the Brazilian 'landless,' The Paraguayan and Ecuadorian peasants, and the Argentine 'picketers.' . . . In this scenario, by 2020 the groups will have grown exponentially and obtained the majority adherence of indigenous peoples in their countries, and a 'demonstration' or 'contagion' effect could cause spillover into other nations. The resulting indigenous irredentism could include rejection of western political and economic order maintained by Latin Americans of European origin, causing a deep social fracture that could lead to armed insurgency, repressive response by counter-insurgent governments, social violence and even political and territorial balkanization." (as cited in Grandin, 2006b:213–214)

the natural resources in their territories available for transnational corporate exploitation.

It is not that there is anything intrinsic in being indigenous—as an historical cultural identity and collective social experience—that makes the indigenous a threat in this way to global capitalism and leads indigenous communities to spearhead twenty-first-century resistance struggles. Rather, the very exclusion and total social control by oppressive colonial and post-colonial states that the indigenous have experienced has forced them to sustain and reproduce a collective community existence in order to survive the past 500 years and that now stands smack in the way of global capitalist expansion in Latin America.

If local paramilitary squads and oligarchs in Colombia, Mexico, and elsewhere respond to this indigenous threat with coercive terror, how has transnational capital responded?

El Indio Permitido and Neoliberal Multiculturalism

The very success of the indigenous movement has led it into a set of quandaries. Its achievements to date in cultural and ethnic rights, in forcing the dominant groups and society at large to recognize those rights, indicate both the advances and the limitations of the multicultural agenda and underscore the limits of what Charles Hale, in his excellent study, *Mas Que Un Indio* (2006), terms the *Indio permitido*. "The rise of a multicultural ethic among Latin American states and political-economic elites has been explained as the outcome of three powerful forces of change," according to Hale: "grassroots and national mobilization from below, with ample support from 'global' allies; neoliberal economic reforms, which eliminated corporate constraints on indigenous politics while accentuating inequality and economic distress; and, finally, democratization, which widened spaces of protest, and necessitated substantive responses from above" (2006:219).

If at first multiculturalism was a threat to the dominant order the transnational elite was able in the 1990s to accommodate itself to the cultural and ethnic demands of indigenous (and Afro-descendant) groups, such as bilingualism, so long as these demands were not part of a more expansive struggle against neoliberalism and capitalist globalization. Indeed, transnational elites and TNS agencies such as the World Bank sought to neutralize such a struggle by raising as its own the banner of multiculturalism and by providing ample funding and other forms of assistance to indigenous organizations and NGOs focusing on multiculturalism and its more limited set of proposals. In this way, the transnational elite appeared as a progressive, pro-indigenous force often at odds with local elites and states that were resisting any change in the racial/ethnic status quo, while multiculturalism becomes the cultural counterpart to neoliberalism in the socioeconomic sphere and polyarchy in the political.

Hale refers to the type of indigenous that the transnational elite sought to support and promote as "el indio permitido," or the permitted/allowed Indian, whereas those challenging the neoliberal socioeconomic order is the unauthorized or "insurrectionary" Indian. "The Maya movement stands at an impasse," he observes, focusing on Guatemala, where 60 percent or more of the population is Mayan. "Powerful institutions well beyond Guatemala are finding ways to contain cultural rights activism through appropriation rather than suppression," or what he terms *neoliberal multiculturalism,* a project "located at higher, more powerful levels of the global system. The World Bank, along with its Latin American counterpart, the Inter-American Development Bank, has championed the notion of 'development with identity,' and devoted significant resources to indigenous organization, participation, and cultural rights. As Hale observes:

> The shift away from national ideologies that promoted assimilation, toward endorsement of cultural rights and intercultural equality, has occurred with striking uniformity across the region [Latin America], beginning in the mid-1980s. This shift has coincided with the ascendancy of economic policies and political practices grouped together by the omnibus term "neoliberalism:. . . . Proponents of neoliberal governance reshape the terrain of political struggle to their advantage, not be denying indigenous rights, but by the selective recognition of them. Far from being exempt from the process of [neoliberal] "subject formation," indigenous peoples (and other protagonists of cultural rights) are their principal targets. While indigenous people engage in widespread and at times intense resistance to the neoliberal establishment, this flow of political activity does not stand outside or immune to processes of neoliberal subject formation. . . . In important respects, *indigenous cultural rights activism and neoliberal economics are neatly compatible.* (Hale 2006:34–35, my emphasis).

It is no wonder, therefore, as Hale observes, that global institutions such as the World Bank support indigenous rights at the same time as they promote policies that deepen indigenous structural poverty, material deprivation, and racial-ethnic inequalities. Indigenous forms of collective land ownership, such as the *comunas* in Ecuador, the *aullus* in Bolivia, the *resguardos* in Colombia, or the *ejidos* in Mexico, are a threat to global capitalism and have become the target of the global capitalist assault even as transnational elites recognize—and offer expanding support to—indigenous cultural and ethnic struggles and demands for political representation. Globalization breaks up non-capitalist forms of land tenure and local community structures and organizations. The 1991 agrarian counter-reform in Mexico, which modified Article 27 of the constitution and eroded communal agrarian ejidos (collective lands), was coupled with reforms to Article 4 of the same constitution that for the first time recognized the multi-ethnic character of the Mexican nation. In that same year, the Agrarian Law approved in Ecuador eliminated from the constitution the definition of the social function of land and water and opened the door to the disappearance of communal lands. A year later in Peru, the Land Law privatized the land market by reversing the constitutional inviolability of community-held lands. Similarly, in Amazonia the penetration by local and transnational investors—loggers, cattle ranchers, agribusiness, oil companies, etc.—facilitated by neoliberal reform threatened indigenous territorial autonomy.

Hale's case study of Mayan struggle in Guatemalan is revealing. Starting in the late 1980s, as the "Mayan effervescence" was taking off, an array of international organizations, from small NGOs to the World Bank, the governments of Scandinavia, Western Europe, and the United States made large-scale funding available and pressured the Guatemalan state to recognize indigenous cultural rights as multiculturalism became the buzzword. In this way transnational forces were able to penetrate and influence the direction of Mayan civil society just as the latter was experience a renaissance in the wake of decades of severe repression and civil war, and when the post-bellicose Maya political project was not yet defined. The 1995 peace accord signed between the government and the URNG insurgent umbrella organization included an Accord on Identity and Rights of the Indigenous Peoples; declared Guatemala a "multicultural, pluri-ethnic, multi-lingual" nation; condemned the country's history of racial discrimination; and granted full language, culture-specific religious, clothing, educational, and other cultural and ethnic rights to the indigenous majority. Yet the very same peace plan also included an Accord on Agrarian and Socio-Economic Affairs that ratified the neoliberal program for the country and proposed solutions to land and other pressing socioeconomic problems within the logic of market forces. In this way, argues Hale, "Maya cultural rights and economic neoliberal restructuring converge to constitute a single political project" (2006:75).

It is important to note that the peace accord granted Mayan demands for collective self-administration of their internal affairs and collective holdings. Similar autonomy and provision for collective ownership of land and management of resources have been granted to the indigenous in Ecuador, Colombia, and elsewhere. But Hale makes the crucially important observation that neoliberal programs involve such flexibility that they are able to accommodate a collective orientation to the imperatives of global capitalism. The key defining feature of neoliberalism "is not strict, market-oriented individualism, as many contend, but rather the restructuring of society such that people come to govern themselves in accordance with the tenets of global capitalism," he argues:

> Compliance with the discipline of the capitalist market can be individual, but may be equally effective as a collective response; if civil society organizations opt for development models that reinforce the ideology of capitalist productive relations, they can embody and advance the neoliberal project as collectivities and not individuals. As long as cultural rights remain within these basic parameters, they contribute directly to the goal of neoliberal self-governance; they reinforce its ideological tenets while meeting deeply felt needs; they register dissent, while directing these collective political energies toward unthreatening ends. (2006:75)

As I have documented elsewhere (Robinson, 2003), the Mayan renaissance unfolded alongside the penetration of global capitalism into the indigenous highlands and the rapid development of the transnational model of accumulation through the establishment of a market in land, commerce, rural and suburban maquiladora industries, non-traditional agricultural exports, and transnational tourism. Local autonomy is not a viable alternative to the national and transnational political system precisely because that system and the neoliberal states that are its local brokers do not intend to allow local indigenous communities to opt out of incorporation into global capitalism.

The challenge facing the indigenous movement became apparent to me during a June 2007 visit to El Cauca, one of the indigenous heartlands in Colombia, invited by the Association of Indigenous Councils of North Cauca. Colombia's indigenous struggle experienced a remarkable renaissance in recent decades. The state was forced to approve a new constitution in 1991 that recognized not only cultural rights but also indigenous rights to collective land and autonomous administration of resources, and millions of acres of land have been reclaimed from landlords. And while the indigenous are only 1 to 2 percent of the Colombian population, they actually spearheaded the national popular mobilization against a free trade agreement between Colombia and the United States. Indigenous identity, levels of internal organization, and self-confidence seems to be at an all time high. Yet more radical ideologies and programs of struggle against neoliberalism and the neo-fascist Colombian state competed with indigenista ideologies and projects, that is, what Hale terms neoliberal multiculturalism. Even more importantly, the movement had reached an impasse in the face of other burning matters, such as what types of alliances it should develop with other popular sectors and whether it should seek to participate in national political struggle or limit itself to protecting and extending local autonomy, and to what extend the indigenous could or should provide leadership outside of their own communities.

If the embrace by the TNS of multiculturalism is a central component of the effort by the transnational elite to co-opt the indigenous movement and construct a hegemonic order in the Americas, in the Gramscian sense, it also exposes in my view the limits (if not the bankruptcy) of identity politics and the pitfall of separating the analysis of race or ethnicity from that of class and from the critique of (now globalized) capitalism. I agree with Hale that "as proponents of neoliberal multiculturalism become ever more deeply invested in shaping cultural rights rather than denying them, this shift helps explain the impasse that many indigenous rights movements now confront." Recognition of indigenous cultural and ethnic rights from the state represented a cutting edge of struggle so long as the state withheld those rights. But the moment when "indigenous identity politics represented a frontal challenge to the state has passed, giving way to a phase of much greater involvement of powerful actors in the formulation of identity-based demands, intense negotiations from within powerful institutions, and inevitably, greater internal dissention within the movements themselves" (2006:37). In Hale's words, neoliberal multiculturalism has "the makings of a menacing political project, informed by deepened knowledge of the [indigenous]. Recognition of certain [indigenous] demands, often adopting the very 'language of contention' that indigenous activists themselves deploy, generates a powerful capacity to punish those demands perceived as militant, unyielding, or dangerous . . . the potential for fragmentation, cooptation, and sheer perplexity is enormous" (2006:44–45).

This is, in sum, a strategy for the hegemonic incorporation rather than the previous coercive exclusion of indigenous populations. Slavoj Žižek (1997) has pointed out that the Universal acquires concrete existence only when some particular content starts to function as its stand-in, and that this link between the Universal and the particular content which functions as is stand-in is contingent in that it is the outcome of a political struggle for ideological hegemony. In order to be effective, "the ruling ideology has to incorporate a series of features in which the exploited majority will be able to recognize its authentic longings. In other words, each hegemonic universality has to incorporate *at least two* particular contents, the authentic popular content as well as its distortion by the relations of domination and exploitation" (Žižek, 1997:29). Žižek reminds us of Etienne Balibar's reversal of Marx's classical formula: the ruling ideas are precisely *not* directly the ideas of those who rule. Rather, these ideas incorporate a series of crucial motifs and aspirations of the oppressed and rearticulate them in such a way that they become compatible with the existing relations of domination. This is precisely what has taken place with the transnational elite's embrace of multicultural indigenous rights; that elite threw the ball back into the court of the indigenous. But the indigenous movement was in the early twenty-first century part of an expansive counter-hegemony sweeping Latin America as its fate became more than ever bound up with that of the popular majority. There is no reason to assume that the "insurrectionary Indian" will not be able to prevail over the "authorized Indian" and push the movement beyond its impasse.

The Immigrant Rights Movement in the United States

A specter is haunting global capitalism—the specter of a transnational immigrant workers uprising. An immigrant rights movement is spreading around the world, spearheaded by Latino/a immigrants in the United States, who have launched an all-out fight-back against the repression, exploitation, cultural degradation and racism they routinely face. A major turning point in this struggle came in Spring 2006 with a series of unparalleled strikes and demonstrations that swept the country. The immediate message emanating from these actions was clear, as marchers shouted, "Aqui estamos y no nos vamos!" [We are here and we are not leaving!]. However, beyond immediate demands, the emerging movement challenged the very structural changes bound up with capitalist globalization that have generated an upsurge in global labor migration, thrown up a new global working class, and placed that working class in increasingly direct confrontation with transnational capital.

The wave of protests began on March 10, 2006, when over half a million immigrants and their supporters took to the streets in Chicago. It was the largest single protest in that city's history and was followed over the next two months with rolling strikes and protests in other cities, large and small, organized through expanding networks of churches, immigrant clubs and rights groups, community associations, Spanish-language and progressive media, trade unions, and social justice organizations. In one "day of national protest" on March 25, 2006, between one and two million people demonstrated in Los Angeles—the single biggest public protest in the city's history—and millions more followed suit in Chicago, New York, Atlanta, Washington, D.C., Phoenix, Dallas, Houston, Tucson, Denver, and dozens of other cities. In addition, hundreds of thousands of high school students around the country staged walkouts in support of their families and communities, braving police repression, and legal sanctions.

Then on May Day, 2006, trade unionists and social justice activists joined immigrants in "The Great American Boycott 2006/A Day Without an Immigrant." Millions—perhaps tens of millions—in over 200 cities from across the country skipped work and school, commercial activity, and daily routines in order to participate in a national boycott, general strike, rallies, and symbolic actions. Hundreds of local communities in the South, Midwest, Northwest and elsewhere, far away from the "gateway cities" where Latino populations are concentrated, experienced mass public mobilizations that placed them on the political map. Agribusiness in the California and Florida heartlands—nearly 100 percent dependent on immigrant labor—came to a standstill, leaving supermarket produce shelves empty for the next several days. In the landscaping industry, nine out of ten workers boycotted work. The construction industry suffered major disruptions. Latino truckers who move 70 percent of the goods in Los Angeles ports did not work. Caregiver referral agencies in major cities saw a sharp increase in calls from parents who needed last minute nannies or baby-sitters. International commerce between Mexico and the United States ground to a temporary halt as protesters closed Tijuana, Juarez-El Paso, and several other crossings along the 2,000-mile border (Robinson, 2006a).

These protests were unprecedented in the history of the United States. The immediate trigger was the introduction in the U.S. Congress of a bill that called for criminalizing undocumented immigrants by making it a felony to be in the United States. It also stipulated the construction of the first 700 miles of a militarized wall between Mexico and the United States, a doubling of the size of the U.S. Border Patrol, and the application of criminal sanctions against anyone who provided assistance to undocumented immigrants, including churches, humanitarian groups, and social service agencies. However, the wave of protest went well beyond opposition to this repressive legislation. It represented the unleashing of pent-up anger and repudiation of deepening exploitation and an escalation of anti-immigrant repression and racism. Immigrants have been subject to every imaginable abuse in recent years. Punitive government legislation approved in 2005, for instance, denied immigrants the right to acquire drivers' licenses. This meant that they had to rely on inadequate or nonexistent public transportation or risk driving illegally; more significantly, the driver's license is often the only form of legal documentation for such essential transactions as cashing checks or renting an apartment. And dozens of local governments around the country passed laws in 2006 for the eviction from housing units of undocumented immigrant families and even for public segregation of immigrants and citizens, while some businesses refused to serve anyone speaking Spanish.

Anti-immigrant hate groups were also on the rise. The FBI reported more than 2,500 hate crimes against Latinos in the United States between 2000 and 2006. Blatantly racist public discourse that only a few years earlier would be considered extreme had by 2005 become increasing mainstreamed and aired on the mass media. The paramilitary organization Minutemen, a modern day Latino-hating version of the Ku Klux Klan, spread in the first decade of the twenty-first century from its place of origin along the border between the United States and Mexico—in Arizona and California to other parts of the country. Minutemen claimed they must "secure the border" in the face of inadequate state-sponsored control. Their discourse, beyond racist, was neo-fascist. Some were even filmed sporting T-shirts with the emblem "Kill a Mexican Today?" and others have organized for-profit "human safaris" in the desert. One video game discovered in 2006 circulating on the Internet, "Border Patrol," let players shoot at Mexican immigrants as they try to cross the border into the United States. Players in the Flash-based game were told to target one of three immigrant groups portrayed in a negative, stereotypical way as the figures rushed past a sign that reads "Welcome to the United States." The immigrants were caricatured as bandoleer-wearing "Mexican nationalists," tattooed "drug smugglers" and pregnant "breeders" who spring with their children in tow. Right-wing organizers, wealthy ranchers, businessmen, and politicians sponsored minutemen clubs. But their social base was drawn from those formerly privileged sectors of the white working class that have been flexibilized and displaced by economic restructuring, the deregulation of labor, and global capital flight. These sectors turned to scapegoating immigrants—with official encouragement—as the source of their insecurity and downward mobility.

Latino immigration to the United States, as I discussed earlier, is part of a worldwide upsurge in transnational migration generated by the forces of capitalist globalization. During the 1980s eight million Latin American emigrants arrived in the United States, nearly equal to the total figure of European

immigrants who arrived on U.S. shores during the first decades of the twentieth century, and making Latin America the principal origin of migration into
the United States. Some 36 million of the 200 million immigrant workers reported worldwide in 2005 were in the United States, at least 20 million of them
from Latin America, which became the largest source of immigration in the
second half of the twentieth century. Among these 36 million, those undocumented were estimated at some 12 million to 15 million, of which 60 percent
were Mexican and another 25 percent from other Latin American countries,
while 9 percent from Asia and the remaining 6 percent from Europe, Canada
and the rest of the world (Passel, 2005:2).

Repression and xenophobia against immigrants from Third World countries,
of course, is ingrained in U.S. (and Western) history. As indirect mechanisms
have replaced colonialism in the mobilization of racialized labor pools, states
assume a gatekeeper function to regulate the flow of labor for the capitalist
economy. U.S. immigration enforcement agencies undertake "revolving door"
practices—opening and shutting the flow of immigration in accordance with
needs of capital accumulation during distinct periods. Immigrants are sucked
up when their labor is needed and then spit out when they become superfluous
or potentially destabilizing to the system. In the late 1800s planters and railroad, canning and packing, mining and industrial companies operating in the
U.S. West drew on the Mexican population that had been forcibly incorporated
into the United States with the annexation of Mexico's northern one-third following the war of 1846 to 1848. They also recruited thousands of Mexicans to
meet labor shortages during World War I. Yet hundreds of thousands were deported during the recession of 1920 to 1921 and up to one million during the
depression of the 1930s. As labor shortages reappeared during World War II,
the U.S. government launched the *Bracero* Program that recruited millions of
Mexican laborers, many of whom were expelled through Operation Wetback
that was implemented during the economic downturn of the late 1950s.

The same economic crisis of the 1970s that paved the way for global restructuring and the new transnational phase of world capitalism also unleashed a
"new nativism" starting in the 1970s and punitive state-sponsored controls over
immigrants in many countries around the world. "The main problem is how to
get rid of those six to eight million aliens who are interfering with our economic
prosperity," declared in 1976 then-U.S. President Gerald Ford (Nevins, 2002:63).
The most recent wave of repression and discrimination, directed largely at Latino/a
immigrants, began in the 1980s, coinciding with the major wave of outmigration
from Latin America. In 1994 the government launched "Operation Gatekeeper,"

which accelerated militarization of the U.S.–Mexico border (Nevins, 2002). Two years later the Clinton government passed the Illegal Immigration Reform and Immigrant Responsibility Act (IIRIRA), which tightened asylum claims, increased penalties on undocumented immigrants, and led to a massive increase in deportations. In that same year, the Welfare Reform Act excluded even legal immigrants from unemployment or health benefits. And in 2005 the U.S. legislature approved the Real ID Act that prohibited undocumented immigrants from holding driver's licenses.

Super-Flexible, Super-Exploitable, and Super-Controllable

It is the "revolving door" function of states in the era of globalization that makes it *appear* that state policy is contradictory. Neither employers nor the state wants to do away with immigrant labor. To the contrary, they want to sustain a vast exploitable labor pool that exists under precarious conditions, that does not enjoy the civil, political, and labor rights of citizens, that faces language barriers and a hostile cultural and ideological environment, and that is flexible and disposable through deportation. It is the *condition of deportable* they wish to create or preserve since that condition assures the ability to super-exploit with impunity and to dispose of without consequences should this labor become unruly or unnecessary. Driving immigrant labor deeper underground and absolving the state and employers of any commitment to the social reproduction of this labor allows for its maximum exploitation together with its disposal when necessary. The punitive features of immigration policy in the 1990s and twenty-first century were combined with reforms to federal welfare law that denied immigrants—documented or not—access to such social wages as unemployment insurance, food stamps, and certain welfare benefits (Binford, 2005:32). In this way the immigrant labor force becomes responsible for its own maintenance and reproduction and—through remittances—for their families members abroad. All this makes immigrant labor low-cost and flexible for capital *and also* costless for the state compared to native-born labor.

A reserve army of immigrant labor must remain just that—*immigrant* labor, and therefore undocumented. Sustaining this reserve army of immigrant labor means creating—and reproducing—the division of workers into immigrants and citizens. This requires contradictory practices on the part of the states. The state must lift national borders for capital but must reinforce these same national boundaries in its immigrant policies and in its ideological activities it must generate a nationalist hysteria by propagating such images as "out of control borders" and "invasions of illegal immigrants." Nation-states become what McMichael (1996) has called "population containment zones." National boundaries are *not* barriers to transnational migration but they are critical to the structural power capital has achieved over an increasingly transnational working class whose ability to exercise its own class power is constrained by the juridical and institutional structures of the nation-state system.

But these "gatekeeper" functions become more complex—and contradictory—as transnational capital becomes increasingly dependent on immigrant labor. Latino and Latina immigrant labor became by the turn of the century structurally embedded in the U.S. (and increasingly the Canadian) economy. Although immigrant labor sustains U.S. and Canadian agriculture, by the 1990s the majority of Latino and Latina immigrants were absorbed by industry, construction, and services as part of a general "Latinization" of the economy. Latino immigrants have massively swelled the lower rungs of the U.S. workforce. They provide almost all of the farm labor and much of the labor for hotels, restaurants, construction, janitorial and house cleaning, child care, domestic service, gardening and landscaping, hairdressing, delivery, meat and poultry packing, food processing, light manufacturing, retail, and so on. New Central American and Mexican agricultural laborers have appeared in the mid-West and the Appalachian region of the United States, and industrial laborers of the same origin have appeared in East and West Coast industries under rigidly segmented labor markets, often displacing African American and white ethnic laborers.

Historically, African Americans were relegated to the lower rungs in the U.S. caste system. But as African Americans fought for their civil and human rights in the 1960s and 1970s they became organized, politicized, and radicalized. Black workers led trade union militancy. All this made them undesirable labor for capital: "undisciplined" and "noncompliant." Starting in the 1980s employers began to push out Black workers and massively recruit Latino immigrants, coinciding with deindustrialization and restructuring (see, e.g., Taylor, 2006). Blacks moved from super-exploited to marginalized—subject to unemployment, cuts in social services, mass incarceration, and heightened state repression—while Latino immigrant labor has become the new super-exploited sector. Employers and political elites in New Orleans, for instance, apparently decided in the wake of Hurricane Katrina to replace that city's historical black working class with Latino immigrant labor. Whereas up to the early 1990s no one saw a single Latino face in such places such as Iowa or Tennessee, Latino workers from Mexico, Central America, and elsewhere had become visible everywhere by the turn of the century. If some African Americans misdirected their anger over marginality at Latino immigrants, the Black community had a legitimate grievance over the anti-Black racism of many Latinos themselves, who often lacked sensitivity to the historic plight and contemporary experience of Blacks with racism, and were reticent to see them as natural allies. (Latinos often bring with them particular sets of racialized relations from their home countries. In this regard, a major challenge confronting the movement in the United States is relations between the Latino and the Black communities.)

The rapidly growing dependence on Latino and Latina labor cannot be over-stated. Between 1980 and 1990, for instance, largely Latino immigrants went from 20 to 64 percent of the state of California's construction workers, from 26 to 49 percent of its janitors, from 58 to 91 percent of its farm workers, from 34 to 76 percent of its maids and other domestic workers, from 20 to 58 percent of child care workers, from 9 to 48 percent of drywall installers, and so on. This dependence intensified in the 1990s (Palerm, 1999:47). At the same time afflu-ent and middle-class sectors have come to enjoy, and depend on, cheap "throw away labor" for their household needs—an army of maids, nannies, gardeners, painters, and so forth. Such dependence—and the arrogance of it being taken for granted by the privileged—was satirically depicted in the film *A Day without a Mexican,* directed by Sergio Arau, a native Mexican. In the satire Californians wake up one day to find that a thick fog has rolled off the ocean and blanketed the state, leading to the disappearance of all Mexicans and people of Mexican heritage. In the ensuing mayhem the state's farms, factories, construction sites, and services grind to a halt, and upper-class Anglo homemakers are hapless as they attempt to cook, clean, tend to their children, and accomplish other tasks in the absence of their Mexican domestic assistants.

In sum, employers, the state, and affluent strata have converged in seeking to sustain a reserve army of immigrant labor. There is a broad social and politi-cal base, therefore, for the maintenance of a flexible, super-controlled and super-exploited Latino immigrant workforce. The system cannot function with-out it. The migrant labor phenomenon will continue to expand along with global capitalism. Just as capitalism has no control over its implacable expan-sion as a system it cannot do away in its new globalist stage with transnational labor. But if global capital needs the labor power of transnational migrants, this labor power belongs to human beings who must be tightly controlled, given the special oppression and dehumanization involved in extracting their labor power as non-citizen immigrant labor. The immigrant issue presents a contradiction for political and economic elites: from the vantage points of dominant group interests, the dilemma is how to deal with the new "barbarians" at Rome's door. This contradictory situation helps explain the frightening escalation of hostilities against Latino/a immigrants. The system needs Latino immigrant labor yet the presence of that labor scares dominant groups and privileged, generally white, strata. Dominant groups and privileged strata fear a rising tide of Latino immigrants will lead to a loss of cultural and political control, becoming a source of counter-hegemony and of instability, as immigrant labor in Paris showed to be in the late 2005 uprising in that European capital against racism and marginality.

But the anti-immigrant bloc also draws in white workers. White labor that historically enjoyed caste privilege within racially segmented labor markets have experienced downward mobility and heightened insecurity. These sectors of the working class feel the pinch of capitalist globalization and the transnationalization of formerly insulated local labor markets. Studies in the early 1990s, for example, found that, in addition to concentrations in "traditional" areas such as Los Angeles, Miami, Washington D.C.–Virginia, and Houston, Central American immigrants had formed clusters in the formal and informal service sectors in areas where, in the process of downward mobility, they replaced "white ethnics," such as in suburban Long Island, in small towns of Iowa and North Carolina, in Silicon Valley and in the northern and eastern suburbs of the San Francisco Bay Area (Robinson, 2006a).

The loss of caste privileges for white sectors of the working class is problematic for political elites and state managers in the United States since legitimation and domination have historically been constructed through a white racial hegemonic bloc. Can such a bloc be sustained or renewed through a scapegoating of immigrant communities? In attempting to shape the public discourse, the anti-immigrant lobby argued that immigrants "are a drain on the U.S. economy." Yet as the National Immigrant Solidarity Network pointed out, immigrants contribute seven billion dollars in social security per year. They earned $240 billion in 2005, reported $90 billion, and were only reimbursed $5 billion in tax returns. They also contributed $25 billion more to the U.S. economy than they receive in healthcare and social services (www.immigrantsolidarity.org/). But this is a limited line of argumentation, since the larger issue is the incalculable trillions of dollars that immigrant labor generates in profits and revenue for capital, only a tiny portion of which goes back to immigrants in the form of wages. Moreover, it has been demonstrated that there is no correlation between the unemployment rate among U.S. citizens and the rate of immigration. In fact, the unemployment rate moved in cycles between 1980 and 2005 and exhibited a comparatively lower rate during the 2000–2005 influx of undocumented workers. Similarly, wage stagnation in the United States appeared starting with the economic crisis of 1973 and continued its steady march since then, with no correlation to increases and decreases in the inflow of undocumented workers. Instead, downward mobility for most U.S. workers is positively correlated with the decline in union participation, the decline in labor conditions, and the polarization of income and wealth that began with the restructuring crisis of the 1970s and accelerated the following decade as Reaganomics launched the neoliberal counterrevolution (Robinson, 2006a).

This is the larger panorama that has produced the dynamic of racialized hostility toward Latinos in which ideological and cultural processes interplay with those of global political economy and with the subjective action of distinct groups caught up in these processes. The twin instruments for achieving the dual goals of super-exploitability and super-controllability are (1) the division of the working class into immigrant and citizen; and (2) racialization of the former. In this way race and class converge. Racialization is an instrument in the politics of domination. It is incorporated into the strategies of ruling groups to manage resistance and maintain order in the face of uncertainty and crisis. The dilemma for capital, dominant groups, affluent and privileged strata is how to "have their cake and eat it" too; how are ruling groups to resolve the contradiction of assuring a steady supply of immigrant labor while at the same time promoting anti-immigrant practices and ideologies?

New World Borders: "Guest Worker" Programs, Criminalization, and Militarization

The state must play a balancing act by finding a formula for a stable supply of cheap labor to employers and at the same time for greater state control over immigrants. The preferred solution for capital and its political representatives are "guest worker" programs that would convert immigrants into a quasi-indentured labor force. Such programs typically provide temporary work visas, rule out legalization for undocumented immigrants, force immigrants to return to their home countries once employment has terminated, and impose tough border controls. There is a long history of such "guest worker" schemes going back to the *Bracero* program, which brought to the U.S. millions of Mexican workers during the labor shortages of World War II only to deport them once native workers had become available again. Similar "guest worker" programs are in effect in several European countries and other labor-importing states around the world. Throughout the 1990s and early twenty-first century, U.S.-based agribusiness, other transnational corporate employers and their allies in the state developed draft legislation and pushed for new "guest worker" programs at the same time as they pushed for more restrictive reforms and tighter enforcement (Ewing, 1999:1). Employers also turned to state immigration officials to block unionization efforts among their workers. "Guest worker" programs that keep immigrants in a state of deportability and such state repressive practices as raids serve to remind workers that they can be replaced should they press for labor rights or wage increases.

The poultry and meatpacking industry is a case in point. During the 1980s and 1990s the industry underwent a transformation, decentralizing from large cities to rural and small town communities, and also upgrading the technological component of slaughtering and quartering so that skilled butchers became replaced by unskilled operators and packers. Animals were now slaughtered and cut apart on disassembly lines involving deskilled labor and Taylorist control and then packed and shipped in small batches. At the same time the industry became increasingly concentrated among the top TNCs such as ConAgra, Cargill, and IBP (owned by Tyson foods). With this shift to flexible accumulation came union busting and the systematic replacement of largely white and some black labor to largely immigrant, Latino/a labor (for these details, see Schlosser, 2001).

Operation Vanguard, launched in 1999 by the then-Immigration and Naturalization Service (INS) with the support of corporate lobbyers, targeted immigrant workers for raids and deportations in poultry and meatpacking plants throughout the U.S. South and Midwest. Here was a shifting political coalition that scapegoated immigrants by promoting ethnic-based solidarities among middle classes, representatives of distinct fractions of capital, and formerly privileged sectors among working classes threatened by job loss, declining income and other insecurities of economic restructuring. As Latino/a immigrants flowed into small towns, working class whites experiencing rising insecurity and downward mobility began to press local officials for ant-immigrant measures. Local political pressures filtered "up" from local communities and "down" from the agribusiness lobby to the INS. In launching Operation Vanguard the INS assured companies that "our intention, of course, is not to harm operations but work in partnership" to maintain a stable workforce, according to one INS handout, and that INS officials would alert employers in advance to unannounced raids (Bacon, 1999). INS official Mark Reed explained that Operation

Vanguard sought to force a political dialogue to build up pressure for guest worker programs that would allow companies to hire contract laborers outside the United States. "If we don't have illegal immigration anymore, we'll have the political support" for such programs (Bacon, 1999). The effect of Operation Vanguard, as Bacon observed, was to wipe out—at least temporarily—efforts that were underway among immigrant workers to organize and demand their rights (ibid.).

But campaigns such as Operation Vanguard were not enough to assure the control and domination of Latino labor as the economy became ever more dependent on that labor and as racialization took its course. Hence the anti-immigrant bloc turned by the new century to criminalizing Latino/a immigrants and to militarizing their control. Criminalization and militarization increasingly drive undocumented immigrants underground, where they become vulnerable to intermediaries in the quest for survival, such as gangs, shady temporary labor agencies, and unscrupulous employers. The array of state and other institutional controls over immigrants further drive down black and informal market wages, working and living conditions and give employers an ever freer hand. There is evidence that as Latinos came to constitute the principal labor force for the reconstruction of New Orleans in the wake of the destruction wrought by Hurricane Katrina in 2005, employers turned to such practices as refusing to pay immigrant workers after they had rendered services, turning them over to immigration authorities for deportation, and employing them in an array of slave-labor like conditions (see, inter alia, Southern Poverty Law Center, 2006). At the same time, borders, in order to be effective instruments for regulating and controlling the supply of immigrant labor, must be militarized. As the U.S.-Mexico border has been increasingly militarized thousands of immigrants have died crossing the frontier. Yet this militarization generates its own contradictions. Many stretches along the 2,000-mile U.S.–Mexico border are akin to a war zone. Rampant militarization of the border provides an environment conducive to the rampant corruption of U.S. officials. According to one report:

A culture of corruption is taking hold along the 2,000-mile border from Brownsville, Texas, to San Diego. At least 200 public employees have been charged with helping to move narcotics or illegal immigrants across the U.S.–Mexican border since 2004, at least double the illicit activity documented in prior years. [An] examination of public records has found thousands more are under investigation. Criminal charges have been brought against Border Patrol agents, local police, a county sheriff, motor vehicle clerks, an FBI supervisor, immigration examiners, prison guards, school district officials and uniformed personnel of every branch of the U.S. military, among others. (Vartabedian, Serrano, and Marosi, 2006:A1)

Class Relations of Global Capitalism and Immigrant Rights

The larger backdrop to all this is transnational capital's attempt to forge post–Fordist-Keynesian global capital–labor relations worldwide based on flexibilization, deregulation, and de-unionization. Capital began to abandon from the 1970s and on earlier reciprocities with labor forged in the epoch of national corporate capitalism precisely because the process of globalization allowed to it break free of nation-state constraints. As I discussed earlier, there has been a vast acceleration of the primitive accumulation of capital worldwide through globalization, a process in which millions have been wrenched from the means of production, proletarianized, and thrown into a global labor market that transnational capital has been able to shape. In drawing on migrant workers, dominant groups are able to take advantage of a global reserve army of labor that has experienced historically unprecedented growth in recent years. At the core of the emerging global social structure of accumulation is a new capital–labor relation based on alternative systems of labor control and diverse contingent categories of devalued labor—subcontracted, outsourced, casualized, informal, part-time, temp work, work, homework, and so on—the essence of which is cheapening and disciplining labor, making it "flexible" and making it readily available for transnational capital in worldwide labor reserves. Workers in the global economy are themselves under these flexible arrangements increasingly treated as a subcontracted component rather than a fixture internal to employer organizations. These new class relations of global capitalism dissolve the notion of responsibility, however minimal, that governments have for their citizens or that employers have toward their employees.

Immigrant workers become the archetype of these new global class relations—the quintessential workforce of global capitalism. They are yanked out of relations of reciprocity rooted in social and political communities that have historically been institutionalized in nation-states. Latino and immigrant workers are reduced to a naked commodity, another flexible and expendable input into globalized production; a transnationally mobile commodity deployed when and where needed throughout North America. As one Canadian agribusiness represented from Ontario bragged: "We can take Mexican tomatoes and ship them up here, you can send a Mexican to California to produce tomatoes there and ship them up here, or you can send a Mexican up here and you grow the tomato here in Ontario" (as cited in Binford, 2005:36).

Labor supply through transnational migration constitutes in this way the *export of commodified human beings*. This commodification goes beyond the more limited concept first developed by Marx, in which the worker's *labor power* is sold to capital as a commodity. To Marx we must add Foucaultian insights. In the classical Marxist construct, the worker faces alienation and exploitation during the time s/he sells this commodity to capital, that is, during the work shift. In between this regularized sale of labor power s/he is not a commodity but an alienated human being, "free" to rest and replenish in the sphere of social reproduction. In its archetypical form, the new immigrant worker as a mobile input for globalized circuits of accumulation is not just selling commodified labor during the time s/he is working; *the whole body becomes a commodity*, mobilized and supplied in the same way as are raw materials, money, intermediate goods, and other inputs. It is, after all, the whole body that must migrate and insert itself into the global accumulation circuits as immigrant labor. Hence, even when each regular sale of labor power concludes—i.e., after each work period—the worker is not "free" to rest and replenish as in the traditional Marxist analysis of labor and capital since he or she remains *immigrant/undocumented* labor 24 hours a day, unable to engage in the "normal" channels of rest and social reproduction due to the whole set of institutional exclusions, state controls, racialized discrimination, xenophobia, and oppression that the undocumented immigrant worker experiences in the larger social milieu.

Immigrant labor pools that can be super-exploited economically, marginalized and disenfranchised politically, driven into the shadows, and deported when necessary are the very epitome of capital's naked domination in the age of global capitalism. Therefore, bound up with the immigrant debate in the United States is the entire political economy of global capitalism in the Western Hemisphere—the same political economy that is now being sharply contested throughout Latin America with the surge in mass popular struggles and the turn to the Left. The struggle for immigrant rights in the United States is thus part and parcel of this resistance to neoliberalism, intimately connected to the larger Latin American—and worldwide—struggle for social justice. No wonder protests and boycotts took place throughout Latin America on May Day 2006 in solidarity with Latino immigrants in the United States. But these actions were linked to local labor rights struggles and social movement demands. In Tijuana, Mexico, for example, maquiladora workers in that border city's in-bond industry marched on May Day in demand of higher wages, eight hour shifts, an end to "abuses and despotism" in the maquila plants, and an end to sexual harassment, to the use of poison chemicals, and to company unions. The workers also called for solidarity with the "Great American Boycott of 2006 on the other side of the border" and participated in a protest at the U.S. consulate in the city and at the main crossing that shut down cross-border traffic for most of the day.

The immigrant rights movement in the United States is demanding full rights for all immigrants, including amnesty, worker protections, family reunification measures, a path to citizenship or permanent residency rather than a temporary "guest worker" program, an end to all attacks against immigrants and to the criminalization of immigrant communities. While some billed the immigrant rights struggle as the birth of a new civil rights movement clearly much more was a stake. In the larger picture, it goes beyond immediate demands; it challenges the class relations that are at the very core of global capitalism. The May Day 2006 immigrant rights mobilization took place on international workers day—which has not been celebrated in the United States for nearly a century—and the significance of this timing was lost on no one. In the age of globalization the only hope of accumulating the social and political forces necessary to confront the global capitalist system is by transnationalizing popular, labor, and democratic struggles. The immigrant rights movement is all of these—popular, pro-worker, and democratic—and it is by definition transnational. In sum, the struggle for immigrant rights is at the cutting edge of the global working class fight against capitalist globalization.

Venezuela and the Bolivarian Revolution

As the battle for the future of global society heated up in the new century, Venezuela was one of the countries on the front line, leading a continental challenge to capitalist globalization. The "Bolivarian revolution" took Latin America by storm with the arrival to power in 1998 of Venezuela's charismatic and enormously popular socialist president, Hugo Chávez. The deepening of the revolution in the tumultuous years that followed came at the strategic moment for Latin America in which the "Washington consensus" had shattered. Venezuela seemed to be putting forward a radical, anti-capitalist alternative to the more reformist post-neoliberal proposals and to be organizing a regional anti-neoliberal power bloc that could tip the balance by encouraging social and political forces in Latin America to move beyond a mild reform of the status quo. A new historic bloc seemed to have ascended to hegemony in Venezuelan society and to be making a major contribution—through cultural and ideological practices and through transnational political action and solidarity—to the rise of counter-hegemonic forces throughout Latin America. The Bolivarian revolution is the first radical, socialist oriented revolution in Latin America—and indeed, the world—since the defeat of the Nicaraguan revolution of the 1980s. The declaration by the *Chavista* leadership for the first time in 2005 that the Bolivarian revolution would seek to build a "twenty-first-century socialism" has major implications for Latin America, and the world, because it put socialism back on the agenda at a time when the global justice movement seemed unable to move beyond a negative anti-capitalism and when the ignominious demise of twentieth-century socialism seemed to discredit the very idea of a socialist project.

The Venezuelan revolution is unique on at least three accounts. First, the old bourgeois state was not "smashed" in the revolution. To the contrary, by winning the presidency through an electoral process in an established polyarchic system and a well-institutionalized capitalist state, Hugo Chávez assumed the highest post in a state bureaucracy that would work over the next few years to resist and undermine the Bolivarian project. What was unfolding appeared to be as much a revolutionary process of the poor majority and their president *against the state* as against the old order. Second, the Venezuelan revolution had impeccable bourgeois democratic legitimacy. Chávez won the 1998 presidential elections by the largest majority in four decades (56.2 percent) and then went on, between 1999 and 2006, to ratify his democratic legitimacy in another eight electoral contests, including three further presidential votes (in 2000, with 59 percent of the vote; in 2004, with 59 percent; and in 2006, with 63 percent), a constitutional referendum, and several parliamentary, gubernatorial, and local elections.[3] And third, the poor majority has been engaged in its own autonomous and often belligerent grassroots and community organizing, especially in the teeming slums of the capital city of Caracas, home to four million of the country's 26 million people, and in other major urban areas. The mass

[3] These elections include presidential elections (December 1998); referendum for the creation of a Constituent Assembly (April 1999); election of the constituents (July 1999); approval of the new constitution (December 1999); presidential mega-elections, deputies, governors, and mayors (July 2000); council members elections (December 2000); union elections (August-October 2001); recall referendum (August 2004); presidential mega-elections elections (December 2006). The class basis of the Chávez government, and the extraordinary class polarization, is reflected in an analysis of these recent elections. One study on the August 2004 recall election, for instance, showed that those in the poorest of five categories in which the population was distributed (A-E, A being the wealthiest "class" of voters and E the poorest), 64 percent of those in E in urban areas and 71 percent in rural areas were against a recall of Chávez,, whereas 62 percent of those in A-B in urban areas and 56 percent of those in rural areas were in favor of recalling the him (Survey for the National Electoral Council, as reported and analyzed by Hellinger, 2005:19–21, and table 1:21).

popular base of the revolution is not subordinated to a state and party at the helm of the process, as they were in most revolutionary experiments of the twentieth century. It is in fact the ongoing and expansive mobilization of this mass base that pushed the *Chavista* leadership forward and led the charge against the decadent capitalist state and social order.

These and other unique aspects of the Bolivarian revolution are rooted, in part, in the country's particular twentieth-century history. With the overthrow of the dictator Marcos Pérez Jiménez in 1958 the leaders of the country's traditional oligarchy signed the Punto Fijo Pact that established a polyarchic system and a power-sharing arrangement among the different factions of the elite. For the next 40 years, power alternated between two multi-class parties: the social democratic Accion Democratica (AD, Democratic Action) and the more conservative Christian Democratic (COPEI) party, in alliance with the Church, military officers, and labor union leaders. Fueled by oil wealth, the country developed a fairly generous corporatist welfare state, a significant ISI industrial base, and relative stability, along with massive corruption and the development of one of the most entrenched clientalist systems in Latin America (see, inter alia, entries in Ellner and Hellinger, 2003).

But the exhaustion of this particularly Venezuelan brand of ISI and populism that emerged from that Pact led to a crisis of the polyarchic system during the 1980s and 1990s. The first signs of trouble came in 1981 with a decline in oil revenues and the onset of economic crisis as Latin America began its "lost decade." Mirroring a tendency throughout the region, Venezuela experienced a rapid process of social polarization, aggravated by the endemic corruption, which progressively worsened as the oil bonanza dwindled. The ratio of the income from salary to the top tenth to that of the lowest tenth, for instance, went from 12.5:1 in 1984 to 23.9:1 in 1991 (Lander, 2005:24). Between 1984 and 1991 total poverty in the country nearly doubled, from 36 percent of the population to 68 percent (Lander, 2005:26). Poverty and inequality continued to escalate throughout the 1990s. Per capita income in 1997 was eight percent less than in 1970; workers' income during this period was reduced by approximately half (Lander, 2005:26). Over half a million people migrated to the cities. The proportion of workers in the informal sector rose from 34.5 percent in 1980 to 53 percent in 1999 (Harnecker, 2004:35).

As globalization set in, the Venezuelan elite was thrown into confusion over how to face the crisis unleashed by the decline of the old model and the rise of neoliberalism. Among the various elite cliques and factions were some stubbornly rooted in the national circuits of accumulation developed in the post

WWII period of oil-driven expansion and ISI. Others, meanwhile, sought a reinsertion of the country into new transnational circuits. The oligarchy became wracked by internal splits and disputes. No one faction could achieve its hegemony over the elite as a whole and nor could the crisis of oligarchic power be contained as the popular classes extended their grassroots mobilization and exerted their own political protagonism. The turning point came in February 1989 with the *Caracazo*—a popular uprising centered in Caracas against an IMF-dictated "shock" austerity program imposed by Carlos Ándres Pérez, the AD leader and former populist president who had been reelected in 1988 on an anti-neoliberal platform. Between 500 and 3,000 people were killed in the government repression that put down the uprising, initiating a decade of popular protest that would eventually be harnessed by Hugo Chávez into the political vehicle for his 1998 electoral victory.

To the popular classes, as Collins observes, "the *Caracazo* is a burning memory of state betrayal and an archetypal fount of class consciousness," and to the middle and upper classes it was proof that the "dangerous classes" could not be trusted (2005:371). If elite hegemony had been eroding throughout the 1980s it collapsed entirely with the *Caracazo*. Popular mobilization and aspirations eventually coalesced around the rise of Hugo Chávez and the Bolivarian government and as a result of a series of conjunctures and circumstances. By shifting the balance in the struggle for hegemony toward the popular classes the *Caracazo* made it impossible to stabilize a neoliberal regime. It was, in effect, the first mass uprising in Latin America against neoliberalism.

The *Caracazo* also led Lt. Colonel Chávez and his comrades, who had been conspiring from within the military against the oligarchic order on the basis of a popular class outlook and inspired by the legacy of Simón Bolívar, into more direct planning to overthrow the decadent Punto Fijo regime (Gott, 2005). Chávez and the young Turks were seared by the orders given to the military to fire on civilians. In Chávez' words, the *Caracazo* marked the beginning of a "real civic-military rebellion" (as cited in Collins, 2005:372). These young officers had formed the Movimiento Bolivariano Revolucionario 200 (MBR-200) several years earlier. They launched a failed coup attempt in 1992 under Chávez' leadership (Gott, 2005). While the coup itself failed and Chávez was sent to jail, the young Bolivarian won mass popular support overnight and became a rallying point around which popular sectors and Leftist groups stepped up their struggles. Pardoned two years later, Chávez and his comrades began traveling around the country, formed a new political party, the Movement for the Fifth Republic (MVR), and eventually won the presidential elections of 1998. Chávez, highly charismatic and a brilliant orator, is of humble black-indigenous back-ground and has been genuinely able to communicate with the poor majority in a way that is hopelessly impossible for the light-skinned upper class members of the traditional elite. He was able to understand the pent-up aspirations of this excluded majority and to tap popular class sentiment at the key national and regional/world historical juncture of crisis and loss of legitimacy of the coun-try's post–World War II political and economic model, and the downward spiral into crisis and delegitimacy of the neoliberal model that replaced it.

The objective of the transnational project in Venezuela prior to the rise to power of Chávez was to salvage oligarchic power, modernize it, and at try to groom new groups among the elite who could resubordinate the popular classes into a dominant neoliberal bloc and insert the country into global capitalism. But the Bolivarian project broke with elitist hegemony and from that point on the primordial objective among the local and transnational elite, led by the U.S. state, became to undermine the Chávez government. The repeated attempts by the elite opposition in Venezuela and its transnational allies to unseat Chávez and restore an elite social and political order included an abortive military coup d'état in 2002, two business strikes during the course of 2003 and 2004, and a recall referendum in 2004 (for detailed discussion, see Golliner, 2006; Gott, 2005). These efforts not only failed to bring down the government but actually had the unintended effect of strengthening the revolutionary process in the country and weakening the anti-Chavista forces. U.S. strategists also turned to a campaign of internal political intervention under the rubric of "democracy promotion," including broad assistance for the ant-Chavista forces—the same ones that were implicated in the 2002 abortive coup and in the mass business strikes (see, e.g., Leight, 2004; Gollinger, 2006). With the failure of the anti-Chavista forces to win the August 2004 referendum and the December 2006 presidential elections, the anti-Chávez strategy shifted from a "war of maneu-ver" that sought the quick overthrow of the government to an extended "war of position" aimed at regrouping the elite opposition, undermining the economy, penetrating the state bureaucracy, eroding the *Chavista* social base, and launch-ing ongoing anti-Chávez media blitzes.

The Bolivarian Program

Beyond its specific policies in favor of the poor majority, the "radical populism" of the Bolivarian government threatened local and transnational elites because cul-tural hegemony and state power were slipping out of the hands of the traditional ruling classes. The revolution reawakened expectations and generated new hopes among the popular majority of poor mestizo, black, and indigenous Venezuelans. As in Nicaragua in the 1980s and other countries that have experienced an empowerment of the popular classes, what most panicked dominant groups was the newfound confidence of these classes, the breaking of the psycho-social chains that reinforce material relations of domination. One grassroots program of the right-wing opposition mounted shortly after Chávez took power, for instance, the Community Plan for Defensive Action, warned that its members should not be "too trusting of domestic help, especially those that are day hires. Remember that many of them have been manipulated and some are beginning to see us as the enemy" (as cited in Ramirez, 2005:91).

Venezuela's ability to launch a transformative project while also sustaining its participation in the global economy is clearly dependent to a significant degree on its oil wealth. Venezuela is the world's fifth-largest producer of oil, a key global resource, with the largest reserves of conventional oil (light and heavy crude) in the Western hemisphere and the largest reserves of non-conventional oil (extra-heavy crude) in the world. This provided the country the resources needed to undertake an internal revolutionary reorganization but it also gave the Bolivarian state a significant international clout. High oil prices—the price per barrel went from some $10 in 1999 to over $70 briefly in 2006—allowed the government to finance a broad array of social programs and gave the revolution some breathing room, as did the U.S. invasion and occupation against Iraq, which made it more difficult for Washington to concentrate political, diplomatic, and material resources in destabilization efforts elsewhere. On the other hand, the *Chavistas* have been able to break foreign and local elite control over the oil industry and to democratize this source of wealth, an experience that poses a powerful example for Bolivia, Ecuador, and Mexico—countries that also have an abundance of energy resources. The struggle over oil in Venezuela—and by extension over energy and other natural resources in Latin America—is instructive of the complexities and contradictions that forces opposed to global capitalism face when they are able to win, or at least influence, state policy, given the impossibility of individual withdrawal from global capitalism.

As the bourgeois order crumbled in Venezuela during the 1990s, and as it became increasingly likely that popular classes could win state power, groups of state bureaucrats and private investors close to the state oil company, PDVSA, began to set up subsidiaries abroad (such as the chain of Citgo Petroleum Company and various refineries in the United States) in conjunction with private transnational oil companies, including Exxon, Shell, and Gulf. The bureaucrats and investors also began to transfer the country's oil wealth out of the country and into the private sector accounts of transnational investors (among them Venezuelan nationals) via price transfers between the company's headquarters in Caracas and this network of worldwide subsidiaries (see, e.g., Lander 2003; Niemeyer, 2004; Mommer, 2003). Local and transnational economic elites were able to bypass the state—wresting control over operations and policy making from the Ministry of Energy and Mines, which became a rubber stamp for decisions made by the company managers—in converting PDVSA into a transnational conglomerate for the generation and private appropriation the country's principal source of wealth (Mommer, 2003). PDVSA succeeded in reorienting public policies by opening up the oil sector to direct foreign investment, increasing the amount of oil marketed internationally in order to capture market shares at the expense of maintaining prices, disregarding Venezuela's OPEC quota commitments, and reducing the tax rate, among other machinations (see various entries in Lander, 2003).

Such a circulation of oil-generated capital only became possible in the globalization phase of capitalism. It was neoliberal structural adjustment from 1989 and on—including liberalization, deregulation, the lifting of capital and currency controls, tax breaks, and privatization—that facilitated this rechanneling of the oil-generated surplus so that it would bypass local state circuits (Parker, 2005). The profits generated by the PDVSA's increasingly abundant investments abroad were never repatriated to the parent company and thus contributed nothing to the state. In 1991, fiscal income was equivalent to 16 percent of GNP but declined to less than 10 percent during the course of that decade and plummeted to less than five percent by 1998. It would seem at the time that Chávez took power in 1999 that the popular classes, even as they won a foothold in the state, were less able to utilize that state as an institutional lever to wrest wealth from a transnationalized bourgeoisie.

However, the Chávez government pursued an aggressive strategy of wresting control back from the PDVSA managers and their backers. The government reestablished control over the company by the Energy and Mines Ministry. It reinvigorated Venezuela's role in the Organization of Petroleum Exporting Countries (OPEC), playing a pivotal role in the successful reimposition of production quotas and consequent rise in world market prices (this was before the U.S. Iraq war sent prices spiraling upward). In 2001, the government passed a Hydrocarbon Law that reduced taxes and increased royalties because the latter was easier to calculate and less susceptible to evasion, price transfer, and other manipulations than the former. Following the December 2002 production stoppage and lockout organized by the PDVSA executives with the backing of the country's business associations and political opposition, the government replaced the PDVSA management. It subsequently introduced measures to favor the participation of local small and medium firms, worker cooperatives, and community organizations in the oil industry and introduced PDVSA-financed social programs in oil-producing regions (Lander, 2003; Parker, 2005).

Macroeconomic policy under Chávez in the first few years of his presidency was heterodox but hardly radical. Currency controls were put in place in 2002 but the government continued to meet its foreign debt obligations, to avoid deficit spending, and to maintain a foreign reserve surplus. Moreover, while mandating state intervention in the economy and directly challenging neoliberalism the new constitution ratified the rights of private property. Yet Chávez himself declared that if his children were starving he would not think twice about committing theft and suggested that the plight of the poor takes priority over the protection of private property (Ellner, 2001:24). The new constitution approved by popular referendum in 1999 prohibited the privatization of public health, education, and utilities, ensured state ownership of all mineral and hydrocarbon deposits and prohibited their transfer or alienation, prohibited the patenting of genome of living beings, and declared the right of indigenous peoples to collective ownership of their lands. In late 2001 Chávez also enacted a package of forty-nine laws with a radical socioeconomic content, including agrarian reform, state control of oil ventures, state support for worker cooperatives and the undoing of the earlier privatization of the social security system (Ellner, 2005:167–168).

During the period between Chávez' inauguration in January 1999 and the abortive coup in April 2002 two positions were in tension within the Chávez movement, according to Ellner. A "soft line" faction led by Luis Miquilena, a longtime businessman and politician who occupied the number two position in the Chavista movement during the government's first few years, advocated a strategy of establishing MVR links with "progressive" capitalists and brought in financial support for the movement from major Venezuelan and transnational economic groups (Ellner, 2005:181). But Miquilena and several other prominent leaders defected to the opposition in 2002, on the eve of the abortive coup, reflecting a shifting correlation of political forces in favor of a "hard line," or elements more inclined to facilitate a deeper transformation of the country's property structure and reconstitution of the political system.

Just as opposition attempts at destabilization—the abortive coup, employee lockouts and strikes, the recall referendum, etc.—had the effect of furthering popular class mobilization and politicization, this self-same mobilization by the popular classes, whether to defend the revolution from its elite opponents or to advance popular class interests, placed pressure to force an ongoing radicalization on the *Chavista* leadership. This is the case, for instance, with worker takeovers of private enterprises abandoned, de-capitalized, or sabotaged by employers, which forced the government to provide state support for an emerging area of workers collective property. It was the poor who streamed down by the thousands during the April 2002 abortive coup from the shantytowns that ring the capital that forced the coup makers to return Chávez to the Miraflores presidential palace just 48 hours after they had removed him. Similarly, peasants have forced the government in a number of instances to back their takeover of lands. Such mobilizations among workers and peasants were common as well in other Latin American revolutionary experiences, such as in Chile (1970–1973) and Nicaragua (1979–1990). They point to an expanding class struggle in Venezuela and to a progressively deepening of the popular class content of the Bolivarian revolution.

"Chávez continues to be popular among non-privileged sectors because his symbolically integrative discourse cultivates an extraordinary sense of belonging," observes Landers. I would concur with Landers on the basis of observations during my own extended visits to Venezuela between 2004 and 2007: "There has been, however, much more than what has been disqualified as a 'merely' symbolic integrating effect. For a large number of the underprivileged, new historical levels of participation and organization have been achieved and, perhaps more significant, a diffuse process of cultural decolonization appears to be taking place among them. The extensive mobilizing and organizing experiences, as well as the significant cultural and political transformations involving the excluded majority of the population, are by far the most significant changes in Venezuelan society during the past four years" (Lander, 2005:33–34).

The cultural transformation among the poor majority augured well for a deepening of political consciousness necessary to allow socioeconomic transformations to occur democratically. Those transformations in the first eight years of the revolution were considerable and include included agrarian reform, the nationalization—or more accurately, re-nationalization after earlier privatizations—of key economic sectors and enterprises, widespread social programs, and an active foreign policy that challenges international economic structures and U.S.–transnational domination. Universal health care is official state policy. Primary schools provide three free meals a day to all students, drawing some million new students to school. *Misiones* (missions and government projects) were extending vital social services like literacy training, food subsidies and rudimentary health care to the poor. Indigenous Venezuelans, homosexuals and women came to enjoy protection in the constitution. Operation *Milagro* (miracle), a joint venture with Cuban doctors, restored eyesight to thousands of blind people in the country. Squatters were granted property rights through an urban deeds program implemented under pressure from urban land committees organized by the poor. There has also been a movement to form cooperatives, both urban and rural, the establishment of local Public Planning Councils, and a national network of community radio stations.

Popular sectors have engaged in a frenzied mobilization since the late 1990s. In early 2002 millions of people, encouraged by the Chávez leadership, began to form "Bolivarian Circles," which were small, self-organized committees within neighborhood and workplace communities; the committees consist of seven to eleven persons committed to defending and carrying out the programs of the Revolution (Ramirez, 2005; Collins, 2005). Their activities ranged from informal forums for political discussion, evaluation, and criticism of the revolutionary project, to assisting people in accessing credit and social services, encouraging the formation of cooperatives, resolving housing problems, pressuring for public accountability from state agencies, and so forth. The Bolivarian Circles also provided leadership of repeated mass mobilizations against elite opposition attempts to undermine the revolution. Following the 2004 referendum, the "Electoral Battle Units" (UBE) that the *Chavistas* had organized for the vote began to convert into "Endogenous Battle Units" to tackle ongoing problems of communities and economic development. They appeared to be organs of popular power that act as counterparts to state programs and policies.

Noteworthy here are a series of crash programs introduced by the Chávez government in 2003 that bypasses the entrenched—and still corrupt—state bureaucracy. These programs, known as Misiones (Missions), many named after national icons, take up some 20 percent of the state's budget (Collins, 2005:390). Mision Robinson, for example, aimed to provide everyone in the country with a basic education. (By 2005 some 1.5 million people had received basic literacy training and Venezuela was preparing to become the second country on the continent, after Cuba, to have eradicated illiteracy.) Mision Ribas prepares high school students to enter universities. Mision Sucre provides university education free of charge. Mision Barrio Adentro brings basic health care and specialized health services to poor and even middle-class neighborhoods. (In 2005, some 30,000 Cuban doctors, dentists, and other health workers helped run clinics in rural villages and urban barrios, while the government trained 40,000 Venezuelan doctors and medical personnel to eventually take over the medical program.)

Mision Vuelvan Caras ("about face") aimed to stimulate grassroots economic development and job growth through what has been called in Venezuela's new popular parlance "endogenous development." This refers to an economic strategy of localized, inward-oriented, and integrative economic activity by self-organized communities that draws on local and national resources, alongside (and apparently subordinated to) trade-related activities, along the lines of what, years earlier, Samir Amin, termed "autocentric accumulation" (Amin, 1977). Clearly an alternative economic model to neoliberalism—in Venezuela and elsewhere—would have to emphasize such a community-centered integrative and self-sustaining economics. Could urban and rural cooperatives, worker-run enterprises, merchants from the informal sector, state enterprises, and peasants covered by the land reform coalesce into an economic bloc of popular enterprises as the kernel of an alternative economy?

One set of transformations was strictly redistributive, a redistribution of resources toward the poor majority through social programs. But as the revolution advanced another set began to challenge directly the fundamental structure of property and production relations. The pace and scope of socioeconomic and political transformations heightened in the period after the failed April 2002 coup, which seems to have radicalized the process, that now came to constitute a more open challenge to elite interests: not only to the neoliberal model but more broadly to the domination of transnational capital and to the logic of global capitalism. There was increasing discussion about nationalizing those industries not being used properly, being sabotaged, or producing below capacity. As peasant communities became restive they mobilized around the country to demand that the land reform laws be implemented more quickly and to protest landlord-organized repression, including paramilitary units that carried out selective assassinations against peasant leaders and even several massacres (Jorquera, 2005:89). By the end of 1994, 2.2 million hectares (5.5 million acres) of land had been distributed to 116,000 families organized in cooperatives.

In December 2002 an oil industry stoppage was organized by the peak business association, the Venezuelan Business Council (Fedecámaras), with the support of the conservative (and U.S.-funded) Confederation of Venezuelan Workers (CTV). A majority of workers did not support the business strike and remained at their posts; some took over factories and workplaces. Following the stoppage, workers and Chavistas formed the National Workers Union (UNT).

The UNT was able to mobilize over a million workers to its May Day 2005 rally while the CTV was barely able to muster a few thousand to its own activity, a sign of the radicalization of the working class and the decline of the old business unionism that had emerged during the Punto Fijo regimes. In late 2005 a law drafted by the UNT was put before the National Assembly on worker co-management in enterprises.

Popular sectors also organized into numerous local and regional organizations, including community associations, students, women's, cultural, Christian base groups, new trade unions, peasant associations, and so forth. As many visitors to Venezuela have observed—I myself made four visits between 2004 and 2007—there has been a rapid process of politicization and self-organization among the poor majority. The anti-neoliberal discourse of the leadership is outpaced by the increasingly revolutionary discourse of popular grassroots sectors that are developing an expanding class-consciousness. Popular sectors, while they may support Chávez and his government, are by no means blindly subservient to the president and have often come out against *Chavista* leaders and state officials. The image of an omnipotent Chávez crafting policy is misleading because it denies the remarkable agency of the poor majority, who are well organized. It is their belligerence that buoys Chávez at the helm of the state and their protagonism that has pushed the process forward. The flourishing grassroots social movements, moreover, predate the Chávez era, with genealogies in the diverse mass, trade union, and guerrilla struggles of the Punto Fijo era. Rural and urban activists, indigenous and Afro-descendant groups, environmentalists, trade unionists and others have taken the initiative repeatedly in protesting against aspects of government policies that go against their interests.

Most would agree that, at least up until 2006, the Bolivarian revolution had managed to avoid state authoritarianism, thanks, in large part, to the ongoing, autonomous mobilization of popular sectors, but also, I would suggest, as a result of the disputed nature of the state and of the Chávez presidency's own efforts to avoid bureaucratism and forge direct ties with popular sectors. *Chavismo* has opened up a remarkable space for mobilization from below. Despite claims by Chávez' opponents it does not seem to be the case that there is an authoritarian one-man rule. Personalistic accounts of the Venezuelan revolution are simplistic (see, e.g., Ramirez, 2005). Chávez is genuinely popular among the poor majority and some sectors of the middle classes, and is as well immensely popular throughout Latin America. Historical processes of social change are the product not of individuals but of collective social forces. These forces throw up individuals whose personal attributes—charisma, brilliance, and foresight—are activated by historical conjunctures. Moreover, as I will discuss in the next section, the discourse critical of Chávez is somewhat contradictory.

A Twenty-First-Century Socialism?

It is clear that intense class struggle is breaking out everywhere. Popular classes in civil society constitute a beehive of organizing and mobilizing. So too are counterrevolutionary right-wing forces, which have, nonetheless, steadily lost initiative. Venezuela may well be in a pre-revolutionary stage still. In its first eight years the revolution was able to reform the political system and pass a new constitution that lays the juridical base for a new society, to break with U.S. domination, recover oil revenues and begin a process of transforming property relations and a new economic model linked to a regional/transnational program of integration and cooperation. A deepening of these developments would entail a more dramatic recreation of the state and the transformation of the means and relations of production.

Chávez himself began to speak ever more openly of a socialist transformation. "It is necessary to socialize the economy, the productive model, to create a truly new model that privileges work over capital and emphasizes social property," he declared in 2006, "that generates new production relations and orients the forces of production to satisfy the necessities of the people" (Chávez, 2006:5). The major turning point—a radicalization—then came in early 2007, following his landslide reelection. Chávez first announced at the January 2005 World Social Forum meeting in Brazil, and then reiterated this goal on May First of that year—that is, on International Workers Day—that the Bolivarian revolution would construct a "twenty-first-century socialism." "It is not possible that we will achieve our goals with capitalism, nor is it possible to find an intermediate path," stated Chávez. "I invite all of Venezuela to march on the path of socialism of the new century. We must construct a new socialism in the 21st century" (Wilpert, 2005). Then after Chávez won the December 2006 presidential elections with nearly 63 percent of the popular vote he announced in a series of speeches in early 2007 that "a new stage in the Bolivarian socialist revolution has begun. The period between 1998 and 2006 was a period of transition. Now begins the stage of building Bolivarian socialism" (Chávez, 2007a:67).

Among the measures Chávez announced were an end to Central Bank autonomy—as we saw earlier in this book the concession of autonomy to Central Banks in Latin America during the neoliberal era has been a key mechanism facilitating transnational state control over internal macroeconomic levers—and the nationalization of the country's telecommunications and electrical systems (which were in any case re-nationalizations as they had been privatized in the early 1990s). As part of a broader plan to "recover strategic means of production as social property," Chávez also called for what would amount to a revolution within the revolution—an opening up of all branches of the state to "popular power" from below and to mechanisms that would permit a "social comptroller" role over state and public institutions by the grassroots. He called for a "war to the death" against corruption and bureaucracy, practices that were "counter-revolutionary currents within the revolution" (Chávez, 2007a:67, 69), and he declared five key pillars that would determine the future of the socialist project in Venezuela.

The first of these pillars was what Chávez called the "mother of all revolutionary laws," or a law allowing the presidency to pass certain measures by decree over an eighteen-month period. "If the [earlier revolutionary] laws impacted on the economic and social scheme of the country, these laws will have a much greater impact on the economic situation of the country, which will include the nationalization of strategic layers of security, sovereignty, and defense" (Chávez, 2007a:68–69). The second was the socialist reform of the constitution. Third was a mass extension of a popular educational system to raise the levels of knowledge, consciousness, and ideological development of the population and to "demolish the old values of capitalism and individualism" (ibid.:70). The fourth and fifth pillars were to be "a new geometry of power on the national map" and a "revolutionary explosion of people's power, of communal power" from below (ibid.). Chávez envisioned a deepening of the role of the Communal Councils and their conglomeration locally, regionally, and nationally into a sort of alternative power structure from below, a Paris Commune on a national scale:

> We must move toward the formation of a communal state and progressively dismantle the old bourgeois state that is still alive and kicking as we put into place the communal state, the socialist state, the Bolivarian state; a state with the ability to steer the revolution. Almost all states came into existence to hold back revolutions, so this is our challenge: to convert the old counterrevolutionary state into a revolutionary state. (Chávez, 2007a:72)

Here we arrive at the marrow of struggle among contending social forces in Venezuela and the contradictions of the Bolivarian process points to broader quandaries for popular alternatives to global capitalism in the twenty-first century. As the struggle for hegemony in global civil society heats up the matter of the state, including national states and the transnational institutions and forums through which they are connected, cannot be avoided. In Venezuela the elite definitively lost its hegemony in civil society. While popular forces managed to grab hold of the capitalist state in the form of the presidency, however, that state remained a bastion of the elite and a major point of penetration by the agents and supporters of a global capitalist order. Such a situation of disunity between civil and political society was not stable. Either, on one hand, the old order would be able to contain the agency of the popular majority and frustrate a socialist transformation of property relations, power structures, culture, values, and ideology through a stranglehold over state institutions and the bourgeois ideological production it would make possible; or, on the other hand, the popular classes and their agents and leaders would have to match hegemony in civil society with the destruction of bourgeois state power and the creation of new forms of revolutionary state power and ideological production. Chávez himself emphasized the connection between the state and the ideological and cultural struggle between the old order not yet dead and the new one trying to be born:

> We have to dismantle the system of privileges. The old customs of capitalism, of the bourgeois capitalist state, are truly obscene. Each one of us must become a motor for bringing down the old bourgeois customs incrusted in the state, in society, in institutions. . . . No matter how many political, economic, and social changes we make, if we are not able to demolish the old customs, the obnoxious class distinctions, the obscene privileges, if we are unable to do this and to generate a new culture of equality, solidarity, and brotherhood, then everything will have been a waste of time. (2007b:2–3)

In late 2006 Chávez called for the formation of a United Venezuelan Socialist Party, or PUSV in its Spanish acronym. The MVR was by 2006 a mass party, with over a million members (Jorquera, 2005:84), and it was the main political force in the pro-revolutionary camp, which involved an alliance of several Left political organizations, including the Venezuelan Communist Party, *Podemos*, and *Patria Para Todos* (PPT, or Homeland for All). Yet neither the MVR nor its allied parties were a statist party: that is, parties fused with state structures. Such a fusion seemed impossible since the state in Venezuela remained a battleground of contending social and political forces, even if under the hegemony of Chávez and the *Chavistas*, especially after the abortive 2002 coup.

The *Chavistas* continuously channeled popular mobilization into electoral contests. "The key to harnessing an electoral process to a revolutionary process in Venezuela was the organic linkage of electoral mobilization with other forms of social class mobilization," observes Hellinger. "Chávez has yet to solve the problem of institutionalizing the relationship between the popular democratic forces that formed in defense of his presidency and the Movimiento Quinta Republica, the *Chavista* party. The participation of the former is needed to prevent *Chavismo* from degenerating into familiar forms of clientelism and populism, but a party is needed to organize Chavista forces on the electoral battlefield" (2005:9). As Max Weber observed, charismatic authority cannot sustain itself indefinitely without creating new institutional arrangements.

The new party would be "a political instrument in the service not of particular interests or banners," according to Chávez, "but of the people and the revolution, of socialism" (Chávez, 2006:11). Chávez announced that his own MVR was to be dissolved and called on the other parties of the revolutionary coalition to do the same:

> Why a party and not a political front? We are beginning a new era in our revolutionary process and need the broadest possible unity in our ranks. If it is true that a political front involves the unity of several political parties around a common program, these parties nonetheless conserve their structures, organizational autonomy, and lines of authority. Let's not forget the experience of Chile. The Popular Unity government was a political front and, while the enemies of the process united to attack it, the contradictions among the distinct parties of that political coalition, the different lines that each one followed even within the same ministry in accordance with the political banner that each served under, seriously weakened the government of President Allende. (Chávez, 2006:11–12)

Some criticized Chávez for the top-down approach in announcing the formation of the PUSV. "Rather than calling for a broad and democratic debate on one of the most important and potentially most polemical aspects of constructing a socialism for the twenty-first century," argued Lander, in cautioning against the Soviet party-state and other failed socialist party models of the twentieth century, Chávez simply "announced that he had decided it was necessary to form a single party among the forces that support the process" (Lander, 2006:2). Chávez, however, criticized the old Soviet model as inappropriate for the Bolivarian revolution:

Some socialist parties copied the experience of the Bolshevik party model because of its relative success at the birth of the Soviet revolution," said Chávez. "However, that party ended as an anti-democratic party and that marvelous slogan, 'All Power to the Soviets,' ended in 'All Power to the Party,' and you can see what happened 70 years afterwards." Karl Marx, argued Chávez, proposed a dictatorship of the proletariat, "but that is not viable for Venezuela in this epoch and will not be the road we go down. Our project is essentially democratic. We are speaking of popular democracy, participatory democracy, 'protagonic' democracy." (Chávez, 2006:32–34)

Some on the Left inside and outside Venezuela, while supportive, criticize Chávez as authoritarian and charge him with cultivating personal rule. The prominent Venezuelan intellectual Margarita López Maya, for instance, has accused Chávez of a "desire to be the one who is essential to the process" and "to perpetuate himself in power" (Rosen, F., 2007). She observes, for example, that in early 2007 Chávez requested of the legislature, and was granted, special powers ("enabling laws") to legislate in eleven areas over a year and a half, bypassing deliberations in the parliament and other formal representative institutions, and that he also attempted to remove limits to his indefinite reelection. These criticisms cannot be dismissed. An authoritarianism of the left, cults of personality, and usurpation from above of popular power from below in the name of subordinate class interests, remain just as much a danger to transformative projects in the twenty-first century as they were in the twentieth century. Yet the discourse critical of Chávez is somewhat contradictory. López Maya acknowledges that "Chávez has successfully mobilized the poor and excluded to fight for first-class citizenship, and among the great majority of Venezuelans, who have never been able to participate in politics and society, many now feel like full citizens" (Rosen, F., 2007). Yet she is troubled by the measures that have moved the country and the popular classes beyond the limits of polyarchic institutions which have historically excluded or co-opted the poor majority.

Popular mobilizations, López Maya observed in early 2007, "have created very conflictive processes, and the country is now experiencing a very powerful polarization. Over the past few months it has tended to deepen as Chávez has proposed a new break with the past, essentially the destruction of the very state he himself brought into being with the Constitution of 1999" (Rosen, F, 2007:5). This, it seems to me, is the crux of the matter. Polarization is less a consequence of Chávez' authoritarianism than an objective and inevitable outcome of the attempt to effect a revolutionary rupture with the old order. The target of Chávez' authoritarianism is not the popular majority but the corrupt and cronyist state of the *ancien régime* and its parasitic bureaucracy through which Chávez came to power: a state he was barely able to modify during his first few years. If there is a strong personal link between Chávez and the masses, it may be explained less by Chávez' desire to cultivate personal rule than by an indication of the historic failure of the institutional Left in Venezuela and the chasm that exists between it and the popular majority.

Smash or Colonize the Capitalist State?

If the Venezuelan revolution's formal democratic legitimacy is impeccable this also presents it with a paradox. The state tended to act through the polyarchic process as a demobilizing and depoliticizing force by institutionally absorbing mass pressure from below. This capacity to institutionally absorb pressure on the social order from subordinate groups is, after all, one of the strengths of the polyarchic system. It is likely the popular sectors that achieved a foothold in the state would have to confront that state on a much more profound level as the process deepens. How such a confrontation will play out—and if it will result in the "smashing" of state institutions, their reconstitution through "colonization" by popular forces, or a combination of both—is not clear. Or will the transnational forces (including elites inside Venezuela) opposed to revolutionary transformation in Venezuela and the old state machinery warp the process into a populist or reformist outcome?

As popular sectors mobilized from below have become concientized and politicized, they confront resistance from this state and its institutions that act to constrain, dilute, institutionalize, and co-opt mass struggles and to reproduce the old order. In opposition to the bankrupt polyarchy of the Punto Fijo era, Chávez has referred to a new participatory or "protagonist" democracy under construction in Venezuela. "Mere representative democracy in Latin America has failed," observed Chávez in 2000:

> If dictatorships do not work for us . . . neither do representative democracies that end up converting themselves into dictatorships based not on a tyrant but on a cabal that governs in a dictatorial manner in the name of democracy. In order to overcome this, it is necessary to promote—and in Venezuela we are doing just this—a democracy that ceases being representative, although it preserves levels of representation, but is one that promotes participation, and that moves toward [popular] decision-making. This process will take years, but we have already begun it—democracy with a popular essence. (cited in Lander, 2005:31)

Can the *consejos comunales* as grassroots organs of popular power take the political system beyond polyarchy? Some of the councils are clearly subordinate to state directives; others are not. Community leaders I met with spoke of the struggle to convert these local councils into autonomous organs of community power that exercise power from below upwards toward state and party institutions, to avoid having these local organs appropriated ("kidnapped/*secuestrado*") from above. They complained that the "process" is moving too slowly, that the "transition" is taking too long. They are keenly aware of the danger of usurpation from bureaucratic and elite forces from above—that it is a danger just as serious as the counterrevolutionary efforts of the old elite and their international allies. The slogan among local activists in the barrios was "no queremos ser gobierno pero queremos gobernar" (we don't want to be the government, but we want to govern [from below]). Community leaders also sought to put into practice Chávez' call for *controlaria popular* (popular comptroller functions)—mechanisms that would allow community councils to prevail over the state's own local structures (the mayorships, local governing councils, juntas parroquiales, consejales).

The model emerging in Venezuela may be one in which social movements play a major role in critical support for the government and participation in the revolutionary process while retaining autonomy from the state and from political parties. What is unfolding in Venezuela is distinct from the old Soviet-statist model, in which political domination emanates vertically from the state downward, the means of production are nationalized and bureaucratically administered, and there is no autonomous space of the working classes. The Venezuelan state is corrupt, bureaucratic, clientalist, and even inert; this was the state inherited from the ancien regime, or the "fourth Republic" as the republic that emerged from the Punto Fijo pact is known in Venezuela. The civil service bureaucracy and old elites remained in control of much of the state. The model defies both traditional socialist models and anarchist-autonomist ideas influential in the global justice movement.

The process in Venezuela raises much larger questions: how do popular sectors push forward social change—or in the case of Venezuela, revolution—without a revolutionary state? This is the challenge in Latin America, and more generally of social change in the age of globalization: how can those who come to power through elections move beyond the constraints of polyarchy and transnationalized capitalist states? Political parties seeking power through the formal institutions of polyarchy have tended to degenerate into internal factional struggles seeking electoral quotas of power—and then to compromise popular interests in name of pragmatism and the need to win votes—when they are not subordinated to social movements and processes. Electoralism converts the winning of votes and elected positions into an end rather than a means for the ends of social transformation and popular empowerment.

Venezuela may be the epicenter of the continental popular ferment. The hegemony of the transnational elite in Venezuela was being displaced by an expanding popular hegemony operating in both political (the Venezuelan state) and civil society. A primordial question is the extent to which a new popular hegemonic bloc could congeal in the region beyond Venezuelan borders. Might such a bloc spread through wars of position—expanding counter-hegemonic influence in civil society—or through wars of maneuver, that is, struggles for control of states? Most likely the battle for hegemony in Latin America will continue to be waged through combinations of both.

Change Society without State Power?

The Venezuelan problematic of revolution and socialism within a capitalist state underscores broader quandaries for popular alternatives to global capitalism in the twenty-first century. As the struggle for hegemony in global civil society heats up the issue of state power and what to do about it, including national states and the transnational institutions and forums through which they are connected with one another, cannot be avoided. Holloway, in *Changing the World without Taking Power* (2005), elevates to theoretical status the Zapatistas' decision not to bid for state power (see below). As long as neoliberalism reigned supreme and the neoliberal states remained impenetrable fortresses the refusal to deal with state power appeared reasonable. The neoliberal national state is not a space for engaging in politics; it is an apparatus for the technocratic administration of transnational capital accumulation, infrastructure, and social control.

Neither Horizontalism nor Verticalism

The claim that social relations can be transformed from civil society alone appears as the inverse of the old vanguardist model in which social and political forces mobilize through political organizations in order to overthrow the existing state, take power, and from the state transform society. That verticalist model, pursued by much of the Latin American Left in the 1960s and 1970s, often through armed struggles, has been recognized by most as a failure and as a dead-end in the new century.

As we saw, the indigenous and other social movements in Latin America, in distinction to the old vertical models, have spearheaded a new model of horizontal networking and organizational relations in a grassroots democratic processes from the bottom up. But at some point popular movements must work out how the vertical and horizontal intersect. A "long march" through civil society may be essential to transform social relations, construct counter-hegemony from the ground up and assure popular control from below. Yet no emancipation is possible without an alternative project, and no such project is possible without addressing the matter of the power of dominant groups, the organization of that power in the state (including coercive power), and the concomitant need to disempower dominant groups by seizing the state from them, dismantling it, and constructing alternative institutions.

The current round of social and political struggle in Latin America highlights the changing relation between social movements of the Left, political parties, the state, and global capitalism. This in turn raises the issue of political organizations that can mediate vertical links between political and civil society, that is, interface between the popular forces on the one hand and state structures on the other? How can internally democratic political instruments be developed to operate at the level of political society and dispute state power without diluting the autonomous mobilization of social movements? The potential for transformation will depend on the combination of independent pressure of mass social movements from below on the state and also on the representatives and allies of those movements taking over the state. The issue is how to assure that political organizations are internally democratic. How can they serve as instruments of social movements and popular class mobilization and not the reverse?

The limitations of strict horizontalism have become evident in Mexico in recent years with regard to the Zapatistas, for whom horizontalism becomes a rigid principle rather than a general emancipatory practice, or in Argentina with regard to the autonomist movement. The Zapatista model generated hope and inspiration for millions throughout Latin America and the world in the 1990s. The January 1, 1994, uprising was an urgent and refreshing response to the capitulation by many on the Left to the "TINA" ("there is no alternative") syndrome: the assertion that there was simply no alternative to the new global capitalist order. The Zapatistas insisted on a new of set non-hierarchal practices within their revolutionary movement and within the communities under their influence, including absolute equality between men and women, collective leadership, and taking directives from, rather than giving them to, the grassroots base, leading by following and listening, and so on. Such non-hierarchal practices must be at the very core of any emancipatory project. Yet they also hold strong appeal to the anarchist currents that have spread among radical forces worldwide in the wake of the collapse of "actually existing socialism" and the old statist-vanguardist Left, and that are unwilling to deal with the wider political system and the state. These currents have a strong influence in the global justice movement and the World Social Forum, as well as among radicalized youth and middle classes in Mexico who provide a base for the Zapatistas beyond Chiapas.

But Zapatismo has not been able to draw in a mass working-class base, and as a result it has experienced a declining political influence in Mexican society. It was still in 2007 a force of counter-hegemony or even of hegemony in some communities inside Chiapas, but the fact is that global capitalism made major headway within Chiapas itself between 1994 and 2007 as the Zapatista movement has stagnated. This conundrum came to a head with the Zapatistas' refusal as a matter of principle to engage with the campaign that the PRD and Manuel López Obrador waged for the presidency in the 2006 elections. As a result the Zapatistas were ill prepared to throw their weight behind the mass struggles against the fraud perpetrated by the Mexican state and its two ruling parties, the PRI and the PAN. If it is true, as the Zapatistas observe, that there is no blueprint for revolution, then it is also true that revolutionaries need to be able to shift strategies and tactics as history actually unfolds.

In Argentina, the late 2001 uprising marked the beginning of a popular rebellion of workers, the unemployed and the poor, along with newly dispossessed sectors of the middle class. In the wake of the rebellion popular sectors created hundreds—perhaps thousands—of neighborhood assemblies, workers occupied and took over hundreds of factories, and the unemployed stepped up their mobilization through *piquetero* and other forms of grassroots struggle. Horizontalist thought makes much of the fact that the rebellion erupted without leadership or hierarchy, and that political parties and elites played no role in the movement (Sitrin, 2006). Nonetheless, in the ensuing years the occupied factories have not been able to present even a remote alternative to the domination of transnational capital over the economy and the country's ever-deeper integration into global capitalism, especially through the soy agro-industrial-financial complex, while assemblies and *piqueteros* have become divided in the face of expanding clientalist networks and co-optation by the state and Kirchner's Peronist faction. It is quite true, as the Argentine autonomists point out, that political parties are bankrupt and corrupt and that local and global elites control the state ("Que se vayan todos!" or "Get rid of them all!" was the popular rallying cry). Yet the *autonomist* movement, with its strict horizontalism, has come no closer to challenging this structure of elite power nor has it been able to hold back the onslaught of global capitalism.

To dismiss political organizations and the state because they are, or can easily become, instruments of hierarchy, control, and oppression is to emasculate the ability of the popular classes and their social movements and mass organizations to transform the institutions of power and to mount a systemic challenge to the social order. Without some political hammer or political vehicle the popular classes cannot operate effectively vis-à-vis political society or synchronize the forces necessary for a radical transformatory process. As the case of Venezuela, and perhaps Bolivia and Ecuador as well, demonstrate, popular forces and classes must win state power and utilize it to transform production relations and the larger social, political, and cultural relations of domination, yet they must do so without subordinating their own autonomy and collective agency to that state. A confrontation with the global capitalist system beyond the nation-state, moreover, requires national state power.

The Ecuadorian and Bolivian experiences are illustrative. Neither the indigenous in Ecuador nor in Bolivia followed the Zapatista example. They did not opt to stay in the highlands and the Amazonian region and forego a frontal struggle against the state. Indigenous and popular sectors in Ecuador, led by the powerful Confederation of Indigenous Nationalities of Ecuador (CONAIE), sustained a virtual permanent mass mobilization against neoliberalism (and for indigenous rights) since the 1990s. On three separate occasions they brought down neoliberal governments between 1997 and 2005. The mass movement had no problem ridding itself of governments that did not meet popular interests, as Luis Macas, CONAIE co-founder, explained to me in 2003. Yet each time these governments were removed they were replaced with yet another neoliberal government whose policies were equally unaccountable to these sectors. This predicament was due, in part, to the lack of a political vehicle that could serve the popular sectors as a mechanism for exercising some form of institutional control over the state beyond oppositional agitation from within civil society. As a result, the CONAIE established a political arm, Pachakutik, in 2002. "We do not only want a plurinational state within in bourgeois state," stated Macas. "It has to be a total transformation, a social and economic transformation."

But events overtook the fledgling Pachakutik. As protests once again escalated the following year the movement placed its bets on an alliance with Lucío

Gutiérrez, an army colonel who promised an alternative to neoliberalism while participating in the popular overthrow of the neoliberal government of Jamil Mahuad. When Gutiérrez betrayed the popular movement and delivered the country to global capitalism, CONAIE lost considerable credibility among its mass base. In the October 2006 elections the indigenous forces faced a dilemma. Should they support another candidate and risk getting burned? Should they put forward an indigenous candidate along the Bolivian model? In the end CONAIE put forward its own candidate in the 2005 vote but supported Correa in a second round of voting. When Correa took office the mass movement provided him with critical support while jealously preserving its own autonomous mobilization and mobilizing to pressure the government to comply with its anti-neoliberal and popular agenda. Similarly, in Bolivia the indigenous and popular movement threw out several neoliberal regimes and in 2005 put Morales in power while continuing to mobilize in an autonomous manner, both against the elite and the right, and to pressure the Morales government.

The Brazilian experience under "Lula" and the Workers Party underscores the importance of continued mass mobilization from below as a countervailing force to such transnational power from above. It also highlights the structural power that transnational capital and its agents are able to leverage over national states even when forces initially in opposition to the global capitalist program come to power. The Workers Party (PT) grew out of the militant labor movement and popular struggles against the military dictatorship in the 1970s and 1980s and enjoyed a close relationship with the country's once-powerful social movements, among them the MST. Prior to its 2002 election, the PT campaigned on an anti-neoliberal platform and called for a major redistribution of land, expanded social programs, in part by redirecting funds earmarked for debt repayment, and popular democracy.

But as I noted earlier, in the lead up to the election that brought the PT to office Lula and his team turned to allaying the fears of global capital markets that there would be any threats to the prevailing property regime or withdrawal from the country's commitment to international creditors. Once elected, Lula appointed a team of neoliberal technocrats to run his economic policy. Instead of postponing debt payments his government adopted a strategy of paying off the country's dollar-linked debt through restrictive and fiscal monetary policies, to the approval of transnational bankers. It also prioritized an expansion of exports over the internal market—exports went from comprising 10.7 percent of GDP prior to the PT government to 18 percent in 2004 (Kirksey, 2006)—legalized genetically modified crops, pushed forward the privatization of state-owned industries, and expanded the presence of low-wage factory zones. In a word, it pursued a policy of deeper integration into global capitalism and on the terms dictated by global capitalism. Brazil remains one of the most unequal countries in the world, ravaged by poverty and brutal violence. Río de Janeiro averages 4,000 murders per year in the face of uncontrolled police and gang violence (Kirksey, 2006). Notwithstanding the introduction of some popular social programs, such as *Zero Fome* and *Bolsa Familiar,* poverty, inequality, and landlessness actually increased during the Lula years (Kirksey, 2006). In any event, these programs, and similar social subsidies of this nature in other pink tide areas tend to weaken autonomous mobilization from below by depoliticizing the question of poverty, turning inequality into an administrative problem, and creating a support base for the state independent of unions and social movements. They generate client—and therefore vertical—relations between "social" ministries and the masses of the poor who become less inclined to mobilize while leaders tapped for low-level jobs in these programs become paternalistic administrators rather than organizers. A November 2003 survey of business elites in Latin America found Lula to be the "best President" in Latin America over the second choice, Chilean President Ricardo Lagos by a wide margin of 39 to 20 percent (Harnecker, 2005:154).

What happened here? The PT took state power largely in the absence of a mass autonomous mobilization from below so that the popular classes could not exert the mass pressure to control the PT government, to force it to confront global capital and implement a popular program. The MST, for example, expecting that the new government would represent its interests, declared a moratorium on new land invasions and went into recess during the early years of the Lula presidency. By the time it reactivated militant struggle the PT government had become deeply exposed to, and co-opted by, transnational capital (Kenfield, 2007). "With the PT's arrival in government Lula's charisma acted as a powerful anesthetic," observes De Oliveira (2006), "bringing about the immediate paralysis of virtually all the social movements." In Uruguay, similarly, many social movements demobilized following the inauguration of the Frente Amplio government of Tabaré Vásquez . The Brazilian and Uruguayan experiences show that, even when revolutionary groups take state power—absent the countervailing force from popular classes below to oblige those groups to respond to their interests from the heights of the state—the structural power of global capital can impose itself on direct state power and impose its project of global capitalism. In other words, global class struggle "passes through" the national state in this way. This lack of mass mobilization to generate popular pressure from below meant that the dominant groups could absorb the challenge to their interests represented by a PT or Frente Amplio government. These parties become administrative apparatuses absorbed into the TNS as local political superintendents of global capital. They did not colonize the state; the (transnational) state colonized them. Counter-posing Brazil and Uruguay to Venezuela, Leftists who came to power in Venezuela faced similar pressures from the global system to moderate structural change. Yet in Venezuela unlike Brazil mass mobilization from below placed pressure on revolutionaries in the state not to succumb to the structural pressures of global capital but rather to carry out a process of social transformation. This is an ongoing process in which the forces of global capital and those of popular majorities are constantly in struggle over the state and its policies.

If the neoliberal national state is not a space for engaging in politics it is necessary to open new political spaces that allow popular forces to challenge elites in that state. What is the possibility of reconstituting national states? How can the popular classes assure the continued accumulation of their autonomous power and at the same time seek to capture local state machineries and transform them into instruments responsive to their interests? How can they undermine the neoliberal national states and challenge the TNS without falling into a resistance grounded in mere rebellion rather than in a coherent and viable alternative project? This means creating imageries and projects that take the popular classes beyond their disruptive powers. Greater webs of interdependence mean greater disruptive powers. Popular forces need to develop constructive power as well, to go beyond the restraining influence of rules in activating both disruptive and constructive powers. The objective potential for popular power has actually increased in the globalization epoch. There is a new wider basis for inter-subjectivities that have been fragmented at the national level by globalization and for a re-territorialization of space in new ways. New spaces are not necessarily transnational spaces. However, popular forces that operate in these new local, national, and regional spaces must link with transnational chains and networks, and moreover, are increasingly empowered to do so by the very nature and dynamics of capitalist globalization.

The challenge, hence, is how to convert a *reactive* global resistance into a *proactive* global program. For poor majorities a resolution to the crisis requires a radical redistribution of wealth and power, predicated on the construction of more authentic democratic structures that allow for popular control over local and TNS institutions. The transformative possibilities that have opened up in Latin America cannot be realized without an organized Left and a democratic socialist program. Yet such possibilities will only end up frustrated by the old vanguardist model of top-down change by command and the military fetishism of the 1960s and 1970s that converted armed struggle from the means to an end into an end itself. No where is this more evident than in the "military hypertrophy" of the Colombian Armed Revolutionary Forces (FARC), which sees independent political mobilization as a threat to its own efforts to hegemonize resistance (Hylton, 2006). The transformative moment of the early twenty-first century in Latin America will depend on the Left's ability to learn the lessons of the previous era of revolution, especially the need to relinquish vanguardism of party and state and to encourage, respect, and subordinate itself to the autonomous mobilization from below of the popular classes and subordinate sectors.

Popular and progressive resistance competes with the spread of reactionary resistance to global capitalism, ranging from religious fundamentalisms to racist and xenophobic right-wing populisms, which may well gain influence if a popular project is unable to cohere. Moreover, we must not conflate neoliberalism with global capitalism. Precisely because the neoliberal phase of global capitalism is coming to a close, resistance must move beyond the critique of neoliberalism. The problem of the particular neoliberal model is in the end symptomatic of the *systemic* problem of global capitalism. If it can be said that the "Washington consensus" had cracked by the turn-of-century then what may replace neoliberalism in Latin America and in global society depends not only on the struggle to *oppose* the neoliberal order but also on the struggle to develop a viable alternative and to *impose* that alternative.

From National to Transnational Projects

As we have seen throughout this book, they new cycle of capitalist expansion is based on a model of accumulation that exhibited increasing structural and social contradictions. Varying degrees of ungovernability and crises of legitimacy characterize country after country in Latin America and in many parts of global society as the dominant groups find it increasingly difficult to maintain governability and assure social reproduction. The crisis and eventual collapse of neoliberalism may create the conditions favorable to winning state power and promoting an alternative. National alternatives, however, are increasing ineffective in transforming social structures, given the ability of transnational capital to utilize its structural power to impose its project even over states that are captured by forces adverse to that project. "Revolution in one country" is certainly even less viable in the twenty-first century than it proved to be in the twentieth century. National economies have been reorganized and functionally integrated as component elements of a new global capitalist economy. Peoples everywhere have experienced heightened dependencies for their very social reproduction on the larger global system.

The objective limitations of projects of popular transformations at the level of the nation-state are apparent in Cuba. Despite the inevitable (and some not so inevitable) problems the Cuban revolution has faced in its half century of existence Cuban society is perhaps the most egalitarian in the hemisphere and certainly one of the most developed in terms of quality of life indicators. Cuba's efforts to transition from a capitalist to a revolutionary socialist society ran up squarely against the limits—nay, the corrosive influence—of global capitalism in the 1990s and on. With no choice but to integrate into world capitalist markets the Cuban government attempted to create a sort of dual economy: one capitalist, linked to the global economy and driven by the law of value; the other socialist, internal, driven by a social logic. Thus it promoted the tourist industry, created a parallel dollar economy where those with access to foreign exchange could purchase scarce goods and services, relaxed controls on private money-making undertakings, and allowed, even encouraged, an expanding informal economy driven by local exchange values.

In theory these measures were innocuous, in the interests of popular majorities, perhaps necessary or even inevitable. The problem is that such reforms were not enacted in the abstract but in the real world of global capitalism and its penetration via these reforms into the structures of Cuban society and the fabric of social and cultural life. Cuba's integration into global capitalism meant growing social inequalities. Those who had access to the capitalist sector, whether in tourist jobs or other forms of association with foreign capital, dollar remittances from family members abroad, the ability to set up a small business, and so forth, inevitably acquired more resources and social privilege over those restricted to the socialist sector. There is gravitation toward the capitalist sector, which could only be suppressed by authoritarian means. It was not possible to insulate the socialist from the capitalist sector. Moreover, those who acquire such privileges form a potential social base for a political opposition to the revolution. Expanding social inequalities combined with the increased availability of scarce goods, luxury items, and conspicuous consumption fuel relative deprivation and social tensions. There were other pernicious influences, such as a renewed racialization process (see Chapter 3), the reappearance of prostitution, largely servicing tourists and other foreign visitors, and corruption. The distorting influence of the law of value or capitalist logic over a system organized along a non-market social logic generated such absurd paradoxes as doctors working as hotel waiters, university professors driving taxis, and engineers running family kitchens.

The Cuban experience underscores the catch-22 that all efforts to challenge global capitalism must address: in an age when "de-linking" or withdrawal from the system is not a viable option, how is transformation from within managed in such a way as to not reproduce the very social and political forces that reproduce global capitalism? How to supersede a system from which one cannot yet de-link, does not control, and cannot confront in its entirety? How to build a democratic socialism in the midst of a global capitalist milieu from which there is no flight? If the (capitalist) state as a class relation is becoming transnationalized then any challenge to (global) capitalist state power must involve a major transnational component. Struggles at the nation-state level are far from futile. They remain central to the prospects for social justice and progressive social change. The key point is that any such struggles must be part of a more expansive transnational counter-hegemonic project, including transnational trade unionism, transnational social movements, transnational political organizations, and so on—able to link the local to the national, the regional, and the global. And they must strive to establish sets of transnational institutions and practices that can place controls on global market and rein in some of power of global capital. This is why permanent mobilization from below that pressures the state to deepen its transformative project "at home" and its counter-hegemonic transnational project "abroad" is so crucial.

Efforts to reform the global order, however, can only be successful when linked to the transformation of class and property relations in specific sets of countries. The formation of the South American Community of Nations under Brazilian leadership in 2003 and the proposal that same year by Lula and his Argentine counterpart, Kirchner, for the "Buenos Aires Consensus" to move forward have been touted by some among the Latin American Left as a step toward a progressive regional challenge to global capitalism. But it is not clear that the CSN or the Buenos Aires Consensus is anything more—at best—than an alternative and perhaps mildly reformist path for regional integration into global capitalism. A regional program that attempts to harness market forces for more regionally balanced accumulation and limited redistribution would be an improvement over the rigid neoliberal model vis-à-vis the interests of popular classes but is hardly a counter-hegemonic alternative to capitalist globalization. Such an alternative would have to be founded on a more fundamental shift in class power at the national and regional levels in Latin America, and would have to involve a transformation of property and production relations beyond limited social redistribution in the phase of surplus circulation. Local class and property relations have global implications. Webs of interdependence and causal sequences in social change link global to local so that change at either level is dependent on change at other level. The struggle for social justice—the hope of humanity—lies in my view with a measure of transnational social governance over the process of global production and reproduction, the first step in effecting a radical redistribution of wealth and power to poor majorities.

To take the example of Venezuela, the oil and financial system is thoroughly integrated into global capitalism. Venezuelan oil is sent to the global capitalist market, and the country's reproduction passes through the global financial system—and it does so inextricably. This means that global capitalism exercises a certain structural power expressed in local political influence. Global capital has local representation everywhere and translates into local pressure within each state in favor of global capital. Those groups most closely tied to global capital—transnationally oriented business groups and state managers, aspiring high-consumption sectors—seek to accumulate enough internal leverage with which to quash a more radical transformative project. Indeed, in Venezuela, the greatest threat to the revolution is not from the right-wing political opposition but that parts of the revolutionary bloc will develop a deeper stake in defending global capitalism over socialist transformation, that state managers will become bureaucratized as their own reproduction will depend on deepening relations with global capital.

In Venezuela's popular parlance, "endogenous development" refers to an economic strategy of localized, inward-oriented, and integrative economic activity by self-organized communities that draws on local and national resources, alongside (and apparently subordinated to) trade-related activities, along the lines of what, years earlier, Samir Amin termed "autocentric accumulation." Clearly an alternative economic model to neoliberalism—in Venezuela and elsewhere—would have to emphasize such a community-centered integrative and self-sustaining economic orientation. Yet the Chavista leadership has also proposed not a withdrawal from international trade and economic integration but an alternative transnational development project: the Bolivarian Alternative for the Americas, known by its Spanish acronym, ALBA. Indeed, the debate about socialism in Venezuela seemed to be centered on the question of how to build a popular economy that can also trade in the international area. The ALBA envisions a regional economic development plan for Latin America and the Caribbean involving solidarity with the weakest national economies so that all can cooperate and benefit from regional exchange networks and development projects. As part of this plan, the Venezuelan government introduced a Compensatory Fund for Structural Convergence that includes subsidized Venezuelan oil and financing. The idea is to transnationalize efforts at "endogenous development." The ALBA rejects the notion of intellectual property rights and rejects any trade agreements that would undermine the use of public policies to regulate the economy and redistribute wealth.

Fundamental change in a social order becomes possible when an organic crisis occurs. An organic crisis is one in which the system faces a structural (objective) crisis and *also* a crisis of legitimacy or hegemony (subjective). An organic crisis is not enough to bring about fundamental, progressive change in a social order (indeed, it has in the past led to social breakdown, authoritarianism, and fascism). A popular or revolutionary outcome to an organic crisis also requires that there be a viable alternative that is in hegemonic ascendance: that is, an alternative to the existing order that is viable and that is seen as viable and preferable by a majority of society. Global capitalism was not experiencing an organic crisis in the early twenty-first century. Nonetheless, I believe the prospects that such a crisis could develop were more palpably on the horizon at the turn of the century than at any time since perhaps 1968. Seen from the viewpoint of capital, neoliberalism resolved a series of problems in the accumulation process that had built up in the epoch of Keynesian capitalism but fueled new crises of over-accumulation and legitimacy. The model is not sustainable socially or politically. Its coming demise may well turn out to be the end of Act I and the opening of Act II in the restructuring crisis that began in the 1970s. As in all historic processes, this act is unscripted.

Barbarism, Socialism, and Alternative Futures

We are living a moment of systemic chaos. The contradictions of global capitalism are indeed explosive. The most salient form of conflict in the global age will not be among nation-states. The crisis of the global system will take the form of escalating transnational social conflicts between popular sectors engaged in diverse forms of resistance—whether spontaneous or organized—and diverse representatives and institutions of the global capitalist elite and the transnational state. Relative deprivation takes place within and between nations. At a time of the communications revolution, the Internet, and the global economy people in every corner of the world experience relative deprivation as the global poor discover how global rich and middle classes consume and live. One of the intractable contradictions of global capitalism is its need, on the one hand, to promote consumerist ideology and culture, including an inundation of advertising that reaches the most remote corners of the globe, and its inability, on the other, to bring about a level of consumption among the majority of the world's people that would satisfy even their most basic needs, much less the urges induced by consumerism.

The crisis has led to a dizzying process of social decomposition as traditional mechanisms of social integration break down in the face of exclusion, segregation, and fragmentation, especially in the teeming cities of global society, that is, the vast global slums (Davis, 2006). The threat represented by the "dangerous classes"—with deeply racist overtones—came to occupy a central place in the global corporate media, fed by cultural and ideological campaigns by dominant groups and the fears of middle classes. The poverty and exclusion that in an earlier period were seen as temporary phenomena pending "development" or "modernization" now came to be seen as permanent features of global society, and the victims of global capitalism were painted as the undeserving, responsible for their own condition. Pedrazzini and Magaly Sanchez (1992) have described a "culture of urgency"—a practical culture of action, in which the informal economy, illegality, illegitimacy, violence, and mistrust of official society are common. This is a useful but simplistic characterization that negates the same culture of urgency that inflicts the dominant classes and middle sectors, who forsake social solidarity for egotistical gratification and denial through social and spatial apartheid and the conversion of those below into diverse Others.

A, or perhaps *the,* paramount concern for dominant classes and privileged layers becomes how to defend property and privilege from threats by the wretched mass of those people who are immiserated. How to contain the excluded population? How to keep the lid on spontaneous and potentially destabilizing protest against the depredations of global capitalism? How to deflect organized resistance? How to ensure that popular or oppositional forces do not capture local states and attempt a withdrawal from the system? The "politics of exclusion" (Hoogvelt, 1997) takes over. Global polarization brings with it increasing residential segregation of the rich, protected by armies of private security guards and electronic surveillance, from the cities of Latin America to those of the United States, Europe, Asia, and elsewhere. There is a shift from the social welfare state to the social control (police) state, replete with the dramatic expansion of public and private security forces, the mass incarceration of the excluded population (disproportionately minorities) [see, inter alia, Winslow,

1999; Chambliss, 2001], new forms of social apartheid maintained through complex social control technologies, repressive anti-immigration and anti-terrorism legislation, and so on. As crime waves have swept Latin American cities, police response has been brutal and, note Hoffman and Centeno (2003), closely correlates with income. In 1992 the São Paulo police killed 1,470 civilians compared with 25 civilians killed by the Los Angeles police department (Hoffman and Centeno, 2003:368). In 1991 violence was the leading cause of death in the adult population in the working-class neighborhoods of Buenos Aires, accounting for more than 30 percent of all mortalities (ibid.). There has been an explosive growth of private security forces in many Latin American countries. Portes and Hoffman report that there are three times as many private security guards in São Paulo as there are policemen, and that the total private expenditure in security in Guatemala is estimated to exceed by 20 percent the public security budget (2003:67).

The upper and middle classes of global society dream of a world in which they will journey joyfully toward global citizenship and First World abundance while preserving the allegiance of the poor and excluded majority whose consent—or at least passivity—is required for the legitimacy and stability of such a world. Should that consent or passivity not be forthcoming—and that is precisely what is happening in the early twenty-first century—then there can be nothing legitimate, nothing stable, nothing peaceful. Where, then, is humanity headed? What solutions might there be to the crisis of the system and the perils that it represents for humanity, from never-ending wars, to mass immiseration and ecological holocaust? In broad strokes, I can envision four alternative futures:

I. GLOBAL REFORMISM BASED ON GLOBAL KEYNESIANISM

Social justice requires, at the minimum, reintroducing a redistributive component into the global accumulation process. What would such a new redistributive component involve, and how would it come about? Certainly it would require a reversal of neoliberal policies at the nation-state level. Achieving social justice requires a state power willing to change the course of public policies. But what configuration of social and political forces could bring about a distributive project at the global level? Already in the late 1990s defectors from the ranks of the transnational elite such as former World Bank Vice President Joseph Stiglitz began to call for neo-Keynesianism or institutionalist measures on a global level that could offset polarizing tendencies, rein in financial chaos, and bring a measure of regulation to the global economy (Robinson, 2004a). Will this left wing (reformist as opposed to conservative and neoliberal) of the transnational elite converge with the right wing (reformist as opposed to radical) of the global justice movement to push for such a program? The pink tide in Latin America would surely constitute a regional component of such a global reformist bloc. A global New Deal is the option considered by many to be the most realistic and pragmatic and would surely be more preferable than the current neoliberal and new war order. But I am hard pressed to disagree with Regalado when he asserts, "History shows that the progressive reform of capitalism has only prospered in those places and at those moments when it was compatible with the process of capital accumulation," and "this compatibility does not exist today, either in Latin America or in any other region of the world" (2007:229).

There is at present no global political authority with an enforcement capacity that could impose a regulatory and redistributive regime on the global economy. In any event, it is hard to see how, in the absence of changes in actual class and property relations, proposals put forward among reformist forces such as a general rise in Third World commodity prices would actually result in a downward redistribution of wealth that could offset polarization and provide a broader demand base for the global economy. A relative shift in prices in favor of commodities, given the current transnational corporate control over the global agricultural and raw materials systems, would only result in a redistribution of profits and rents among fractions of global capital. Similarly, no matter how genuine the reformist call for "fair trade" and "market access" it is difficult to imagine truly *fair* trade—meaning a more equitable exchange of values—under the prevailing global *production relations*. We would have to see a change in class and property relations and in the social and political content of local states, such as what is taking place in Venezuela, for such reform measures in global market relations to ameliorate the global crisis, which is why I asserted above that local class and property relations have global implications. Moreover, it is not clear if a mere reform of global capitalism could avert an ecological holocaust.

2. GLOBAL FASCISM BASED ON A NEW WAR ORDER

The outlines of a twenty-first-century neofascism seemed to be congealing in the years of the Bush presidency in the United States and more generally as an ascendant tendency in global society. A descent into barbarism, driven by military spending, multiple forms of repression, and wars to contain the downtrodden, to seize new territories, resources, and labor pools, and to maintain social control has already begun. What makes this particularly frightening is that we could imagine a global fascism not necessarily incompatible with an economic program involving a redistributive component. Could a neofascist project that moves in this direction organize enough support to put in place a hegemonic bloc? Some of the tell-tale signs of such a neofascist project are the fusion of transnational capital with reactionary political power, a mass base among economically insecure and socially disaffected sectors animated by a fanatical ideology, in this case Christian fundamentalism and race and culture supremacy embracing an idealized and mythical past, and a racist mobilization, especially, in the case of the United States and France, among other countries, against immigrants as the new racialized scapegoats.

A twenty-first century neofascism would not be a repetition of its twentieth-century predecessor. The role of political and ideological domination through control over media and the flow of images and symbols would make any such project more sophisticated and—together with new panoptical surveillance and social control technologies—probably allow it to rely more on selective than generalized repression. Stan Goff (2006), a retired twenty-six-year veteran of the U.S. Army Special Forces, observes in a chilling analysis of the "seeds of fascism in America" that many of the historical precursors of fascism—white supremacy, militarization of culture, vigilantism, masculine fear of female power, xenophobia, economic destabilization, and concomitant social anxiety among a privileged strata of the working class—were ascendant in the United States in the early twenty-first century. This fusion of militarization and extreme masculinization—what Goff calls "martial masculinity"—has invaded the sphere of mass culture. An increasingly fascistic pop culture combines this celebration of militarization and masculinity with fantasy, mysticism, and irrationality, as epitomized in the mass appeal of extremely violent computer games, the proliferation of reality TV shows, and the glorification of military aggression, social violence, and domination in mainstream Hollywood cinema.

"Social cleansing" or doing away through repression with those most marginalized from and superfluous to the new social order—street children, the homeless—takes many different forms, including the conversion of natural disasters such as Hurricane Katrina that destroyed the city of New Orleans in 2005 into opportunities for dominant groups to reorganize space in function of spatial control. In Latin America, the twenty-first-century neofascist alternative seemed to be unfolding in Colombia and threatens ascendancy in El Salvador, and perhaps Mexico, among other countries. Those targeted by state repression and death squads are now as much the most marginalized and superfluous as they are political dissidents and social movement and working-class leaders. It seemed as the new century progressed that security forces in Latin America no longer even felt the need to hide their war against the poor and the marginalized. The mayor of São Paulo, José Serra, launched in 2006 "Operation Cleansing," which involved the forcible removal of homeless residents from poor inner city *favelas* to make way for urban development (Kirksey, 2006). The police in Brazil's major cities have long practiced unofficial *faxinas*, or such social cleansing operationsas vigilante operations and death squad raids, to relieve the streets of "undesirables."

As dominant groups in Latin America feel power slip from their hand they are likely to turn with more frequency to violent methods in defense of their interests. These groups' resistance to change is likely to take increasingly extra-institutional forms especially in those cases where the threat they face, beyond redistributive reform, involves property relations. Recent anti-terrorism laws have been passed in most Latin American countries that criminalize social protest, such as in El Salvador, where terrorism is defined by such legislation as "any pressure on authorities to make certain decisions" (COMPA, 2007). In the Venezuelan countryside and in Bolivia's eastern region landlords have already organized armed paramilitary squads that have clashed with peasants demanding agrarian reform. We cannot rule out military intervention and new coup d'états in countries such as Bolivia and Ecuador. In Colombia, upward to four million people have been violently uprooted from the countryside by state security forces and right-wing paramilitary armies to make way for transnational agribusiness and mining concerns, while it has been disclosed that such TNCs as Coca Cola, Chiquita Brands International, and several U.S.-based mining companies have regularly hired the paramilitary armies to block unionization and eliminate dissent among their workers (Hylton, 2006).

3. GLOBAL ANTI-CAPITALIST ALTERNATIVE—A DEMOCRATIC SOCIALIST PROJECT

What configuration of social and political forces could bring about a post-capitalist global order? It is an irony that the crisis of global capitalism has followed in the wake of the crisis and collapse of the Left in most countries around the world and the discrediting, until recently, of socialist ideology. In Latin America a twenty-first-century neofascist project is taking place in Colombia while right next door, in Venezuela, a twenty-first-century socialist project is under way. A socialist alternative is not at odds with a struggle for global reformism, and in fact such an alternative would most likely snowball out of efforts to bring about a reform of the system, such as we may be seeing in

Venezuela, and perhaps even in Bolivia and Ecuador. What is crucial is for popular, radical, and socialist-oriented forces in the global justice movement to put forward an alternative vision that goes beyond reformism and to have such a vision achieve hegemony within any counter-hegemonic bloc to global capitalism. Redistributive reform, it is worth reiterating, is not viable without structural changes that move a counter-hegemonic bloc from challenging the "fairness" of the market to replacing the *logic of the market* with a *social logic.*

A democratic socialist alternative would require a renewal of critical and radical thinking along with a capacity to operate as much on the cultural and ideological as on the political terrain. More than ever before, political and economic processes are globalized, as Levine (2005) observes, to the extent that they are "culturized." Global accumulation is increasingly reliant on symbolic and cultural exchanges that make possible the rapid circulation of commodities. But that alternative also requires renovated political vehicles that provide the popular classes in civil society with instruments for invading state structures. Moreover, no matter how unpopular with post-modernists, a global transformative project requires, as Boswell and Chase-Dunn argue, a new universalism. The axis of an ant-capitalist and universalist struggle must be the new global working class, with its rainbow and heavily female face, one that is transnationally organized. I am convinced that if there can be no socialism without democracy in the twenty-first century it is equally true that democracy is not possible without socialism. A democratic socialism founded on a popular democracy is in my view the only real alternative to disaster—to collective suicide.

4. COLLAPSE OF GLOBAL CIVILIZATION—A NEW DARK AGES

Will there be a predatory degeneration of civilization if neither forces from above nor those from below are able to bring about a resolution of crises and conflicts? Are we already seeing this? There are many historical precedents in which a civilization collapses when it is unable to resolve its internal contradictions. Chew has written extensively on recurrent "dark ages" in human history: that is, periods when particular civilizations have reached ecological exhaustion as a result of or resulting in chronic social and military conflict that makes impossible systemic change that could avert collapse. Such periods have been characterized by the collapse of centralized authority, a sharp regression in social organization and the forces of production, the death of many, and a drastic reduction in population levels (see, inter alia, Chew 2007). What makes such a prospect in our particular historical times most frightening is that a civilizational collapse would now be global, encompassing all of humanity, and the level of ecological destruction involved suggests there may be no easy recovery, if indeed, any would be possible. Images of Hurricane Katrina and its aftermath, of a global *Blade Runner* society, to evoke the dystopian imagery of the 1982 Ridley Scott film, or more recently of the 2006 film *Children of Men,* written and directed by Alfonso Cuaron, come to mind.

The possibility of such an outcome is terrifying. But we would be foolish to dismiss it as a possibility rather than to take such prospects as a dire warning for collective action against those social, political, and ideological forces that prevent a change, to use William Greider's phrase (1997), in the "manic logic of global capitalism." I am reminded of Žižek's chilling observation that "the true horror [of global capitalism] does not reside in the particular content hidden beneath the universality of global Capital, but rather in the fact that Capital is effectively an anonymous global machine blindly running its course, that there is effectively no particular Secret Agent who animates it" (1997:45). This implies, however, that even if their command over resources allows them to exercise a disproportionate influence over outcomes, ruling groups and the powerful do not actually control their own—or collective outcomes. The future is not predetermined; we are all its collective agents. As frightening as the current course of events may seem, we should also recall that the crisis opens up tremendous new possibilities for progressive change. It is at times of crisis rather than stability and equilibrium in a system that the power of collective agencies to influence history is most felt.

Whatever humanity's future, we should keep our eyes on Latin America, as it will surely play a vital role in what is to come.

Adams, Richard, H. 2006. "Remittances, Poverty, and Investment in Guatemala." In Caglar Ozden and Maurice Schiff (eds.), *International Migration, Remittances, and the Brain Drain*. Washington, DC, and New York: World Bank and Palgrave Macmillan, pp. 53–80.

Agencia France Presse (AFP). 2007. "Mexican Tycoon Passes Bill Gates as Planet's Richest Person." Dispatch datelined July 4, accessed on July 6, 2007, at http://news.yahoo .com/s/afp/20070704/ts_afp.liefstulemexico_0707.

Agency for International Development (AID). 1991. *Economic Assistance Strategy for Central America: 1990 to 2000*. Washington, DC: AID.

———. 1994. *Harvest of Progress: A Quiet Revolution in Latin America and Caribbean Agriculture*. Washington, DC: AID.

Aglietta, Michel. 1979. *A Theory of Capitalist Regulation*. London: Verso.

AIDEnvironment. 2005. *Soy Production in South America*. Amsterdam: AIDEnvironment: Partners in Development and Environment. Accessed at www.aidenvironment.org/ soy/03_factsheet_soy_aug05.pdf on March 1, 2006.

Alcala Iberri, Maria del S. 2004. *Las Muertas de Juarez*. San Diego: Libra.

Altenburg, Tilman, and Jorg Meyer-Stamer. 1999. "How to Promote Clusters: Policy Experiences from Latin America." *World Development* 27(9):1693–1713.

Amin, Ash, ed. 1994. *Post-Fordism: A Reader*. London: Blackwell.

Amin, Samir. 1977. *Unequal Development: An Essay on the Social Formations of Peripheral Capitalism*. New York: Monthly Review Press.

Appelbaum, Richard, and William I. Robinson. 2005. *Critical Globalization Studies*. New York: Routledge.

Arrighi, Giovanni. 1994. *The Long Twentieth Century*. London: Verso.

———. 1996. "Workers of the World at Century's End." *Review* 19(3):348.

Arrighi, Giovanni, and Beverly J. Silver. 1999. *Chaos and Governance in the Modern World System*. Minneapolis and London: University of Minnesota Press.

Austin, Amanda A. 1996. "Guatemala Expects Tourist Boom." *Hotel and Motel Management* 21(20):8.

AVANCSO. 1994. *Apostando al Futuro Con los Cultivos No Tradicionales de Exportacion*, vol. 1. Guatemala: AVANCSO.

Bacon, David. 1999. "INS Declares War on Labor." *The Nation*, October 25, 1999, accessed at www.thenation.com/doc/19991025/bacon on October 10, 2006.

———. 2006. "Mexican Workers Want a Recount." *San Francisco Chronicle*, July 17, 2006, accessed at www.sfgate.com/cgi-bin/article.cgi?f=/c/a/2006/07/17/EDGOBIPTNB1 .DTL& on November 30, 2006.

Baer, Werner. 1972. "Import Substitution and Industrialization in Latin America." *Latin American Research Review* 7(1):95–122.

Balch, Oliver. 2006. "Seeds of Dispute." *The Guardian*, February 22, 2006, Internet edition, accessed at www.guardian.co.uk/argentina/story/0,1715330,00.html on February 27, 2006.

Balussa, Bela. 1981. *The Newly Industrialized Countries in the World Economy*. New York: Pergamon.

———. 1989. *Comparative Advantage, Trade Policy and Economic Development*. London: Harvester Wheatsheaf.

Baran, Paul, and Paul Sweezy. 1966. *Monopoly Capital*. New York: Monthly Review Press.

Barham, Bradford, Mary Clark, Elizabeth Katz, and Rachel Schurman. 1992. "Nontraditional Agricultural Exports in Latin America." *Latin America Research Review* 27(2):43–82.

Barker, Kathleen, and Kathleen Christensen, eds. 1998. *Contingent Work: American Employment Relations in Transition*. Ithaca: Cornell University Press.

Barkin, David, Irene Ortiz, and Fred Rosen. 1997. "Globalization and Resistance: The Remaking of Mexico." *NACLA Report on the Americas* 30(4):14–27.

Barnet, Richard, and John Cavanagh. 1994. *Global Dreams: Imperial Corporations and the New World Order*. New York: Simon and Schuster.

Barrera Pérez, Oscar. 1998. "Tourismo y Globalization: Un Reto para Nicaragua." *Encuentro* 30(7):46–53.

Barrientos, Stephanie. 1997. "The Hidden Ingredient: Female Labor in Chilean Fruit Exports." *Bulletin of Latin American Research* 16(1):71–81.

Barry, Tom. 1999. *Inside Guatemala*. Albuquerque: The Resource Center.

Bartu, A. 1999. "Redefining the Public Sphere through Fortified Enclaves: A View from Istanbul." Istanbul: WALD International Conference.

Basch, Linda, Nina Glick Schiller, and Cristina Szanton Blanc. 1994. *Nations Unbound: Transnational Projects, Postcolonial Predicaments, and De-territorialized Nation-States*. New York: Gordon and Breach.

Bee, Anna. 2000. "Globalization, Grapes and Gender: Women's Work in Traditional and Agro-Export Production in Northern Chile." *Geographic Journal* 166(3):255–265.

Bee, Anna, and Isabel Vogel. 1997. "*Temporaras* and Household Relations: Seasonal Employment in Chile's Agro-Export Sector." *Bulletin of Latin American Research* 16(1):83–95.

Bello, Walden. 2006a. "Micro Credit, Macro Problems." *Focus on the Global South* 124(October) (monthly electronic bulletin of Bangkok-based Focus on the Global South), accessed at www.focusweb.org.

———. 2006b. "The Rise of the Relief-and-Reconstruction Complex." *Journal of International Affairs* 59(2):281–296.

Bewería, Lourdes, and Shelly Feldman, eds. 1992. *Unequal Burden: Economic Crises, Persistent Poverty, and Women's Work*. Boulder: Westview.

Berberoglu, Berch, ed. 2002. *Labor and Capital in the Age of Globalization*. Lanham, MD: Rowman and Littlefield.

Beveridge Report (full title: *Social Insurance and Allied Services*). 1942. As summarized in an executive summary posted at www.fordham.edu/halsall/mod/1942beveridge.html by Internet Modern History Sourcebook, accessed at www.fordham.edu/halsall/mod/modsbook.html on September 25, 2005.

Binford, Leigh. 2005. "A Generation of Migrants: Where They Leave, Where They End Up." *NACLA Report on the Americas* 39(1):31–37.

Bisang, Roberto. 2003. "Difussion [*sic*] Process in Networks: The Case of Transgenic Soybean in Argentina" *Globelics*, November (published proceedings of Conferencia Internacional Sobre Sistemas de Inovacao E Estrategias de Desenvolvimento para o Terceiro Milenio), accessed at www.probio.ungs.edu.ar/sub/Papers/Bisang,%20R.%20(2003)2.pdf on February 27, 2006.

Blackstock, Sarah. 1999. "Bandaid Bandwagon." *New Internationalist* 314 (July):23.

Blakely, Edward J., and Snyder, Mary G. 1997. *Fortress America: Gated Communities in the United States*. Washington, DC: Brookings, and Cambridge, MA: Lincoln Institute of Land Policy.

Bonnano, Alessandro, Lawrence Busch, William Friedland, Lourdes Gouveia, and Enzo Mingione, eds. 1994. *From Columbus to ConAgra: The Globalization of Agriculture and Food*. Lawrence: University Press of Kansas.

Borocz, Jozsef. 1996. *Leisure Migration: A Sociological Study on Tourism*. Oxford: Pergamon.

Bose, Sukanya. 2005. "Banking FDI in Latin America: An Economic Coup." *International Development Economics Association (IDEAS)*, accessed at www.networkideas.org/focus/mar2005/fo21_Banking_FDI.htm on June 25, 2005.

Bourdreaux, Richard. 2006. "The New Foreign Aid: The Seeds of Promise." *Los Angeles Times* (April 14):1A.

———. 2006. "The New Foreign Aid: The Seeds of Promise." *Los Angeles Times* (April 16):A1, A12–15.

Bowles, Samuel, David M. Gordon, and Thomas E. Weisskopf. 1990. *After the Waste Land*. Armonk, NY: M.E. Sharpe.

Braga, Helson C. 2002. "Prospects for Free Trade Zones under FTAA." Paper presented at Integration in the Americas Conference, Latin American Institute, University of New Mexico, Albuquerque, April 2, accessed at http://laii.unm.edu/conference/braga.php on March 6, 2006.

Braga, Ruy. 2007. "Information Work and the Proletarian Condition Today: The Perception of Brazilian Call Center Operators." *Societies without Borders* 2(1):27–48.

Brandt, Don. 2003. *Maquilas throughout the Americas: Economic Development or Human Rights Nightmare?* New York: World Vision International.

Brennan, Denise. 2002. "Selling Sex for Visas: Sex Tourism as a Stepping Stone to International Migration." In Barbara Ehrenreich and Arlie Russell Hochschild (eds.), *Global Woman: Nannies, Maids, and Sex Workers in the New Global Economy*. New York: Henry Holt, pp. 154–168.

Brenner, Robert. 2002. *The Boom and the Bubble*. London: Verso.

Briody, Dan. 2003. *The Iron Triangle: Inside the Secret World of the Carlyle Group*. New York: John Wiley and Sons.

Britton, S. 1982. "The Political Economy of Tourism in the Third World." *Annals of Tourism Research* 9:331–358.

Broad, Robin, and Richard Cavanagh. 2003. "The Death of the Washington Consensus?" In Broad (ed.), *Global Backlash: Citizen Initiatives for a Just World Economy*. Lanham, MD: Rowman and Littlefield.

Brockett, Charles, D. 1998, 2nd edition. *Land, Power, and Poverty: Agrarian Transformation and Political Conflict in Central America*. Boulder: Westview.

Bronstein, Arturo, S. 1997. "Labor Law Reform in Latin America: Between State Protection and Flexibility." *International Labor Review* 136(1):5–26.

Bruton, Henry J. 1998. "Reflections on Import Substitution Industrialization." *Journal of Economic Literature* 36:903–936.

Brysk, Alison. 2000. *From Tribal Village to Global Village: Indian Rights and International Relations in Latin America*. Stanford: Stanford University Press.

Bull, Benedicte. 2004. "Business Regionalization and the Complex Transnationalization of the Latin American States." Working Paper No. 2004/02. Oslo: Center for Development and the Environment, University of Oslo.

———. 2005. *Aid, Power, and Privatization: The Politics of Telecommunication Reform in Central America*. Cheltenham, UK, and Northampton, MA: Edward Elgar.

Bulmer-Thomas, Victor, ed. 1996. *The New Economic Model in Latin America and Its Impact on Income Distribution and Poverty*. New York: St. Martin's Press.

———, ed. 2001. *Regional Integration in Latin America and the Caribbean: The Political Economy of Open Regionalism*. London: Institute of Latin American Studies, University of London.

Business Week. 2004. "Made in the *Maquilas* Again." August 16 on-line issue, www.businessweek.com/magazine/content/04_33/b3896079.

Carletto, Calogero, Alain de Janvry, and Elisabeth Sadoulet. 1999. "Sustainability in the Diffusion of Innovations: Smallholder Nontraditional Agro-Exports in Guatemala," *Economic Development and Cultural Change* 47(2):345–369

Carroll, William K., and Colin Caron. 2003. "The Network of Global Corporations and Elite Policy Groups: A Structure for Transnational Capitalist Class Formation?" *Global Networks* (3)1:29–57.

Carroll, William K., and Meindert Fennema. 2002. "Is there a Transnational Business Community?" *International Sociology* 17(3):393–419.

Carter, Michael R. 1997. "Intellectual Openings and Policy Closures: Disequilibria in Contemporary Development Economics." In Frederick Cooper and Randall Packard (eds.), *International Development and the Social Sciences: Essays on the History and Politics of Knowledge*. Berkeley: University of California Press, pp. 119–149.

Castañeda, Jorge. G. 2006. "Latin America's Left Turn." *Foreign Affairs* (May/June).

Castells, Manuel. 2000, 2nd edition. *The Rise of the Network Society*, vol. 1. Oxford: Blackwell.

Castells, Manuel, and Alejandro Portes, eds. 1989. *The Informal Economy: Studies in Advanced and Less Developed Countries*. Baltimore: Johns Hopkins University Press.

Castillo, Manuel Angel. 1996. "Migration, Development and Peace in Central America." In Alan B. Simmons (ed.), *International Migration, Refugee Flows and Human Rights in North America: The Impact of Free Trade and Restructuring*. New York: Center for Migration Studies, pp. 137–155.

Castles, Stephen, and Mark J. Miller. 2003, 3rd edition. *The Age of Migration: International Population Movements in the Modern World*. New York: Guilford Press.

Centeno, Miguel A. 1994. *Democracy within Reason: Technocratic Revolution in Mexico*. University Park: Pennsylvania State University Press.

———. 2003. "The Lopsided Continent: Inequality in Latin America." *Annual Review of Sociology* 29:363–390.

Centeno, Miguel A., and Patricio Silva, eds. 1997. *The Politics of Expertise in Latin America*. London: Macmillan.

CEPAL (Comision Economica para America Latina). [various years.] *Panorama Social de America Latina*. Santiago, Chile: CEPAL/United Nations.

———. 1994. *El Regionalismo Abierto en America Latina y el Caribe: la Integracion Economica al Servicio de la Transformacion Productiva con Equidad*. Santiago, Chile: CEPAL.

———. 2000. *Equity, Development, and Citizenship*. Santiago, Chile: United Nations.

Cevallos, Diego. 2005. "Mexico: Wal-Mart's Plans for Indigenous Areas under Fire." *CorpWatch*. 25 August. Accessed at http://corpwatch.org/article.php?id=12589 on October 22, 2005.

Chambliss, William J. 2001. *Power, Politics, and Crime*. Boulder: Westview.

Chávez, Hugo. 2006. *El Discurso de la Unidad*, speech delivered in the Teresa Carreño Theatre on December 15, published and distributed by the Venezuelan Ministry of Communications and Information.

———. 2007a. *Entramos a Una Nueva Era: El Proyecto Nacional Simon Bolivar*, speech on the occasion of the swearing in of the executive cabinet, Caracas, on January 8, published and distributed by the Venezuelan Ministry of Communications and Information.

———. 2007b. *Poder Popular: Alma de la Democracia Revolucionaria*, speech delivered in the Teresa Carreño Theatre in Caracas on January 17, published and distributed by the Venezuelan Ministry of Communications and Information.

Cheru, Fantu. 1989. *The Silent Revolution in Africa: Debt, Development, and Democracy*. London: Zed Books.

Chew, Sing, C. 2007. *The Recurring Dark Ages: Ecological Stress, Climate Changes, and System Transformation*. Lanham, MD: AltaMira Press.

Choski, A. M., and D. Papageorgiou, eds. 1986. *Economic Liberalization in Developing Countries*. Oxford: Blackwell.

Chossudovsky, Michel. 1997. *The Globalization of Poverty: Impacts of IMF and World Bank Reforms*. London: Zed Press.

Cid Aguayo, Beatriz Eugenia. 2006. "Global Villages and Rural Cosmopolitanism: Exploring Global Ruralities." Paper presented at the 101st Annual Meeting of the American Sociological Association, Montreal, August 11–14.

Clairmont, Frederic. 2001. "USA: The Making of the Crisis." *Third World Resurgence* (January–February):46.

Clark, Mary A. 1995. "Nontraditional Export Promotion in Costa Rica: Sustaining Export-Led Growth." *Journal of Inter-American Studies and World Affairs* 37(2): 181–223.

Cohen, Robin. 1988. *The New Helots: Migration in the International Division of Labor*. Avebury: Gower Publishers.

Collins, Joseph, and John Lear. 1995. *Chile's Free Market Miracle: A Second Look*. San Francisco: Food First.

Collins, Sheila D. 2005. "Breaking the Mold: Venezuela's Defiance of the Neoliberal Agenda." *New Political Science* 27(3):367–395.

COMPA (Convergencia de Movimientos de los Pueblos de las Americas). 2007. "La Represion en El Salvador y las Leyes Antiterroristas en el Continente." Press release, accessed at http://movimientos.org/ on July 17, 2007.

Conaghan, Catherine M., and James M. Malloy. 1994. *Unsettling Statecraft: Democracy and Neoliberalism in the Central Andes*. Pittsburgh: University of Pittsburgh Press.

Conroy, Michael E., Douglas L. Murray, and Peter M. Rosset. 1996. *A Cautionary Tale: Failed U.S. Development Policy in Central America*. Boulder: Lynne Rienner.

Corden, Max W. 1982. "Booming Sector and Deindustrialization in a Small Open Economy." *Economic Journal* (Royal Economic Society, York, England) 92:825–848.

Cornia, Giovanni A., and Julius Court. 2001. *Inequality, Growth, and Poverty in the Era of Liberalization and Globalization*. Policy Brief No. 4. Helsinki: United Nations University, World Institute for Development Economics Research.

Cornia, Giovanni, Richard Jelly, and Frances Stewart, eds. *Adjustment with a Human Face*. Oxford: Oxford University Press, 1987.

Cortes, Fernando. 2001. "La Metamorfosis de los Marginales: Discusion sobre el Sector Informal en America Latina." In Viviene Brachet-Marques (ed.), *Entre Polis y Mercado*. Mexico, D.F.: El Colegio de Mexico.

Cox, Robert W. 1979. "Ideologies and the New International Economic Order: Reflections on Some Recent Literature." *International Organization* 33(2):267–302.

———. 1983. "Gramsci, Hegemony and International Relations: An Essay in Method." *Millennium: Journal of International Relations* 12(2):162–175.

———. 1987. *Production, Power, and World Order: Social Forces in the Making of History*. New York: Columbia University Press.

Cravey, J. Altha. 1998. *Women and Work in Mexico's Maquiladoras*. Lanham, MD: Rowman and Littlefield.

Crozier, Michel, Samuel P. Huntington, and Joji Watanuki. 1975. *The Crisis of Democracy: Report on the Governability of Democracies to the Trilateral Commission*. New York: New York University Press.

Dahl, Robert A. 1971. *Polyarchy: Participation and Opposition*. New Haven: Yale University Press.

Damian, Araceli, and Julio Boltvinik. 2006. "A Table to Eat On: The Meaning and Measurement of Poverty in Latin America." In Eric Hershberg and Fred Rosen, *Latin America after Neoliberalism: Turning the Tide of the 21st Century*. New York: New Press, 144–170.

D'Andrea, Guillermo E., Alejandro Stengel, and Anne Goebel-Krstelj. 2004. "Six Truths about Emerging-Market Consumers." *ePhilantrropy eZine* 4(14):1–13, accessed at www.imakenews.com/ephilantrhopy/e_article000240937.cfm on October 25, 2005.

Datamonitor. 2004. Opportunities in Caribbean and Latin American Call Centres Markets to 2007, on-line report, accessed at www.datamonitor.com on April 9, 2007.

Davis, Mike. 1999. *Ecology of Fear: Los Angles and the Imagination of Disaster*. New York: Metropolitan Books.

———. 2006. *Planet of Slums*. London: Verso.

Deere, Carmen Diana. 2005. *The Feminization of Agriculture? Economic Restructuring in Rural Latin America*. Geneva: United Nations Research Institute for Social Development (UNRISD). Policy Report on Gender and Development: 10 Years after Beijing, Paper No. 1.

Deere, Carmen Diana, and Magdalena Leon de Leal. 1979. *Rural Women and State Policy: Feminist Perspectives on Latin American Agricultural Development*. Boulder: Westview.

De la Fuente, Alejandro. 2001a. *A Nation for All: Race, Inequality, and Politics in Twentieth Century Cuba*. Chapel Hill: University of North Carolina Press.

———. 2001b. "The Resurgence of Race in Cuba," *NACLA Report on the Americas* 31(6):29–34.

Del Cit, Nelly, Caria Castro, and Yadira Rodriguez, 1999. "Maquila Workers: A New Breed of Women." *Envío* 18(218):25–31.

Delgado-Wise, Raul, and James M. Cypher. 2005. "The Strategic Role of labor in Mexico's Subordinated Integration into the U.S.: Production System Under NAFTA." Working Paper No. 12/11/2005. Zacatecas, Mexico: Red Internactional de Migracion y Desarrollo/International Network on Migration and Development, Autonomous University of Zacatecas.

Delgado-Wise, Raul, and Oscar Mañan Garcia. 2006. "Migracion Mexico-Estados Unidos: Eslabon Critico de la Integracion." Zacatecas, Mexico: Red Internactional de Migracion y Desarrollo/International Network on Migration and Development, Autonomous University of Zacatecas.

De Oliveira, Francisco. 2006. "Lula in the Labyrinth." *New Left Review* 42.

De Soto, Hernando. 1987. *El Otro Sendero: La Revolucion Informal*. Lima: Instituto Libertad y Democracia.

Devlin, Robert, and Antoni Estevadeordal. 2001. "What's New in the New Regionalism in the Americas? In Bulmer-Thomas (ed.), *Regional Integration in Latin America and the Caribbean*. London: Institute of Latin American Studies, pp. 17–44.

Diamond, Larry, Juan J. Linz, and Seymour Martin Lipset. 1989. *Democracy in Developing Countries: Latin America*. Boulder: Lynne Rienner.

Diamond, Larry, and Mark F. Plattner, eds. 1993. *The Global Resurgence of Democracy*. Baltimore: Johns Hopkins University Press.

Dicken, Peter. 1998, 3rd edition. *Global Shift*. 1998. London and New York: Guilford Press.

———. 2003, 4th edition. *Global Shift*. London and New York: Guilford Press.

Dickerson, Marla. 2005. "Instant Ramen Noodles Are Supplanting Beans and Rice for Many in Mexico." *Los Angeles Times* (October 21):A1.

———. 2006a. "On the Stump, Not the Ballot, in Mexico." *Los Angeles Times* (June 29):A1.

———. 2006b. "Chile Holds Own in Global Market." *Los Angeles Times* (October 14):C1.

Di Martino, Vittorio. 2004. *El Teletrabajo en America Latina y El Caribe*. Geneva: OIT.

Domínguez, Jorge I., ed. 1997. Technopols: Freeing Politics and Markets in Latin America in the 1990s. University Park: Pennsylvania State University Press.

Domínguez, Virginia. 1998. "Asserting (Trans)Nationalism and the Social Conditions of Its Possibility." *Communal/Plural* 6:(2):139–156.

Dros, San Maarten. 2004. *Managing the Soy Boom: Two Scenarios of Soy Production Expansion in South America*. Amsterdam: AIDEnvironment.

Dugger, Celia W. 2004. "Guatemalan: Supermarket Giants Crush Farmers: Survival of the Biggest." *New York Times* (December 28):A1.

Dypski, Michael Cornell. 2002. "The Caribbean Basin Initiative: An Examination of Structural Dependency, Good Neighbor Relations, and American Investment." *Journal of Transnational Law and Policy* 12(1):96–136.

Ecocentral. 1997. "U.S. Efforts to Crack Down on Illegal Immigration Creates Alarm in Central American Countries." 2(9), March 6, Latin America Data Base, Latin American Institute, University of New Mexico, Albuquerque.

Economic Commission for Latin America and the Caribbean (ECLAC). 1983. *Economic Survey of Latin America and the Caribbean*. Santiago, Chile: United Nations.

———. 1998a. *Economic Survey of Latin America and the Caribbean*. Santiago, Chile: United Nations.

———. 1998b. *Social Panorama of Latin America*. Santiago, Chile: United Nations.

———. 1999. *Economic Survey of Latin America and the Caribbean*. Santiago, Chile: United Nations.

———. 2000a. *Economic Survey for Latin America and the Caribbean*, table IV.1, p. 80.

———. 2000b. *Preliminary Overview of the Economies of Latin America and the Caribbean*, table A-18, p. 104. Santiago, Chile: United Nations.

———. 2002. *Preliminary Overview of the Economies of Latin America and the Caribbean*. Santiago, Chile: United Nations.

———. 2004. *Statistical Yearbook for Latin America and the Caribbean*. Santiago, Chile: United Nations.

———. 2005. *Statistical Yearbook for Latin America and the Caribbean*. Santiago: United Nations

———. 2006. *Preliminary Overview of the Economies of Latin America and the Caribbean*. Santiago, Chile: United Nations.

The Economist. 1998a (March 21). "Great Reforms, Nice Growth, but Where Are the Jobs?" pp. 37–38.

———. 1998b (November 14). "The Central Bank as God," pp. 23–25.

———. 1998c (January 10). "A Survey of Tourism," special supplement.

———. 2003 (February 22). "Make or Break: A Survey of Brazil," special section, and pp. 1–16, after p. 54.

Ehrenreich, Barbara, and Arlie Russell Hochschild, eds. 2004. *Global Woman: Nannies, Maids, and Sex Workers in the New Economy*. New York: Owl Books.

Ellner, Steve. 2001. "The Radical Potential of Chavismo in Venezuela," *Latin American Perspectives* 28(5):5–32.

———. 2005. "Revolutionary and Non-Revolutionary Paths to Radical Populism: Directions of the Chavista Movement." *Science and Society* 69(2):160–190.

Ellner, Steve, and Daniel Hellinger, eds. 2003. *Venezuelan Politics in the Chavez Era: Class, Polarization, and Conflict*. Boulder: Lynne Rienner.

Elton, Catherine. 2006. "Remittances: Latin America's Faulty Lifeline." Working Paper. Cambridge, MA: MIT Center for International Studies.

English, E. Philip. 1986. *The Great Escape? An Examination of North-South Tourism*. Ottawa: North-South Institute.

Envío (the editors). 1999. "Mitch, Foreign Debt, Disasters, Emigrants and Remittances in Central America." *Envío* 18(212):46–54.

———. "Is the Game All Sown Up? Questions and Contradictions." *Envío* 18(218):10.

Escoto, Jorge, and Manfredo Marroquin. 1992. *La Aid en Guatemala*. Managua: CRIES.

Espiritu, Yen Le. 2003. *Home Bound: Filipino American Lives Across Cultures, Communities, and Countries*. Berkeley: University of California Press.

Ewing, Walter. 1999. "A New Bracero Program for the 21st Century." *The Washington Report on the Hemisphere* 19(19). Washington, DC: Council on Hemispheric Affairs, on-line edition, accessed at www.coha.org on November 11, 1999.

Fatemi, Khosrow, ed. 1990. *The Maquiladora Industry: Economic Solution or Problem?* New York: Praeger.

Fernández Jilberto, E. Alex, and Barbara Hogenboom. 2004., "Conglomerates and Economic Groups in Neoliberal Latin America." *Journal of Developing Societies* 20(3–4):149–171.

Fernández-Kelly, Maria Patricia. 1983. *For We Are Sold, I and My People: Women and Industry in Mexico's Frontier*. Albany: SUNY Press.

———. 1994. *Political Economy and Gender in Latin America: The Emerging Dilemmas*. Baltimore: Johns Hopkins University, Latin American Program Working Papers, no. 207.

———. 2006. "Introduction." In Fernández-Kelly and Jon Shefner (eds.), *Out of the Shadows*.

Fernández-Kelly, Maria Patricia, and Jon Shefner, eds. 2006. *Out of the Shadows: Political Action and the Informal Economy in Latin America*. University Park: Pennsylvania State University Press.

Figueroa, Hector. 1996. "In the Name of Fashion: Exploitation in the Garment Industry." *NACLA Report on the Americas* 29(4):34–41.

Firebaugh, Glenn. 2003. *The New Geography of Global Income Inequality*. Cambridge: Harvard University Press.

Fishlow, Albert, Carlos F. Diaz-Alejandro, Richard R. Fagen, and Roger D. Hansen. 1978. *Rich and Poor Nations in the World Economy.* New York: McGraw-Hill.

Fitzgerald, Valpy. 1998. Asia's Financial Crisis: What It Can Teach Us. *Envío* 17(200): 33–38.

Folker, Fröbel, Jurgen Heinrichs, and Otto Kreye. 1980 [first published in German in 1977]. *The New International Division of Labour.* Cambridge: Cambridge University Press.

Forest Working Group. 2005. *Relation between Expansion of Soy Plantations and Deforestation.* São Paulo: Friends of the Earth-Brazilian Amazonia.

Foster, John Bellamy. 2006. *Naked Imperialism: U.S. Pursuit of Global Dominance.* New York: Monthly Review.

Frank, Andre Gunder. 1980. *Crisis in the World Economy.* New York: Heinemann.

———. 1981. *Crisis in the Third World.* New York: Heinemann.

Freeman, Alan. 2002. "The New Political Geography of Poverty." Paper presented at the annual international economics conference of the Middle Eastern Technical University, September 11–14, Ankara.

Freeman, Alan, and Boris Kagarlitsky. 2004. *The Politics of Empire: Globalisation in Crisis.* London: Pluto Press.

Freeman, Richard. 2005. "China, India, and the Doubling of the Global Labor Force: Who Pays the Price of Globalization?" *The Globalist* (June 3), posted at *Japan Focus*, August 26, and accessed at www.japanfocus.org/article.asp?id=377 on October 13.

Friedmann, Harriet. 1991. "Changes in the International Division of Labor: Agri-food Complexes and Export Agriculture." In Friedland et al., *Towards a New Political Economy of Agriculture.*

Friedman, Milton. 1962. *Capitalism and Freedom.* Chicago: University of Chicago Press.

———. 1974. *Monetary Correction.* London: Institute of Economic Affairs.

Friedmann, Roberto, Codas. 1991. *Exportaciones Agricolas No Tradicionales en El Salvador.* San Salvador: UCA.

Friends of the Earth International (FOEI). 2005. "Bacon and Beans: How Trade in Pork and Soy Causes Hunger, Pollution, and Human Rights Violations." *Link Magazine* 109, December, on-line edition, accessed at www.foei.org/publications/link/trade-hongkong.19–20.htm on February 27, 2006.

Fuentes, Claudia Dary. 1991. *Mujeres Tradicionales y Nuevos Cultivos.* Guatemala: ASIES.

Fund for the Promotion of Exports (Proexport). 2006 (February 16). *Informe de Tendencias: Comportamiento de las Exportaciones Colombianas.* Bogotá: Proexport. Accessed at www.proexport.com.co on February 21, 2006.

Gabetta, Carlos. 2002 (January 16). "Argentina: IMF Show State Revolts." *Le Monde Diplomatic.* Accessed at www.mondediplo.com/2002/01/12argentina on January 16, 2002.

Galbraith, James, K. 2002. "A Perfect Crime: Global Inequality." *Daedalus* 131 (Winter):11–25.

Galhardi, Regina, M.A.A. 1998. *Maquiladora Prospects of Regional Integration and Globalization, Employment, and Training Papers 12.* Geneva: International Labor Organization (ILO).

Garst, Rachael, and Tom Barry. 1990. *Feeding the Crisis: U.S. Food Aid and Farm Policy in Central America.* Lincoln: University of Nebraska Press.

Gaspar de Alba, Alicia. 2005. *Desert Blood: The Juarez Murders*. Houston: Arte Publico Press.

Gelinas, Jacques B. 1998. *Freedom from Debt: The Reappropriation of Development through Financial Self-Reliance*. London: Zed.

George, Susan. 1992. *The Debt Boomerang: How Third World Debt Harms Us All*. Boulder: Westview.

Gereffi, Gary. 1997. "Global Shifts, Regional Response: Can North America Meet the Full-Package Challenge?" *Bobbin* (November):1–4.

Gereffi, Gary, and Lynn Hemple. 1996. "Latin America in the Global Economy: Running Faster to Stay in Place." *NACLA Report on the Americas* 29(4):7–18.

Gereffi, Gary, and Miguel Korzeniewicz, eds. 1994. *Commodity Chains and Global Capitalism*. Westport: Praeger.

———. Gereffi, Miguel Korzeniewicz, and Roberto Korzeniewicz, 1994. "Introduction." In Gereffi and Korzeniewicz, *Global Commodity Chains*.

Gill, Stephen, ed. 1993. *Gramsci, Historical Materialism, and International Relations*. Cambridge: Cambridge University Press.

Gill, Stephen, and David Law. 1993. "Global Hegemony and the Structural Power of Capital." In Gill, *Gramsci, Historical Materialism, and International Relations*, pp. 93–124.

Global Exchange. 2006. "Benilda Flower Company Continues de Discriminate Against Unionists in Colombia," San Francisco: Global Exchange. Accessed at www.globalexchange.org/countries/americas/colombia/Colom on February 21, 2006.

Glover, David, and Ken Kusterer. 1990. *Small Farms, Big Business: Contract Farming and Rural Development*. New York: Palgrave Macmillan.

Goesling, Brian. 2001. "Changing Income Inequalities within and between Nations: New Evidence." *American Sociological Review* 66:745–761.

Goff, Stan. 2006. "Sowing the Seeds of Fascism in America." *Truthdig* (Internet magazine), posted on October 3 and accessed at www.truthdig.com/dig/item/200601003_white_supremacism_sexism_militarism/ on July 21, 2007.

Gollinger, Eva. 2006. *Bush vs. Chavez: La Guerra de Washington Contra Venezuela*. Havana: Editorial Jose Martí.

Gonzales-Estay, Manolo. 1998. "The Californization of Chilean Farms: Preliminary Study of the Social Consequences of Chilean Campesinos in a Global System of Production." Paper presented at the XXI International Congress of the Latin American Studies Association, September 24–26, Chicago.

Goodman, D. B. Sorj, and J. Wilkinson. 1987. *From Farming to Biotechnology: A Theory of Agro-Industrial Development*. Oxford: Blackwell Publishers.

Goodman, D., and M. Watts (eds.). 1997. *Globalizing Food: Agrarian Questions and Global Restructuring*. London: Routledge.

Gore, Charles. 2000. "The Rise and Fall of the Washington Consensus as a Paradigm for Developing Countries." *World Development* 28(5):789–804.

Gott, Richard. 2005. *Hugo Chavez: The Bolivarian Revolution in Venezuela*. London: Verso.

Gramsci, Antonio. 1971. *Selections from Prison Notebooks*. New York: International Publishers.

Grandin, Greg. 2006a. "How Donald Rumsfeld Discovered the Wild West in Latin America." ALIA New Services, 17 May. Accessed at www.alia2.net/article139038.html on April 29, 2007.

———. 2006b. *Empire's Workshop: Latin America, the United States, and the Rise of the New Imperialism.* New York: Metropolitan Books.

Grau, Ricardo H., T. Mitchell Aide, and N. Ignacio Gasparri. 2005. "Globalization and Soybean Expansion into Semiarid Ecosystems of Argentina." *Ambio* 34(3):265–266.

Green, Duncan. 1995. *Silent Revolutions: The Rise of Market Economics in Latin America.* London: Cassell/Latin America Bureau.

Greider, William. 1997. *One World Ready or Not: The Manic Logic of Global Capitalism.* New York: Simon and Schuster.

Grimson, Alejandro. 2001. "A Hard Road for Argentine's Bolivians." *NACLA Report on the Americas* 35(2):33–35.

Gwynne, Robert, N. 1999. "Globalization, Commodity Chains, and Fruit Exporting Regions in Chile." *Tijdschrift voor Economische en Sociale Geografie* 90(2):211–225.

———. 2002. "Transnational Capitalism and Local Transformation in Chile." *Tijdschrift voor Economische en Sociale Geografie* 94(3):310–321.

Habel, Janette. 2002 (January 16). "U.S. Demands a Secure, Compliant Hemisphere." *Le Monde Diplomatique.* Accessed at www.mondediplo.com/2002/01/13latinamerica on January 18, 2002.

Hacher, Sebastian. 2004 (February 26). "Argentina Water Privatization Scheme Runs Dry." *Corpwatch.* Accessed at www.corpwatch.org/print_article.php?id=10088 on October 14.

Hale, Charles R. 2006. *Mas Que Un Indio: Racial Ambivalence and Neoliberal Multiculturalism in Guatemala.* Santa Fe, NM: School of American Research.

Halevi, Joseph. 2002. "The Argentine Crisis." *Monthly Review* 53(11):18, 21.

Hannum, Ann Barger. 2002. "Tricks of the Trade: Sex Tourism in Latin America." *ReVista* (Winter issue, "Tourism in the Americas"). Cambridge: Center for Latin American Studies, Harvard University. Accessed at www.fas.harvard.edu/~drclas/publications/revista/Tourism/hannum.html on April 26.

Hansen-Kuhn, Karen. 1993. *Structural Adjustment in Central America: The Case of Costa Rica.* Washington, DC: The Development Gap.

Hardt, Michael, and Antonio Negri. 2000. *Empire.* Cambridge, MA: Harvard University Press.

Harnecker, Marta. 2004. "After the Referendum: Venezuela Faces New Challenges." *Monthly Review* 56(6):34–48.

———. 2005. "On Leftist Strategy." *Science and Society* 69(2):142–152.

Harris, Nigel. 1995. *The New Untouchables: Immigration and the New World Worker.* London: Penguin.

———. 2002. *Thinking the Unthinkable: The Immigration Myth Exposed.* New York: I. B. Tauris and Co.

Harrison, Bennett. 1994. *Lean and Mean: The Changing Landscape of Corporate Power in the Age of Flexibility.* New York: Basic Books.

Harrison, David, ed. 2001. *Tourism and the Less Developed Countries*. London: CABI Publishing.

Harrison, Lynn C., and Winston Husbands, eds. 1996. *Practicing Responsible Tourism: Planning, Policy, and Development*. London: Wiley.

Harvey, David. 1982. *The Limits to Capital*. Chicago: University of Chicago Press.

———. 1990. *The Condition of Postmodernity*. London and New York: Blackwell.

———. 2003, 2nd edition. *The New Imperialism*. Oxford: Oxford University Press.

Hayek, F. 1978. *New Studies in Philosophy, Politics, Economics, and the History of Ideas*. Chicago: Chicago University Press.

Held, David. 1995. *Democracy and the Global Order: From the Modern State to Cosmopolitan Governance*. Cambridge: Polity Press.

Hellinger, Daniel. 2005. "When 'No' Means 'Yes to Revolution': Electoral Politics in Bolivarian Venezuela." *Latin American Perspectives* 32(3):8–32.

Hilferding, Rudolf. 1981 [1910]. *Finance Capital: A Study of the Latest Phase of Capitalist Development*. London: Routledge.

Hobsbawm, Eric. 1962. *The Age of Revolution*. New York: Mentor.

———. 1977. *The Age of Capital*. London: Sphere.

———. 1987. *The Age of Empire*. New York: Pantheon.

———. 1994. *The Age of Extremes*. New York: Vintage

Hoffman, Kelly, and Miguel Angel Centeno. 2003. "The Lopsided Continent: Inequality in Latin America." *Annual Review of Sociology* 29:363–390.

Honey, Martha. 1999. *Ecotourism and Sustainable Development: Who Owns Paradise?* Washington, DC: Island Press.

Hoogvelt, Ankie. 1997. *Globalization and the Post–Colonial World: The New Political Economy of Development*. Baltimore: Johns Hopkins University Press.

Hopkins, Terrence K., and Immanuel Wallerstein. 1994. "Commodity Chains: Construct and Research." In Gereffi and Korzeniewicz, *Commodity Chains and Global Capitalism*.

Horn, John. 2005. "Filmmakers Are Swept Away by Romania." *Los Angeles Times* (October 2):A1.

Hylton, Forrest. 2006. *Evil Hour in Colombia*. London: Verso.

Iglesias Prieto, Norma. 1997. *Beautiful Flowers of the Maquiladora: Life Histories of Women Workers in Tijuana*. Austin: University of Texas Press.

Inter-American Development Bank (IDB). 1997. *Latin America after a Decade of Reforms: Economic and Social Progress, 1997 Report*. Washington, DC: IDB. 2006

———. *Remittances 2005: Promoting Financial Democracy*. Washington, DC: IDB.

International Financial Corporation (IFC) [a World Bank agency]. 2000. "Latin America and the Caribbean: Summary of Project Information, Project Number 10651, Inka Terra. "Peru S.A.C." Washington, DC: IFC. Accessed at www.ifc.org/ifcext/lac.nsf/ Content/ SelectedProject?OpenDocument & UNID = B42BD-D74E7A0AA4585256992007CAA3C on June 20, 2006.

International Labor Organization (ILO). 1998. *La Industria Maquila en Centroamerica*. Geneva: ILO. Accessed at www.ilo.org/public/spanish/dialogue/actemp/papers/1998/ maquila/capi-2.htm on August 17, 2000.

————. 2005. *2005 Labor Review: Latin America and the Caribbean*. Geneva: ILO.

Iritani, Evelyn. 2000. "High-Paid Jobs Latest U.S. Export." *Los Angeles Times* (April 2):A1, A18.

Isacson, Adam, Joy Olson, and Lisa Haugaard. 2004. *Blurring the Lines: Trends in U.S. Military Programs with Latin America*. Washington, DC: Latin American Working Groups, Center for International Policy, and Washington Office on Latin America.

Itzigsohn, José. 1995. "Migrant Remittances, Labor Markets, and Household Strategies: A Comparative Analysis of Low-Income Household Strategies in the Caribbean Basin." *Social Forces* 74(2):633–656.

Jaquette, Jane S. 1994. *The Women's Movement in Latin America*. Boulder: Westview.

Jelin, Elizabeth, ed. 1990. *Women and Social Change in Latin America*. London: Zed Press.

Jenkins, Mauricio, Gerardo Esquivel, and Felipe Larrain B. 1998. "Export Processing Zones in Central America," *Development Discussion Papers*. No. 646, Central America Project Series. Cambridge, MA: Harvard Institute for International Development, Harvard University.

Joekes, Susan. 1987. *Women in the World Economy*. New York: Oxford University Press.

Jones, Richard C. 2001. "Maquiladoras and U.S. –Bound Migration in Central Mexico." *Growth and Change* 32(Spring):193–216.

Jorquera, Roberto. 2005. "Notes on the Bolivarian Revolution." *Links* 28(May–August): 82–90.

Kaplan, Karen. 2006. "U.S. Prison Numbers up 35% in 10 Years." *Los Angeles Times*(December 1):A24.

Kaplinsky, Raphael. 1993. "Export Processing Zones in the Dominican Republic: Transforming Manufactures into Commodities." *World Development* 21(11):1851–1865.

Kay, Cristobal. 2002. "Chile's Neoliberal Agrarian Transformation and the Peasantry." *Journal of Agrarian Change* 2(4):464–501.

Kearney, Michael. 1995. "The Local and the Global: The Anthropology of Globalization and Transnationalism." *Annual Review of Anthropology* 24 (1995):547–565.

Kempadoo, Kamala. 1999. *Sun, Sex, and Gold: Tourism and Sex Work in the Caribbean*. Lanham, MD: Rowman and Littlefield.

Kenfield, Isabella. 2007. "Landless Rural Workers Confront Brazil's Lula: Vow to Continue Struggle for Land and Against Agribusiness Interests." Oakland: CENSA, on-line. Accessed at http://globalalternatives.net/news/landless_workers_confront_lula On June 18.

Kennedy, Paul, and Victor Roudometof, eds. 2002. *Communities across Borders: New Immigrants and Transnational Cultures*. London: Routledge.

Kentor, Jeffrey. 2005. "The Growth of Transnational Corporate Networks, 1962 to 1998." *Journal of World-Systems Research* 11(2):262–286.

Kentor, Jeffrey, and Yong Suk Jang. 2004. "Yes, There Is a (Growing) Transnational Business Community." *International Sociology* 19(3):355–368.

Key, Nigel, and David Runsten. 1999. "Contract Farming, Smallholders, and rural Development in Latin America: The Organization of Agroprocessing Firms and the Scale of Outgrower Production." *World Development* 27:381–401.

Kim, Chul-Kyoo, and James Curry. 1993. "Fordism, Flexible Specialization and Agri-Industrial Restructuring." *Sociologia ruralis* 33(1):37–45.

King, Anthony. 1999. *Suburb/Ethnoburb/Globurg: Framing Transnational Urban Space in Asia.* Istanbul: WALD International Conference.

Kinnaird, Vivian, and Derek Hall, eds. 1994. *Tourism: A Gender Analysis.* New York: John Wiley.

Kirksey, Emily. 2006 (June 21). "Lula—Brazil's Lost Leader." Press release. Washington, DC: Council on Hemispheric Affairs.

Klein, Naomi. 2005a (November 21). "The Threat of Hope in Latin America." *The Nation.* Accessed at www.thenation.com/doc/20051121/klein on November 28, 2005.

———. 2005b (May 2). "The Rise of Disaster Capitalism." *The Nation.* Accessed at www .thenation.com/doc/20050502/klein on January 7, 2007.

Kolko, Joyce. 1988. *Restructuring the World Economy.* New York: Pantheon.

Kopkinak, Kathryn. 1998. *Desert Capitalism.* Tonawanda, NY: Black Rose Books.

Korovkin, Tanya. 1992. "Peasants, Grapes, and Corporations: The Growth of Contract Farming in a Chilean Community." *Journal of Peasant Studies* 19(2):228–254.

———. 1997. "Taming Capitalism: The Evolution of the Indigenous Peasant Economy in Northern Ecuador." *Latin American Research Review* 32(3):89–110.

———. 2003. "Cut Flower Exports, Female Labor, and Community Participation in Highland Ecuador." *Latin American Perspectives* 131(30):18–42.

———, ed. 2004. *Efectos Sociales de la Globalizacion: Petroleo, Banano y Flores en Ecuador.* Quito: CEDIME.

———. 2004. "Globalizacion y Pobreza: Los Efectos Sociales de la Floricultura de Exportacion." In *Efectos Sociales de la Globalizacion.*

Korzeniewicz, Roberto P., and Timothy P. Moran. 1997. "World Economic Trends in the Distribution of Income, 1965–1992." *American Journal of Sociology* 102(4):1000–1039.

Korzeniewicz, Roberto P., and William C. Smith. 2000. "Poverty, Inequality, and Growth in Latin America: Searching for the High Road to Globalization." *Latin American Research Review* 35(3):7–54.

Kotz, David M., Terrence McDonough, and Michael Reich, eds. 1994. *Social Structures of Accumulation: The Political Economy of Growth and Crisis.* Cambridge: Cambridge University Press.

Kraul, Chris. 2006. "China to Invest $5 Billion in Venezuelan Oil Projects." *Los Angeles Times* (August 29):A1.

Kruger, Ann O. 1978. *Foreign Trade Regimes and Economic Development: Liberalization Attempts and Consequences.* Cambridge: Ballinger.

Kurtz-Phelan, Daniel. 2006. "The Return of the Sandinistas: Former Guerrillas Are Trying to Foment a Tourism Boom in Nicaragua, but It's Not Costa Rica Yet." *Wall Street Journal* (March 11):P7.

Kyle, David. 2000. *Transnational Peasants: Migrations, Networks, and Ethnicity in Andean Ecuador.* Baltimore: Johns Hopkins University Press.

LaBotz, Dan, and Robin Alexander. 2005. "The Escalating Struggles over Mexico's Labor Laws." *NACLA Report on the Americas* 39(1):16–22.

Laclau, Ernesto. 1977. *Politics and Ideology in Marxist Theory: Capitalism, Fascism, Populism.* London: New Left Books.

———. 2004. "Populism: What's in a Name?" On-line Papers, Center for Theoretical Studies in the Humanities and Social Sciences, University of Essex. Accessed at www.essex.ac.uk/centres/TheoStud/ on January 11, 2006.

Laibman, David. 2005. "Theory and Necessity: The Stadial Foundations of the Present." *Science and Society* 69(3):285–315.

Lander, Edgardo. 2005. "Venezuelan Social Conflict in a Global Context." *Latin American Perspectives* 32(2):20–38.

———. 2006 (December). "Venezuela: Creacion del Partido Unico." *La Jornada* 29:1–4. Accessed at www.jornada,unam.mx/2006.12/29/index.php?section=opinion on January 2, 2007.

Lander, Luis E. (ed.). 2003. *Poder y Petroleo en Venezuela.* Caracas: Faces-UCV.

Lanfant, Marie-Francoise Lanfant. 1980. "Tourism in the Process of Internationalization." *International Social Science Journal* 32(1):14–43.

Lash, Scott, and John Urry. 1987. *The End of Organized Capitalism.* Cambridge: Polity Press.

Latin America Data Base (LADB). 1999. "Honduras: Government Abandons Controversial Development Scheme after Police Fire on Protesters." *Notisur* 4(41). Albuquerque: Latin American Institute, University of New Mexico.

———. 2002 (March 10). "Study Shows Significant Growth in Informal Economy Since Early 2001." *Sourcemex* 13(10). University of New Mexico.

———. 2004. "U.S. Military Officials Seek Expanded Military Presence in Latin America." *Notisur* 14(22).

Latinobarametro. 2004 and 2006 (annual reports). Informe latinobarometro. Santiago, Chile: Corporacion Latinobarometro. Accessed at www.latinobarametro.org/.

Leight, Jessica. 2004. "Promulgating Democracy of Another Variety." *Council on Hemispheric Affairs* 14 July. Accessed at www.venezuelanalysis.om/articles.php?artno=1218.

Lenin, V. I. 1970 [1917]. *Imperialism: The Highest Stage of Capitalism.* Moscow: Progress Publishers.

Let's Go. 2006. "Discover Central America." Advertisement posted on commercial tourist Web site *Let's Go.* Accessed at www.letsgo.com/destinations/latin%5Famerica/central/ on June 22, 2006.

Levine, Mark. 2005. *Why They Don't Hate Us: Lifting the Veil on the Axis of Evil.* Oxford: One World.

Levitt, Peggy. 2001. *The Transnational Villagers.* Berkeley: University of California Press.

Lichtenstein, Nelson. 2006. "Wal-Mart: A Template for Twenty-First–Century Capitalism." In Lichtenstein (ed.), *Wal-Mart: The Face of Twenty-First-Century Capitalism.* New York: New Press, pp. 3–30.

Lindsay, Reed. 2005. "Divided Bolivia Likely Close to a Showdown." *San Francisco Chronicle* March 19, on-line edition. Accessed at http://archives.econ.utah.edu/archives/marxism/2005w11/msg00318.htm on March 23, 2005.

Lindsay-Poland, John. 2004. U.S. Military Bases in Latin America and the Caribbean. *Foreign Policy in Focus* August 2. Accessed at http://americas.irc-online.org/am/1670 on April 28, 2007.

Linz, Juan, and Arturo Valenzuela, eds. 1994. *The Failure of Presidential Democracy.* Baltimore: Johns Hopkins University Press.

Lipietz, Alain. 1987. *Mirages and Miracles: The Crisis of Global Fordism.* London: Verso.

López, José Roberto, and Mitchell A. Seligson. 1991. "Small Business Development in El Salvador: The Impact of Remittances." In Sergio Diaz-Briquets and Sidney Weintraub, *Migration, Remittances, and Small Business Development: Mexico and the Caribbean Basin Countries.* Boulder: Westview, pp.175–206.

López-Alves, Fernando, and Diane E. Johnson. 2007. *Globalization and Uncertainty in Latin America.* New York: Palgrave Macmillan.

Lowell, Lindsay B., and Rodolfo O. De la Garza. 2000. *The Developmental Role of Remittances in U.S. Latino Communities and in Latin American Countries.* Washington, DC: Inter-American Dialogue and Thomas Rivera Policy Institute.

Lungo, Mario E. 1996. *El Salvador in the Eighties: Counterinsurgency and Revolution,* Philadelphia: Temple University Press.

Lungo, Mario E., and Susan Kandel. 1998. "International Migration, Transnationalism and Socio-Cultural Changes in El Salvador's Sending Towns." Paper presented at the 1998 meeting of the Latin America Studies Association, Chicago, September 24–26, 1998.

Mahler, Sarah J. 1998a. "Transnationalizing Community Development: The Case of Migration between Boston and the Dominican Republic." *Nonprofit and Voluntary Sector Quarterly* 26(4):509–526.

———. 1998b. "Theoretical and Empirical Contributions Toward a Research Agenda for Transnationalism." In Michael Peter Smith and Luis Eduardo Guarnizo (eds.), *Transnationalism from Below.* New Brunswick, NJ: Transaction, 1998.

Maimbo, Samuel Munzele, and Dilip Ratha 2005a. "The Regulation and Supervision of Informal Funds Transfer Systems." In Maimbo and Ratha, *Remittances: Development Impact and Future Prospects,* pp. 211–241.

———. 2005b. *Remittances: Development Impact and Future Prospects.* Washington, DC: World Bank.

Malloy, James M., ed. 1977. *Authoritarianism and Corporatism in Latin America.* Pittsburgh: University of Pittsburgh Press.

Mandel, Ernest. 1975. *Late Capitalism.* London: New Left Books.

Marglin, Stephen A., and Juliet B. Schor, eds. 1990. *The Golden Age of Capitalism: Reinterpreting the Postwar Experience.* Oxford, UK: Clarendon Press.

Marichal, Carlos. 1989. *A Century of Debt Crises in Latin America: From Independence to the Great Depression, 1820–1930.* Princeton: Princeton University Press.

———. 1997. "The Vicious Cycles of Mexican Debt." *NACLA Report on the Americas* 31(3): 28.

Markoff, John. 1997. "Really Existing Democracy: Learning from Latin America in the Late 1990s." *New Left Review,* 223:48–68.

Marston, Joshuya, director. 2004. *Maria Full of Grace.* New York: Fine Line Features.

Martin, Brendan. 1993. *In the Public Interest? Privatization and Public Sector Reform.* London: St. Martin's Press.

Martinez, Alonso, Ivan de Souza, and Francis Liu. 2003. "Multinationals: Latin America's Great Race." *Strategy and Competition* 32. Accessed at www.uky/~wallyf/multilatinas. pdf on October 21, 2005.

Martínez Valle, Luciano, ed. 2000. *Estudios Rurales*. Quito: FLACSO.

Massey, Douglas S., Joaquin Arango, Graeme Hugo, Ali Kouaouci, Adela Pellegrino, and J. Edward Taylor. 1998. *Worlds in Motion: Understanding International Migration at the End of the Millennium*. Oxford: Clarendon Press.

McAfee, Kathy. 1991. *Storm Signals: Structural Adjustment and Development Alternatives in the Caribbean*. Boston: South End.

McClenaghan, Sharon. 1997. "Women, Work, and Empowerment: Romanticizing the Reality." In Elizabeth Dore (ed.), *Gender Politics in Latin America: Debates in Theory and Practice*. New York: Monthly Review Press, 19–35.

McLaren, Deborah. 2003, 2nd edition. *Rethinking Tourism and Ecotravel: The Paving of Paradise and What You Can Do to Stop It*. West Hartford, CT: Kumarian Press.

McMichael, Philip. ed. 1994. *The Global Restructuring of Agro-Food Systems*. Ithaca: Cornell University Press.

———. 1996. *Development and Social Change: A Global Perspective*. Thousand Oaks: Pine Forge.

———, ed. 1995. *Food and Agrarian Orders in the World Economy*, Westport: Praeger.

McNeill, William H. 1986. *Polyethnicity and National Unity*. Toronto: University of Toronto Press.

Mena, Norma, and Silvia Proaño. 2005. *Sexual Harassment in the Workplace: The Cut Flower Industry. Case Study Northern Sierra of Ecuador*. Washington, DC: International Labor Rights Fund.

Méndez, Jose, A. 1991. *The Development of the Colombian Cut Flower Industry*. World Bank Working Papers, WPS 660. Washington, DC: World Bank, Country Economics Department.

Meyers, Deborah Waller. 1998. *Migrant Remittances to Latin America: Reviewing the Literature*. Washington, DC: Inter-American Dialogue/The Thomas Rivera Policy Institute.

Mies, Maria. 1999, 2nd edition. *Patriarchy and Accumulation on a World Scale: Women in the International Division of Labor*. London: Zed.

Milanovic, Branko. 2002. *True World Income Distribution, 1988 and 1993: First Calculation Based on Household Surveys Alone*. World Bank Research Paper, reproduced in Lee, Marc. (2002, April 18). "The Global Divide: Inequality in the World Economy." *Behind the Numbers: Economic Facts, Figures, and Analysis* 4(2). Canadian Centre for Policy Alternatives.

Moghadam, Valentine M. 2005. *Globalizing Women: Transnational Feminist Networks*. Baltimore: Johns Hopkins University Press.

Mommer, Bernard. 2003. "Subversive Oil." In Ellner and Hellinger (eds.), *Venezuelan Politics in the Chavez Era*, pp. 131–145.

Monahan, Jane. 2005. "Soybean Fever Transforms Paraguay." *BBC News*, on-line dispatch, 6 June 2005. Accessed at http://news.bbc.co.uk/2/hi/business/4603729.stm on February 25, 2006.

Mondragon, Hector. 2007. "Democracy and Plan Colombia." *NACLA Report on the Americas* 40(1):42–44.

Montecinos, Veronica, and John Markoff. 2001. "From the Power of Economic Ideas to the Power of Economists." In Miguel Angel Ceneno and Fernando Lopez-Alves, *The Other Mirror: Grand Theory through the Lens of Latin America*. Princeton: Princeton University Press.

Monthly Review. 2004. "Note from the Editors." November, inside front cover and pp. 64–65.

Moody, Kim. 1997. *Workers in a Lean World: Unions in the International Economy*. London: Verso.

Morales, Abelardo. 1997. *Los Territorios del Cuajipal: Frontera y Sociedad Entre Nicaragua y Costa Rica*. San Jose: FLACSO.

Morales, Abelardo, and Carlos Castro, eds. 1999. *Inmigracion laboral Nicaraguense en Costa Rica*. San Jose: FLACSO.

Mouzelis, Nicos. 1985. "On the Concept of Populism: Populist and Clientelist Modes of Incorporation in Semiperipheral Politics." *Politics and Society* 14(3):329–348.

Mowforth, Martin, and Ian Munt. 1998. *Tourism and Sustainability: New Tourism in the Third World*. London: Routledge.

Munck, Ronaldo. 2002. *Globalization and Labor: The New "Great Transformation."* London: Zed.

Murray, Kevin. 1995. *Inside El Salvador*. Albuquerque: The Resource Center.

Murray, Warwick E. 1997. "Competitive Global Fruit Export Markets: Marketing Intermediaries and Impacts on Small-Scale Growers in Chile." *Bulletin of Latin American Research* 16(1):43–55.

NACLA Report on the Americas. 1998 (March/April). Issue title: The Wars Within: Counterinsurgency in Chiapas and Colombia 31(5).

———. 2002 (July/August). Issue title: Crisis in the Americas 36(1).

Naim, Moises. 1995. "Latin America: The Second Stage of Reform." In Larry Diamond and Marc F. Plattner (eds.), *Economic Reform and Democracy*. Baltimore: Johns Hopkins University Press, pp. 28–44.

Naipaul, V. S. 2002 (1962). *The Middle Passage*. New York: Vintage.

Nash, Dennison. 1989, 2nd edition. "Tourism as a Form of Imperialism." In Valene L. Smith (ed.), *Hosts and Guests: The Anthropology of Tourism*. Philadelphia: University of Pennsylvania Press.

Nash, June, and Maria Patricia Fernández-Kelly, eds. 1983. *Women, Men, and the International Division of Labor*. Albany: SUNY Press.

Nathan, Deborah. 1999. "Work, Sex, and Danger in Ciudad, Juarez." *NACLA Report on the Americas* 33(3):24–31.

Nederveen-Pieterse, Jan. 2002. "Global Inequality: Bringing Politics Back In." *Third World Quarterly* 23(6):1023–1046.

Nevins, Joseph. 2002. *Operation Gatekeeper: The Rise of the "Illegal Alien" and the Making of the U.S.–Mexico Boundary*. New York: Routledge.

The New Internationalist. 1993. "Tourism: The Final Brochure" (special issue), no. 245, July.

Niemeyer, Ralph T. 2004. *Morning Dawn in Venezuela*. New York: Universe Inc.

Norsworthy, Kent. 1993. *Inside Honduras*. Albuquerque: The Resource Center.

Noticen. 2006a (June 22). "Epistemicide: Under CAFTA, Indigenous Heritage Becomes First World Intellectual Property." *Noticen* 11(24). Latin America Data Base, University of New Mexico, Albuquerque.

———. 2006b (March 23). "The Shadow of Wal-Mart Lengthens in Central America." *Noticen* 11(12). Latin America Data Base, University of New Mexico, Albuquerque.

———. 2004a (May 13). "ECLAC Reports Privatization Has Been Bad for Regional Power" *Noticen* 9(18). Latin America Data Base, University of New Mexico, Albuquerque.

Notisur. 2006a (April 28). "Argentina: Buenos Aires Cracks Down on 'Slave Labor' Shops after Fire Kills Six Bolivian Immigrants." *Notisur* 16(16). Latin America Data Base, University of New Mexico, Albuquerque.

———. 2007 (March 9). "Colombia and U.S. Focus Military Spending on Plan Colombia." *Notisur* 17(10). Latin America Data Base, University of New Mexico, Albuquerque.

O'Donnell, Guillermo. 1973. *Modernization and Bureaucratic Authoritarianism.* Berkeley: University of California Press.

Ohmae, Kenichi. 1996. *The End of the Nation State: The Rise of Regional Economies.* New York: Free Press.

Orozco, Manuel. 2002. "Globalization and Migration: The Impact of Family Remittances in Latin America." *Latin American Politics and Society* 44(2):41–66.

———. 2003. "Worker Remittances in an International Scope." Working Paper, March. Washington, DC: Inter-American Dialogue and Multilateral Investment Fund of the Inter-American Development Bank.

———. 2005. "Transnationalism and Development: Trends and Opportunities in Latin America." In Maimbo and Ratha, *Remittances: Development Impact and Future Prospects,*, pp. 307–329.

Orozco, Manuel, Rodolfo de la Garza, and Miguel Barahona. 1997. *Inmigracion y Remesas Familiares.* San Jose: FLACSO.

Overbeek, Henk, ed. 1993. *Restructuring Hegemony in the Global Political Economy: The Rise of Transnational Neoliberalism in the 1980s.* London.

Overholt, William H. 2006 (December 21). "Globalization's Unequal Discontents." *Washington Post.* Accessed at www.washingtonpost.com/wp-dyn/content/article/2006/12/20/AR2006122001307.html?referrer=emailarticle on January 7, 2007.

Ozden, Caglar, and Maurice Schiff. 2006. "Overview." In Ozden and Schiff (eds.), *International Migration, Remittances, and the Brain Drain.* Washington, DC, and New York: World Bank and Palgrave Macmillan, pp. 1–16.

Palan, Ronen, ed. 2000. *Global Political Economy: Contemporary Theories.* London: Routledge.

Palast, Greg.. 2001. "The WTO's Hidden Agenda." *CorpWatch,* November 9, retrieved on December 5, 2001, from www.zmag.org/palastwto.htm.

———. 2003. *The Best Democracy Money Can Buy.* New York/London: Plume.

Palerm, Juan Vicente. 1999. "The Expansion of California Agriculture and the Rise of Peasant-Worker Communities." In Susanne Jonas and Suzie Dod Thomas, *Immigration: A Civil Rights Issue of the Americas.* Wilmington, DE: Scholarly Resources.

Palic, Deanna. 2002 (March). "Latin America—Marketing Tourist Travel to Peru." *International Travel News,* on-line edition, accessed at www.intltravelnews.com/ on April 26, 2006.

Palmisano, Samuel F. 2006. "The Globally Integrated Enterprise." *Foreign Affairs* 85(3):127–136.

Parker, Dick. 2005. "Chavez and the Search for an Alternative to Neoliberalism." *Latin American Perspectives* 32(2):39–50.

Passel, Jeffrey S. 2005. *Estimates of the Size and Characteristics of the Undocumented Population*. Washington, DC: PEW Hispanic Center.

Pattullo, Polly. 2005, 2nd edition. *Last Resorts: The Cost of Tourism in the Caribbean*. New York: Monthly Review Press.

Paus, Eva, ed. 1988. *Struggle against Dependence: Nontraditional Export Growth in Central America and the Caribbean*. Boulder: Westview.

Pedrazzini, Ivez, and Magaly Sanchez. 1992. *Malandros, Bandas y Niños de la Calle: Cultura de Urgencia en la Metropolis Latinoamericana*. Valencia: Hermanos Vadell Editores.

Pengue, Walter. 2000. *Cultivos Transgenicos: Hacia Donde Vamos?* Buenos Aires: Lugar Editorial, UNESCO.

———. 2001. "The Impact of Soy Expansion in Argentina." *Seedling* 18(3):1–5.

———. 2005. "Transgenic Crops in Argentina: The Ecological and Social Debt." *Bulletin of Science, Technology and Society* 25(4):314–322.

Peredo Leigue, Antonio. 2006 (April 10). "Las Tragedias del Exilio." ALAI, accessed at http://alainet.org/docs/11102.html on October 15, 2006.

Pérez Saínz, Juan Pablo, ed. 2002. *Encadenamientos Globales Y Pequeñas Empresas en Centroamerica*. San Jose, Costa Rica: FLACSO.

Pérez Saínz, Juan Pablo, and Katharine E. Andrade-Eekhoff. 2003. *Communities in Globalization: The Invisible Mayan Nahaul*. Lanham, MD: Rowman and Littlefield.

Peru's Challenge. 2005. "Projects," accessed at Web site of Peru Challenge, Cuzco-based development NGO, www.peruschallenge.com/projects.html, on June 20, 2006.

Petersen, Kurt. 1992. *The Maquiladora Revolution in Guatemala*. Occasional Paper Series 2. New Haven: Yale Law School, Orville H. Schell Jr. Center for International Human Rights.

Petras, James. 2001. "The Geopolitics of Plan Colombia." *Monthly Review* 53(1), digital edition, available at http://findarticles.com/p/articles/mi_no1132/is_53/ai_74826973; accessed on April 21, 2007.

Petras, James, Ignacio Leiva Fernando, and Henry Veltmeyer. 2004. *Democracy and Poverty in Chile: The Limits to Electoral Politics*. Boulder: Westview Press.

Petrovic, Misha, and Gary G. Hamilton. 2006. "Making Global Markets: Wal-Mart and its Suppliers." In Nelson Lichtenstein (ed.), *Wal-Mart: The Face of Twenty-First-Century Capitalism*. New York: New Press, pp. 107–141.

Pettman, Ralph. 1996. *Understanding International Political Economy*. Boulder: Lynne Rienner.

Pew Hispanic Center. 2003. *Remittance Senders and Receivers: Tracking the Transnational Channels*. Washington, DC: Pew Hispanic Center/Multilateral Investment Fund.

Philip, George. 1993. "The New Economic Liberalism and Democracy in Latin America." *Third World Quarterly* 14 (3):555–571.

Phinney, David. 2005. "Blood, Sweat and Tears: Asia's Poor Build U.S. Bases in Iraq." *CorpWatch*, October 3, downloaded from http://www.corpwatch.org/article.php?id=12675 on 10/5/2005.

Pinto, Edivan, Larluce Melo, and Maria Luisa Mendonca. 2007 (March 13). "El Mito de los biocombustibles." ALAI on-line news service. Accessed at http://colombia.indymedia. org/news/2007/03/60228.php on March 13, 2007.

Piras, Claudia, ed. 2004. *Women at Work: Challenges for Latin America*. Washington, DC: Inter-American Development Bank.

Pizarro, Jorge Martinez. 2003. *El Encanto de los Dats: Sociodemografia de la Inmigracion en Chile Segun el Censo de 2002*. Santiago, Chile: United Nations.

Portes, Alejandro. 1995 (April). "Transnational Communities: Their Emergence and Significance in the Contemporary World-System." Working Papers no. 16. Baltimore: Johns Hopkins University, Department of Sociology.

———. 1996. "Global Villagers: The Rise of Transnational Communities." *American Prospect* 25(March–April):74–77.

———. 1997. "Immigrant Theory for a New Century: Some Problems and Opportunities." *International Migration Review* 3(4):799–825.

Portes, Alejandro, and Jozsef Borocz. 1990. "Contemporary Immigration: Theoretical Perspectives on Its Determinants and Modes of Incorporation." *International Migration Review* 23(3):606–630.

Portes, Alejandro, Luis Eduardo Guarnizo, and Patricia Landolt. 1999. "The Study of Transnationalism: Pitfalls and Promise of an Emergent Research Field." *Ethnic and Racial Studies* 22(2):217–237.

Portes, Alejandro, and Kelly Hoffman. 2003. "Latin American Class Structures: Their Composition and Change During the Neoliberal Era." *Latin American Research Review* 38(1):41–82.

Portillo, Lourdes. 2001. *Señorita Extraviada*. New York and San Francisco: Xochitl Films.

Potts, Lydia. 1990. *The World Labor Market: A History of Migration*. London: Zed.

Poulantzas, Nicos. 1975. *Political Power and Social Classes*. London: New Left Books.

Prakash, Aseem, and Jeffrey A. Hart. 2000. "Indicators of Economic Integration." *Global Governance* 6(1):95–105.

Proexport. See Fund for the Promotion of Exports, above.

Psacharopoulos, George, and Harry A. Patrinos, eds. 1994. *Indigenous People and Poverty in Latin America: An Empirical Analysis*. Washington, DC: World Bank.

Ramirez, Cristobal Valencia. 2005. "Venezuela's Bolivarian Revolution: Who Are the Chavistas?" *Latin American Perspectives* 32(3):79–97.

Ram's Horn: A Monthly Journal of Food Systems Analysis. 2005. "Sustainable Soy." Editorial. Sorrento, British Columbia: Ram's Horn.

Ratha, Dilip. 2004. "Workers' Remittances: An Important and Stable Source of External Development Finance." In Maimbo and Ratha, *Remittances: Development Impact and Future Prospects*, pp. 19–52.

Raynolds, Laura. 1994. "Institutionalizing Flexibility: A Comparative Analysis of Fordist and Post-Fordist Models of Third World Agro-Export Production." In Gereffi and Korzeniewicz, *Commodity Chains and Global Capitalism*, pp. 143–161.

———. 1998. "Harvesting Women's Work: Restructuring Agricultural and Industrial Labor Forces in the Dominican Republic." *Economic Geography* 74(2):149–169.

Reardon, Thomas, and Julio A. Berdegue. 2002. "The Rapid Rise of Supermarkets in Latin America: Challenges and Opportunities for Development." *Development Policy Review* 20(4):371–388.

Reddy, Sanjay G., and Thomas W. Pogge. 2002 (August 15). "How Not to Count the Poor." Accessed at www.columbia.edu/~sr793/count.pdf on March 9, 2003.

Regalado, Roberto. 2007. *Latin America at the Crossroads: Domination, Crisis, Popular Movements, and Political Alternatives.* New York: Ocean Press.

Rettberg, Angelinica. 2005. "Business Versus Business? Grupos and Organized Business in Colombia." In *Latin American Politics and Society* 47(1):31–54.

Reyes, Gerardo, ed. 2003. *Los Dueños de America Latina.* Mexico, D.F.: Ediciones B.

Reygadas, Luis. 2006. "Latin America: Persistent Inequality and Recent Transformations." In Eric Hershberg and Fred Rosen, *Latin America after Neoliberalism: Turning the Tide of the 21st Century.* New York: New Press, pp. 120–143.

Rincon, Alejandro, Susanne Jonas, and Nestor Rodriguez. 1999. "La Inmigracion Guatemalteca en los EEUU: 1980–1996," manuscript prepared for and summarized in United Nations Development Program (UNDP, 1999), *Guatemala: El Rostro Rural del Desarrollo Humano,* Guatemala City, as discussed in Jonas, *Of Centaurs and Doves* (Boulder: Westview), pp. 224–225.

Roberto, Lopez Jose, and Mitchell A. Seligson. 1991. "Small Business Development in El Salvador: The Impact of Remittances." In Sergio Diaz-Briquets and Sidney Weintraub, *Migration, Remittances, and Small Business Development: Mexico and the Caribbean Basin Countries.* Boulder: Westview, pp. 175–206.

Roberts, Bryan, Reanne Frank, and Fernando Lozano-Ascencio. 1999. "Transnational Migrant Communities and Mexican Migration to the U.S." *Ethnic and Racial Studies* 22(2):238–266.

Roberts, Kenneth. 2002. "Social Inequalities without Class Cleavages in Latin America's Neoliberal Era." *Studies in Comparative International Development* 36(Winter):3–33.

Robinson, William I. 1993. "The Global Economy and the Latino Populations in the United States: A World Systems Approach." *Critical Sociology* 19(2):29–59.

———. 1996a. *Promoting Polyarchy: Globalization, U.S. Intervention, and Hegemony.* Cambridge: Cambridge University Press.

———. 1996b. "Globalisation: Nine Theses of Our Epoch." *Race and Class* 18(2):13–31.

———. 1996c. "Transnational Politics and Global Social Order: A Reassessment of the Chilean Transition in Light of U.S. Intervention." *Journal of Political and Military Sociology* 24(2):1–30.

———. 1998. "Beyond Nation-State Paradigms: Globalization, Sociology, and the Challenge of Transnational Studies." *Sociological Forum* 13(4):561–594.

———. 1999. "Latin America in the Age of Inequality: Confronting the New Utopia." *International Studies Review* 1(3): 41–67.

———. 2000. "Promoting Capitalist Polyarchy: The Case of Latin America." In M. Cox, J. G. Ikenberry, and T. Inoguchi (eds.), *American Democracy Promotion: Impulses, Strategies, and Impacts.* New York: Oxford University Press.

———. 2001a. "Social Theory and Globalization: The Rise of a Transnational State." *Theory and Society* 30(2):157–200.

———. 2001b. "Transnational Processes, Development Studies, and Changing Social Hierarchies in the World System: A Central American Case Study." *Third World Quarterly* 22(4):529–563.

———. 2002. "Remapping Development in Light of Globalization: From a Territorial to a Social Cartography." *Third World Quarterly* 23(6):1047–1071.

———. 2003. *Transnational Conflicts: Central America, Social Change, and Globalization.* London: Verso.

———. 2004a. *A Theory of Global Capitalism: Production, Class, and State in a Transnational World.* Baltimore: Johns Hopkins University Press.

———. 2004b. "The Crisis of Global Capitalism: How it Looks From Latin America." In Alan Freeman and Boris Kagarlitsky (eds.), *The Politics of Empire: The Crisis of Globalization.* London: Pluto Press.

———. 2004c. "Global Crisis and Latin America." *Bulletin of Latin American Research* 23(2):135–153.

———. 2005. "Gramsci and Globalization: From Nation-State to Transnational Hegemony." *Critical Review of Social and Political Philosophy* 8(4):1–16.

———. 2006a. "Aqui Estamos y No Nos Vamos: Global Capital and Immigrant Rights." *Race and Class* 48(2):77–91.

———. 2006b. "Promotion Democracy in Latin America: The Oxymoron of 'Market Democracy.'" In Eric Hershberg and Fred Rosen, *Latin America after Neoliberalism.* New York: New Press, pp. 96–119.

———. 2006c. "Critical Globalization Studies." In Judith Blau and Keri E. Iyall Smith (eds.), *Public Sociologies Reader.* Lanham, MD: Rowman and Littlefield, pp. 21–36.

———. 2007a. "Theories of Globalization." In George Ritzer (ed.), *The Blackwell Companion to Globalization.* London and New York: Blackwell.

———. 2007b. "Beyond the Theory of Imperialism: Global Capitalism and the Transnational State." *Societies without Borders* 2:5–26.

———. Forthcoming. *Theories of Globalization.* Thousand Oaks: Pine Forge.

Robinson, William, I., and Jerry Harris. 2000. Towards a Global Ruling Class? Globalization and the Transnational Capitalist Class. *Science and Society* 64(1):11–54.

Rodríguez, Marta (producer/director). 1988. *Love, Women and Flowers* (documentary video). Distributed by Women Make Movies (New York).

Rosamond, Ben, ed. 2002. *New Regionalism in the Global Political Economy.* London: Routledge.

Rosen, Fred. 2007. "Breaking with the Past: A 40th-Anniversary Interview with Margarita Lopez Maya." *NACLA Report on the Americas* 40(3):4–8.

Rosen, James. 2007 (March 19). "Defense Spending Soars to Highest Levels Since World War II." *McClathy Newspapers,* accessed at www.realcities.com/mld/krwashington/16935815.htm?template=contentModules/printstory.jsp on April 27, 2007.

Ross, Robert J.S., and Kent C. Trachte. (1990). *Global Capitalism: The New Leviathan.* Albany: SUNY Press.

Rothkopf, David. 1997. "In Praise of Cultural Imperialism." *Foreign Policy* 107:38–53.

Rouse, Roger. 1991. "Mexican Migration and the Social Space of Postmodernism." *Diaspora* 1:8–24.

Ruesga, Santos, and Gerardo Fujii. 2006. "El Comportamiento del Mercado de Trabajo en America Latina en el Contexto de la Globalizacion Economica." Research Papers, Center for U.S.–Mexican Studies, University of Californa–San Diego, accessed from University of California Scholarship Repository at http://repositories.cdlib.org/usmex/ ruesga_fujii on December 12, 2006.

Rupert, Mark. 1995. *Producing Hegemony.* Cambridge: Cambridge University Press.

Sachs, Jeffrey D., ed. 1989. *Developing Country Debt and Economic Performance,* vols. 1 and 2. Chicago: Chicago University Press.

Safa, Helen. 1995a. "Economic Restructuring and Gender Subordination." *Latin American Perspectives* 22(2):35–50.

———. 1995b. "The New Women Workers: Does Money Equal Power?" In Fred Rosen and Deidre McFayden (eds.), *Free Trade and Economic Restructuring in Latin America.* New York: Monthly Review Press, pp. 129–140.

Salzinger, Leslie. 2003. *Genders in Production: Making Workers in Mexico's Global Factories.* Berkeley: University of California Press.

Sánchez-Anocochea, Diego. 2004. "Developing Through Manufacturing Exports? Limitations of the New External Specialization of Small Latin American Countries in the Global Economy." Paper presented at the Congress of the Latin American Studies Association, October 6–9, Las Vegas.

Sandinista National Liberation Front (FSLN). 2007. *Cuaderno Sandinista No. 1: El Nuevo Proyecto Sandinista (Document de Consulta y Debate.* Managua: FSLN.

Sandovál, Carlos Garcia. 2004. *Threatening Others: Nicaraguans and the Formation of National Identities in Costa Rica.* Athens: Ohio University Press.

Santiso, Javier. 2006. "Multilatinas in the Global Economy." Report presented to "Expert Meeting," OECD Development Centre, March 27. Paris: OECD.

Sassen, Saskia. 1988. *The Mobility of Labor and Capital: A Study in International Investment and Labor Flows.* Cambridge: Cambridge University Press.

———. 1991. *The Global City: New York, London, Tokyo.* Princeton: Princeton University Press.

———. 1996. *Losing Control? Sovereignty in the Age of Globalization.* New York: Columbia University press.

Sawer, Larry. 2005. "Nontraditional or New Traditional Exports: Ecuador's Flower Boom." *Latin American Research Review* 40(3):40–67.

Sawyer, Mark Q. 2005. *Racial Politics in Post-Revolutionary Cuba.* Cambridge: Cambridge University Press.

Saxe-Fernández, John. 2002. *La Compre-Venta de Mexico.* Mexico: Plaza y Janes.

Schiller, Nina Glick. 1999. "Transmigrants and Nation-States: Something Old and Something New in the U.S. Immigrant Experience." In Charles Hirschman, Philip Kasinitz, and Josh de Wind (eds.), *The Handbook of International Migration: The American Experience.* New York: Russell Sage Foundation, pp. 94–119.

Schiller, Nina Glick, and Georges E. Fourton. 2001. *Georges Woke Up Laughing: Long Distance Nationalism and the Search for Home.* Durham, NC: Duke University Press.

Schlosser, Eric. 2001. *Fast Food Nation*. New York: Harper.

Schmitz, Hubert. 1995. "Collective Efficiency: Growth Paths for Small Scale Industry." *Journal of Development Studies* 31(4):529–566.

Schmitz, Hubert, and Peter Knorringa. 2000. "Learning from Global Buyers." *Journal of Development Studies* 27(2):177–205.

Schneider, Ben Ross. 2001. "Business Politics and Regional Integration: The Advantages of Organization in NAFTA and MERCOSUR." In Bulmer-Thomas, *Regional Integration in Latin America and the Caribbean*, pp. 167–193.

Schumpeter, Joseph A. 1942. *Capitalism, Socialism and Democracy*. New York: Harper and Row.

Schurman, Rachel A. 2001. "Uncertain Gains: Labor in Chile's New Export Sectors." *Latin American Research Review* 36(2):3–29.

Schwartzman, Kathleen C. 2006. "Globalization from a World-System Perspective: A New Phase in the Core—A New Destiny for Brazil and the Semiperiphery?" *Journal of World-System Research* 12(2):265–307.

Scott, James, C. 1976. *The Moral Economy of the Peasant*. New Haven: Yale University Press.

Secretaría de Turismo. 2005. *Compendio Estadistico del Turismo en Mexico*. Mexico City: Secretaría de Turismo.

Segovia, Alexander. 2004. "Centroamerica Despues del Cafe: El Fin del Modelo Agroexportador Tradicional y el Surgimiento de un Nuevo Modelo." *Revista Centroamericana de Ciencias Sociales* 2(1):5–38.

———. 2006. *Integracion Real y Grupos de Poder Economico en America Central: Implicaciones para la Democracia y el Desarrollo en la Region*. San Jose, Costa Rica: Fundacion Friedrich Ebert America Central.

Seldeman, Tony. 2004 (June 1). "Despite Globalization Traumas, Flower Industry Blooms." *World Trade Magazine*, on-line edition, accessed at www.worldtrademag.com/CDA/Archives/4e61cf5149af7010 on February 21, 2006.

Shaw, Timothy, and Fredrik Soderbaum, eds. 2004. *Theories of New Regionalism: A Palgrave Reader*. Basingstoke: Palgrave Macmillan.

Silva, Eduardo. 1996. *The State and Capital in Chile*. Boulder: Westview Press.

Sitrin, Marina, ed. 2006. *Horizontalism: Voices of Popular Power in Argentina*. Oakland: AK Press.

Sklair, Leslie. 1993. *Assembling for Development: The Maquiladora Industry in Mexico and in the United States*. San Diego: Center for U.S. –Mexican Studies, University of California at San Diego.

———. 2000. *The Transnational Capitalist Class*. London: Blackwell.

———. 2002. *Globalization: Capitalism and Its Alternatives*. New York: Oxford University Press.

Smith, Alan, K. 1991. *Creating a World Economy: Merchant Capital, Colonialism, and World Trade, 1400–1825*. Boulder: Westview.

Smith, Michael Peter, and Luis Eduardo Guarnizo, eds. 1998. *Transnationalism from Below*. New Brunswick, NJ: Transaction.

Smith, Robert C. 1998. "Mexican Immigrants, the Mexican State, and the Transnational Practice of Mexican Politics and Membership." *LASA Forum* 29(2):19–21.

Smith, W. Rand. 2002. "Privatization in Latin America: How Did It Work and What Difference Did It Make?" *Latin American Politics and Society* 44(4):153–166.

Soederberg, Susanne. 2006. *Global Governance in Question: Empire and the New Common Sense in Managing North-South Relations*. London: Pluto Press.

Southern Poverty Law Center. 2006. "Center Exposes Exploitation of Immigrant workers" (posted August 16) and "Rebuilding New Orleans" (posted August 19). Accessed at www.splcenter.org/ on October 28, 2006.

Souza, Cesar. 2005. "Las Empresas en America Latina Estan Cambiando Rapidamente." Interview with Center for International Private Enterprise. Accessed at www.cipe.org/publications/fs/ert/s31/s31-9.htm on October 21, 2005.

Spritzer, Dinah A. 1994. "Nicaragua Seeks Investment to Expand Tourism Infrastructure." *Travel Weekly* 20(76):94–95.

Stalker, Peter. 2000. *Workers without Frontiers: The Impact of Globalization on International Migration*. Boulder: Lynne Rienner.

Stallings, Barbara. 1987. *Banker to the World: U.S. Portfolio Investment in Latin America, 1900–1986*. Berkeley: University of California Press.

Standing, Guy. 1989. "Global Feminization through Flexible Labor." *World Development* 17(7):1077–1095.

Stavrianos, L. S. 1981. *Global Rift: The Third World Comes of Age*. New York: William Morrow.

Stefoni, Carolina. 2003. *Inmigracion Peruana en Chile: Una Oportunidad a la Integracion*. Santiago, Chile: FLACSO–Editorial Universitaria.

Stiglitz, Joseph, E. 2002. *Globalization and Its Discontents*. New York: W. W. Norton and Co.

Stokes, Doug. 2005. *America's Other War: Terrorizing Colombia*. London: Zed.

Stonich, S., J. Sorenson, and A. Hundt. 1995. "Ethnicity, Class and Gender in Tourism Development: The Case of The Bay Islands, Honduras." *Journal of Sustainable Development* 3(1):1–28.

Strange, Susan. 1986. *Casino Capitalism*. Oxford: Oxford University Press.

———. 1996. *The Retreat of the State: The Diffusion of Power in the World Economy*. Cambridge: Cambridge University Press.

Talcott, Molly. 2005. "Report from the Post-Stan, Post-Wilma Mexican South: Disaster Capitalism in the Yucatan Peninsula Meets the Politics of Neglect in Chiapas?" Unpublished report. 23 October. Write to Molly Talcott at Department of Sociology, University of California, Santa Barbara, California, 93106, USA, or at mtalcott@umail.ucsb.edu, for a copy.

Tamayo, Eduardo, G. 2006a (February 8). "Industria de las Flores en Ecuador: Dolares para Empresarios, Espinas para Trabajadores." *Minga Informativa de Movimientos Sociales*. Accessed at http://alainet.org/docs/10559.html on February 12, 2006.

———. 2006b. "America Latina: Boom Minero, Desastres y Resistencias." *America Latina en Movimiento* 412:22–27.

Taplin, Ian M. 1994. "Strategic Reorientations of U.S. Apparel Firms." In Gereffi and Korzeniewicz (eds.), *Commodity Chains and Global Capitalism*.

Taylor, Keeanga Y. 2006 (May 9). "Life Ain't Been No Crystal Stair: Blacks, Latinos, and the New Civil Rights Movement." *Counterpunch*. Accessed at www.counterpunch.org/taylor05082006.html on May 18, 2006.

Teichman, Judith A. 2001. *The Politics of Freeing Markets in Latin America: Chile, Argentina and Mexico*. Chapel Hill: University of North Carolina Press.

Tello, Mario D., and William Tyler, eds. 1997. *La Promotion de Exportaciones en Nicaragua, 1997–2010: Experiencias y Alternativas*. Managua: Ediciones Nicargo.

Thank-Dam, Truong. 1990. *Sex, Money, and Morality: Prostitution and Tourism in Southeast Asia*. London: Zed.

Thomas, Jim. 1996. "The New Economic Model and Labor Markets in Latin America." In Victor Bulmer-Thomas (ed.), *The New Economic Model in Latin America and Its Impact on Income Distribution and Poverty*. New York: St. Martin's Press, pp. 79–102.

Thrupp, L. A. 1995. *Bitter-Sweet Harvests for Global Supermarkets*. Washington, DC: World Resources Institute.

Tiano, Susan. 1994. *Patriarchy on the Line: Labor, Gender, and Ideology in the Mexican Maquiladora Industry*. Philadelphia: Temple University Press.

Tilly, Chris. 2006. "Wal-Mart in Mexico: The Limits to Growth." In Nelson Lichtenstein (ed.), *Wal-Mart: The Face of Twenty-First-Century Capitalism*. New York: New Press, pp. 189–209.

United Nations Conference on Trade and Development (UNCTAD). Various years. *World Investment Report*. New York: United Nations/UNCTAD.

United Nations Development Program (UNDP). 1995. *Human Development Report*. New York: Oxford University Press/UNDP.

————. 2000. *Human Development Report*. New York: Oxford University Press/UNDP, table 1, p. 7.

————. 2002. *Human Development Report*. New York: Oxford University Press/United Nations.

————. 2004. *Democracy in Latin America: Towards a Citizens' Democracy*. New York: UNDP.

————. 2005. *Human Development Report*. New York: Oxford University Press/UNDP.

United Nations Environmental Program (UNEP). 2002. "Negative Socio-Cultural Impacts from Tourism." Nairobi: UNEP (summary of report is available on-line at www.upeptie.org/pc.tourism/sust-tourism/soc-drawbacks.htm).

United States Bureau of the Census. 1997. Current Population Survey, March, table 3–4, "Country or Area of Birth of the Foreign-Born Population From Latin America and Northern America, 1997," at www.census.gov/population/ socdem/foreign/98/tab 03 -4.pdf; and INS, "Illegal Alien Resident Population, table 1," at www.ins.usdoj.gov/ graphics/ aboutins/statistics/illegalalien/index.htm.

United States Department of Agriculture. 2005a (August 29). "The Competition in 1997: Chile." Washington, DC: USDA, accessed at www.fas.usda.gov/cmp/com-study/1997/ comp97-cl.htm on February 3, 2006..

————. 2005b. *World Wine Situation and Outlook*. Washington, DC: International Strategic Marketing Group, USDA.

United States Department of Labor. 2006 (February 22). "Colombia," report by the U.S. Department of Labor, Bureau of International Labor Affairs." Washington, DC, Accessed at www.dol.gov/ilab/media/reports/iclp/sweat/colombia.htm on February 22, 2006. Valente, Marcela. 2006 (February 28). "Soy Overruns Everything in Its Path."

Inter-Press Service (IPS News Agency), on-line dispatch, accessed at www.ipsnews/net/print.asp?idnews=24977 on February 28, 2006.

van der Pijl, Kees. 1997. "The History of Class Struggle: From Original Accumulation to Neoliberalism." *Monthly Review* 49(1):28–44.

Vartabedian, Ralph, Richard A. Serrano, and Richard Marosi. 2006. "Rise in Bribery Tests Integrity of U.S. Border." *Los Angeles Times* (October 23):A1, A16–17.

Veltmeyer, Henry. 1997. "Latin America in the New World Order." *Canadian Journal of Sociology* 22(2): 197–242.

Venutelo, Patricia Alvarenga. 1997. *Conflictiva Convivencia: Los Nicaraguenses en Costa Rica*. San Jose: FLACSO.

Verdezoto, Maria Elena. 2005 (June). "Building Anew: Ecuador Is Betting Nearly US$900 Million on Airports and Roads to Capture a Slice of World Trade." *Latin Trade* on-line issue, accessed at www.findarticles.como/p/articles/mimOBEK/is613/ain14791766? on February 21, 2006.

Vertovec, Steven. 1999. "Conceiving and Researching Transnationalism." *Ethnic and Racial Studies* 22(2):447–462.

Victoria International Development Education Association (VIDEA). 2002. *Deceptive Beauty: A Look at the Global Flower Industry*. Victoria (British Columbia): Canadian International Development Agency/Canadian Auto Workers' Social Justice Fund.

Videla, Nancy Plankey. 2005. "Following Suit: An Examination of Structural Constraints to Industrial Upgrading in the Third World." *Competition and Change* 9(4):397–327.

———. 2006. "It Cuts Both Ways: Workers, Management and the Construction of a 'Community of Fate' on the Shop-Floor in a Mexican Garment Factory." *Social Forces* 84(4):2099–2120.]

Vilas, Carlos. 1997. "Inequality and the Dismantling of Citizenship in Latin America." *NACLA Report on the Americas* 31(1):57–63.

Visser, Evert-Jan. 2004. *A Chilean Wine Cluster? Governance and Upgrading in the Phase of Internationalization*. Santiago: ECLAC, Division of Production, Productivity and Management.

Wade, Peter. 1997. *Race and Ethnicity in Latin America*. London: Pluto.

Wallerstein, Immanuel. 1974. *The Modern World System*, New York: Academic Press.

———. 2004. *World-Systems Analysis: An Introduction*. Durham: Duke University Press.

Walton, John, and David Seddon. 1994. *Free Markets and Food Riots: The Politics of Global Adjustment*. Oxford: Blackwell.

Waters, Malcolm. 1995. *Globalization*. London: Routledge.

Watkins, Kevin. 2001 (August 29). "Deadly Blooms: Colombia's Flower Industry is Based on the Exploitation of its Women Workers." *The Guardian*, accessed at http://society.guardian.co.uk/society/guardian/sotry/0,,543351,00.html on February 22, 2006.

Weaver, Frederick Stirton. 2000. *Latin America in the World Economy: Mercantile Colonialism to Global Capitalism*. Boulder: Westview.

Webber, Michael J., and David L. Rigby. 1996. *The Golden Age Illusion: Rethinking Postwar Capitalism*. New York: Guilford.

Weersma-Haworth, Teresa S. 1996. "Export Processing Free Zones as an Export Strategy for Central America and the Caribbean." In Rudd Buitelaan and Pitou van Dijck (eds.), *Latin America's New Insertion in the World Economy*. New York: Palgrave Macmillan.

Weisbrot, Mark. 2006. "Latin America: The End of an Era." *International Journal of Health Services* 36(4).

Went, Robert. 2002. *The Enigma of Globalization*. London: Routledge.

Weyland, Kurt. 1996. "Neopopulism and Neoliberalism in Latin America: Unexpected Affinities." *Studies in Comparative International Development* 9(2):108–121.

Whitaker, Morris D., and Dale Colyer. 1990. *Agriculture and Economic Survival: The Role of Agriculture in Ecuador's Development*. Boulder: Westview.

Wilkie, James A., ed. 1995. *Statistical Abstracts for Latin America* (SALA), vol. 31. Los Angeles: UCLA Latin American Center Publications.

Williamson, John, ed. 1990. *Latin American Adjustment: How Much Has Happened?* Washington, DC: Institute for International Economics.

———. 1993. "Democracy and the "Washington Consensus'." *World Development* 21(8): 1329–1336.

———. 2002 (November 6). "Did the Washington Consensus Fail?" Speech at the Center for Strategic and International Studies. Washington DC, Accessed at www.iie.com/publications/papers/paper.cfm?ResearchID=488 on March 9, 2007.

Willmore, Larry. 1997. "Reflexiones Sobre la Promocion de Exportaciones en Centroamerica." In Tello and Tyler, *La Promocion de Exportaciones*.

Wilpert, Gregory. 2005. "Chavez Affirms Venezuela Is Heading Towards Socialism of 21st Century." *Venezuelanalysis* May 5, accessed at www.venezuelanalysis.com/news.php?newsno=1607 on May 10, 2005.

Winn, Peter, ed. 2004. *Victims of the Chilean Miracle: Workers and Neo-Liberalism in the Pinochet Era, 1973–2002*. Durham: Duke University Press.

Winslow, George. 1999. *Capital Crimes*. New York: Monthly Review Press.

Witte, Benjamin. 2005. "Multinational Gold Rush in Guatemala." *NACLA Report on the Americas* 39(1):8–11.

Wolf, Eric. 1997. *Europe and the People without History*. Berkeley: University of California Press.

Wood, Ellen, Meiksins. 2003. *Empire of Capital*. London: Verso.

World Bank. 1991. *World Development Report*. Washington, DC and New York: World Bank and Oxford University Press.

———. 1992. *World Development Report*. Washington, DC and New York: World Bank and Oxford University Press.

———. 1997a. *Poverty and Income Distribution in Latin America: The Story of the 1980s*. Washington, DC: World Bank.

———. 1997b. *The State in a Changing World*. Washington, DC: World Bank.

———. 1998. *World Development Indicators, 1998*, table 2.7. Washington, DC: World Bank.

———. 2001a. *World Development Indicators, 2001*. Washington, DC: World Bank.

———. 2001b. *World Development Report*. Washington, DC, and New York: World Bank and Oxford University Press.

———. 2002. *World Development Report*. Washington, DC, and New York: World Bank and Oxford University Press.

———. 2005. *PREM Note—Chilean Wine Industry*. Washington, DC (Program of Advisory Support Services for Rural Livelihoods, Department of International Development, WB0199/08): World Bank.

———. 2006a. Privatization Database (World Bank on-line database), "Privatizations by Region: Latin America and the Caribbean," accessed at http://rru.worldbank.org/Privatization/Region.aspx?regionid=435 on November 28, 2006.

World Tourism Organization. 1990, *Economic Review of World Tourism: Tourism in the Context of Economic Crisis and the Dominance of the Service Economy*. Madrid: WTO/United Nations.

———. 2005. *Tourism Market Trends*. Madrid: WTO.

World Trade Organization. *Trade Policy Review*. Geneva: WTO Secretariat. Various years and various country reports.

World Travel and Tourism Council (WTTC). 2005a. *Latin America Travel and Tourism: Sowing the Seeds of Growth*. London: WTTC.

———. 2005b. *Travel and Tourism: Sowing the Seeds of Growth*, various Latin America country reports. London: WTTC.

Wright, Angus Lindsay, and Wendy Wolford. 2003. *To Inherit the Earth: The Landless Movement and the Struggle for a New Brazil*. Oakland: Food First.

Yashar, Deborah J. 2005. *Contesting Citizenship in Latin America: The Rise of Indigenous Movements and the Post-Liberal Challenge*. Cambridge: Cambridge University Press.

Yates, Michael D. 2003. *Naming the System: Inequality and Work in the Global Economy*. New York: Monthly Review Press.

Zibechi, Raul. 2006. "America Latina: La Nueva Gobernabilidad." ALAI news service, June 23 dispatch, datelined Montevideo, accessed at www.paginadigital.com.ar/articulos/2006/2006prim/noticias6/america-latina-260606.asp on June 23, 2006.

Žižek, Slavoj. 1997. "Multiculturalism, or, the Cultural Logic of Multinational Capitalism." *New Left Review* 225:28–51.

Zolberg, Aristide. 1989. "The Next Waves: Migration Theory for a Changing World." *International Migration Review* 23(3): 403–430.